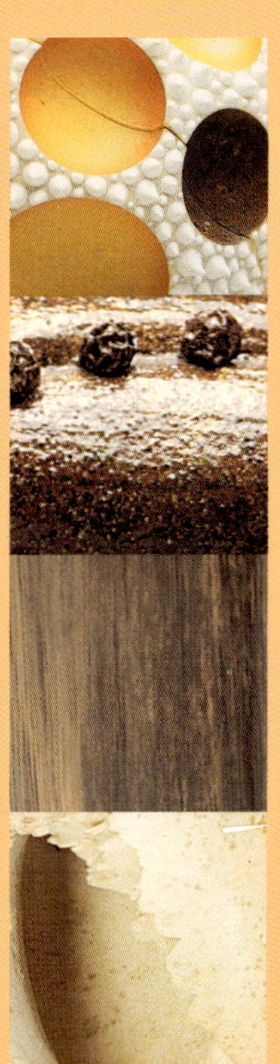

# Challenge VI— Roots:
## Insights & Inspirations in Contemporary Turned Objects

Michelle Holzapfel, Curator/Essayist

Robin Rice, Essayist

Christopher D. Tyler, Curator/Essayist

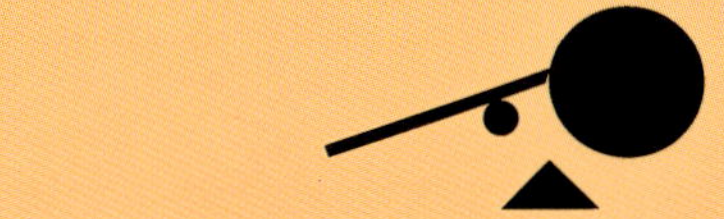

Wood Turning Center

Albert LeCoff, Executive Director

CHALLENGE VI— ROOTS:
INSIGHTS & INSPIRATIONS IN CONTEMPORARY TURNED OBJECTS

The Wood Turning Center of Philadelphia is a nonprofit membership organization, founded in 1986, dedicated to the education, preservation and promotion of the art and craft of lathe turning through the aquisition of collections and organization of exhibitions, conferences, a residency program, symposia and outreach programs. The Center's goal is to encourage and promote the work of established and developing artists and to cultivate, among the public, a deeper understanding and appreciation of lathe turning.

Contact the Wood Turning Center for more information about this book and exhibition, other publications produced by the Center, or the art of lathe turning.

501 Vine Street
Philadelphia, Pennsylvania 19106 USA
Telephone 215-923-8000
Fax 215-923-4403
Email turnon@woodturningcenter.org
http://www.woodturningcenter.org



Library of Congress Control Number: 2001094648

ISBN 0-9624385-6-1

# Table of Contents

## Lisa Tremper Hanover, *Director*

### Philip and Muriel Berman Museum of Art at Ursinus College

In 1994 the Philip and Muriel Berman Museum of Art at Ursinus College presented *Challenge V: International Lathe-Turned Objects*, the first of what has been a long and successful collaboration with The Wood Turning Center. Since that time, our respective institutions have joined together to present six International Turning Exchange exhibitions with accompanying symposia. In 1997, the Museum hosted *Curators' Focus: Turning in Context* and the accompanying World Turning Conference. These innovative exhibitions have introduced our audiences to an exciting art form, which redefines the language of sculptural objects.

*Challenge VI— Roots: Insights & Inspirations in Contemporary Turned Objects* is the third major installation the Berman Museum of Art has hosted in eight years and we are proud to be the inaugural venue for this multidimensional approach to investigating the lathe-turning genre. Curators Michelle Holzapfel and Christopher Tyler faced the daunting task of selecting work with aesthetic merit while also evaluating the inspirational origins of the piece as articulated by the artist. Relating a visual composition to tangible and intangible sources adds an exciting dimension to our interpretation of a piece. The installation seeks to create a context for this relationship.

The participants selected for representation in *Challenge VI* are both accomplished and emerging artists who have blended their personal stories and influences with imagery that is dynamic and challenging. Such non-traditional media as metal and glass, manipulated by the lathe, take the field to another level.

We are grateful for the generous support received by both the Wood Turning Center and the Berman Museum of Art to produce this important exhibition and publication. We extend our appreciation to the Arcadia Foundation, the Friends of the Wood Turning Center, John and Robyn Horn, a congressionally directed grant from the Institute of Library and Museum Services, the Pennsylvania Council on the Arts, and the Windgate Charitable Foundation. In addition, we congratulate the Wood Turning Center on the opening of its new facility in Philadelphia, which elevates the program to a level of visibility and stewardship. It has become the locus of tremendous outreach efforts, which are part of its mission to serve the lathe-turning community.

## Albert LeCoff, *Executive Director*

### Wood Turning Center

The *Challenge VI— Roots: Insights & Inspirations in Contemporary Turned Objects* exhibition represents the Wood Turning Center's continued commitment to furthering lathe artists' growth and public awareness of the lathe turning field. The *Challenge* series evolved from encouraging artists to seek new personal areas of exploration and presenting it in gallery settings to putting the call out for entries and inviting curators, critics, and scholars to select the work and write essays on lathe art. The *Challenge* series includes works from both established and emerging international artists who seek to redefine function, decoration and sculptural forms.

*Challenge VI* is exciting because we asked the artists to explain what inspired them to do the work that they submitted for the exhibition. Anything could be the source of inspiration, but they had to figure out how to convey it in a tangible form. Exciting hand drawings, photographs, magazine articles, and even a CD of a piano composition came in with slides of their work. We present the work and inspirations of fifty artists from ten countries around the globe.

The Wood Turning Center once again appreciates the opportunity to work with Lisa Tremper Hanover and the Philip and Muriel Berman Museum of Art in staging the *Challenge* exhibition. The members of the curatorial team, who graciously provided their time and insights — internationally known American writer and sculptor Michelle Holzapfel, and Canadian curator Christopher Tyler, discussed, examined, probed for meaning and then selected the work you see from hundreds of entries. Inspired by the artists' words and objects, their essays capture the work from their unique perspectives. Michelle's poetic essay is drawn directly from the artists' descriptions of very personal inspirations. Art historian Robin Rice's essay puts the artists' work in historic perspective.

The arts are fortunate to have many recent publications, including several glamorous ones, which document lathe art. This book captures the inspirations before and during the physical work, a way of recording the spirit within the objects. We read about the muse, we wonder over the work, and we understand how it fits into evolving contexts. This is the reader's challenge: to contemplate the artists' thoughts and resulting works. Enjoy!

# Acknowledgements

*by Fleur Bresler, President,*
*on behalf of the Wood Turning Center Board of Trustees*

The Wood Turning Center is in the midst of one of the most exciting periods in its fifteen year history. There are a number of people and organizations who we can not thank enough for their ongoing involvement and assistance. First, thanks and recognition must be extended to Albert LeCoff, Executive Director of the Center, who oversaw the development and implementation of the *Challenge VI— Roots: Insights & Inspirations in Contemporary Turned Objects* exhibition and catalogue, along with the assistance of the WTC's devoted staff.

Next to be thanked are the members of the Exhibition and Publication Committees, with a special thank you to Judson Randall, the Head of the Publication Committee, for the editorial expertise he brought to this entire catalogue.

The *Challenge VI* curators, Chris Tyler and Michelle Holzapfel, have brought together one of the most groundbreaking *Challenge* shows, and have both provided extraordinary, insightful essays for this catalogue. Robin Rice also contributed the fruits of her research and involvement, and in doing so, brought a very valuable historical context to the exhibition.

Lisa Tremper Hanover's continued cooperation continues to be an invaluable resource for the Center, and we are thrilled that the Philip and Muriel Berman Museum, under her leadership, will be the opening venue for *Challenge VI*.

We would also like to acknowledge the financial support of the Arcadia Foundation, the Friends of the Wood Turning Center, John and Robyn Horn, the Pennsylvania Council on the Arts, the Philadelphia Cultural Fund and the Windgate Charitable Foundation.

Last, and certainly not least, we want to extend our sincerest gratitude to all of the artists whose wonderful work brought about this exhibition, as well as all of the artists who submitted their work for consideration. Without their dedication to the field, we would not be writing this today.

# Creating a Portrait of Our Field

*by Michelle Holzapfel*

Watching an interview on PBS recently, I heard the commentator, Clarence Page, say, "...fight for the right to be complex...," and I thought, "that's what I'm trying to do here."

I see *Challenge VI* as a rare opportunity in the history of the movement. The wood turning field has grown and flourished over the last two decades. But in recent years, as the stakes have grown, a great deal of effort and expense has been lavished on the concerted "legitimization" of the field.

Although a well-meant and worthy effort, it has also succeeded in alienating the actual makers' voices, replacing them with the voices of "expert" commentators. The critical/historical viewpoint is certainly vital, but its authority tends to drown out the more tentative voices of many makers whose work is often stronger than their verbal analyses.

So, before the field evolves from a rigorous confederacy into a rigid hierarchy in which craft/technique/skill — perceived as the "bastard" child of Art — gets a good scrubbing before being presented to those who confer legitimacy, perhaps we can make a document/portrait of the state of the art and/or craft of our field today based on the evidence presented by its actual inhabitants.

# Hearing the Artists' Voices

*by Christopher D. Tyler*

"Well," said Michelle, as the waiters in the Vietnamese restaurant hurried about placing an abundance of dishes on the table, "this is a lot like curating — too many choices at once!"

Michelle Holzapfel and I had just concluded the last day of the second phase of curating *Challenge VI* and were beginning to sink into a contented haze at what we felt we had accomplished. Both of us felt we had never had such a satisfying experience of this sort before. Despite quite different perspectives and approaches, and being strangers, we had found our way to a coherent and joined vision through the work. This was a kind of affair, a whirlwind intellectual affair — all the stages from acquaintance and now to imminent parting — in a total of four days, as we sat with Albert LeCoff and his wife, Tina, among the scattered and emptied dishes in the restaurant. No wonder we were tired!

There were several possible shows to choose from inherent in the same works and several different ways at getting at each. Early on, we agreed that we wanted to avoid the "dog's breakfast" juried show, in which the "best" pieces were included regardless of whether they had any connection with one another. We decided to try to curate rather than jury, for our aim was to assemble an artistically coherent show. This involved much discussion, not just about the work, but about our strategy. Did we want to go round separately, give a score, and just add 'em up? Or could we agree together on each piece? Would we begin by eliminating or by choosing the strong pieces and letting them determine the kind of statement by which the others would be selected? Although we disagreed about some pieces at the beginning, we eventually persuaded each other, and in the end there were no compromises and only strong joint approval.

We also had to get to know one another's cast of mind, our preferences and possible blind spots. I had plenty of these, for sure, as I was trained as a potter and had virtually no experience with wood turning as a maker. Michelle's tolerance for this vast ignorance was truly gracious, and I think we found a way to complement one another. I want to say that this was one of the most remarkable experiences of this sort I have had. This is very rare in life and even rarer in art! I learned so much from Michelle, and we finished the task with a sense of having grown in many important ways.

We agreed later that we had been able to approach the selection very much as collaborative artists approach an art work. The act of selection seemed inclusive as well as subtractive. We also began to intuit the show's cohesion before we had finished, and before we could articulate it to one another. The artists were "speaking" to us. At the beginning, we heard this both as a collective babble and as two hundred and thirty individual statements. Gradually, we were able to give each artist a platform for his or her statement. We felt we were able to edit, to orchestrate silences, and to bring out rhythms so that the babble became words, then sentences, and then debates where both the roars and the whispers could be heard.

As someone with previously only a superficial acquaintance with the field, I found the whole experience invigorating, truly fascinating, and exciting in scope. It has been a great privilege to be so closely involved and to work so closely with Michelle, Robin Rice and Albert.

# A Conversation of Great Excitement

*by Christopher D. Tyler*

A ceramist and arts administrator, Christopher Tyler is manager of Crafts, Design and Publishing Programs for the Province of Nova Scotia, which includes managing the Nova Scotia Centre for Craft and Design. He has written articles and reviews on contemporary crafts, and also works as an independent curator. Several years ago, he was curator of contemporary work in all media from eastern Canada called "The Poetry of the Vessel."

In 2000, he was the resident scholar with the Wood Turning Center's International Turning Exchange.

A native of England, Tyler immigrated to Canada in 1966. Teaching at a community college in Ontario for some years, he was co-author of a book on contemporary Raku pottery, the first book on contemporary ceramics by a Canadian.

In 1975-1976, he worked on a research project and continued his own ceramic work at the ceramics department of Ohio University in Athens, and moved to Halifax,in Nova Scotia, to earn an MFA in ceramics at the Nova Scotia College of Art and Design in 1978.

**Introduction**

If this exhibition is any indication, and I am sure it is, then the wood turning community is becoming increasingly aware of its potential. *Challenge VI— Roots: Insights and Inspirations in Contemporary Turned Objects* shows that artists in this medium are turning to increase their interaction with surface beyond the discovery and presentation of beautiful grain. Once this emancipation has begun, the artist steps from being a "discoverer" to being a "creator". Turners are aware of architectural references and recent developments. They play with ideas of repetition and repeated forms (which are at the root of the history of the medium), and they are open to a wide variety of influences, which are likely to be personal and autobiographical, formal, or derived from the precedents of other artists. Their awareness of the preciousness of the environment is an especially strong theme. It is obviously related to their deep connection with the living material in which they work, and is different in character, though not in strength, from that of the feelings of the potter who uses inert, recyclable, but non-renewable resources.

In their entries, the artists were "speaking" to us. At the beginning, we heard them both as a collective babble and as 230 individual statements. Gradually, we were able to give each artist a platform for his or her statement; we felt we were able to edit, orchestrate silences, and bring out rhythms, so that the babble became words, then sentences, then debates where both the roars and the whispers could be heard. As a result, we do not have, I think, a unified chant, or an incantation, or even a chorus, but a continuing conversation where everyone's remarks have a connection and a contribution to make, and where statements made today may very well resonate differently tomorrow. Included in this overall conversation are sub-conversations, where a particular aspect of the dialogue has caught the excited attention of a few.

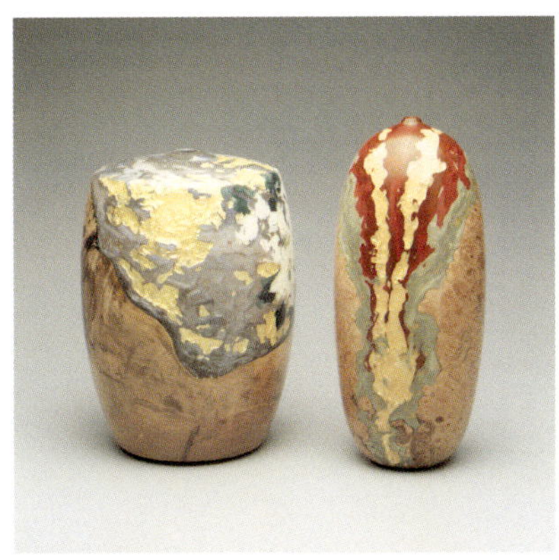

1
Robert Chatelain
*Dogwood,* 2000 and *Wrapt,* 1999
H: 12 1/2", Diam: 8 1/2";
H: 14", Diam: 5 1/4"
Red maple burl, big leaf maple burl, epoxy resin, powdered pigments, mica and gold leaf
lent by the artist

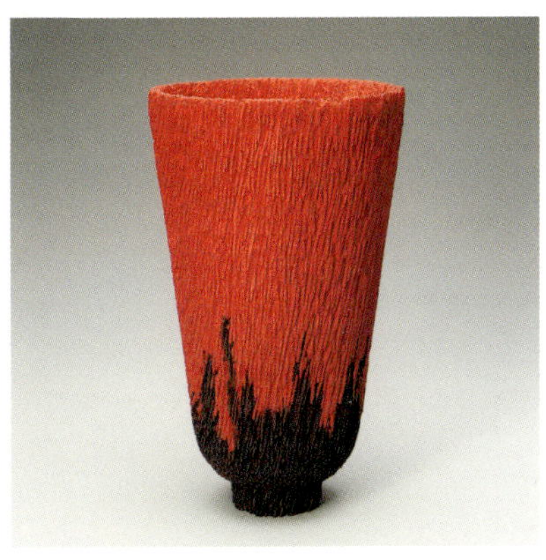

2
Dewey Garrett
*Rouge et Noir,* 1999
H: 12", W: 7", D: 7"
Palm and aniline dyes
lent by the artist

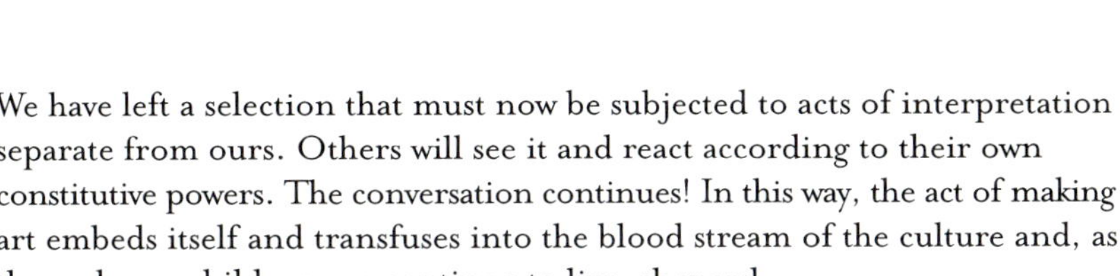

We have left a selection that must now be subjected to acts of interpretation separate from ours. Others will see it and react according to their own constitutive powers. The conversation continues! In this way, the act of making art embeds itself and transfuses into the blood stream of the culture and, as through our children, we continue to live, changed.

**Surface**

The appeal of wooden objects is obviously due in part to the surface appearance of the wood itself. Today, beyond the time-honored appeal of grain markings, and the particular beauty of typical markings, some wood turners are exploring other effects. This was remarked upon in the 2000 International Turning Exchange (ITE) exhibition, *allTURNatives*, where the interest in surface went beyond the normal enhancement and appreciation of grain, and was felt to be a noticeable feature of that year's program.

The classic treatment of wood, from at least the 18th century, revered polished grain and figure. This was acknowledged by Ed Moulthrop (born 1916) when he said, "Unlike clay, glass, metals and fiber, where the material is shifted and re-arranged to the artist's desire, my works 'have always been there.'[1] The wood you see is the wood exactly as it was created. I simply uncover it and there it is!" Moulthrop saw himself as a discoverer of the surface, and not its creator. Since, the evolution of surface intervention in wood has been marked by the work of David Ellsworth (born 1944)—who went further in the incorporation and acknowledgement of defects & freestyle turning, Todd Hoyer (born 1952), and others who continued to develop interventionist strategies.

In *Challenge VI*, the work of William Hunter probably has the most classic luscious surface, although his forms continue to evolve. Robert Chatelain, Andrew Curle, George Peterson, Rolly Munro, Louise Hibbert, Helen Shirk, Mark Sfirri, Jason Marlow, James Thurman, Dewey Garrett and arguably Virginia Dotson, continue to extend the active creation of surface. In making this grouping, I considered carved pieces as a different category.

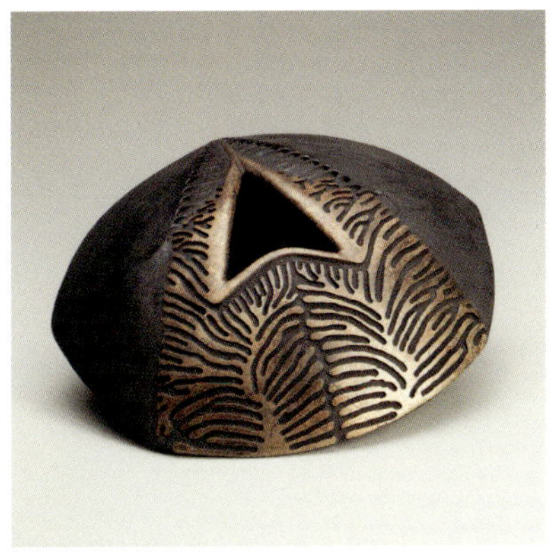

3
Rolly Munro
*Sea Biscuit Form II,* 2000
H: 3", Diam: 11"
Walnut, gold leaf and pigments
lent by the artist

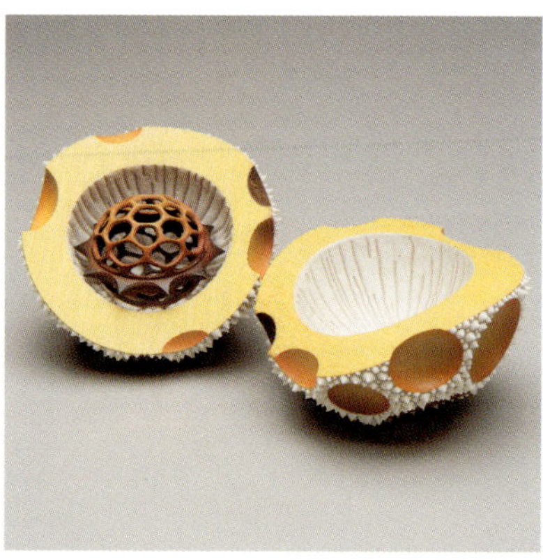

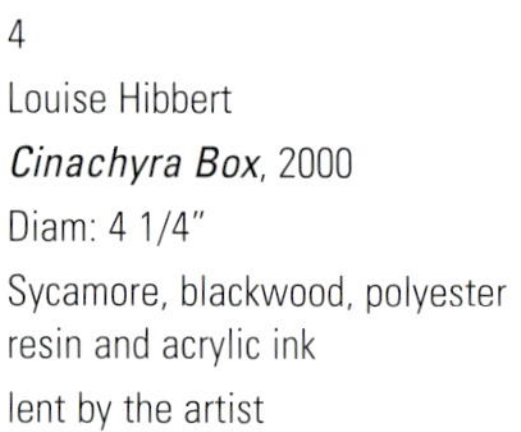

4
Louise Hibbert
*Cinachyra Box*, 2000
Diam: 4 1/4"
Sycamore, blackwood, polyester resin and acrylic ink
lent by the artist

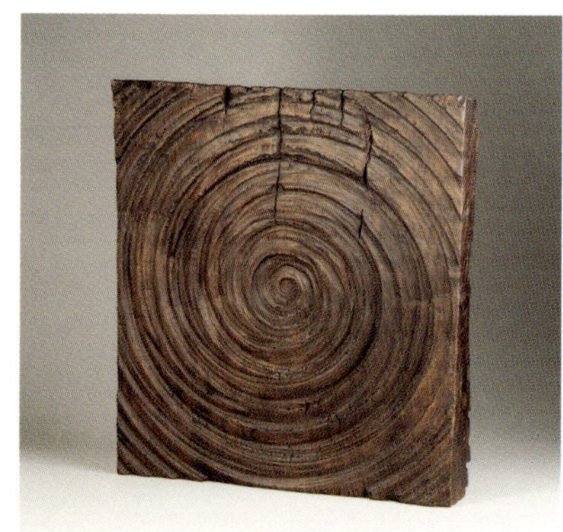

5
George Peterson
*Buddha's Mirror*, 2000
H: 24", W: 21", D: 4"
Charred maple
lent by the artist

Robert Chatelain's vase forms [1] in themselves illustrate the transition I am referring to in a quite pivotal way. The grain is acknowledged but not sacrosanct. Beginning with a green burl, the pieces are turned, kiln dried and turned again. The resulting gaps in the burl are filled with colored epoxy and finished so that the surface is smooth. In this way, the elements of the natural grain are not denied, but intensified by artificial[2] means. For his sources, Chatelain cites Japanese kimonos by Itchiku Kubota, gold leaf, and screens designed by Frank Lloyd Wright, all of which share a sheer gorgeousness and lushness of surface which is in a different mode from that of Moulthrop's. Chatelain's effects are not unlike those of ceramist Brother Thomas in their courage, but nevertheless remain true to the suggestions of the material.[3] Dewey Garrett's *Rouge et Noir* [2] is similarly bright, but the heavy texture of the palm fiber form is entirely dyed so that the effect is as much like crepe, or some other textile, as it is like classic turned wood. Exploitation of bold, bright-applied color is a significant departure in turned wood forms.

Rolly Munro's [3] and Louise Hibbert's [4] surfaces are detailed essays in three dimensional surface pattern loosely based on organic sources, which support, in a smaller scale of the surface, the focused and carefully realized forms. George Peterson's work [5] contrasts strongly, with chain sawn texture so heavy that the deep grooves cut into the wood, splintering and carving, achieve a hacked and gestural surface that almost becomes form, and in which sculptural form approaches a free state of three dimensional drawing. His final treatment of scorching the surface (an increasingly common effect in our field), eliminates color and visual grain, enhancing the grain to a dramatic tactile experience. James Thurman [6] further asserts the texture of the grain by eroding it until its depth is literal as well as visual.

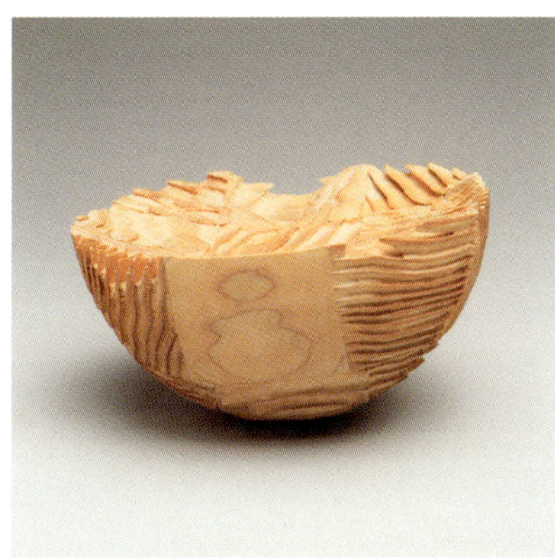

6
James Thurman
*Boolean Ia*, 2000
H: 5", Diam: 8"
Laminated fir
lent by the artist

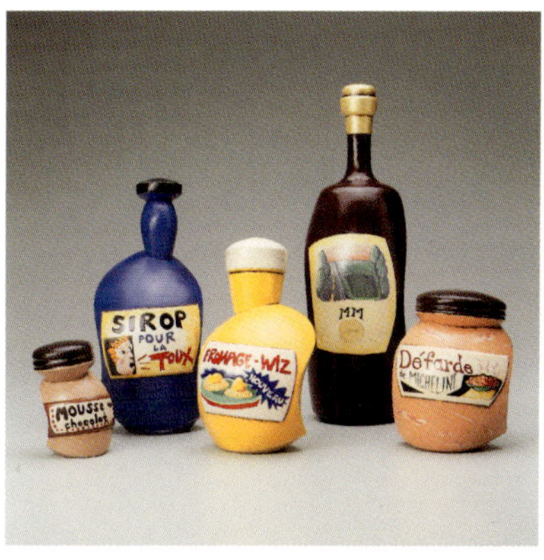


7
Mark Sfirri
*French Vessel Series*, 2000
H: 13 1/2", W: 26", D: 6"
Poplar and paint
lent by the artist

None of these methods deny the nature of the wooden surface, but intensify some aspects of it through an act of "creative intervention". The increasing interest in the wood turning community in surfaces achieved through pro-active participation is an indication of a wider embrace of artistic practice than Moulthrop's example. Almost all artists, however, maintain a connection with the wood and with the wood turning tradition, and do not ignore or deny the grain. Mark Sfirri, in a sense, goes further, in that he paints the surface almost obscuring the element of wood entirely [7]. Conscious and extremely thoughtful about the evolution of wood turning and the development of a range of issues which both extend the tradition and connect it with *avant garde* thinking in the visual arts, he employs in his *French Vessel Series* his trade mark multiple-axis turning techniques, which he has now begun to use with an element of self parody. This exploitation of a "trick of the trade" positions the work well within the context of traditional wood turning, while deploying the irony in two directions: that of the tendency to rely on "tricks of the trade" for difficult effects, and the use of turning techniques and conventions for the purposes of a statement. The negation of grain and the insistence on technique provides a suitably ironic tension in the pieces.

The range of surface interests in this show, from Hunter's classic exploration of wooden turned form, to Sfirri's detached but still respectful use of the material, demonstrates the increasingly exploratory nature of wood turning today.

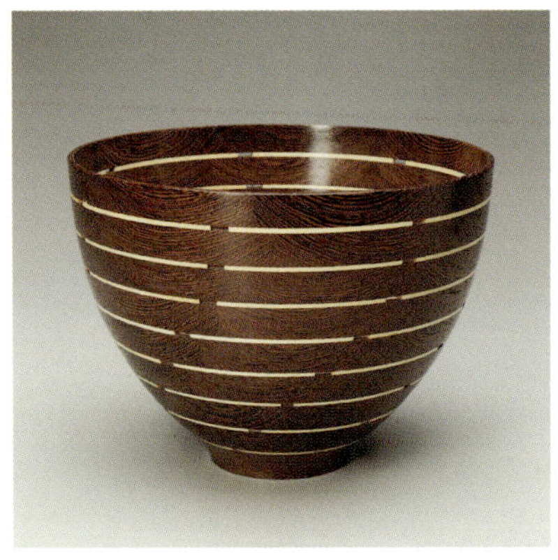

8
Yosh Sugiyama
*Untitled*, 1999
H: 7 1/4", Diam: 9 7/8"
Wenge and holly
lent by the artist

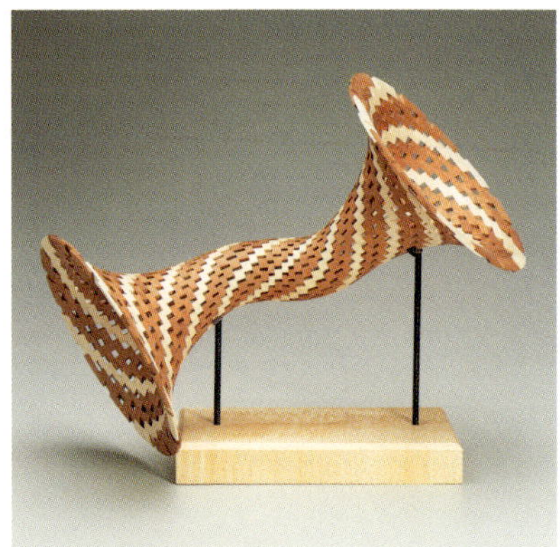

9
William Smith
*Down The Rabbit Hole*, 2000
H: 13", W: 16", D: 9"
Mahogany, maple and brass
lent by the artist

**Architecture, Decoration and Ornament**

Architecture has long been a dominant force for the visual arts, and claims have been made that it "comprehends" and dominates the other arts which may appear on it, in it or otherwise adorning it. The relationship of the craft movement to architectural developments is close but not always clear. William Morris himself was trained, though he never practiced, as an architect. In an age when decoration was prominent in architecture, most of Morris' designs, except for his stained glass, were not integrated into buildings; although they were respectful of the relationships with them. The contribution of the Arts and Crafts movement was closely associated with making functional items that had an aesthetic dimension, and also with the idea that function itself could provide a proper arena for aesthetic expression.

Not until the 19th century did works of art become more autonomous from the building, and with the advent of Modernism, were displayed in galleries specially designed to show the works in as neutral a setting as possible. Also with Modernism, architectural form became monolithic and coherent in a collateral way, so that ornament became, in Adolph Loos' words, a crime.[4] The art work and the expressive object, while it gained some independence, also contracted its references, while the idea of decoration became, if not a crime on everyone's mind, at least a second rate and relatively trivial pleasure based on its literal superficiality to the structural and aesthetic integrity of the building.

In the meantime, as craft theory faltered and veered in various directions after Morris, developments in the field of design provided an ideological arena for craft. In the Post-Modern period, the craft revival has associated itself with theories of design just as much as with the theories of visual art, as represented in the work of furniture makers Wendell Castle and John Makepeace.[5] Recently, an increased emphasis on ornament and decoration

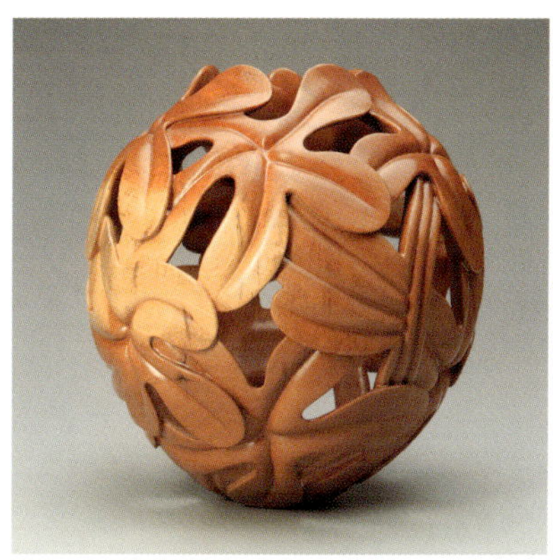

10
Ron Fleming
***Orpheus***, 2000
H: 12", Diam: 10"
Brazilian mahogany
lent by the artist

has also been embraced in visual art and architecture, thereby re-emphasizing a viable role for craftspeople. In 1982, Robert Jenson and Patricia Conway wrote, "Modernist prescription is against ornament. To ornament or decorate today is a radical act, quite the opposite of the conservative act it has been for most of the century."[6] This statement represents a pivotal stage in a shift of hierarchies in the 20th century that significantly affected all media arts. As the vigor of Modernism has faded, decoration has come to be viewed in a more respectable light and, in fact, has become a principal "vocabulary" for personal statement and a means for making buildings and places legible. Today, the role of ornament or decoration has assumed a significance closer to what it had in pre-Modern periods, but it is only now being recognized by the craft community as an essential validation of the craft aesthetic and as a key opportunity for works in fine craft.

Recently, the paradigm for architectural form has been affected by a number of influences; particularly, by virtual reality software, and there has been at least one trend that I know of which sees architecture and textiles as related (see Gehry's Guggenheim building in Bilbao, and the new one to be built in New York). Toronto architect and theorist Philip Beezely has for some time been interested in exploring the idea of "porous architectural space," which extends the Modernist quest for lightness and transparency, which he says has defined the past century's "progressive" mainstream into a kind of cloud or foam structure[7]—an architecture of weakness in which the filigree nature of the form has become both ornament and structure.

In this exhibition, many of the artists cited architectural interest as being implicated in their work, while others explored a decorative vocabulary for turned wood. Many pieces either cited an architectural precedent consciously, or have explored porous forms as a natural extension of the artist's own directions, where the turned walls are pierced. Some pieces, such as Yosh Sugiyama's *Untitled* [8] or William Smith's *Down the Rabbit Hole* [9], use piercing as a way of relating inside and outside in a systematic rhythm, whereas the porosity in

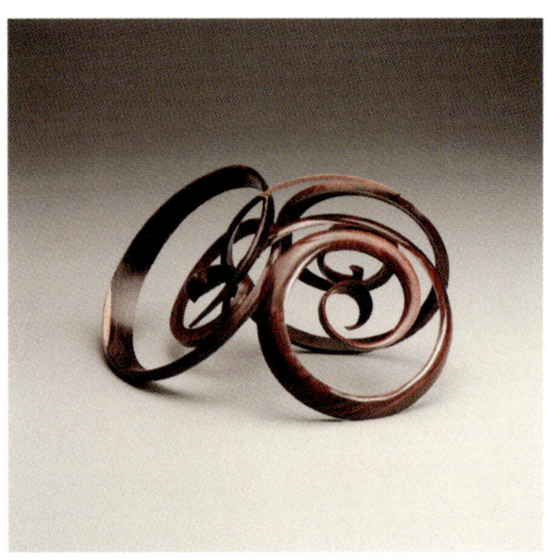

12
Phillip Wall
*Music to My Ears*, 2000
H: 6 1/4", W: 14", D: 11"
Cocobolo
lent by the artist

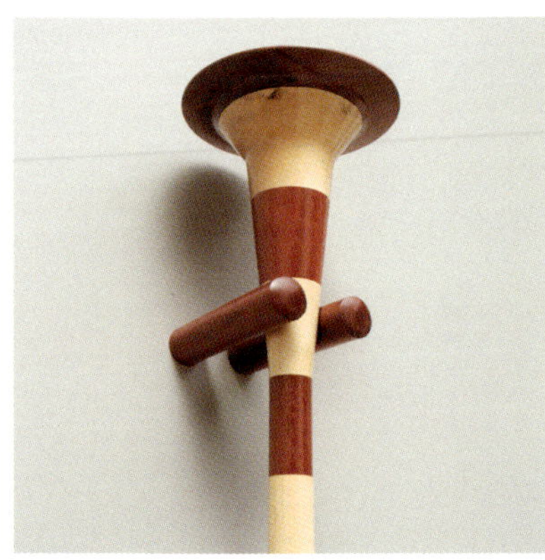

13
Peter R. Thibeault
*Liar's Poker*, 1999
H: 61", W: 9 3/4", D: 10"
Maple, purpleheart and veneer ebony
lent by the artist

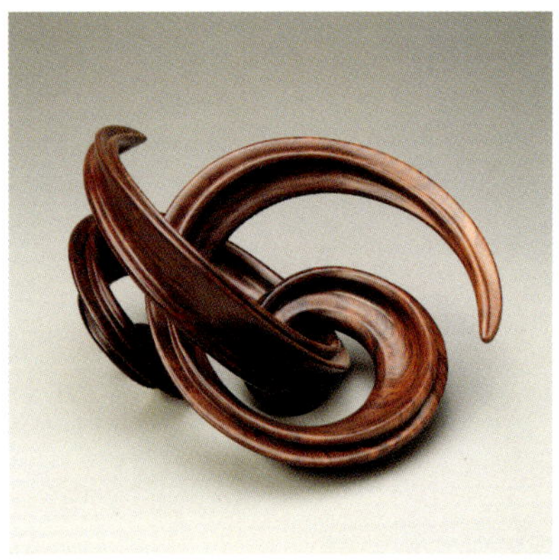

11
William Hunter
*Reciprocal Helix*, 2000
H: 12", W: 12", D: 24"
Cocobolo rosewood
lent by the artist

Ron Fleming's *Orpheus* [10] is not only organic in origin and more extensive, but goes almost as far as possible to fracture the turned form without totally disassembling it. William Hunter's [11] and Phil Wall's [12] pieces take the penultimate step in deconstructing and dissolving turned form.

Peter Thibeault writes of his "lifelong pre-occupation with towers, elongated forms, and vivid graphic contrasts." He takes a camera with him on his travels and finds that what he has taken "is a consistent recording of color juxtapositions, simple structures, and architectural details."[8] His various photos exemplify that, and he also cites the work of Austro-Hungarian architect, Joze Plecnik as an inspiration. His monolithic pieces [13,14,15] demonstrate his faith in the power of the elongated form and utilize the turner's ability to create spindles of scale. Dewey Garrett's piece *Colosseo* [16], is based partly on his first encounter with the Coliseum, but "is not a representation of a particular place but a collage of architectural elements from my memories and impressions.... The challenge addressed in this work is to incorporate familiar, classical architectural elements within a vessel form to evoke feelings of a distant past.... There is something about architecture which resonates with us."[9] The juxtaposition of this fairly literal piece with his more abstracted works also based on building construction and construction sites, confers a power to each piece derived from their similar sources. The other pieces, however, go much further with a creation of a new kind of porous architectural space. In contrast with Thibeault's work of minimalist gravity based on undervalued and somewhat uncommon sources, the starting point of Garrett's work is common construction scaffolding and contemporary buildings under construction, or a cliché like the Coliseum. His interest is "how the apparent complexity and confusion are ultimately arranged into a purposeful construction," but is also an exploration of constructed architectural space.

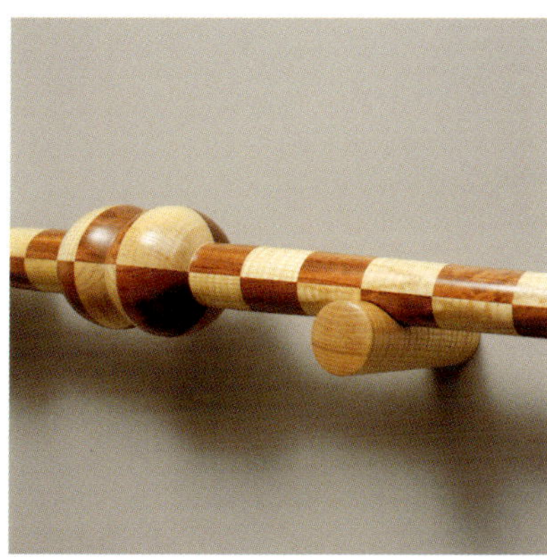

14
Peter R. Thibeault
***Recumbant Monolith***, 1999
H: 5 3/4", W: 79 1/2", D: 13 1/2"
Curly ash and bubinga
lent by the artist

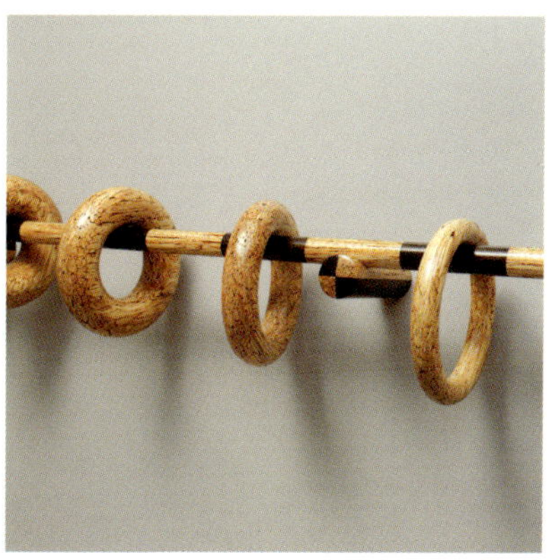

15
Peter R. Thibeault
*Toroidal Entropy*, 1999
H: 15 1/2", W: 76 1/4", D: 13 1/2"
Ebonized walnut and engineered lumber
lent by the artist

Steve Loar's piece [17], in collaboration with Sfirri and F. Sudol, also derives its inspiration in part from architecture — in this case the early Gothic jamb figures from the west portal of Chartres Cathedral. While he also cites the influence of his collaborators (with whom he has worked before), and the illustrations for the *Wizard of Oz*, by Lisbeth Zwerger, which connected him with the idea of totems, the architectural influence in the piece is the most significant. The rhetoric of architecture informs his piece, in that its height (above our heads) and its verticality condition our approach to be one of reverence and respect. Its pedestal, like the steps of a public building, also asserts its seriousness and importance, and its pole-like form (unlike the horizontal mounting of Thibeault's pieces of a similar dimension) asserts the authority of a mace or a processional cross. Of further interest in this piece is the ambiguity which this rhetoric sets up. The iconic references to Christian art are strong: the vestments of the figure, the symbolic blues and reds, the halo, and even the use of purple heart wood which is "bleeding" down onto the little Calvary of a burl that provides the base of the staff.[10] The figure itself, however, is remote, unforgiving and made into an authoritarian figure by its location and by the blankness of its tiny face. The association with the Wizard of Oz, who was also a snake oil salesman, the fraud behind a screen, in the innermost holy of holies in a fortress of highly rhetorical architecture, sets up a skepticism which counteracts the plain and reverential implications of the first impression.

Many makers in the exhibition are converging on architecture as source because of the possibility today of re-integration of the art object with architectural issues and decorative roles, as well as a new understanding of form. This moves the handcrafted object out of the realm of the isolated "super object" into a work with more capacity for exchanging meaning with other objects and other media and, ultimately, with the viewer.

Many makers turn to architecture as a source for decorative ideas. J. Paul Fennell's work [18] references specifically an article by Eva Zeisel from *The Sourcebook of Architectural Ornament*, and the marble pierced screens of mosques in India.

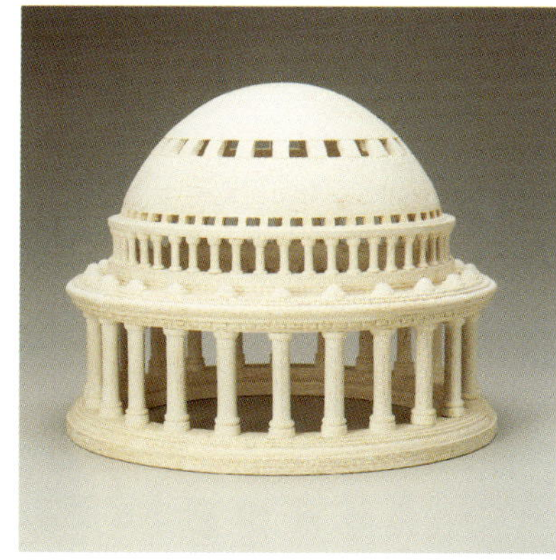

16
Dewey Garrett
*Colosseo*, 1999
H: 7 1/2", W: 13 1/2", D: 13 1/2"
Oak (bleached)
lent by the artist

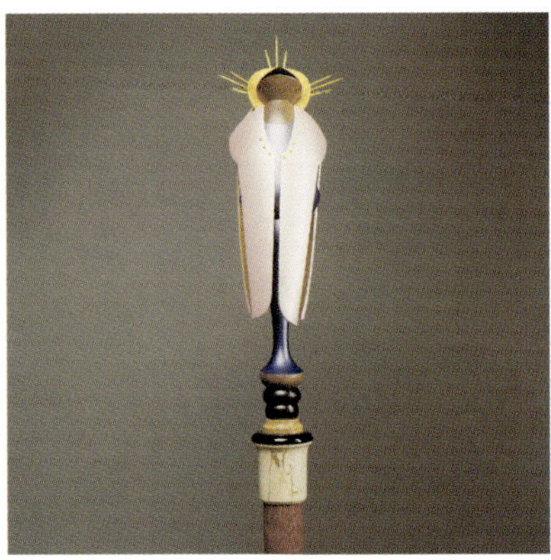

17
Steve Loar, in collaboration with Mark Sfirri and Frank Sudol
*Chatres Revisited*, 2000
H: 85", W: 19", D: 14"
Walnut, walnut burl, birch, spalted elm, satinwood, Plexiglas, Corian and purpleheart veneered struct-tube
lent by the artist

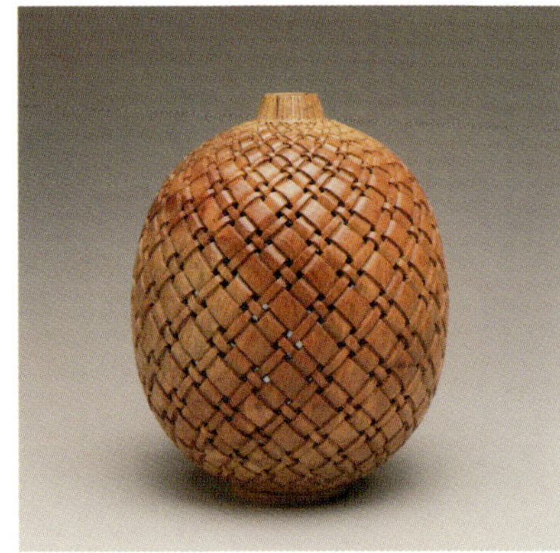

18
J. Paul Fennell
*Untitled*, 2000
H: 10", Diam: 8"
Carob
Collection of Marilyn Friedman, New York, NY

He further notes the influence of "designs found in architectural ornament and patterns abstracted from woven items of everyday use."[11] In combining textiles and architecture, Fennell is in touch with one of the most recent paradigms for architectural structure, but also taps into the fertile connection, already mentioned, between architecture and decoration.

Other artists in this exhibition embrace the decorative theme more completely, with less reference to architecture. Louise Hibbert's piece [4] is based on microscopic marine life forms that she studies and then reinvents in her work. Influenced by the 19th century illustrations of Ernst Haekal, her *Cinachyra Box* is protected "for its journey [with] a hard, spiny exoskeleton, enclosing a delicate interior, to encourage careful handling."[12] Hidden magnets make its closure definite, and the urgency with which it closes simulates life. Like Munro's own marine-influenced forms [3], which are covered with detailed and exquisite decorative, textured patterns, Hibbert's communicates the power and expressiveness of ornate objects packed with meaning for the artist. Gorst du Plessis' *Seattle Series (variations)* [19], are objects so perversely yet satisfyingly decorative that the functional elements (the lids) overwhelm the spherical containers to such a degree that its use would require exaggerated care to avoid breakage, and great patience to extract the contents through the small openings. The sheer decorativeness of them becomes a statement about the enjoyment of luxury for its own sake. Fleming's *Orpheus* [10] has a simple but convincing program, based visually on foliage, and thematically on the "spirit ditties of no tone" played by the mythical Orpheus, as imagined by Fleming. The piece is a graceful and decorative vessel fulfilling its purpose, and answering, rather than asking, questions, while testing the limits of turned form.

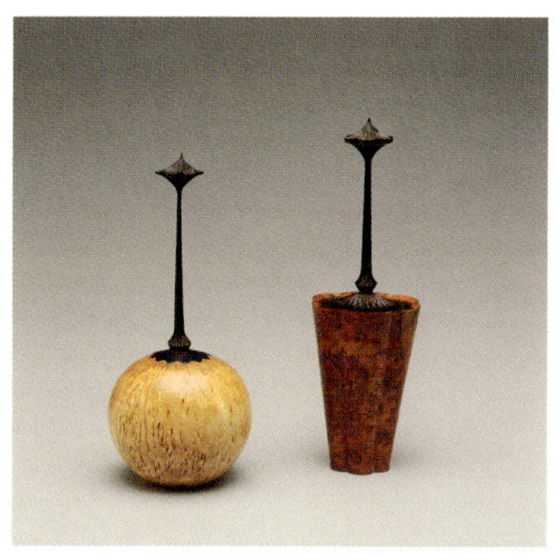

19
Gorst du Plessis
*Seattle Series (Variation)*, 2000
H: 7 1/2", Diam: 3 1/2"
Masur birch and African blackwood
lent by the artist

*Seattle Series (Variation)*, 2000
H: 8 1/2", Diam: 2 5/8"
Paela burl and African blackwood
lent by the artist

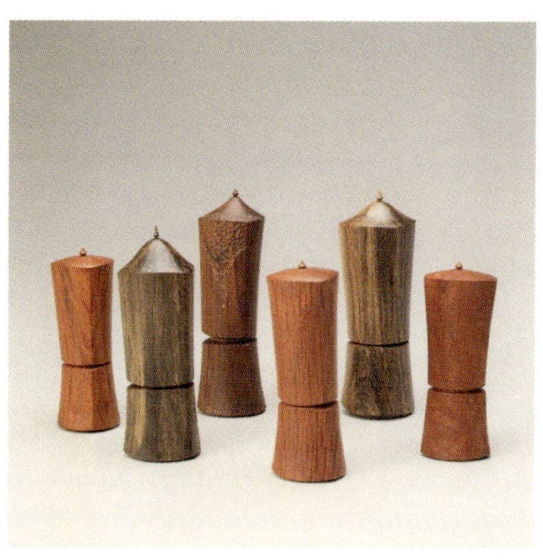

20
Andrew Potocnik
*Emperor Boxes*, 2000
Each H: 4", Diam: 1 3/4"
She oak and red gum
lent by the artist

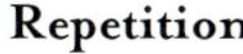

## Repetition

The production of multiples has traditionally been an important component of craft practice. Closely connected to it is the whole cluster of craft issues, especially functionality, with which the non-craft fine artist typically has so much difficulty. Perhaps in its rapid recent evolution, the wood turning community may be undecided about how to engage its historical origins. Similarities may be found to other craft media, such as ceramics, where the makers of place settings and household ware in the Leach tradition have discovered that the market is limited and that the art galleries simply do not accept the idea that the issues inherent in limited production are interesting enough. Yet in ceramics, some of the makers have found that one answer to their search for craft issues can be found in the history and practice of their own medium as differentiated from fine art issues.

Gerald Pocius, a folklorist from Memorial University in St John's, Newfoundland, has put his finger on our difficulty when he writes that our society's difficulty with cultural symbols of shared identity may be "because we have broken with the common link with our artifact past."[13] Artifacts as a class, he argues, have a different and lesser role in society than they once did.

Walter Ostrom, an influential ceramic artist and craft theorist based in Nova Scotia, proposes as a solution that the artists engage with the past. "A potter without ceramic history is a potter with amnesia.... History is one of the greatest ways to learn what is possible."[14] While the majority of wood turners preoccupy themselves with making an object in the "tradition of the new," some are clearly engaged in the origins of the medium, and in the implications of these origins on their possibilities for making a personal statement.

Andrew Potocnik's *Emperor Boxes* [20] are based on a combination of sources, which include Chinese Ming Dynasty hats, and cairns from Nepal. These sources appear to provide interesting forms which he has adapted to small elegant containers that are closely alike in size. These are one of only two entries which address the classic craft agenda of elegant and useful objects

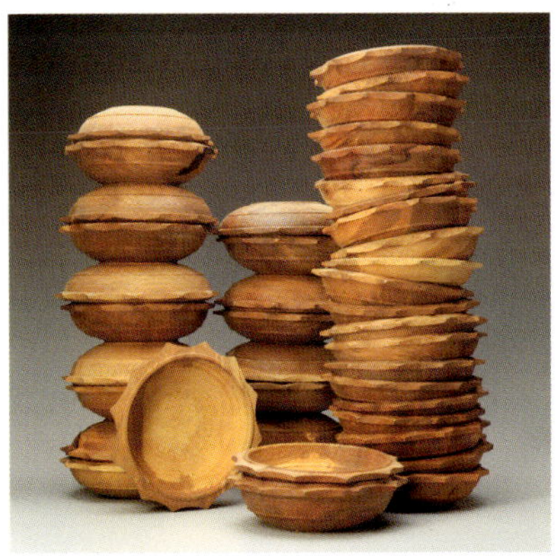

21
Robin Wood
*Star Bowls*, 2000
Each H: 2 1/2", Diam: 8"
(fifty-one bowls)
Pear wood
lent by the artist

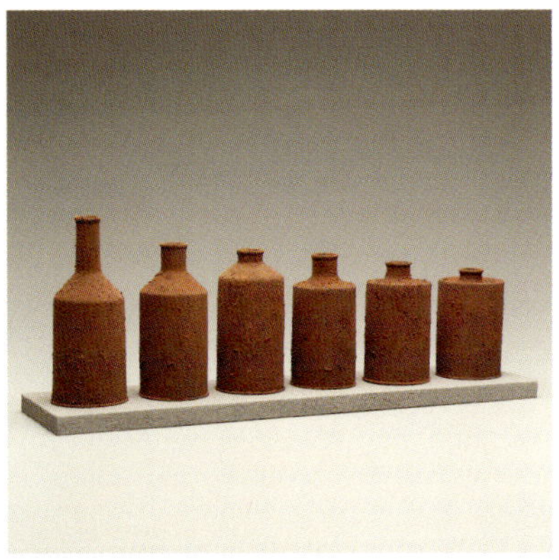

22
Richard Tuttle
*Pop-A-Top* (From the Junk Can Series), 2000
H: 7 1/4", W: 18 5/8", D: 4 1/2"
Oak, iron oxides, MDF and acrylics
lent by the artist

handmade in multiples from primary raw materials, the other being Robin Woods' *Star Bowls* [21]. Together with Richard Tuttle's *Pop-A-Top* [22], John Jordan's *Black/White Pair* [23], Merryll Saylan's *Tribute: Hans Coper* [24] and arguably Sfirri's *French Vessel Series* [7], they represent the continuation of the engagement with repetition and function of the wood turning tradition.

While Potocnik's works are functional and decorative pieces which unquestioningly acknowledge the influence of other cultures in providing domestic comfort and elegance for ours, Wood's *Star Bowls* represent a different sort of engagement with the specific history of wood turning practice. In referring to an actual artifact dating from the mid 15th century and other late medieval/early Renaissance sources, Wood says, "The humble wooden bowl is as much a part of our cultural identity as fine ceramics are for the Chinese."[15] His use of the pole lathe to produce multiples is not only historically accurate but also symbolically important for the maker. The resulting fifty-one pieces, based on an actual historical design, are as alike and as heart-warming as slices of crusty bread. As the maker says, "...to me subtle differences in balance and form make one bowl sing whilst another doesn't. Like fine wine, it is often the barely perceivable that makes the difference and like fine wine, it is the variation which makes them interesting." This is the heart of the case for craft. The awkward fact that this argument does not change is perhaps the main reason why its appeal tends to fade in a critical context. However, while the essential artifact has not changed in three hundred years, the context for it continues to change, and the subtleties ripen if we care to attend to them.

Tuttle has only been turning since 1995, and claims to have been involved in "one-of-a-kind" pieces since that time. In his *Junk Cans* series, he found a starting point in an old, industrially produced can that he found in the woods. Out of this find, came a discovery of the idea of repetition, the rhythm of multiples, "the paradox between the time it took to make the individual pieces compared to the original concept of mass production"[16] and the challenge of formulating an appropriate surface to express the rusted actuality of the

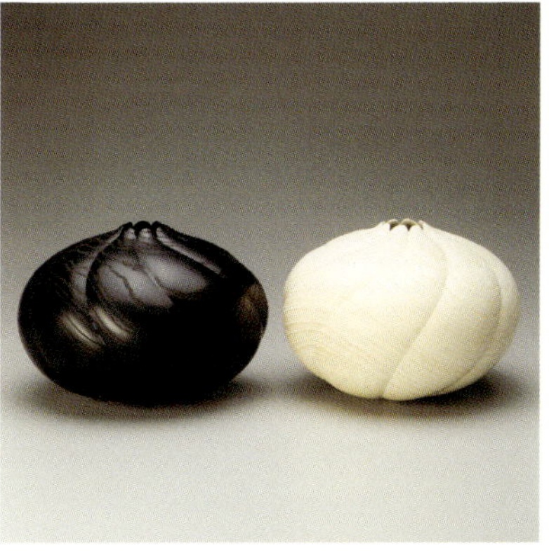

23
John Jordan
*Black/ White Pair*, 2000
H: 7", W: 10", D: 10"
Ash
lent by the artist

found can. Saylan's *Tribute: Hans Coper* [24] juxtaposes similar forms based on the great Modernist ceramist's work .[17] "Somehow," she says, "there is a power in the sheer number and repetitions of one form against another."[18]

In his work, Tuttle reflects on the idea of repetition and the proto-industrial nature of the bodger, a traditional English wood-turning craftsman, and yet does not attempt Wood's historicist strategy or Potocnik's volume of product. The work of Potocnik, Wood, Saylan, and Tuttle together demonstrates the notion that wood turning's heritage can provide a source of contemporary elegant living, of lively traditional practice, and also of commentary on contemporary issues.

**Influences**

"Curators will evaluate submissions in terms of the success of the object's evolution from the source into a unique statement." So says the Call to Entry for *Challenge VI*. As a curator, while I was not part of the decision to establish this criteria, when I accepted the role I accepted the emphasis. Subsequently, some artists contacted me to discuss this. Some were puzzled about how to do it; others were opposed to it and felt it excluded them; others felt that their particular sources — ephemeral experiences or memories, for example — were unreproducible. One or two were angry. Others supplied a poor quality Xerox copy as a source, indicating a passing interest in the source itself.

Clearly, some artists are more introspective in their creative process than others. I don't think anyone would discount or minimize the seminal role played by the intuitive, non-verbal processes in making art. Some clearly see exploring the roots of an idea as destructive to the flower and fruit: "The stories you tell you never write," said novelist William Faulkner.

On the other side of this question, many artists find value in reflecting on their ideas. Many, as this show indicates, work their sources intensely, recognizing their voices as artists' through the process of tracing the source. Poet

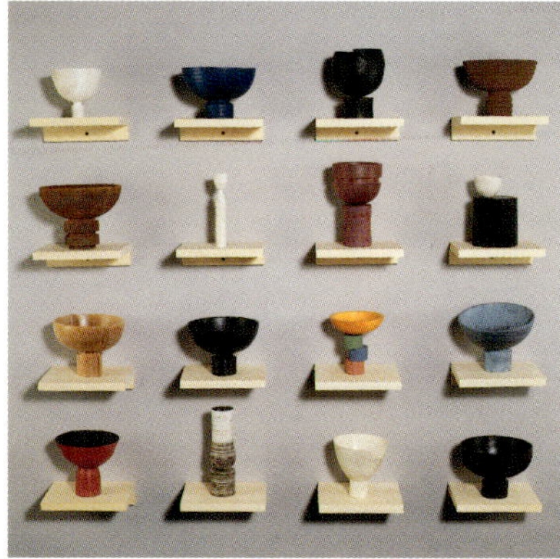

24
Merryll Saylan
*Tribute: Hans Coper*, 2000
H: 54", W: 47", D: 8"
Wood, paint and dye
lent by the artist

W.H. Auden's question "How do I know what I mean until I see what I said?" is one of my very favorites. Perhaps this is another way of stating Kierkegaard's aphorism that "Life is lived forwards and understood backwards." The idea of intuition and reflection, or of two very different sorts of creative phases is an old idea, and we find in Pope, for example, the tension between the two, apparent in 1711:

> "For Wit and Judgement often are at strife,
> Tho' meant each other's Aid, like Man and Wife"[19]

Searching for sources can, at the very least, be an important way to understanding oneself. In addition, it can bring the artist's own critical faculties to bear on his or her own work. It can provide a useful distance between the work and the artist, which may enable the artist to work closer to his original intention.

The dangers of encouraging the purely intuitive and non-introspective process of making art may include works that are impulsive and poorly thought through. On the other hand, the dangers of encouraging reflective art may result in works that lack passion or the marks of the white heat of creation.

In this show we have tried to recognize a blend of the two. There were some pieces that were rejected because we felt the account of them was laborious and forced, just as we rejected others because there did not seem to be a convincing resonance between the claimed source and the piece. Nevertheless, there were some specific problems. The question of influence of one artist on another was a case in point. One exhibitor had proposed a homage to the work of another artist who had influenced and inspired him. We felt that the homage was, though sincere, derivative and added nothing to the source. This piece was rejected.

Another entry was perhaps a more resolved and powerful piece, but clearly resembled a fairly well known piece by a distinguished artist in wood. However, the derivation was not acknowledged, despite an otherwise well

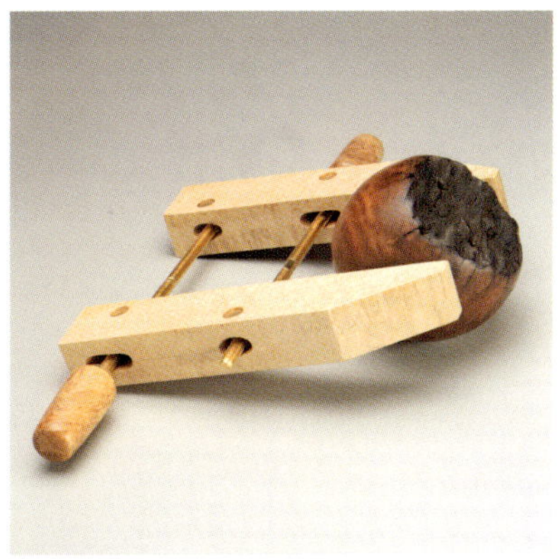

25
Steve Bishop
*Portrait of an Artist as a Middle Aged Man...*, 2000
H: 5 1/2", W: 19", D: 3 1/2"
Birdseye maple, redwood, maple burl and 24k gold-plated hardware
lent by the artist

researched account of the sources. We felt that the similarity was so obvious that, while we did not suspect the applicant of consciously plagiarizing, we felt there was a responsibility to know and to acknowledge primogeniture.

Several artists acknowledged a debt and were accepted. Wall's respectful reference to Hunter's works was accepted because we felt he had made a personal contribution to a type of form Hunter had created. Wall's work was similar in technique, but different in feeling and was presented differently, being suspended and not resting on a horizontal surface.

Wood's *Star Bowls* [21] are virtually copies of a traditional type. Here, originality is not an issue at all, but the penetration and continuation of historical practice into contemporary life. Loar's piece[17] references the sculptures at Chartres and the *Wizard of Oz*, and consciously manipulates them in an original piece.

Steve Bishop's piece *Portrait of the Artist as a Middle-Aged Man (with a stressful job, a wife, a house, two mortgages, two cars, five cats and a neurotic dog)* [25] was accompanied by a found image of oppressively suburban, stereotypical family life from the 1950's.[20] The source image was so strong that it combined brilliantly with the title and the giant nut cracker made by the artist into a two-part piece – one of the few works in the show where the source became part of the final piece, rather than an informative adjunct to it.

Thibeault's [13, 14, 15] and Garrett's [16] architectural references have been dealt with earlier as two of several artists who have been influenced in that way. Thibeault's work does not seem directly autobiographical, but it does draw attention to unusual forms and to a set of formal interests which convince me they will repay further consideration. Garrett's work, dealing with constructions and the nature of creation out of disorder, leads him to reflect on the nature of his interest, and he comes to a conclusion about the nature of thought itself: "The organizing process that transforms a complex framework into a simpler form seems to me to be representative of the processes of thought, invention, and creativity."[21] To find such startlingly effective forms which are

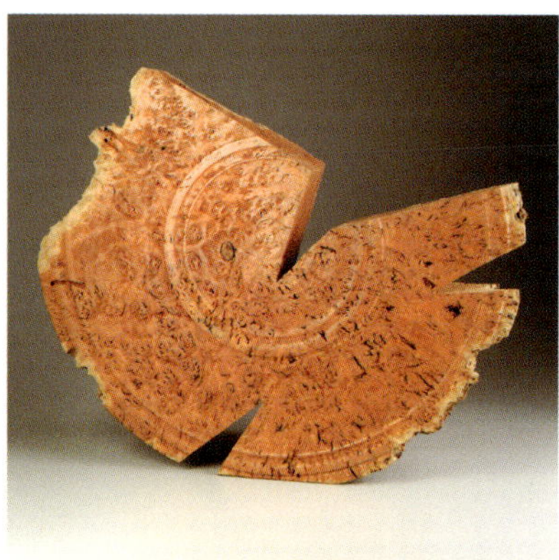

26
Robyn Horn
*Fractured Millstone*, 2000
H: 24", W: 24", D: 7"
Jarrah burl
lent by the artist

themselves a result of a reaction and reflection of the very processes of human thought seems to me to answer any concerns about the value of inquiring into an artist's sources.

Today, visual art is seen as a language, and the critical audience demands a knowledge of the overall discourse which artists are engaged in. Artistic statements are not only personal but relate to points in the discourse just as, in a conversation, we expect that each person's comments move the discussion forward a little, or move it backwards usefully to elucidate something which went before. The crafts, on the other hand, have been less successful in establishing the idea of a discourse between themselves or with others. Confused, perhaps, with various agendas, craft tends to remain either dependent on a nostalgic view of the world — remaining stuck with technology which was becoming an anachronism when William Morris began the Movement – or fixated on material and process to re-live their Modern Golden Age when Abstract Expressionism blessed these aspects of all art work. In addition, various craft media advanced at different rates, with perhaps ceramics and textiles leading the way for most of the second half of the 20th century. Potters such as Bernard Leach and Peter Voulkos led their own revolutions of taste and approach in clay, while textile artists such Ethel Mairet and Claire Zeisler did the same. Coming, as I did, to wood turning from ceramics with a general acquaintance with fine crafts, my impressions are that wood turning is progressing at its own pace, and undergoing several developments which bear some comparison to other media.

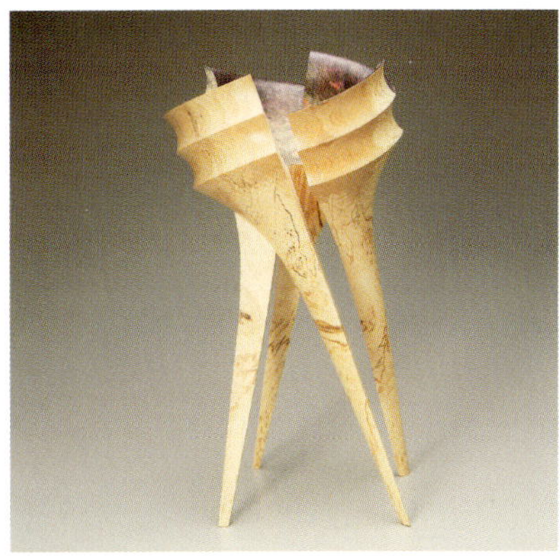

27
Stephen Hogbin
*Progress of Walking: Happen Stance*, 2000
H: 19", W: 9", D: 9"
Spalted maple
lent by the artist

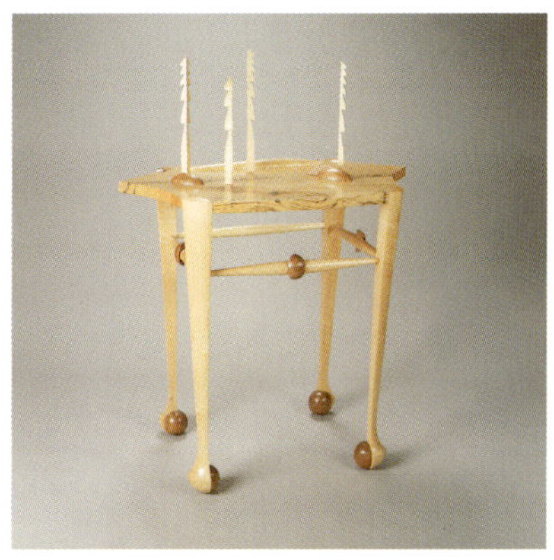

28
Stephen Hogbin
*Conversation through a Table*, 2000
H: 48", W: 36", D: 21"
Beech, maple and walnut
lent by the artist

**Finale**

In every exhibition, there are probably several pieces which one returns to time and time again, because they exemplify many aspects of the exhibition which other pieces perhaps only touch on singularly, or with less force.

Robyn Horn's work, both her writing and her making in wood, is well known for its influential character. Her *Fractured Millstone* pieces [26], follow on from several series of earlier works and are not explained by the artist in terms of definite outside references. She refers to the series *Geodes*, their successors *Millstone*, and *Stepping Stones*. She seems still preoccupied with working through from a starting point which is fresh in her mind, and the pieces have the resonance of constant thought about a single and very powerful cluster of meanings whose meaning she is still trying to capture and understand for herself. This stillness and density is appropriate to the subject that she refers to as that of the oldest and most durable of human artistic materials: stone. She writes of the negative spaces showing "the strength of stone and the 'livingness' and cohesiveness of wood."[22] Other references to arches make clear that the architectural use of stone, as well as its monumental qualities, are part of the aura of the pieces. Erected on end like standing stones, they are pre-architectural in presence and impact.

Also partaking similarly is the work of George Peterson whom I met briefly during the ITE 2000. While Horn is contemplative and still, though implying motion and activity, Peterson's work is extremely gestural and boisterous with energy and activity. His method of working is highly intuitive and improvised rather than reflective. His account, however, shows his awareness of his method and his confident reliance on his power to relate and interact with the wood. He refers to Bob Stocksdale, Mark Lindquist, Del Stubbs, and Hap Sakwa as inspirations, and also notes his tendency to move from one piece to another, retaining the highly exploratory nature of each piece. His introduction to turning came through the bowl form. He still connects to simple open forms and sees his piece, *Buddha's Mirror* [5], as a bowl form. His ambitious and bold

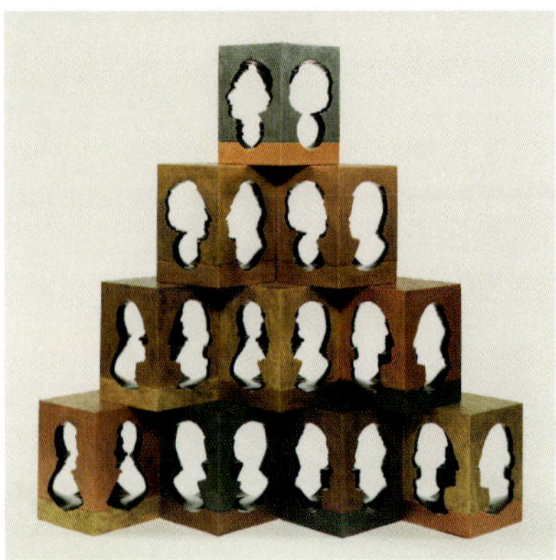

29
Gene Kangas
*Rushmore*, 2000
H: 64", W: 66", D: 16 1/2"
Painted poplar and basswood
lent by the artist

use of very large pieces of wood, and the voracious and fearless use of heavy tools, such as a chain saw for the making of surface marks, develops pieces which have the monumental presence of Horn's, while establishing a graphic surface in which the intervention of the artist is the dominant element in the partnership with the wood.

The contrast of Stephen Hogbin's pieces could not be more striking. Hogbin, from Ontario, has an established reputation as one of the most influential makers and thinkers — if that separation makes any sense in Hogbin's case — in wood turning today. His pieces, *Progress of Walking: Happen Stance* [27], and *Conversation through a Table* [28], are in their deliberation a contrast to Peterson's, and in their finished appearance a contrast to both Peterson's and Horn's. In respect to the turning process, both of Hogbin's pieces explore forms that can be attained by cutting the turned piece apart. He achieved both the bowl and the table legs in this way. His explanation contrasts the active result ("walking") with the reflective ("conversation") in the two pieces, and also notes the similarity in the words for his two main concerns: conversation and conservation. He is almost certainly aware of the Latin derivations, where "conserve" is from *servare: to keep* and conversation is from vertare, *versum: to turn*, so that a conversation becomes about turning as well as about keeping the earth in a good state. Taken together, the pieces make a symmetrical statement about active and reflective states and responsibilities by using wood turning as a medium: a medium which itself depends both on the stillness of the axis and the movement of the surface. The table is a fine example of Hogbin's ability to carry though an intellectual program into actual form. Intended as a hall or side table, the integral placing of stylized trees and "erratic" boulders occupies, but does not clutter, the surface. Such a table, as Hogbin points out, is meant to be used for the laying down or picking up of keys or letters. "The activity of exchange is like a conversation. In this conversation, too many objects will spoil the image of the land by cluttering the space. The quantity, juxtaposition, and balance of the objects is everything."[23] And so, as we use the table, our behavior is conditioned by it, as it is or should be by the same considerations of the

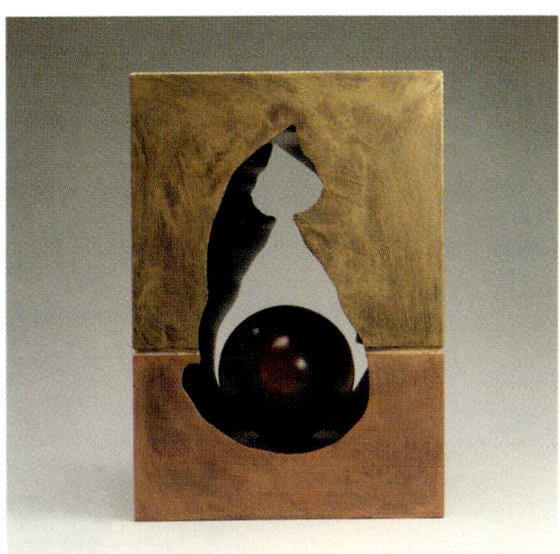

30
Gene Kangas
***Daisy Turns***, 1999
H: 15", W: 10 1/2", D: 10 1/2"
Painted basswood and maple
lent by the artist

environment itself. Hogbin's program is so carefully thought through and deeply felt in itself, and so well translated into the objects, that his work is an exceptional example of the interrelation between concept and object. It is notably not just a slick or strained explanation imposed on the piece and the viewer, but a mutually enriching convergence of thought and object.

Perhaps the most striking piece in the show is Gene Kangas' *Rushmore 2000* [29], supported by *Daisy Turns* [30], and *Hutch* [31]. We often see a craft medium follow in the tracks of fine art, but here Kangas — a sculptor in flat steel — has found a craft medium which extends his explorations. "Wood turning has provided the opportunity to transform the two-dimensionality of flat steel into three-dimensional volume"[24] By recognizing that spindle turning creates a profile, he has used that ability to create portraits from the negative space. By creating portraits of politicians of iconic stature, and adding Albert Einstein and the atomic mushroom cloud, a weighty political statement derives directly from the potential of the technique and language of turning. Not just a clever trick, but a convincing and complex statement about human achievement and risk, the piece is an overt acknowledgement from a distinguished American sculptor of the potential of turning as a medium for artistic statement.

Following on Suzanne Ramljak's important essay "As the World Turns: Wood Turning in an Expanded Context,"[25] which marks perhaps the first serious attempt to put the issues of wood turning into a broader intellectual context, this exhibition may mark an important stage in the wood turning field as it stretches its scope. To return to the metaphor of conversation at the beginning of this essay, I write sensing the great excitement in the turning field as the people practicing in it find new directions to engage one another in a way which does not negate the history of the medium, nor the work of the individuals who were the pioneer artists.

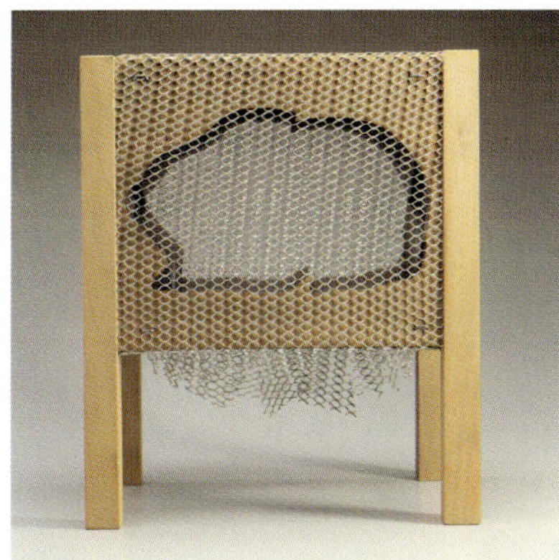

31
Gene Kangas
***Hutch***, 2000
H: 17", W: 14 1/4", D: 10 1/2"
Poplar and wire screen
lent by the artist

1 Quoted by Suzanne Ramljak in "As the World Turns: Wood Turning in an Expanded Context" in *Turning Wood into Art: The Jane and Arthur Mason Collection* (NY: Harry N Abrams, and The Mint Museum of Craft + Design, 2000) p. 21, referencing S Hogbin et al, *Curator's Focus* WTC, 1997, p. 112.

2 "Artificial" in the original sense of "being made by art."

3 See *Creation out of Clay: the ceramic art of Brother Thomas*, ed. Rosemary Williams (Boston: Pucker Gallery in association with Wm. B Erdmans Publishing Co., Grand Rapids, MI., 1999) ISBN 0-8028-3870-7. Thomas' work is notable for its subtle management of bold glaze effects.

4 A. Loos, *Ornament und Verbrechen (Ornament and Crime)*, 1908.

5 See Fiell, *Charlotte and Peter, Design of the 20th Century*, (Koln: Taschen, 1999), p. 183. In this text, representative of a standard view of the field, the authors note: "During the 1980's, the Craft Revival was stylistically accomplished by Post Modernism and designers such as Fred Baier who combined technical virtuosity with bizarre forms to create objects which were the very antithesis of "the good citizen's furniture" that had been espoused by Morris and Ruskin."

6 Jenson, Robert and Conway, Patricia, *Ornamentalism – The New Decorativeness in Architecture and Design*, (NY: Clarkson and Potter Inc, 1982) p. 1.

7 Beezely cites Ignasi de Sola-Morales, *Weak Architecture*, in "Differences: topographies of Contemporary Architecture," ed. Sarah Whiting, trans. Graham Thompson, (Cambridge: MIT Press, 1996).

8 Artist's statement for this exhibition.

9 Artist's statement for this exhibition.

10 Roman Catholic iconography is redolent of various blood and heart motifs, including The Immaculate Heart of Mary, The Sacred Heart of Jesus, and the Precious Blood.

11 Artist's statement for this exhibition

12 Artist's statement for this exhibition

13 Gerald Pocius, "Craft and Cultural Meaning", in *Making and Metaphor: A Discussion of Meaning in Contemporary Craft*, ed G Hickey (Hull: The Canadian Museum of Civilisation and the Institute for Contemporary Canadian Craft, 1994), p. 131.

14 Quoted by Ann West in *Walter Ostrom: The Advocacy of Pottery* (Halifax:Art Gallery of Nova Scotia, 1996) p. 32. West comments that Ostrom's approach to history was "Not merely a registration of the past, but a productive reclamation and interpretation in terms of one's own age, vision and intention."

15 Artist's statement for this exhibition.

16 Artist's statement for the exhibition.

17 Coper was a German who escaped Nazism and worked in England before and after WWII. His work explored simplified and stylized vessel forms based on Cycladic sculpture.

18 Artist's statement for the exhibition.

19 Alexander Pope, *Essay on Criticism*, ll.82-3 ed J Butt (London: Methuen, 1963) p. 146.

20 "Yes," says the artist, "sometimes I feel like my life is in a clamp, but isn't it a beautiful clamp?"

21 Artist's statement for this exhibition.

22 Artist's statement for this exhibition.

23 Artist's statement for this exhibition.

24 Artist's statement for this exhibition.

25 From *Turning Wood into Art: The Jane and Arthur Mason Collection* ed. Mark Richard Leach, (New York: Harry M Abrams, 2000, in association with the Mint Museum of Craft and Design) pp.17-31. I would like to acknowledge here my deep debt to this essay for its ambitious scope, valuable information, and groundbreaking scholarship.

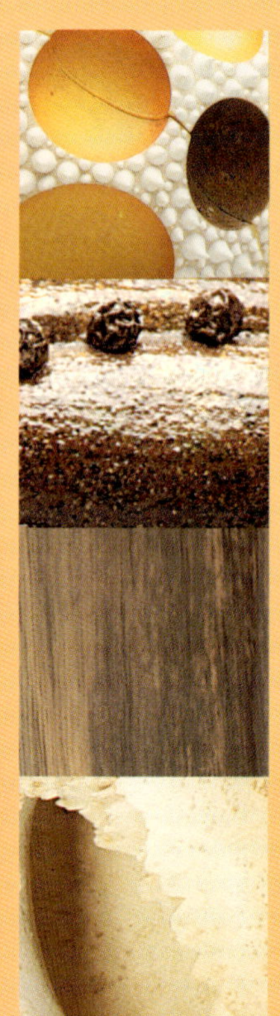

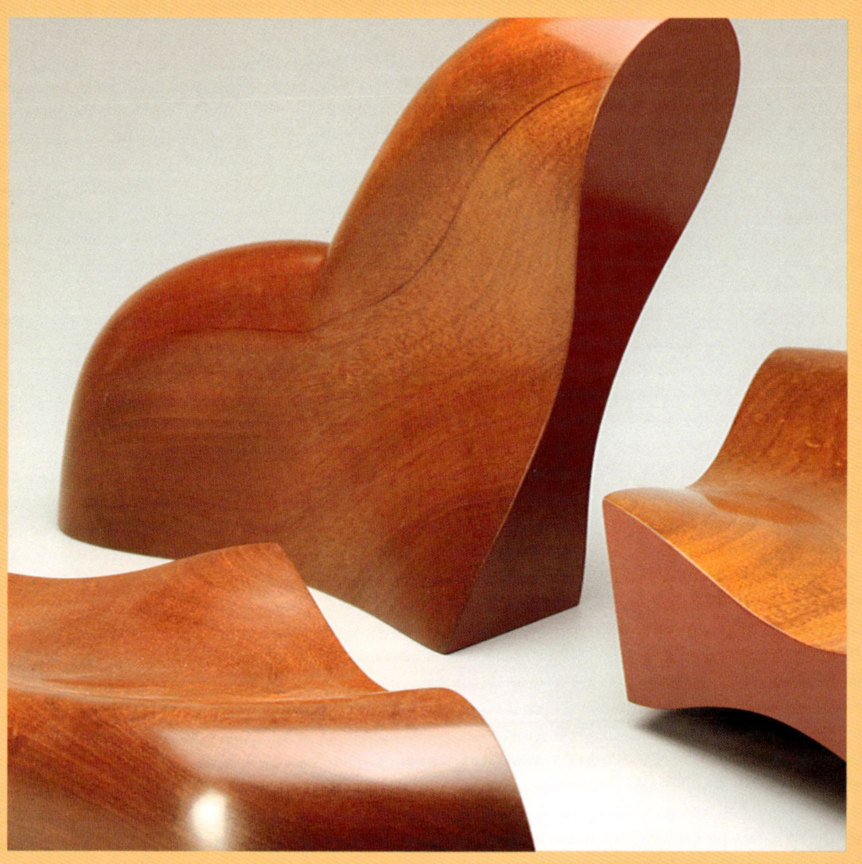

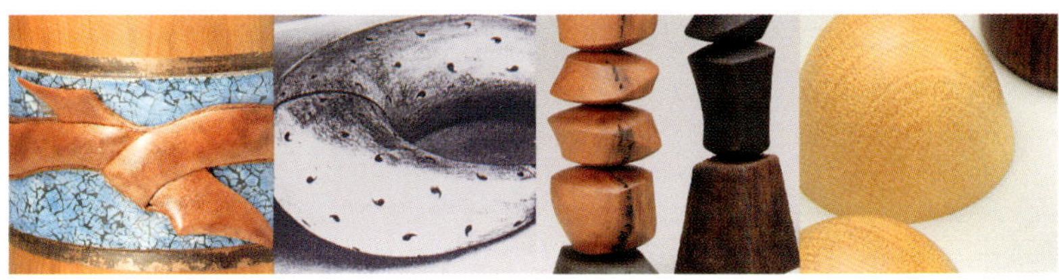

# A Mosaic Love Letter ?

*by Michelle Holzapfel*

Michelle Holzapfel has over two decades of experience turning and carving native hardwoods in Southern Vermont, where she lives. Her work has been exhibited in museums and galleries in the United States and Europe, and been acquired by the Museum of Fine Arts, Boston, the Rhode Island School of Design Museum, Yale University Art Gallery, the Smithsonian's Renwick Gallery, and other public and private collections.

Ms. Holzapfel's work has been in many Wood Turning Center exhibitions, including the first four *Challenge* exhibitions through 1991. An object of hers will be in the *Wood Turning in North America Since 1930* exhibition sponsored by the Wood Turning Center and the Yale University Art Gallery, opening in October at the Minneapolis Institute of Arts.

Publications featuring her work include *House Beautiful*, *American Craft*, and *Fine Woodworking*. She has lectured and taught at events sponsored by local and national craft organizations. Her writings have been published in *American Craft* and *Turning Points* magazines.

The process of making a composite statement is a lot like my working process — and that of many other makers. First, I closely examined the materials that came with each maker's application — statements, photos, sketches. While mindful of their uniqueness and respectful of their integrity, my effort was aimed at arranging this 'raw' material into a different form for use in this book. I would attempt to engender the voice of a "Meta-Maker," or "Uber-Maker," to speak for all. This process began with a careful search of each maker's statements for the most vivid, honest words about all aspects of making things. I copied these words, phrases, and sentences onto paper; then cut them apart and sorted and re-sorted — striving to group allied ideas, and connect kindred subjects.

This felt a lot like the moments in my own work-process in which a piece seems simultaneously to be coming together and coming apart — a moment of both sweet possibilities and grave self-doubts. Slowly the pieces began to cohere, flow, and support each other — attracted or repelled by their magnetic valences. The full statements from each maker can be found throughout this book.Like a beautiful piece of timber, these rare and rich materials could have been formed into a hundred different statements, in the hands/minds of a hundred different makers. In the end, I'm still wondering what this effort reflects. My foremost aim was to serve as the agent of each maker's voice, the ambassador for their clarity and strength. Is this an act of ventriloquism? Am I assembling a mosaic love letter? Or are all my little pieces of paper the streamers and confetti of a celebration of our vital and varied field?

# Introduction

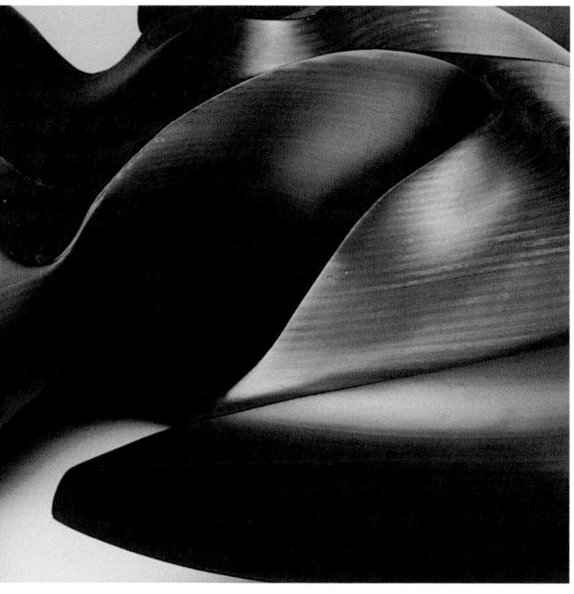

The Idea: a cup sitting in a ring.//...the perfect confluence of curves...

the life-affirming curves, curves familiar to 1st century Mediterranean carpenters.

I wanted to make it fragile... rather fragile...

the entrancing purity of the egg's blending of sphere and ellipse

...the beauty of the wood was exploited...at the expense of form and aesthetics.

The form lacked excitement so I looked at Moebius forms...

I then started 'doodling' on the outside of the form...

...no pretense of circular perfection...

...I dissolved the walls of the vessel...

the negative space slashed through the middle.

I could easily have changed...the form to make it 'my own,' but feel no need. I could re-make the bowl a thousand times, and still no two would be the same, and still I would be developing, refining...

...portraying ripeness.

An egg balancing between my forefinger and my thumb.

...its sensuousness, strangeness and intimate details.

The fingerprint-like incisions..

...engage the hand and imagination of the recipient...

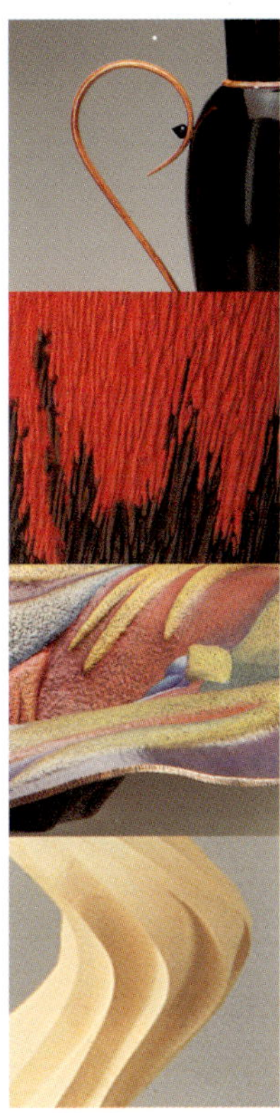

...to encourage careful handling.//...to inspire tactile desire...

...carry a human touch; carry spirit.

...I have handled thousands of Medieval wooden bowls...

...touched the heart...

...thicker and tactile 'Celtic Touch Bowls'...more functional yet still sensitive...

...pick them up, feel the marks of the tools, feel where the weight lies.

I did have a concept...strands of form undulating from right to left, up and down.

...a sense of movement, balance, tension...//...the contrast of obese and thin...

Playful, energetic, and centrally focused...visually dynamic...

...emphasizing contrast..Black with White..Big with Small.

a form, texture or colour that I find... irresistible.

...visual, tactile and in some instances, smell.

Like fine wine...//...made to whisper, not shout...

# Surface
## One: materials and color

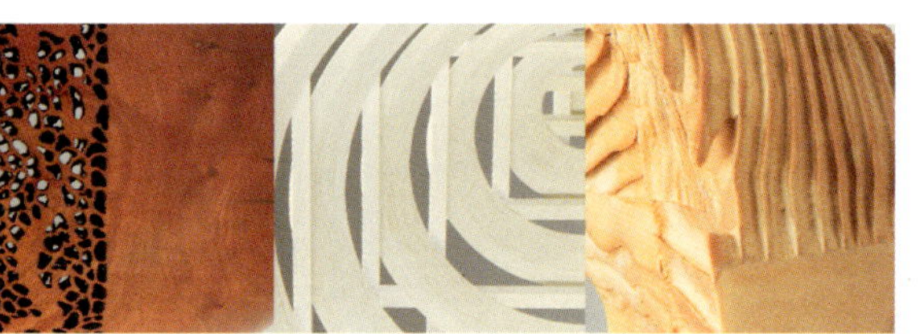

...wood....as long as I can remember

...rhododendron/spalted hackberry/carob...

...the life of a tree can be read in the trunk.//...close to the bole...

...Pink Ivory...//...the walnut was saved from a pile of firewood...

...firewood oak...a neighbor's woodpiles or arborist's leavings.

black persimmon...lignitized cedar...japanese zelkova...sarusuberi

...a tree taken down in a street renovation....

sirari and guatambu, wenge and holly//olives, lemons....

...pale, even-grained sycamore to act as a blank canvas...

...the whitened wood...Roots embedded in the dark hidden bosom of earth...

the 'livingness' and cohesiveness of wood.

the wood, I collaborate with it.//a relationship with a particular piece of wood...

...begins as a chunk of fresh green burl//still green, a pleasure to cut and handle.

...a soft, wet, pithy substance dotted with long, stringy fibers.

...a piece of wood I had admired for years but couldn't bring myself to alter

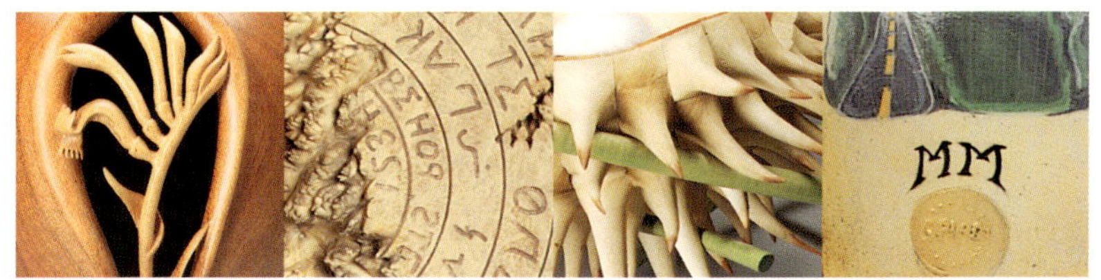

...hard to tame...the wildest wood I have ever used.//any woodturner's nightmare!

...responding to the challenge of this odd material

...it accepts guidance but resists any attempt to make it conform.

...thorns...I have long been aware of their figural properties.

Plexiglass, Corian,//...cast leaded crystal.//...toothpicks.

...shell, stone, silver, sharks' teeth...//...coppered peppercorns,

found metal//copper vessel...//...linen thread...telegraph wire

...carnuba wax/...lacquer.../a light oil finish, buffed and waxed.

...Cherokee red and earth green...//...stained by a moldy growth.

...the colors hearken back to my paintings of 20 years ago.

brightly colored resin/freshly mixed with pigments

...translucent with an amber color.../...vibrant stains and markings...

...the symbolic blues and reds used in Medieval Christian paintings.

Experiment with...bleaching, dyeing.//...remove all its color...

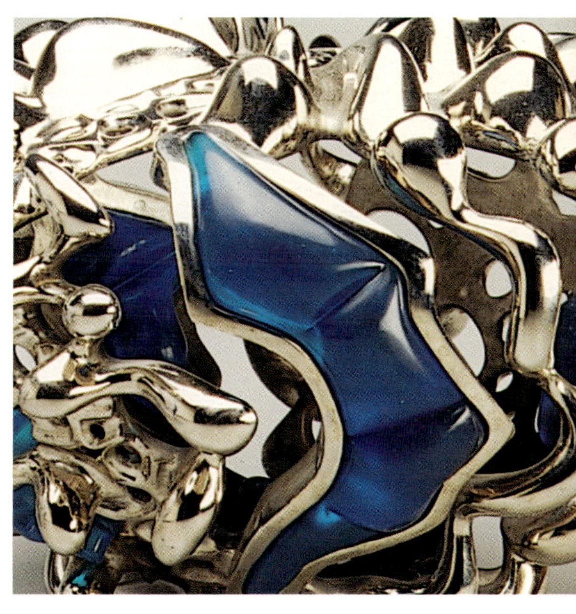

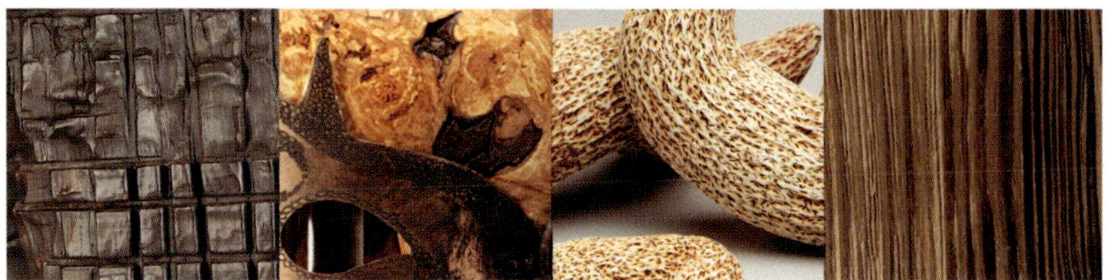

# Two: tools

...focused on the physical effort...//...and the love of process.

...a 'classical machinist' who creates his own machines.

Turning exists at the core of my works...

Faceplate turning is akin to thrown pottery...

...rotational processes./...multi-axis turning./...multiple-axis techniques...

spindle turning...the more ancient form of lathe work...

I use the tools used five hundred years ago: the pole lathe, the axe, the knife, not out of some nostalgic vision but because they work efficiently and give the variation in texture and form which I desire.

One-way/General/Holtzapffel...1842/Armbruster Rose Engine lathe.

...Origins traced to ancient Mesopotamia....a line of descent may be drawn from this era to the complexities of late industrial machine work.

...I use no measuring tools...I turn and carve them by eye.

...treat the lathe as a carving tool.

...removing the recognizable relationship of the scupltures to the lathe.

...Sandblasting and beadblasting.../...engraving and texturing...

...scorched and rough/...wire brushing./...subtle scoring and perforations

...one section masked...steamed and bent.//...off the lathe augmentation...

...possibilities revealed through process.

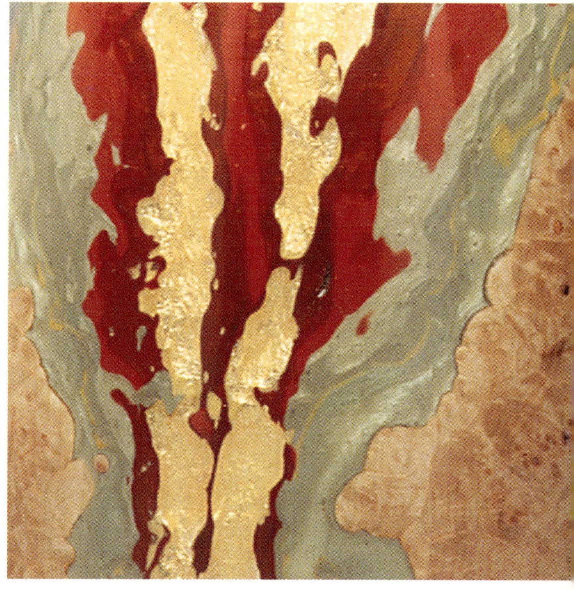

## Three: nature

...from galaxies to spiralling hawks to DNA...

the smooth lines of a full sail...the force that moves the vessel forward.

I was drawn to the river: the power, vitality, and endurance of the river.

living near...a tidal marsh-striations, movement, patterns

a seed pod/burr//a seed pod bursting open

tortoise carapaces//radiolarians and echinoderms

exoskeleton enclosing a delicate interior//sand dollars and sea biscuits

bird-of-paradise//avian forms//an amalgamation of different creatures

hommage rocks and cairns from Everest

stones and their strong, solid shapes//geological strata...expose the layers within

...provoke a power which might be called the providence of nature in my work.

# Architecture One:

lighting patterns in a New Jersey convention hall.

Egyptian and Mayan pyramids...//a modern, functioning office building

Bernini's Baldiccino at St. Peter's in Rome

pierced marble screens of the mosques//a concrete decorative wall...

domes with their concavity and their axial symmetry....

the 12 columns of King Solomon's Temple//the Seattle ... Space Needle

the jamb figures of the West Royal Portal of Chartres Cathedral...

my life-long preoccupation with towers...

...architrave....awning...clerestory

...there is something about architecture that resonates with us...

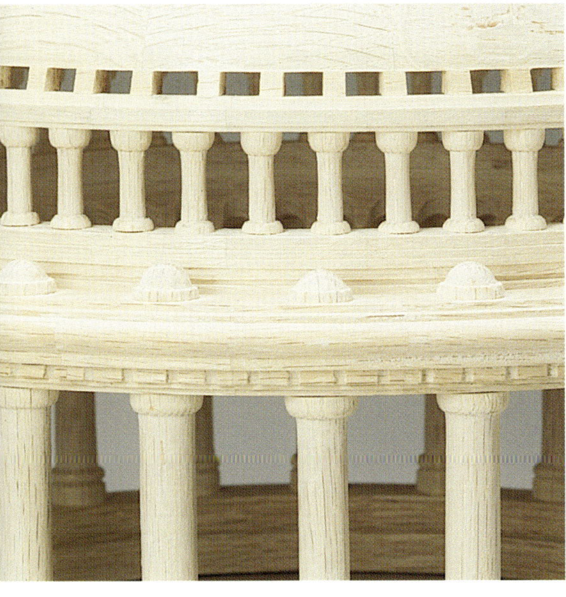

# Two:

...a minimal intrusion of structure...a non-supporting exo-skeleton.

...the idea of structure and enclosure...//...a more complex helix form...

...a reverse wood-turned sculpture consisting of ten figural blocks.

...one turning made from four blanks fixed together and turned.

...graceful tapers, and linear frame construction.

... to refine the dimensions of form by freeing it from the constraints of function...

...the large scale...allows the viewer to enter that place...and explore...

...a maze of sinus-like cavities...

...its appearance changes greatly as you walk by...

...viewers are challenged to look through and around...

...to experience the interplay between the inner and outer surfaces...

...a visual tour from the exterior to the Sculpture's inner voids.

...the eye is...drawn to...its voids...

...cutting through the walls...//...to discover fresh visual material../.

...the...windows are entrance to another world.

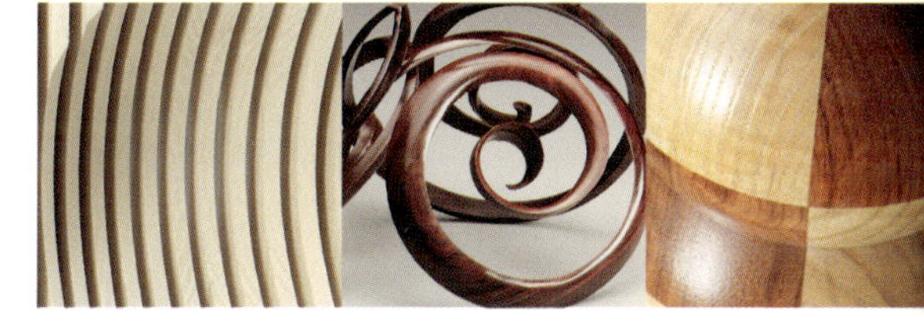

# Repetition

...there is a power in the sheer number and repetitions of one form against another.

...to produce objects in multiples like the potter's wheel and weaver's loom.

...multiples. No longer do I see them as dreaded, dull and uninteresting.

...the everyday vessels of industrial culture: the bottle, the jar and the can.

Plates and platters serve as a canvas.

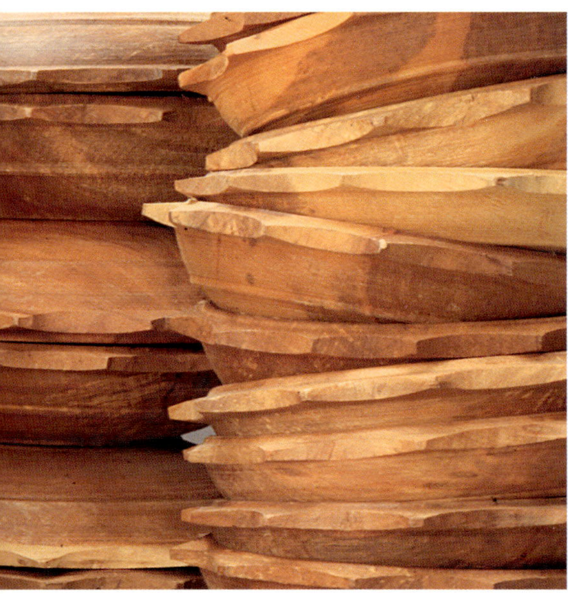

...the relationship of 'classical' shapes used in 'industrial' context.

This general sense of a bottle is intended to be a contradiction within itself.

...an interpretation of an everyday, throwaway object...made of a highly figured piece of curly maple.

...a wood bowl can be so much more than it appears

...learning to look at small details, just at details.

...many hours of contemplation during the glue-up stage...this quiet...time allows my mind to wander.

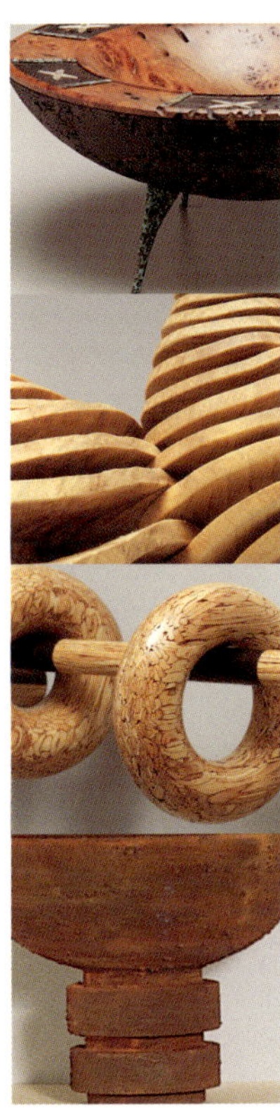

# One: design

Drawing #2...made during a long and uninteresting phone conversation

...computer modeling/wire frame depiction...//...a fiber optics system...

I'm not interested in making hard mathematically generated models.

...twelve sine wave tapered...six scalloped with 3 scallops on the 6.

...fragmentals...a new configuration....Fibonacci numbers or Golden rule

...inscribed or milled decaying mathematical functions onto spiralling surfaces.

...simply an exploration of making lines or tool paths on cones.

...the cross-over was given a Moebius twist & then transposed onto an egg profile

...legs that form two flat planes with a bowl slung between them

...one section of a log, which was split to make the two pieces...having grown foot-to-foot...opposing spirals...black and white contrast.

A footed bowl with a natural rim...//...elevated on patinated copper legs...

...the classic Etruscan ewer...//The humble wooden bowl: our cultural identity...

...my first venture into the 'vessel' form.

What would happen if the base dominated and there was only a teeny bowl on top?

...the piece would appear to have grown that way.

... a normal turning that evolves into a meandering convoluted turning impossibility.

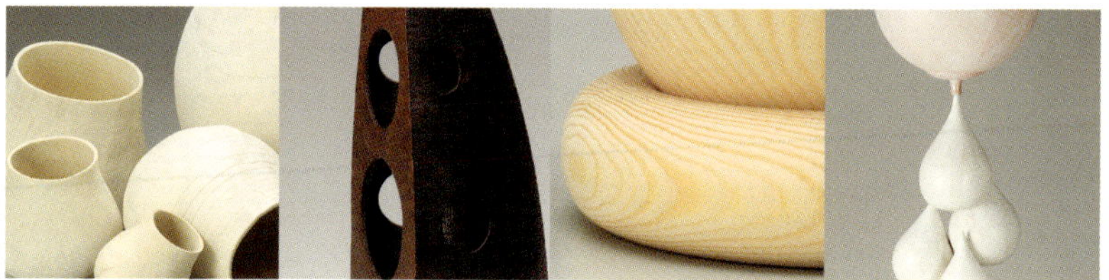

# Two: form

Production work? Not me!

...an element of surprise.//...is deceptively simple...

...simple white forms—their shadows, their details, their differences.

...simple, open shapes still appeal.

...a simple base form and the air or space about it...

...negative spaces...represent the unseen weight of the unknown.

...complexity and confusion... arranged into a purposeful construction.

The tabletop is the ground...?//To make tables or overturn them?...

...a ridiculously exaggerated protrusion.//...a fantasy lathe attachment....

...various heads and face forms mounted atop high poles

...a sphere in the grips of a clamp//...a dragon's claw grasping a pearl...

...a progression of profiles...

...negative portraiture...hybrid profiles...Janus-faced...

...portrait, caricature, silhouette.../... not a replica or counterfeit...

# Influence
# One: colleagues

Tribute.../ /...admiration and respect.../ /...homage...

...a homage.../ /...a gift that I treasure.../ /...an exceptional gift...

...respectfulness.../ /...deep respect../ /..in collaboration.../

...working collaboratively.../ /...the comradery...the shared struggles...

I am mindful of the obligation.

...the activity of exchange.../ /...encouraged me to 'try stuff'...

The chief inspiration is the wood turning movement itself.

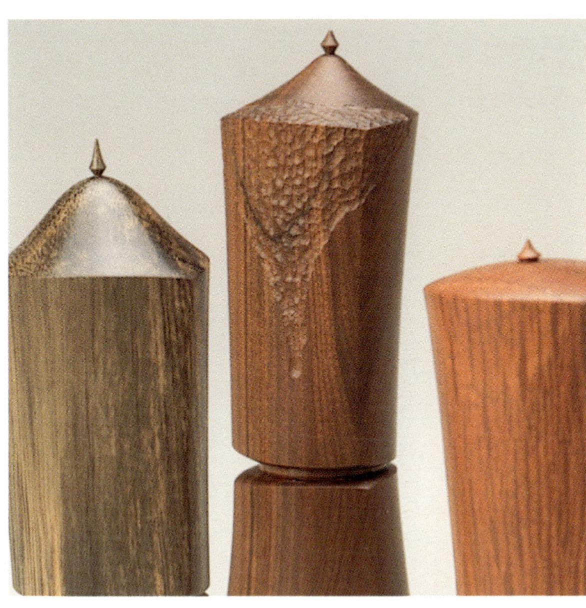

## Two: time

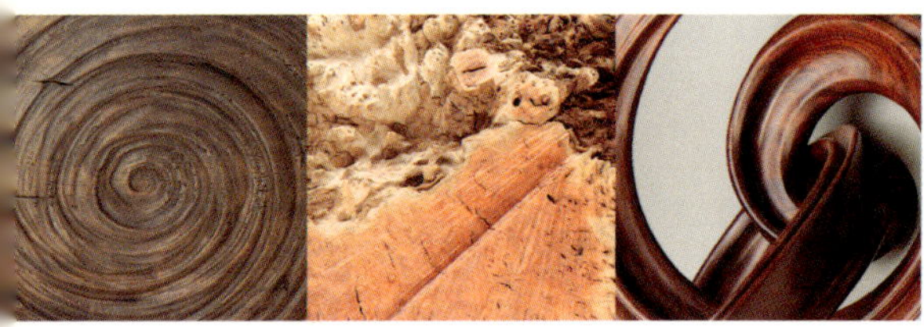

I am deeply interested in the roots of woodturning.

...the achievements (and the horrors) of a forgotten time...

Time: ...kind or harsh, ordered or chaotic...

...a large time lag between the impetus and the object that emerges...

...these cycles...their progressions through time...suggest spiral forms.

When spiralling lines ascend, they also converge and diminish until, at the top, they approach a straight line.

...a symbol to move from the past to the future...

...a repeating cyclical theme which changes subtly with each rotation...

In this way, one can describe infinity on a finite object.

No more than a tree can change its location, we cannot change our past.

...thirty generations of Europeans ate from turned wooden bowls...

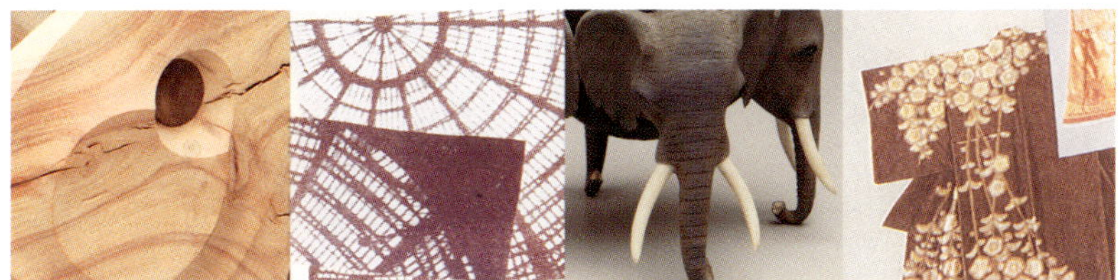

# Three: material culture

...sitting on dusty museum shelves...

...in the basement of the Smithsonian's Museum of Natural History.

Fragments of a forgotten civilization...

Animals in cave paintings chased by running figures arc across the interior space...

...an archaeological dig.../...ancient stone...tablets...a monumental stele from Elam

...a bowl in use from a playing card made in 1460...

...richly decorated, engraved...patterns...from a few workshops... nine hundred years ago.

...the furrows dressed into the face of the Millstone./jade...Maori symbol for eternity

Ming Dynasty hats/Pacific tapa cloth//Northwest Coast Indian baskets

Morandi//Nakashima//Albrecht Dürer//Ernst Haeckel

...kimonos as a continuous landscape...the seasons changed from one kimono to the next...and...return to its beginning...making a circular trip through space and time.

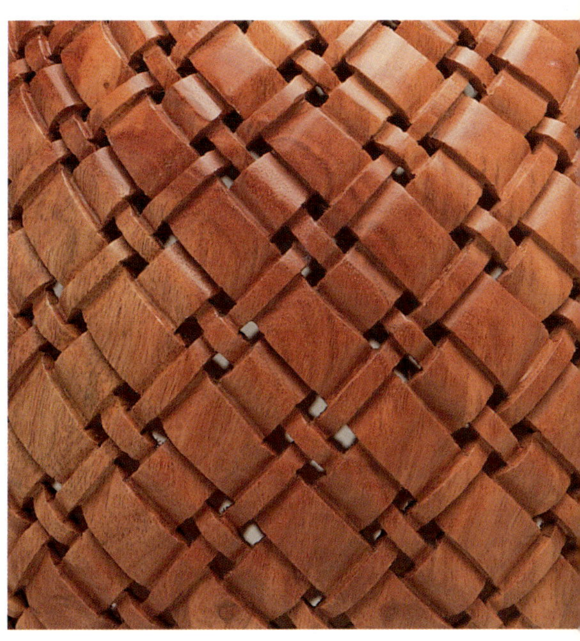

# FOUR: LANGUAGE / MUSIC / DANCE

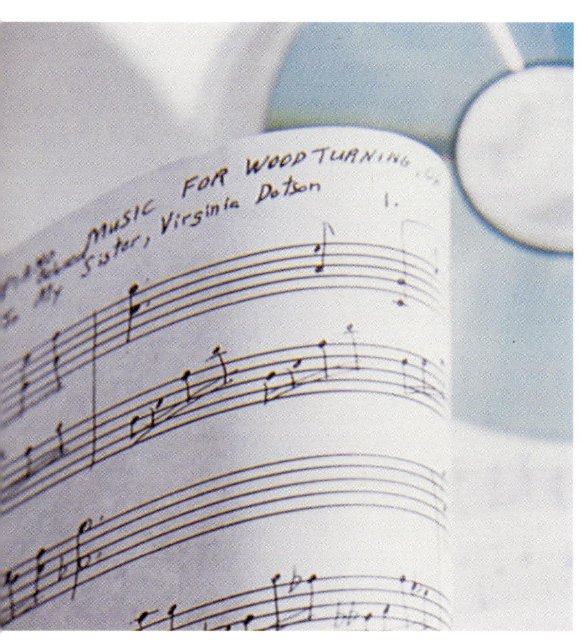


My descent into woodturning coincided with the purchase of a book.

...parallel translations in old Persian, Elamite, and Babylonian.

...the rhythm and narrative./...a dialogue between disclosure and enclosure.

...previously unused voices//speak a language that all can understand...

...we e-mailed comments back and forth through cyberspace...

"call and response"//make one bowl sing whilst another doesn't.

The wood has a voice, and I have a voice; we interact/...as a jazz musician...

...hear the differences in resonance as they touch the table.

...the rhythms, contrasts and repeating patterns...often suggest visual equivalents.

"...that's how I feel when I dance."

...a foot reaching for its next step.//being grounded while experiencing the earth

...a point of perfect balance and spin.//...the relationship of art to walking.

...the purest balance of proportion...//...a simple find during an afternoon walk...

...the illusion of motion.../...the amplification of motion...

...motion and suspension..../...implied motion...

...the apparent movement noted on a non-moving object.

...walking, stepping, skipping, leaping, hopping, sprinting, jumping...

...or rest within, or encroach upon or embrace...defy gravity...

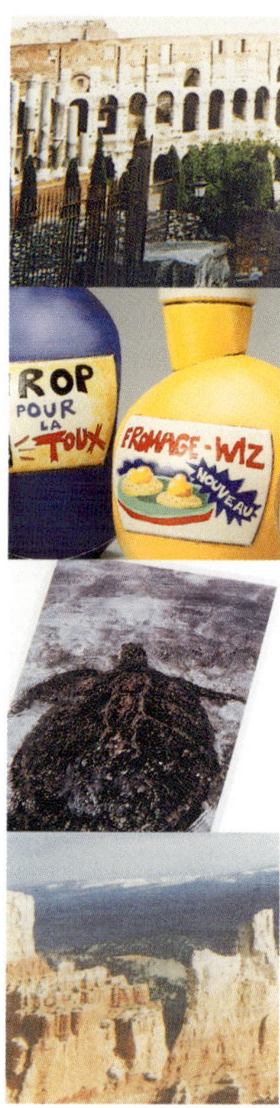


# Five: travel

"I travel for travel's sake." — (Robert Louis Stevenson)

...to explore and drink in the travel experience.

I have been intrigued when travelling...The grocery store is a highlight. I am challenged.

...a community artist.../...inspired by the historic Waterworks on the Schulkyll River.

I have traveled extensively, always with a camera in hand.

...Mardi Gras...//...Emma Lake...//Fatehpur Sikri in India.

Western Australia,...the richest and most varied wildflower area—in the world.

...my first views of the Colisseum in Rome...a humbling experience...

...5 years in Japan and 2 years in Thailand...//...Cartography Diploma...

"a kind of jeopardized map-making, bringing chaos and order into close quarters."

...this fascination with unfamiliar groceries./...ripe with possibilities for exploration.

...a need to explore form./...it is difficult to escape/...no escape from references./

...perhaps escaped to freedom...//Freedom!

# Six: future

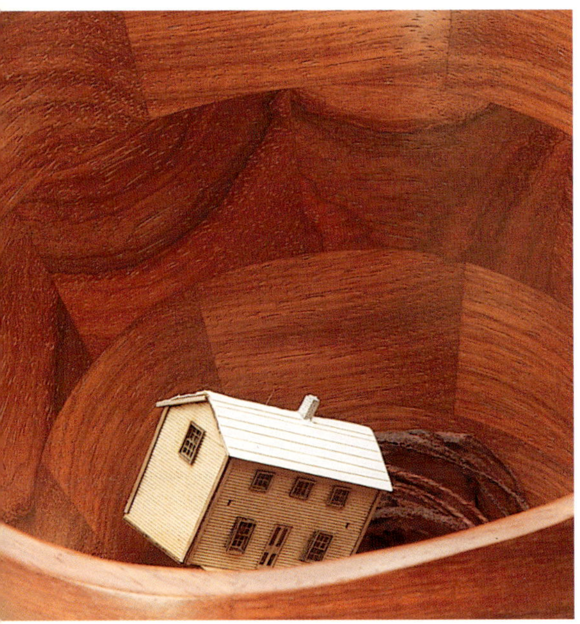

Historically, woodturning has been confined by various restraints, yet the ripping open...is an indication of potential movement outward.

my response to the stiffness of wooden objects./The stiffness...the closed compositions.

Transcending the round object...//...letting the wood find its own shape

hinting at possible use/...using more of the whole

to marry the elements of form with the raw beauty of the medium.

...to mine the potential that exists in juxtaposition of wood and metal...

...to find a different treatment./...relinquish control...

the challenge of unpredictability...which...patterns would emerge.

the relationship between materials and processes

...the distant but distinct reflection of what originally inspired me to woodturning.

...an approximation of the perfect star bowl that lives in my mind as it lived in the mind of the turner of the original five hundred and fifty years ago.

...this process yields the expression I sought.

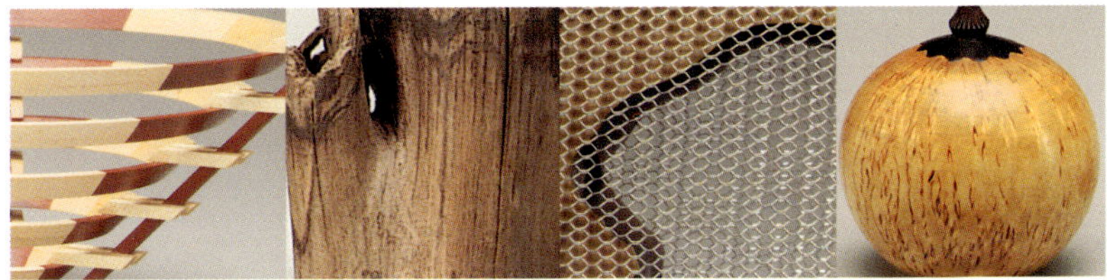

# Finale One:

...we're all swimming around in the same ocean...or adrift in the maelstrom.

...the anchor chain has been cut and one drifts...

...the South Pacific where I live...// I was raised in the Midwest...

...when I was seven or eight and saw my first tornado on the Kansas farm where I grew up.

I am a lucky man...

...helped my Granddad repair bamboo fly rods.../...my father's furniture factory

...his brother gave him an unneeded lathe.

/Living with a portrait painter for the past twenty years...

*Portrait of the Artist as a Middle-Aged Man...*

Family is a grouping of objects...//...an inseparable bond that encompasses all.

...the canoe form, the spaces inside...conjure the homesickness..

...broken hearts, tears, and feeling of rootlessness..

...the death of friends and family..//...personal tragedy...I have persevered...

...because my father said that I couldn't.//I started my life all over again.

...I saw the sonogram...I felt that strong urge to cradle and protect...

My child Eli, his adventures of independence and return to his father... gathering strength for his next exploration.

when the light comes into the mother's body, every time sun rises, new life will come into the world.

...bring this idea to full term.../...still in its infancy...

...fertility, renewal, rebirth// Selfishly we suckle...

...to create a family of physical forms.

# Two:

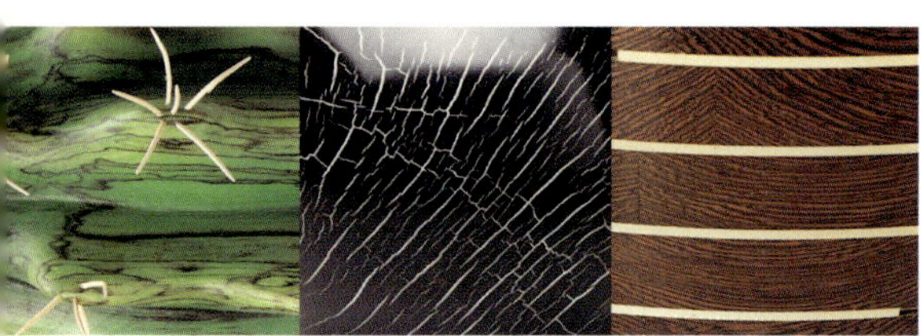

So please understand,...I may be wondering about their source as much as you are...

...happen stance.../Standing Stones/The...balance of objects is everything.

Perfection can be impossible to improve upon...that elusive element ...is lost...

Life defies definition.

Yet one man's horror is another one's delight.

...a mythical beast.../...my own mythical organisms...

...eventually developing its 'self.'

I look to the center of the work where there exists something elusive yet... captivating.

...burned into my subconscious.../...I had forgotten about it totally...

...it was in the 'memory vault'...below conscious level.

...a wordless connection.../...an intuitive and spontaneous approach..

...with neither ordered thoughts nor rational purpose...

...something magical had occured...a living entity that also touched the heart..

...a transformation of complexity.

...transforming...rough timber into a kind of poetry.

It's simple yet complex./...pure elegance and closure...

...ceremony or offering//...self-rewarding...

...the unanticipated change that occurred...A little fantastic, a little odd.

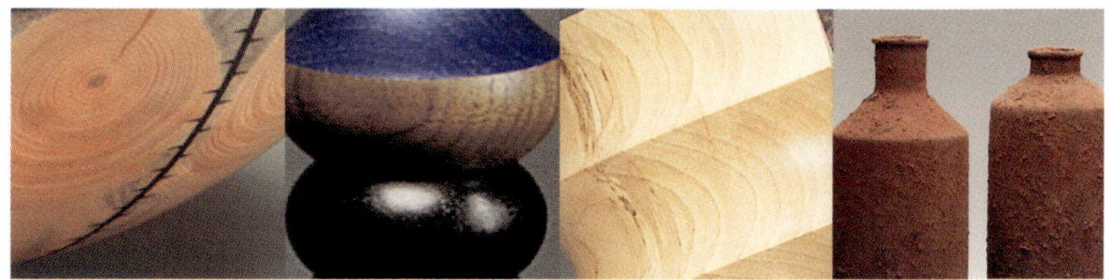

...more alive, difficult to predict.../highly unlikely, with a life of their own.

...to cause a moment of confusion followed by a quick assessment, then understanding.

Everything fell into place!

...what may have been the catalyst.

...everything from mystery unraveling (or deepening) to the innocent pleasure of a toy...and

memories of things seen.

...that feeling of not needing to improve on nature.

...healing.../...and finally dismissal.

I...don't think about the work much...after it is finished. I am...involved with the next piece./

...and I can't wait to see what comes next.

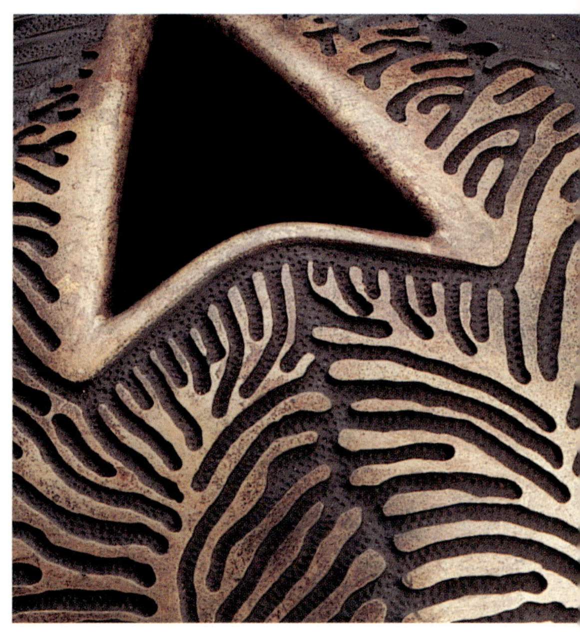

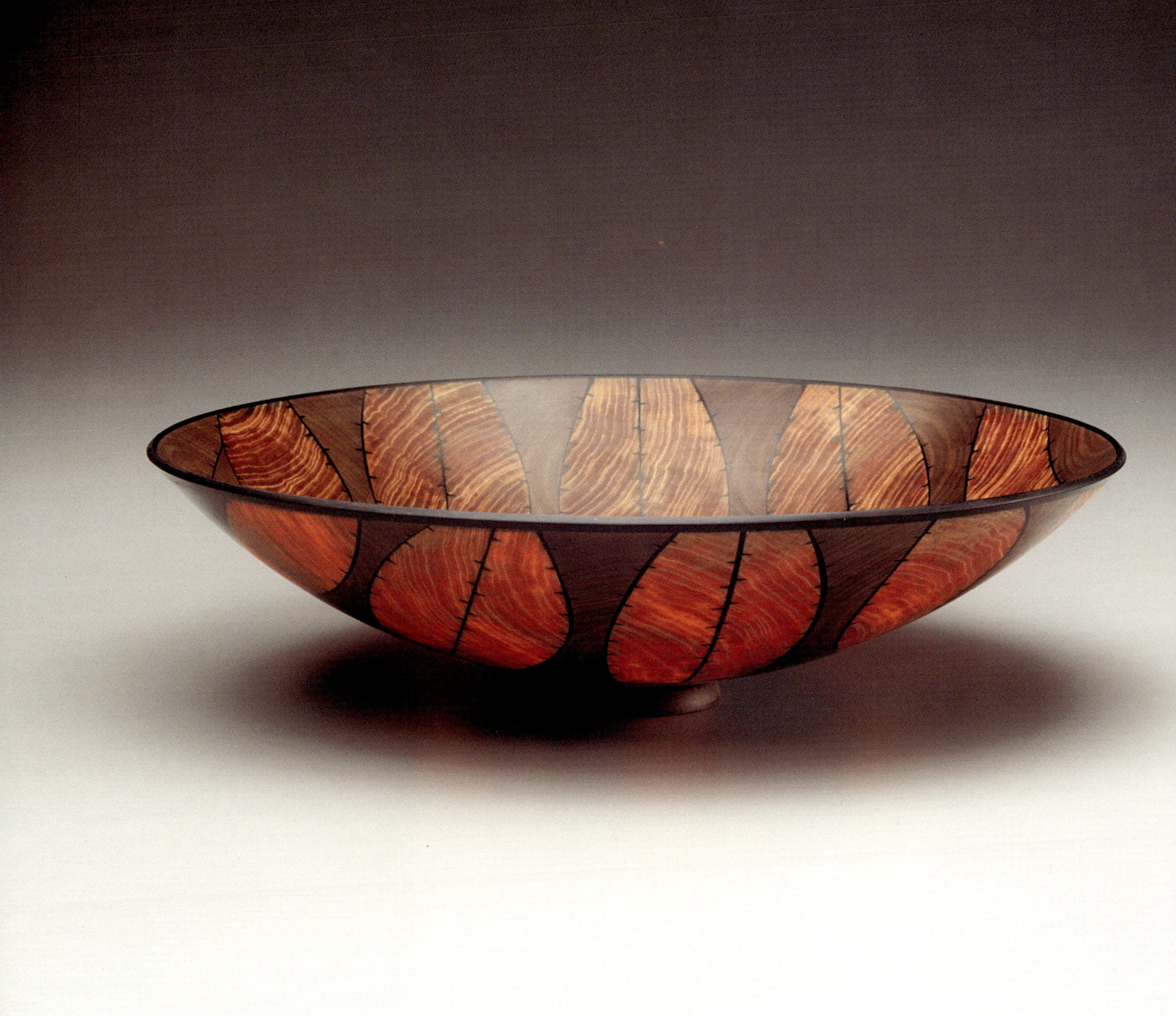

*Walnut Pitch Pine Bowl*
1999
H: 4", Diam: 13 1/2"
Walnut, pitch pine, epoxy resin and cotton yarn

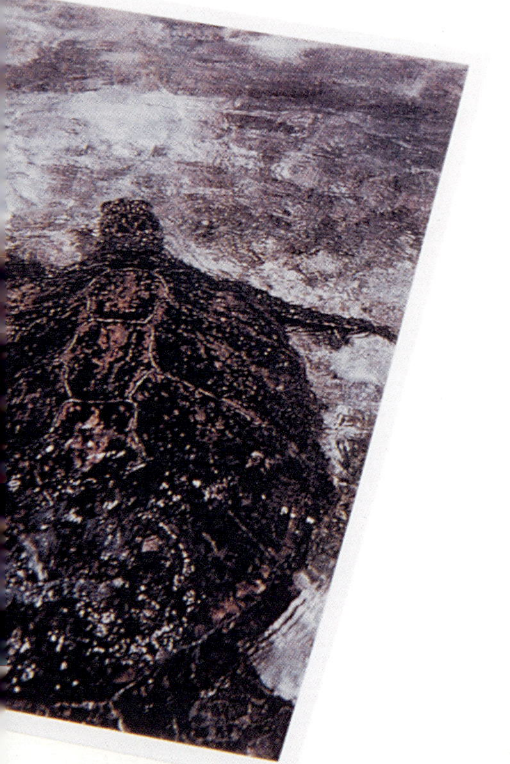

## Gianfranco Angelino [*Italy – b. 1938*]

The infinite variety of shapes, structures, and colors which nature offers to our view, is for me a permanent source of inspiration. In particular, since I am interested in hollow forms, shells of various kinds are a source of aesthetic suggestion. Turtle or tortoise carapaces are extraordinarily appealing to me since they are formed by geometrical scales, as in my typical way of building bowls. If nature employed millions of years to determine the best way of subdividing a hemispherical form, I made numberless attempts aiming at the same goal. Segments, hexagons, squares, irregular shapes were all used to construct my bowls. Furthermore, pieces of turtle shell, observed against the sun, look translucent with an amber color. I obtain a similar effect when I use my pitch-pine, resin soaked, timber.

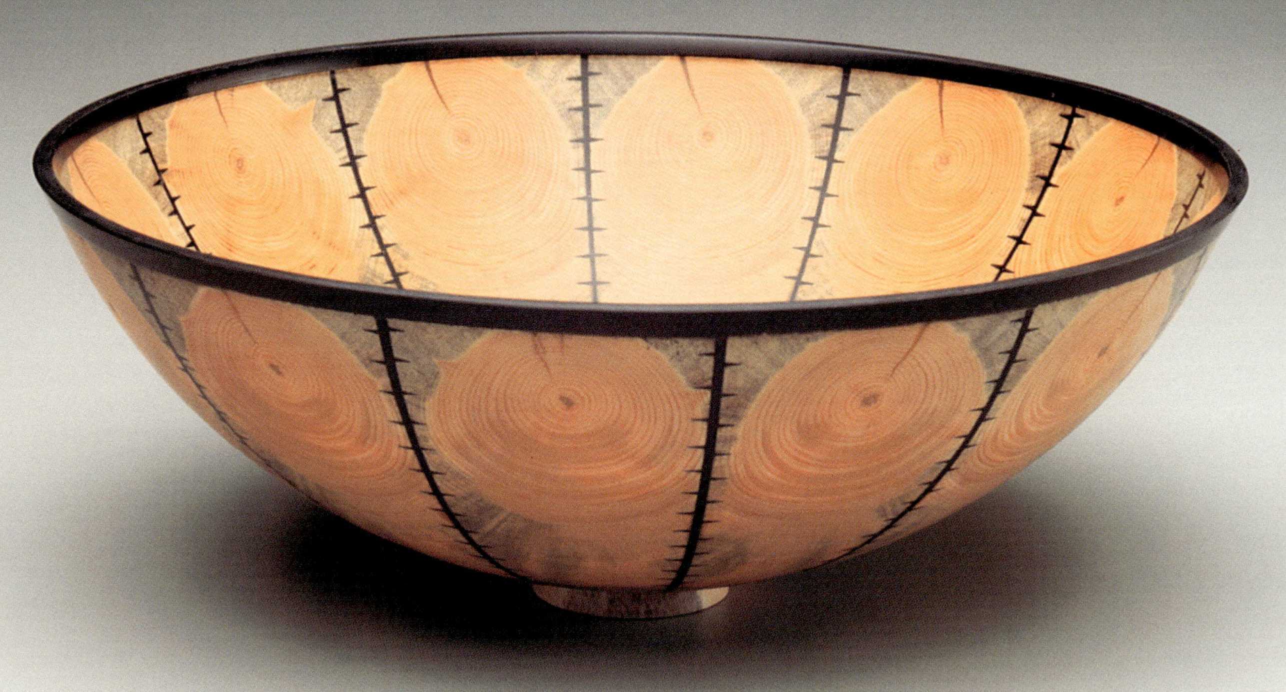

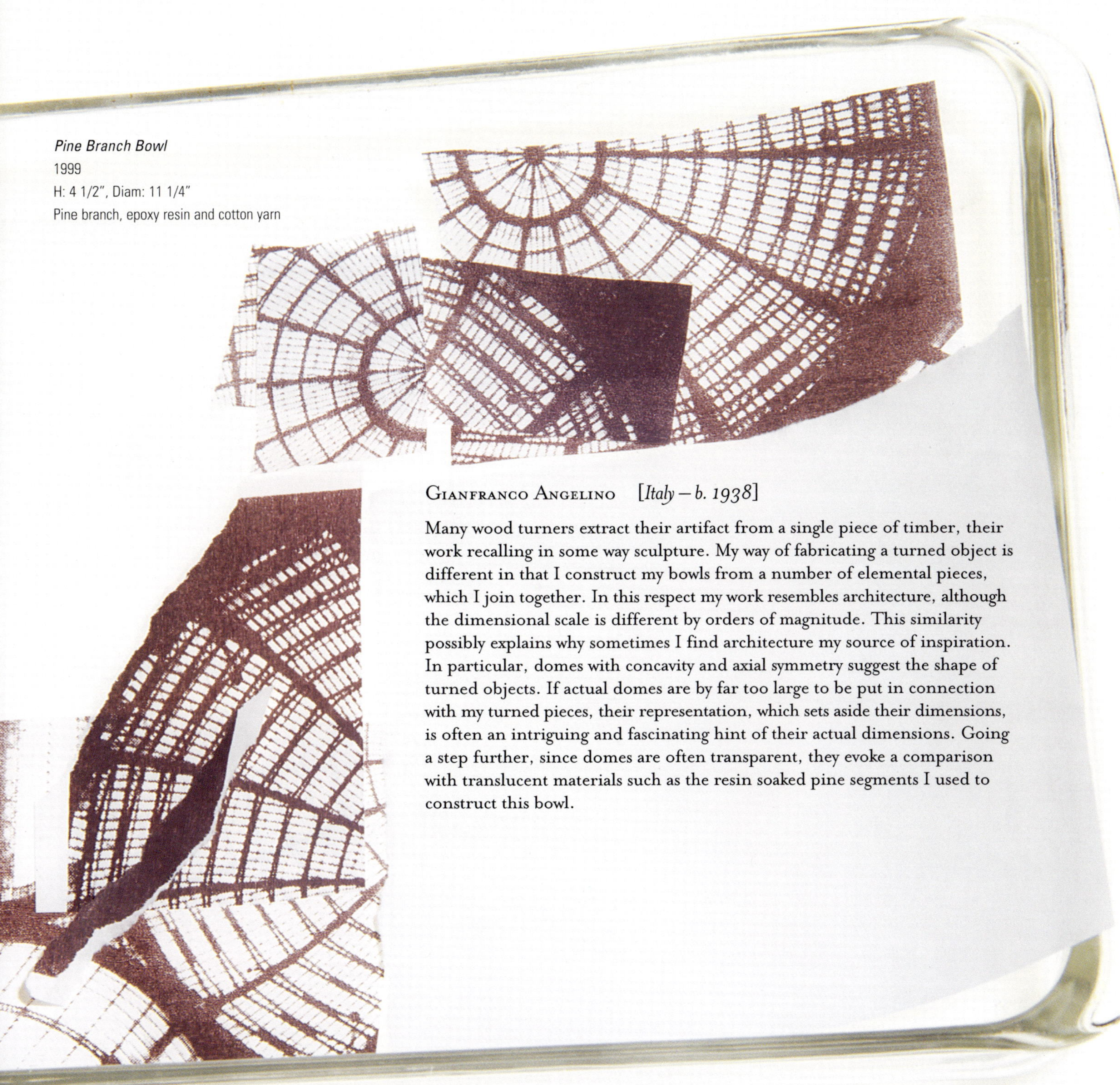

*Pine Branch Bowl*
1999
H: 4 1/2", Diam: 11 1/4"
Pine branch, epoxy resin and cotton yarn

## Gianfranco Angelino [*Italy – b. 1938*]

Many wood turners extract their artifact from a single piece of timber, their work recalling in some way sculpture. My way of fabricating a turned object is different in that I construct my bowls from a number of elemental pieces, which I join together. In this respect my work resembles architecture, although the dimensional scale is different by orders of magnitude. This similarity possibly explains why sometimes I find architecture my source of inspiration. In particular, domes with concavity and axial symmetry suggest the shape of turned objects. If actual domes are by far too large to be put in connection with my turned pieces, their representation, which sets aside their dimensions, is often an intriguing and fascinating hint of their actual dimensions. Going a step further, since domes are often transparent, they evoke a comparison with translucent materials such as the resin soaked pine segments I used to construct this bowl.

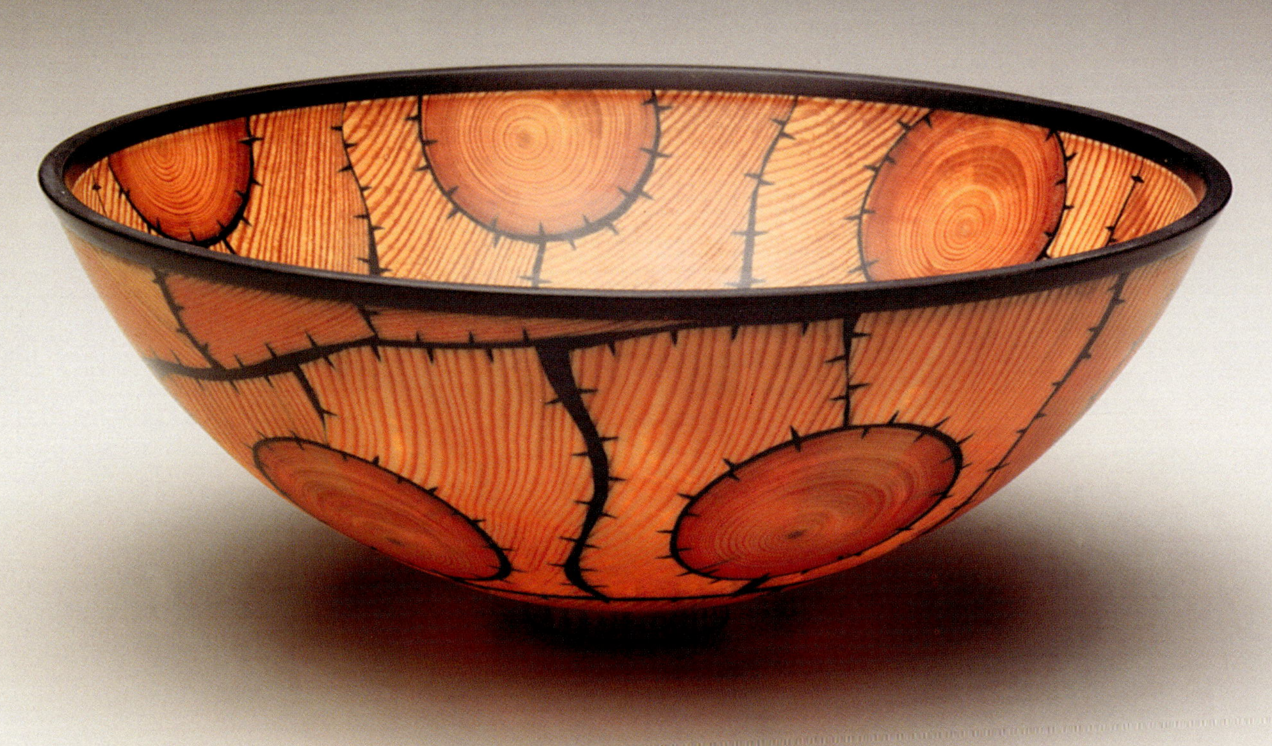

*Pine, Pine Branch Bowl*
1999
H: 3 1/2", Diam: 9"
Pine and pine branch

GIANFRANCO ANGELINO [*Italy – b. 1938*]

Walking in a pine forest, I once found a piece of wood almost dissolved by weather, which, in my hands, seemed unnaturally heavy. I looked more carefully and I found that within it there was a chunk of perfectly sound wood, which was preserved from decay by a thorough impregnation of resin. Freely speaking, it was a sort of "fossilized" wood. With time I learned how to find usable pieces of this kind of timber in this manner and I thought that it would be appealing to preserve within the artifact the concept of the archaic material that was used. Since I am also keen on true fossils, I looked in my books on the subject for suggestions. It was easy to recognize that many fossils, mainly belonging to the ammonite class, exhibit a neat spiral shape closely resembling a bowl structure. If, for the old creature the spiral form was its way of building a shell with larger and larger rooms, for the turner, it seemed a natural way of building a round blank starting from small elemental pieces.

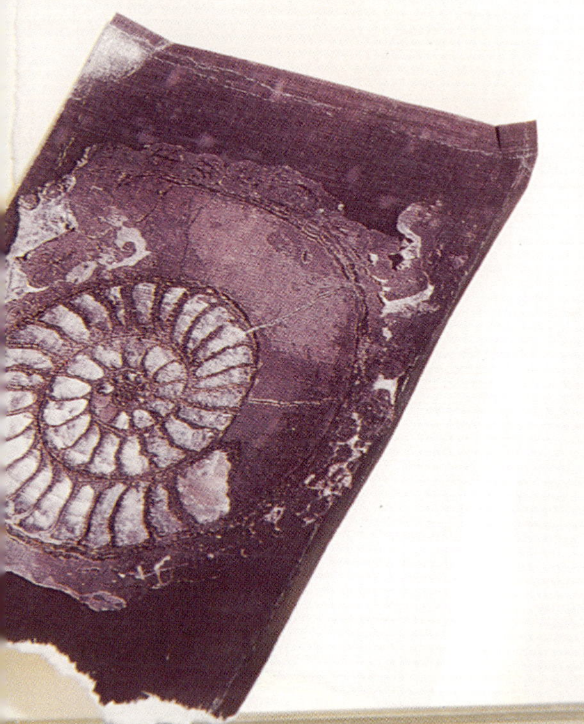

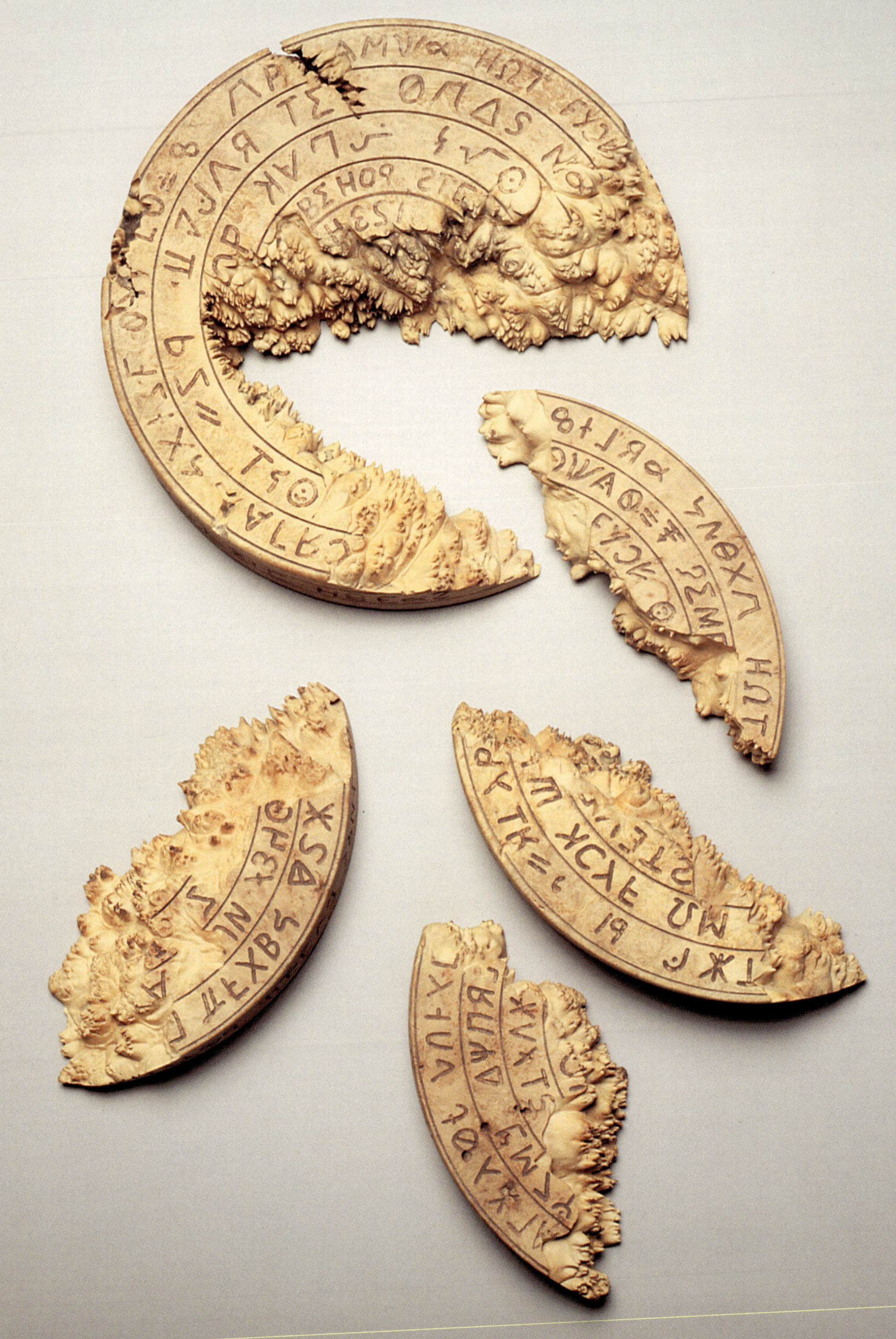

*Fragments of a Forgotten Civilization*
1997
H: 32", W: 20", D: 3 1/2"
Maple burl

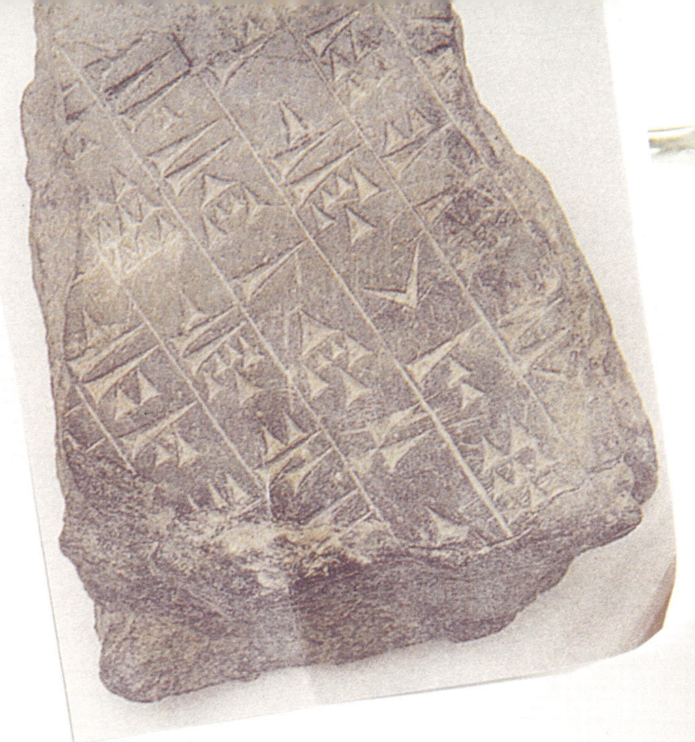

Steve Bishop [*Virginia, USA – b. 1960*]

The inspiration for *Fragments of a Forgotten Civilization* came from fragments of ancient stone or clay tablets, such as the one in the picture, which is a piece of a monumental stele from the ancient Near Eastern region of Elam (western Iran). The fragment is the Elamite version of a trilingual inscription of Darius I, and appears originally in parallel translations in Old Persian, Elamite, and Babylonian.

When one imagines clay tablets, they are usually thought to come in the form of square or rectangular shapes, but the archaeological remnants of this civilization indicate that their people were skilled in making objects thrown on a potter's wheel, and that is probably why its clay tablets were round. The language of my "civilization" is also untranslatable, as its "Rosetta stone" has not been discovered, so scholars have yet to make sense of the inscriptions.

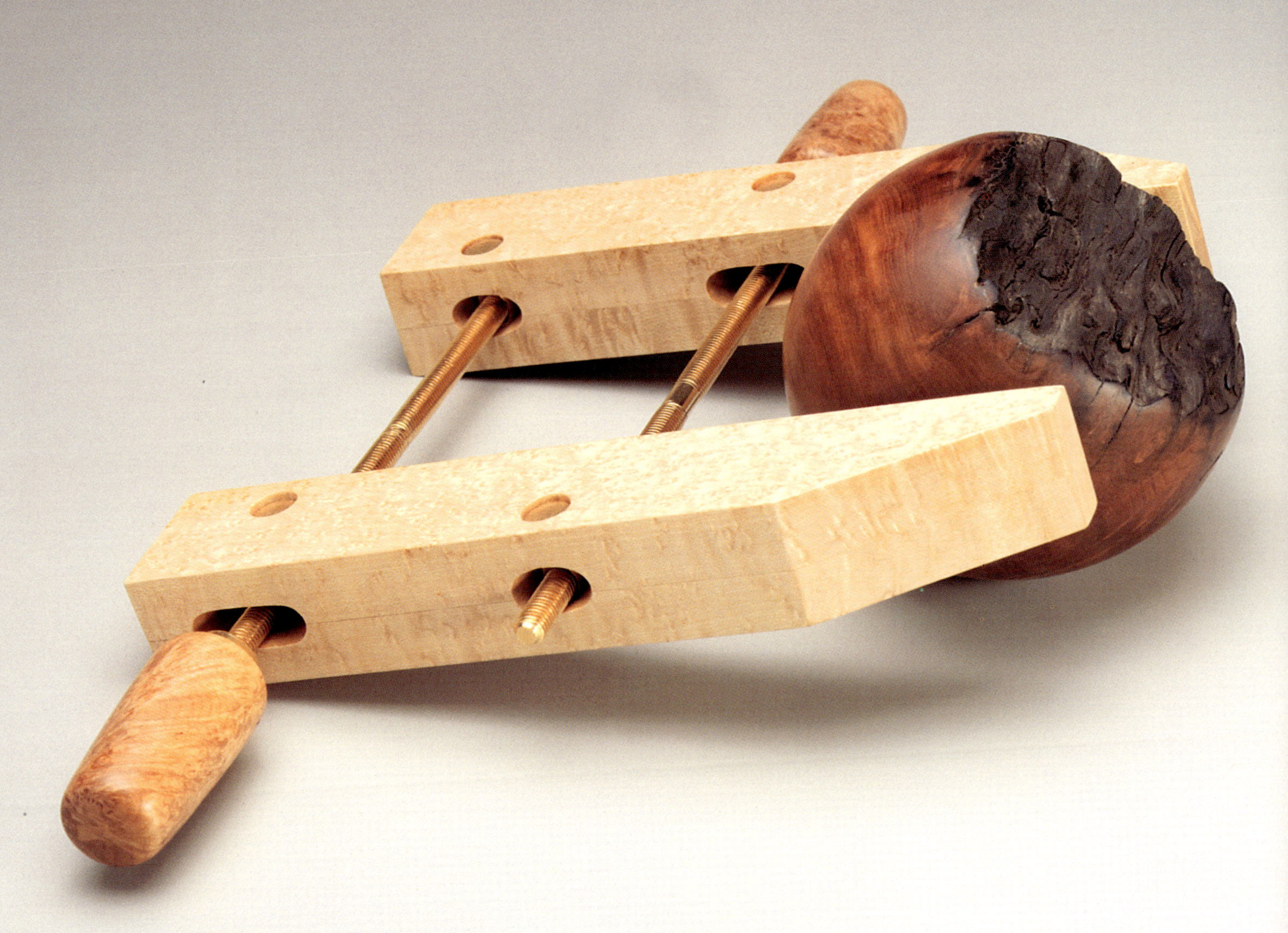

*Portrait of an Artist as a Middle-Aged Man (with a stressful job, a wife, two kids, a house, two mortgages, two cars, five cats, and a neurotic dog)*
2000
H: 5 1/2", W: 19", D: 3 1/2"
Birdseye maple, redwood, maple burl and 24k gold-plated hardware

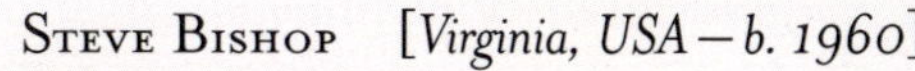


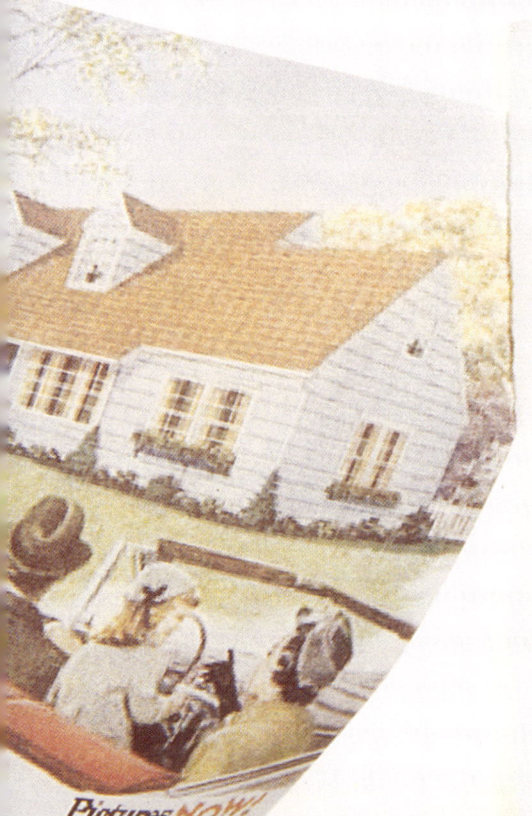


STEVE BISHOP [*Virginia, USA – b. 1960*]

My inspiration for this piece comes from a cliché, or an ideal, depending on how you look at it: the "American Dream." It can mean different things to different people, but the picture I cite as an inspiration exemplifies that dream common to many people: a happy family, a house in the suburbs, a nice car. *Portrait of an Artist* strives to interpret the "American Dream" as it applies to myself in particular, and to others in similar circumstances.

What this picture does not show, however, is the pressure placed upon a successful man by the expectations of his family, himself, and society. By placing a sphere in the grips of a clamp, I am striving to show that these expectations and responsibilities have me (and others like me) in their grip, from which it is difficult to escape. The piece is also a reflection of the hold that materialism has on the concept of the "American Dream."

The choice of redwood for the sphere was made quite deliberately. The redwood tree is naturally resistant to fire, and the scorched and rough surface of the sphere is especially symbolic of personal tragedy in my life. Through it all, however, I have persevered and will continue to do so. The choice of highly figured woods and gold-plated hardware for the clamp is indicative of the privileged status I have achieved. Yes, sometimes I feel like my life is in a clamp, but isn't it a beautiful clamp?

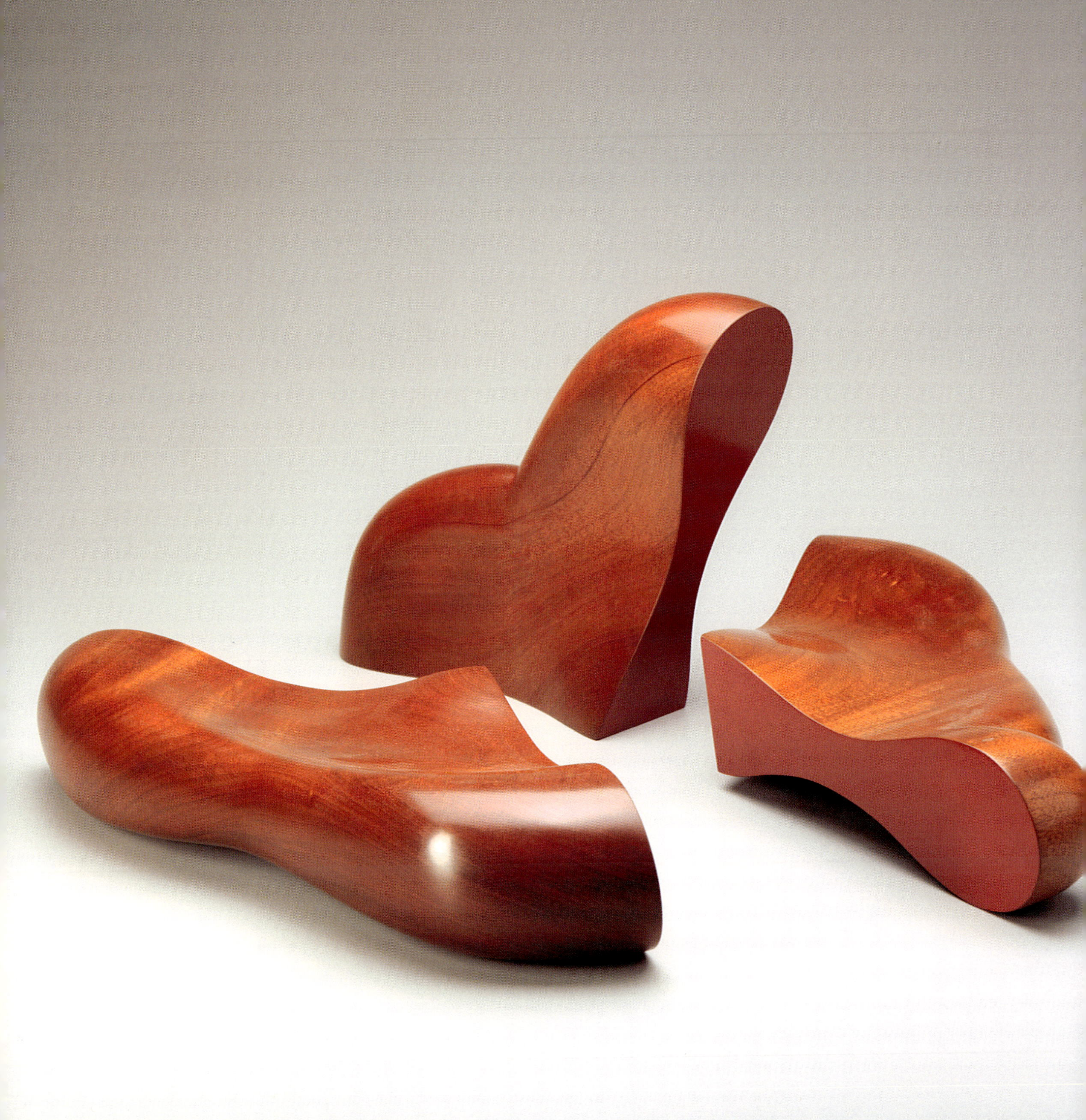

*Broken Heart*
1999
H: 22", W: 22", D: 24"
Mahogany and paint

Michael Brolly [*Pennsylvania, USA – b. 1950*]

When relationships end, often there are broken hearts, tears and the inevitable feeling of rootlessness. The anchor chain has been cut and one drifts, aimlessly it seems, at the whim of the winds. When my marriage dissolved, I hoped that eventually I would meet someone else and be able to pick up the pieces and go forward. When that finally happened, I knew that I had to make a piece, a symbol to move from the past to the future: to admit the hurts and move with the healing. This piece is my attempt at that healing. Hearts lay broken, they sometimes realign in odd ways but if you "turn it over" they become whole again, as does this one.

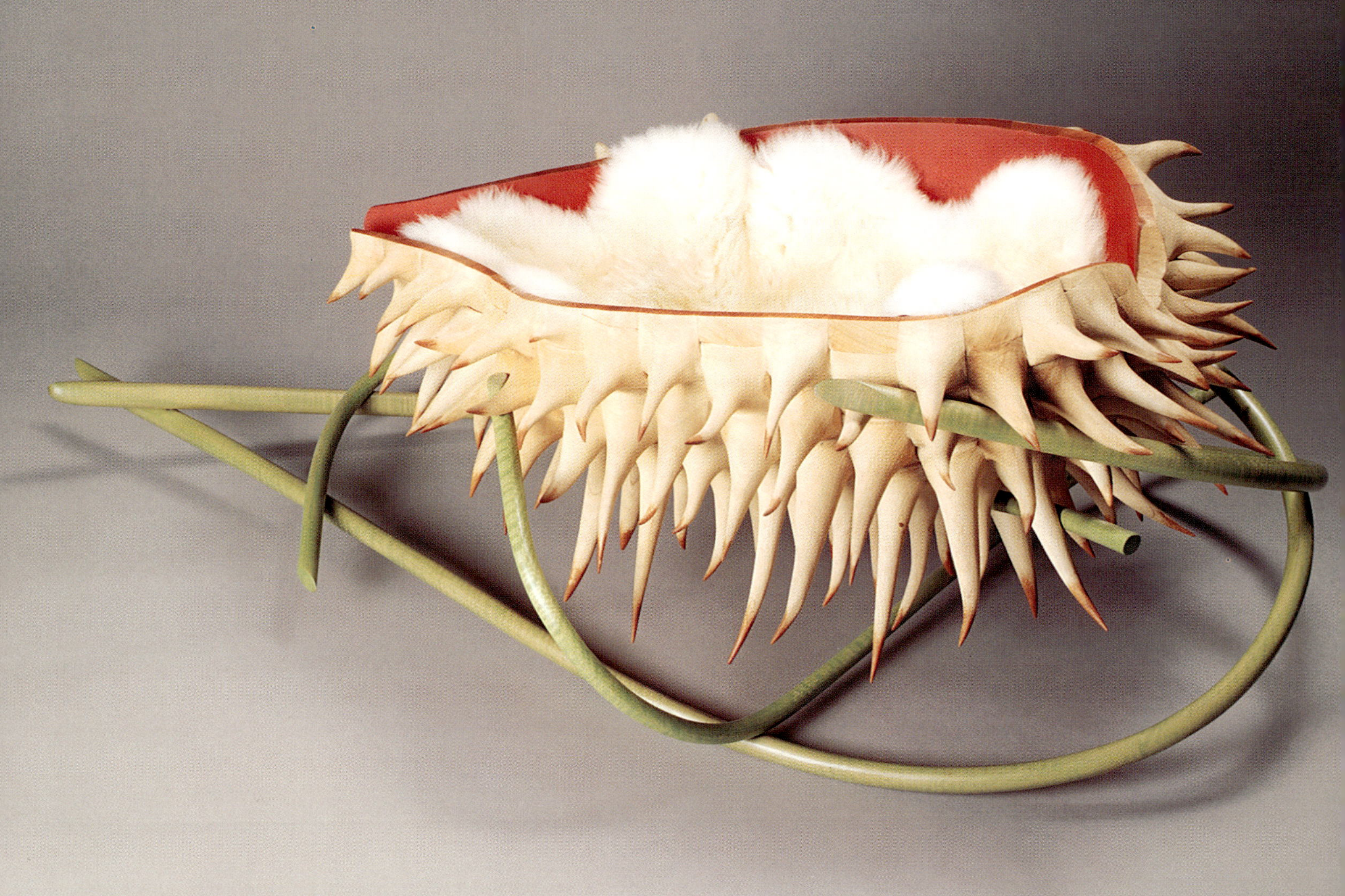

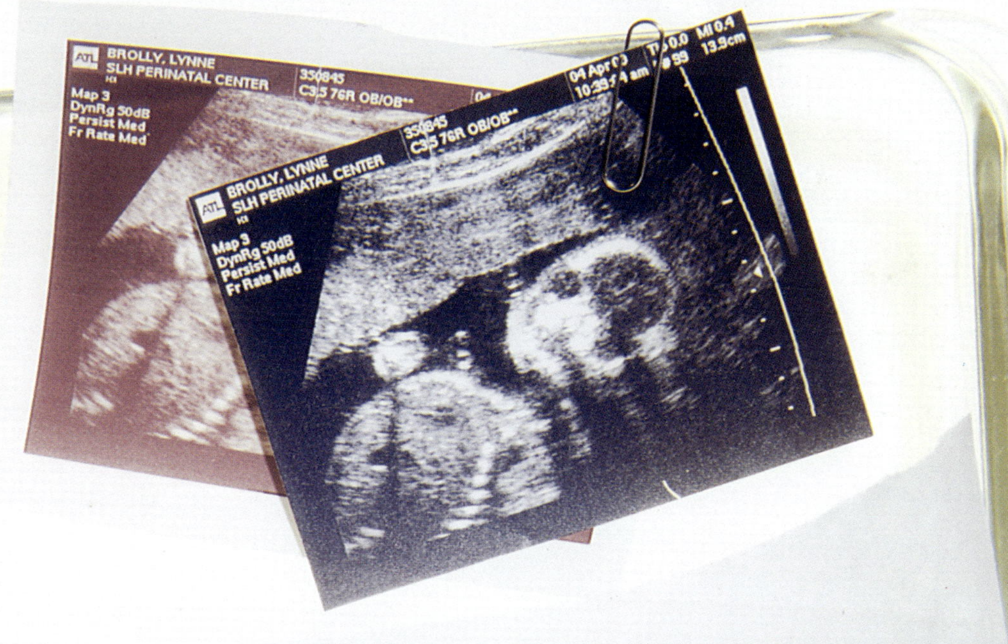


*Cradle*
2000
H: 36", W: 24", D: 20"
Mahogany, paint and ash

Michael Brolly [*Pennsylvania, USA – b. 1950*]

My sister had a string of miscarriages, then adopted a daughter. I made her a cradle, probably because my father said that I couldn't, which eventually led me to woodworking and the lathe. When I saw the sonogram of our soon to be first child, I felt that strong urge to cradle and protect.

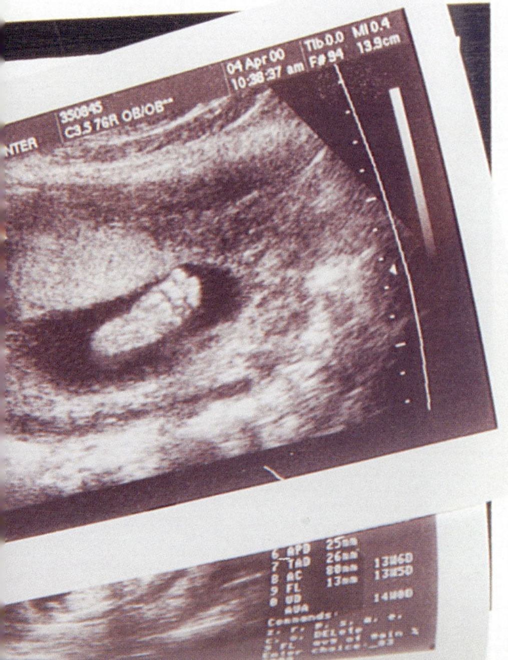

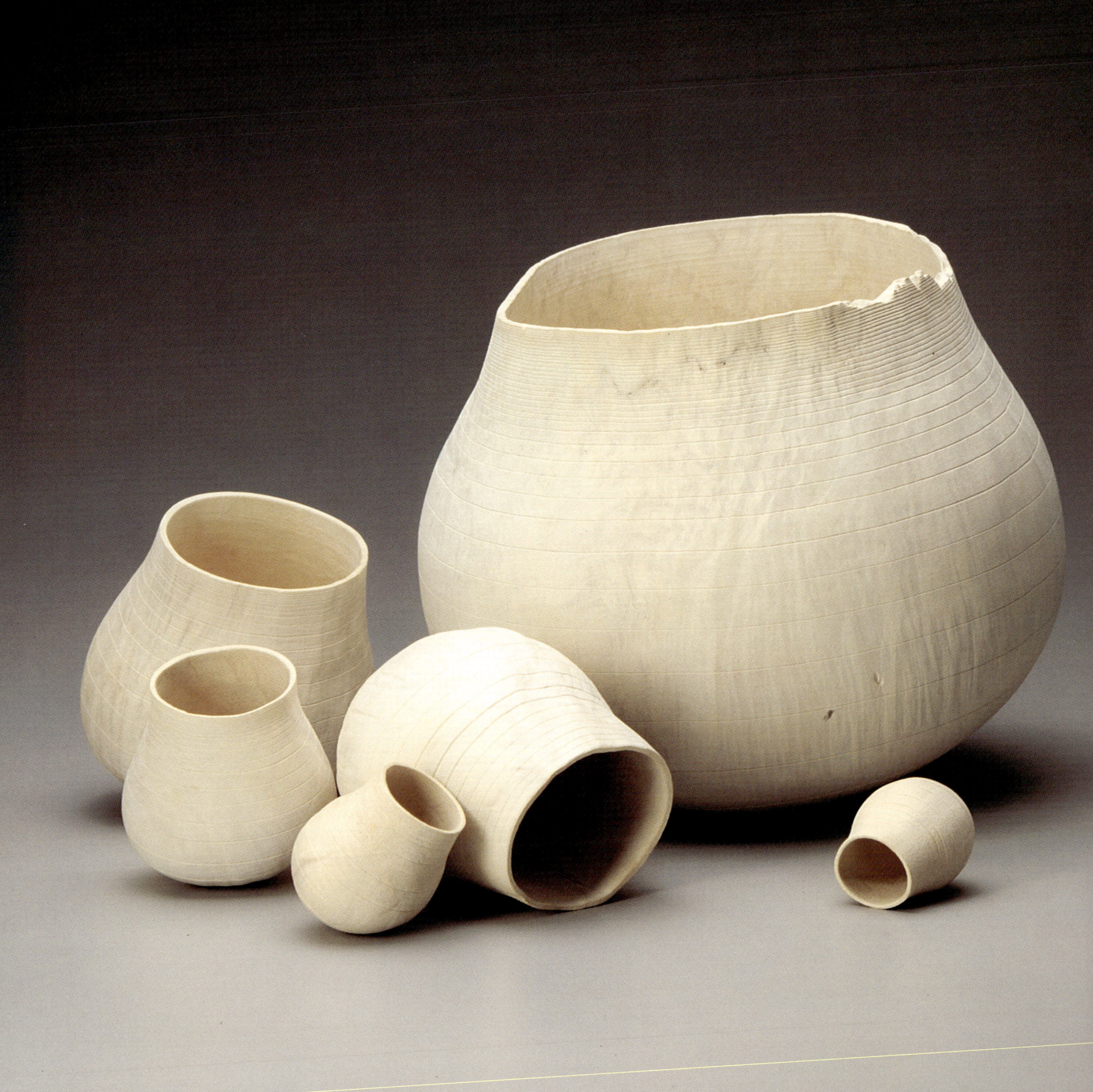

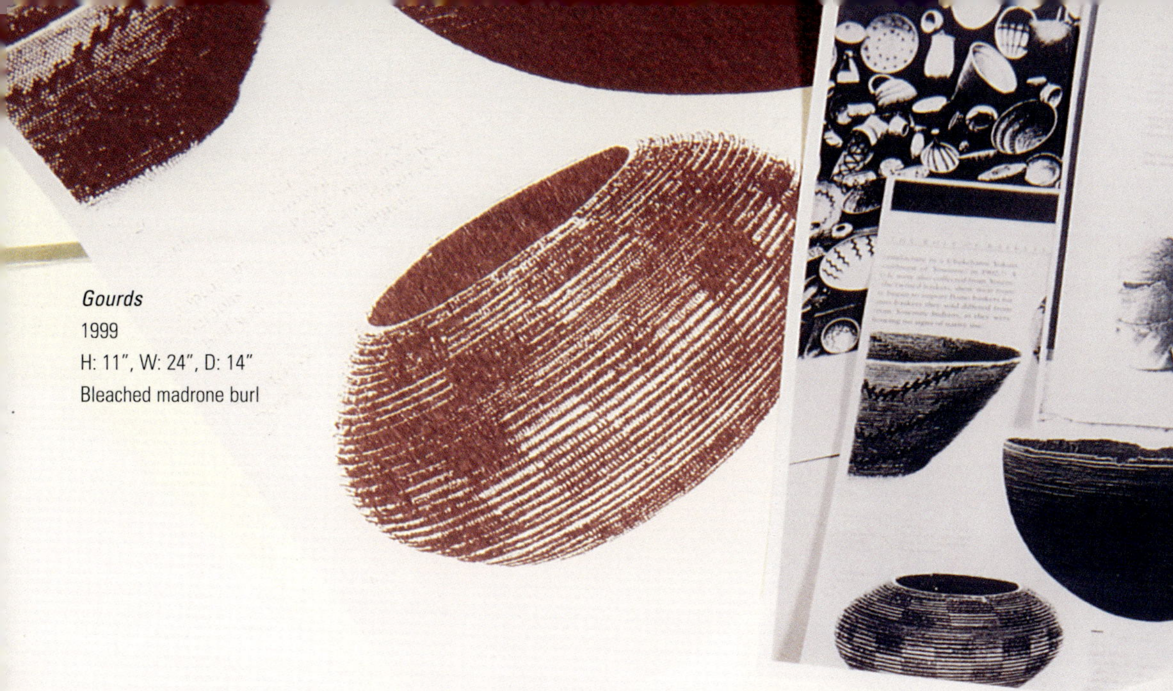

*Gourds*
1999
H: 11", W: 24", D: 14"
Bleached madrone burl

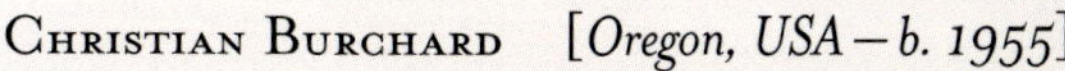

Christian Burchard [*Oregon, USA – b. 1955*]

This set of white gourds is part of a series of basket and gourd forms that I have been working on for a few years. At times the strength of the wood, its color and grain pattern can be overwhelming. Through a simple bleaching process I have taken just about all the color out and made the surface subtle and soft. I wanted to allow the simplicity of the gourd forms to stand out, emphasizing their quietness, their loose and gentle relationships.

Not one source but many. Russian dolls and Chihuly Baskets, but most strongly Northwest Coast Indian Baskets used for storage, for cooking, for food gathering. Sitting on dusty museum shelves, worn and sagging. The wood, Pacific madrone, hard to tame, the wildest wood I have ever used, requiring me to loosen up, giving it space. No pretense of circular perfection, but hinting at possible use. Intricate relationships and balances, gestures. Many influences over many years, connections at 5 a.m.

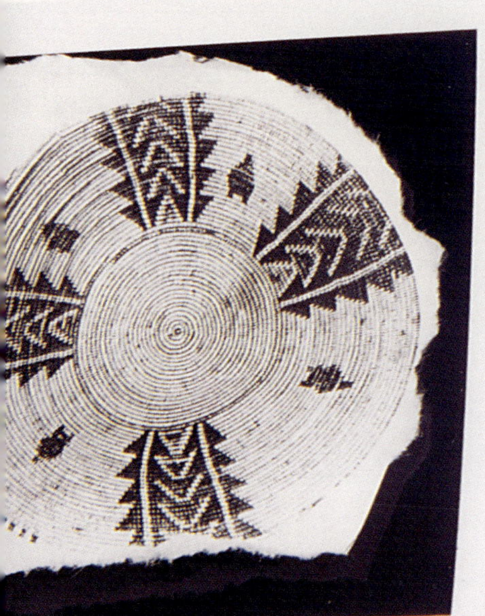

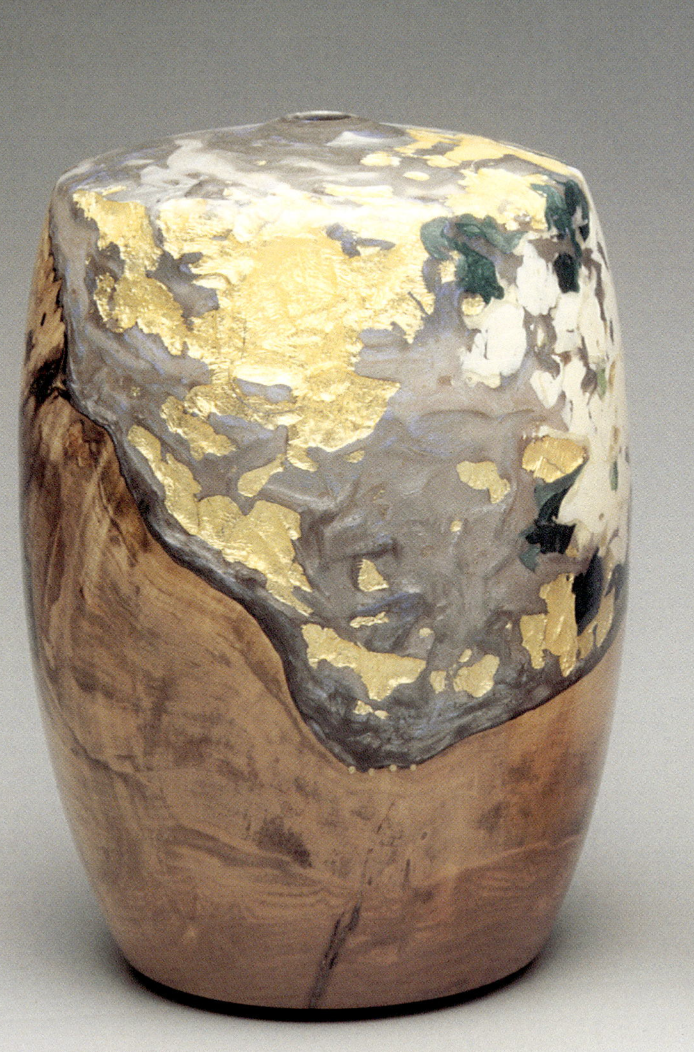
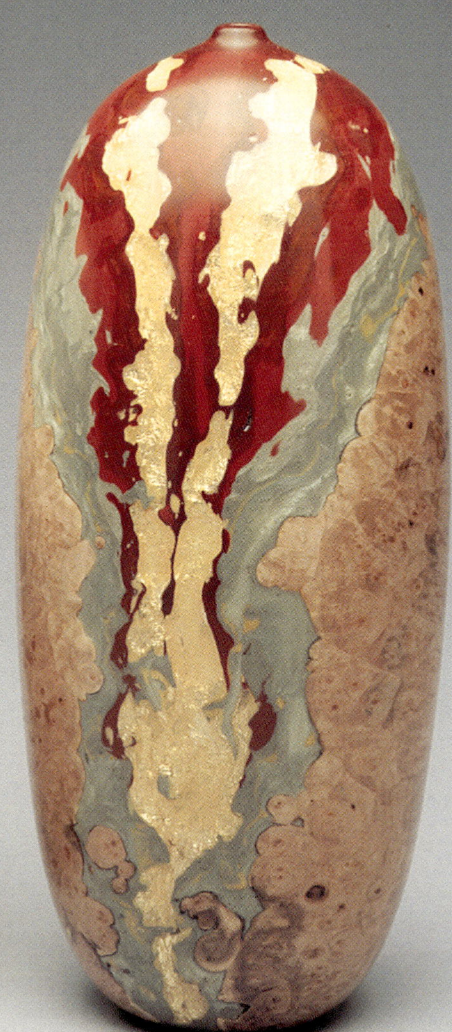

*Dogwood*
2000
H: 12 1/2", Diam: 8 1/2"
Red maple burl, epoxy resin, powdered pigments, mica and gold leaf

*Wrapt*
1999
H: 14", Diam: 5 1/4"
Big leaf maple burl, epoxy resin, powdered pigments, mica and gold leaf

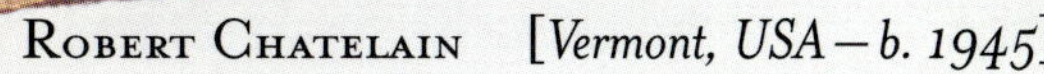

## Robert Chatelain [*Vermont, USA – b. 1945*]

There are multiple inspirations to my turnings. The common thread in many of my pieces is the use of gold leaf. This is derived from the sliding doors and folding screens used in Japanese architecture. Which in turn was used by Whistler in his Peacock Room, Frank Lloyd Wright as decoration in his earlier houses, and numerous others in art nouveau/deco style art/craft pieces. The second thread is my interest in decorative clothing. That is the use of over-the-top wearable art as a traditional means of ordaining authority.

Most directly, the kimonos of Itchiku Kubota are the inspiration for *Dogwood*. A few years back I came across a show of Kubota's kimonos in the basement of the Smithsonian's Museum of Natural History. The kimonos were made by a tie-dye method that rendered them beautifully decorated by luminescent abstract landscapes. I have picked up on his abstract style and used mica to produce the luminescence.

The feel that what I am striving for with *Wrapt* is the robed figure, not unlike Rodin's *Balzac* or the high garb of clerics with their decorative collars. The gold leaf is like a collar draped over the shoulder of the vessel.

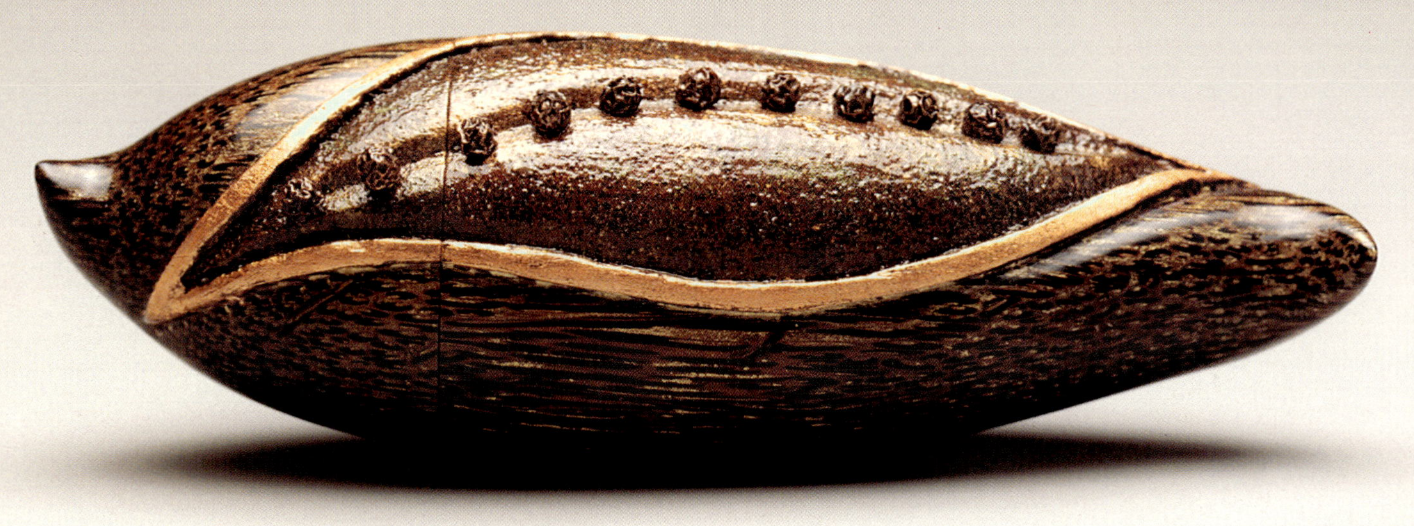

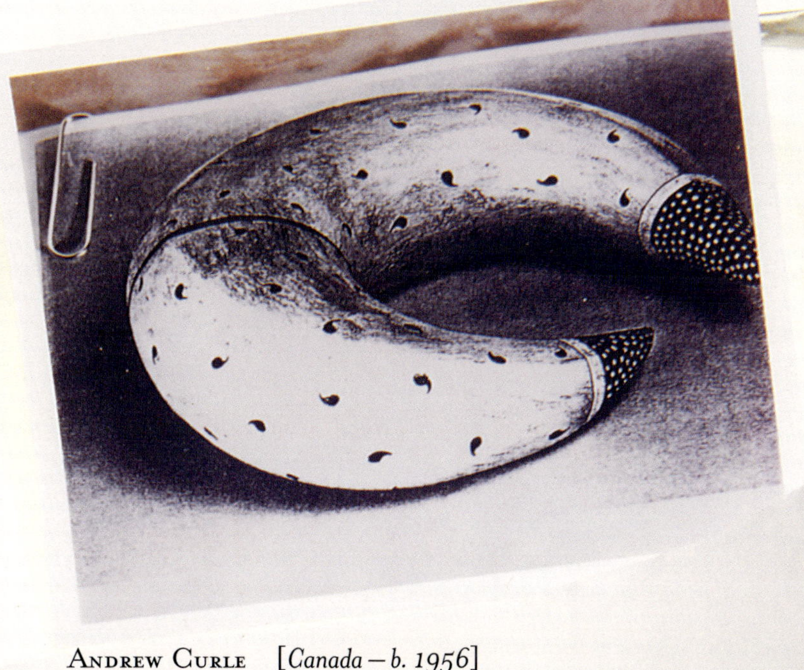

*Full of Life Series: Jewel Pod #7*
2000
H: 2 1/2", W: 6", D: 2"
Black palm, coppered peppercorns, sand, pigment, copper powder, copper leaf and lacquer

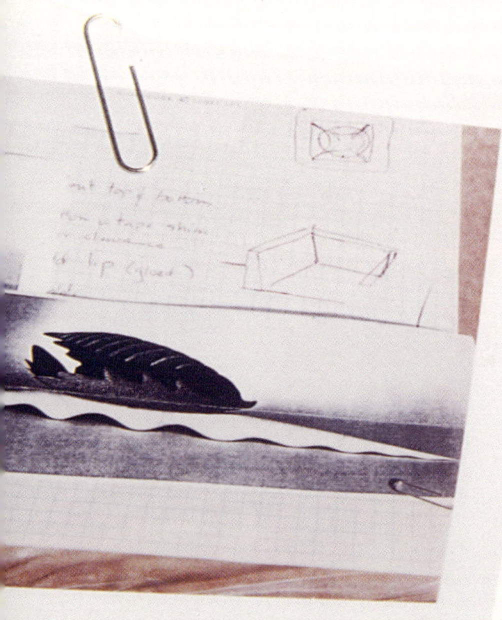

## Andrew Curle [*Canada – b. 1956*]

This series began with only a vague idea of portraying "ripeness." In fact, the original sketch that inspired the series was for an incense container for a Japanese tea ceremony to be constructed and carved, not turned. That item has yet to be made, as I decided to try the concept in a turned piece; which became something that to my mind resembled a seed pod bursting open.

I would have said that an influence for this piece might have been Louis Armstrong's "What a Wonderful World," as the cycle of renewal in nature is a wonderful mystery to me. However, talking with Jamie Russell at the *Turning on Furnishing 2000* opening, he remarked that he thought it was influenced by a piece done by Helen Shirk and William Leete at Emma Lake 1998. I said that I had seen and really liked the piece, but had forgotten about it completely. It was in my "memory vault," but if it had an influence, it was at work subconsciously. I am always surprised when others see things I don't in my work. For during the creating, I tend to be either focused on the physical effort or improvising as it progresses. I don't usually think about the work much after it is finished, as I am involved with the next piece.

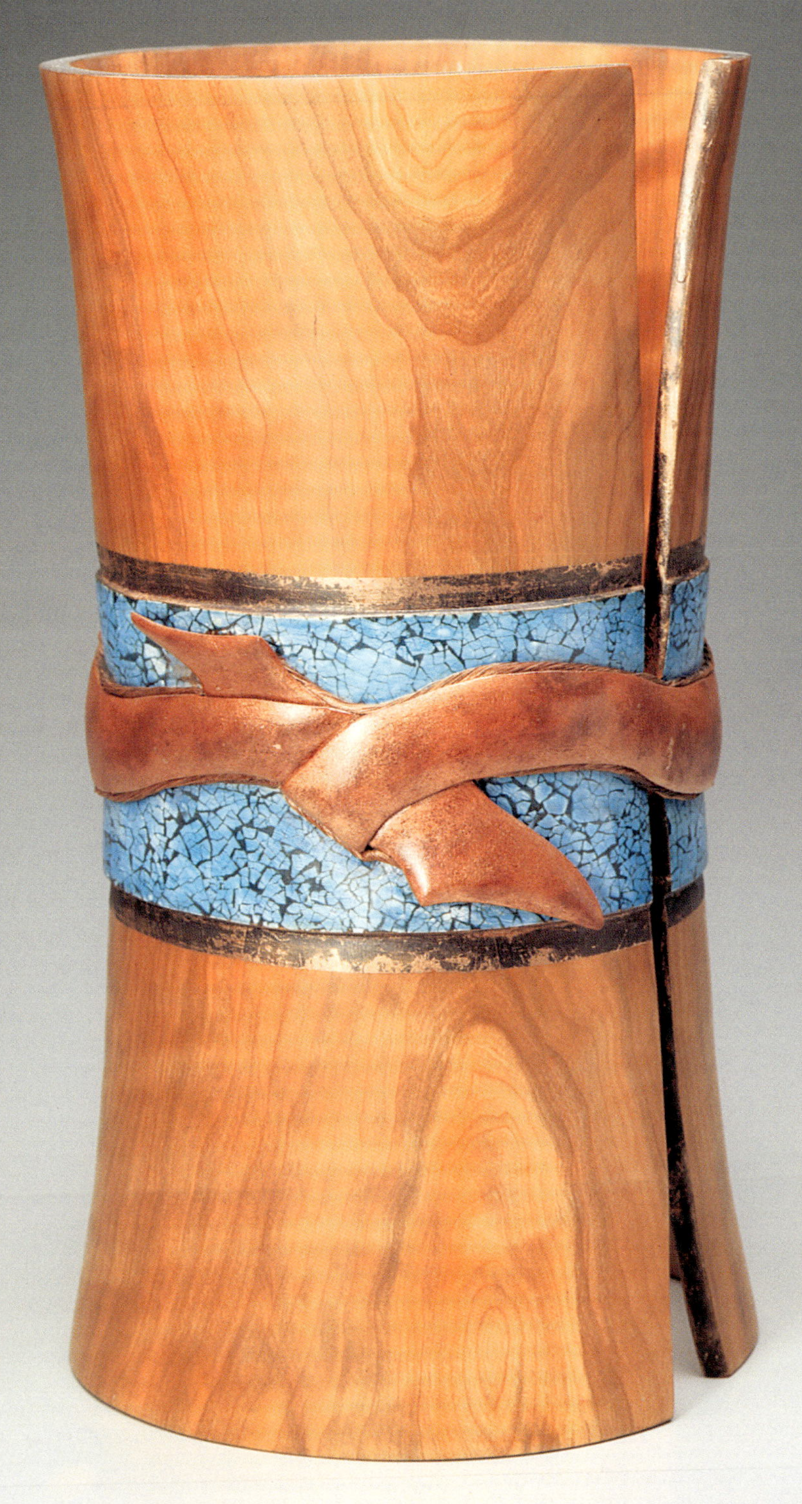

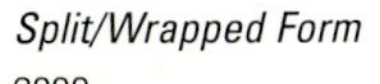

*Split/Wrapped Form*
2000
H: 16 1/2", Diam: 9 1/8"
Curly cherry, eggshell, copper wire, copper leaf, copper flake, red oxide powder and varnish

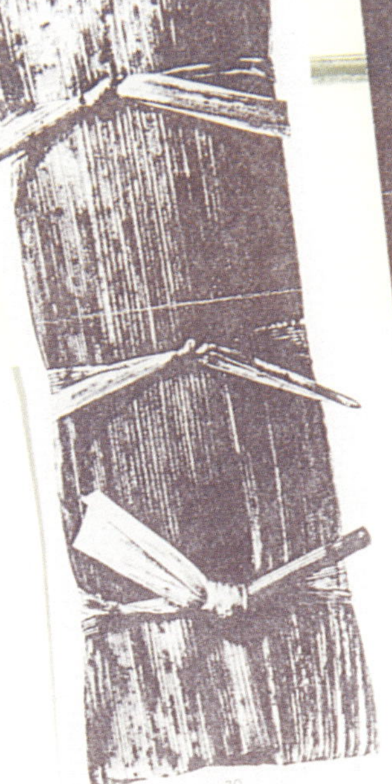

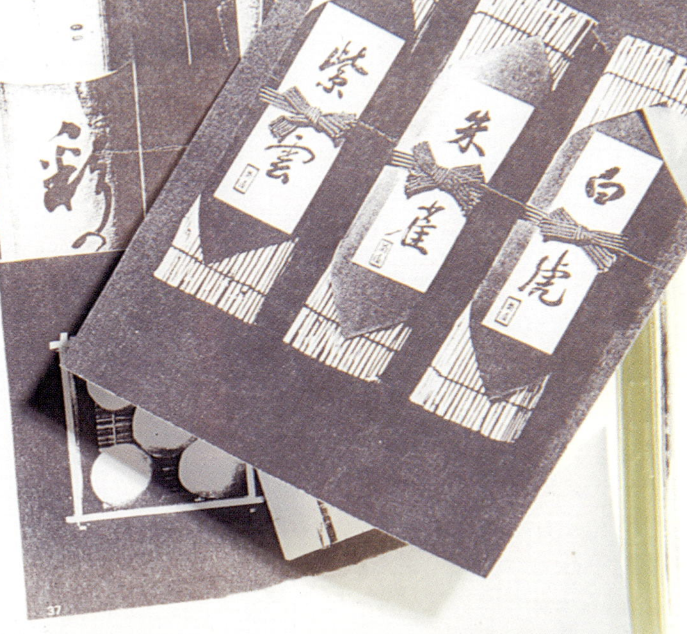


## Andrew Curle [*Canada – b. 1956*]

Many years ago, before I went to Japan, I had seen a book entitled *How To Wrap Five Eggs* on traditional Japanese packaging. I remember being intrigued by the often simple, always beautiful methods of holding things together. Since then, I had not seen the book again until I borrowed it from a friend to find a visual source for the form. I have always admired the surface decoration techniques of Japanese urushi artists using natural materials in amazing ways. When I began turning this form, I had only a general idea of wanting a simple shape held together with a band of some sort. After carving away everything that wasn't a band, I realized that the band disappeared visually because of the grain. Thinking of the eggshell work I had seen, I thought it might set off the band from the form. During all this, I was working with twenty-year-old memories, so I felt it wouldn't be too direct a source, and would allow me more freedom to re-interpret the form. Looking at the book, I was surprised by how much I had been influenced, and perhaps the decision to use eggshell was connected to the title (although the book shows none of this type of work). It did take more than 5 eggs to get it right though...

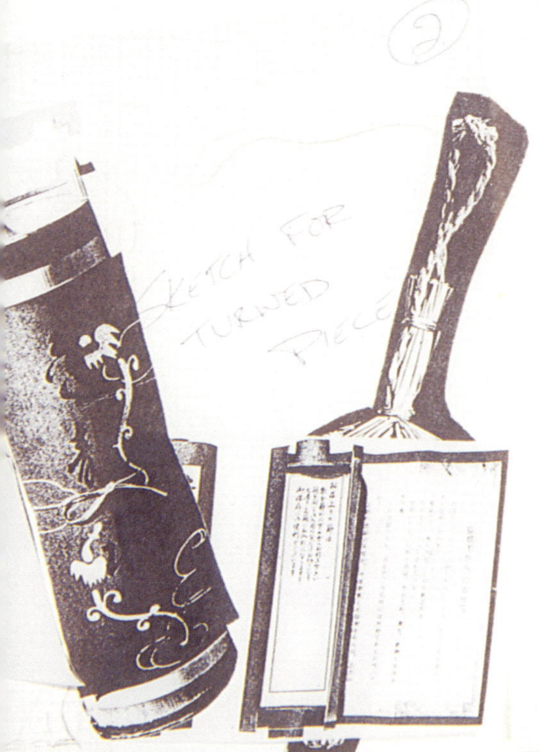

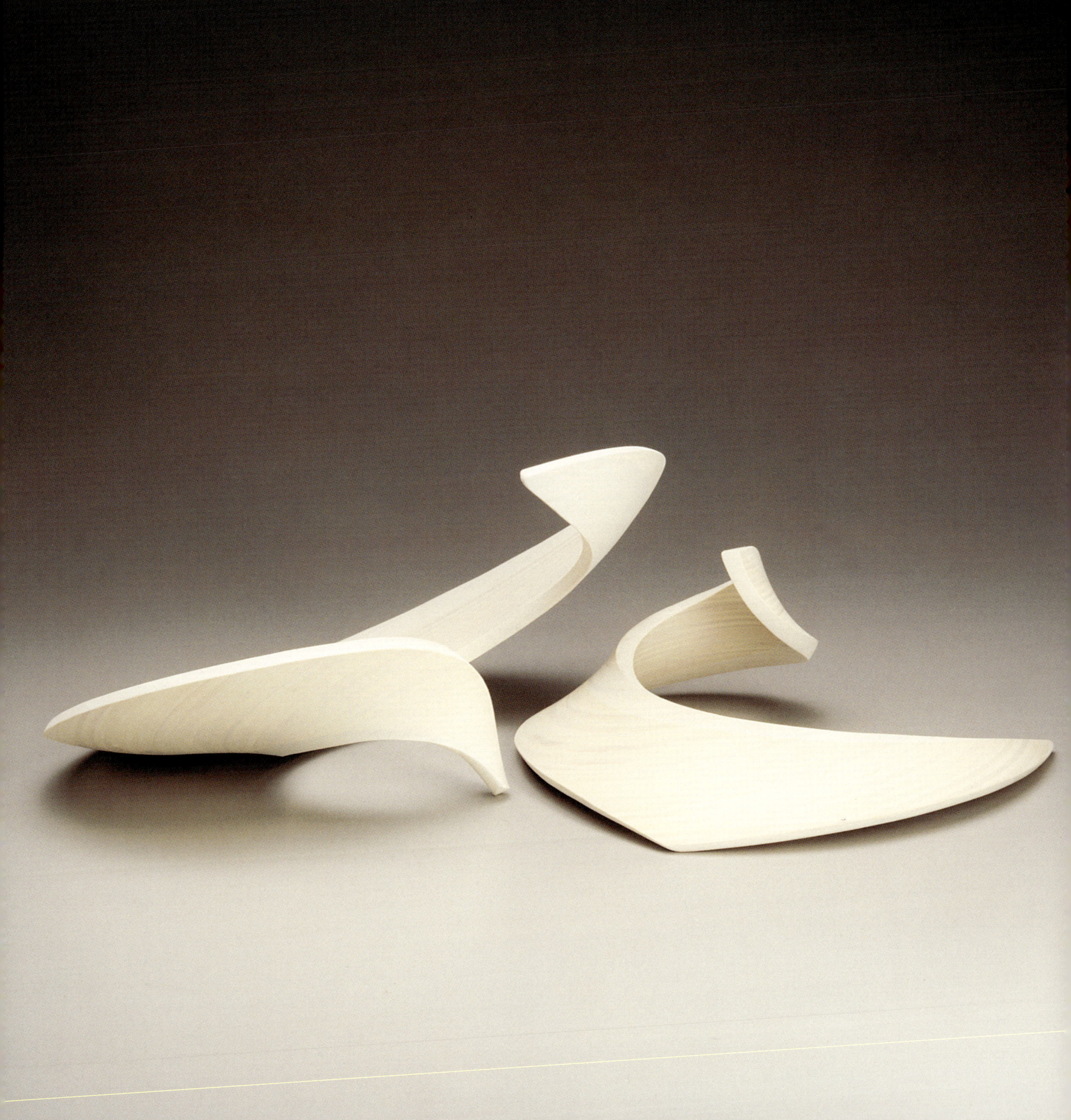

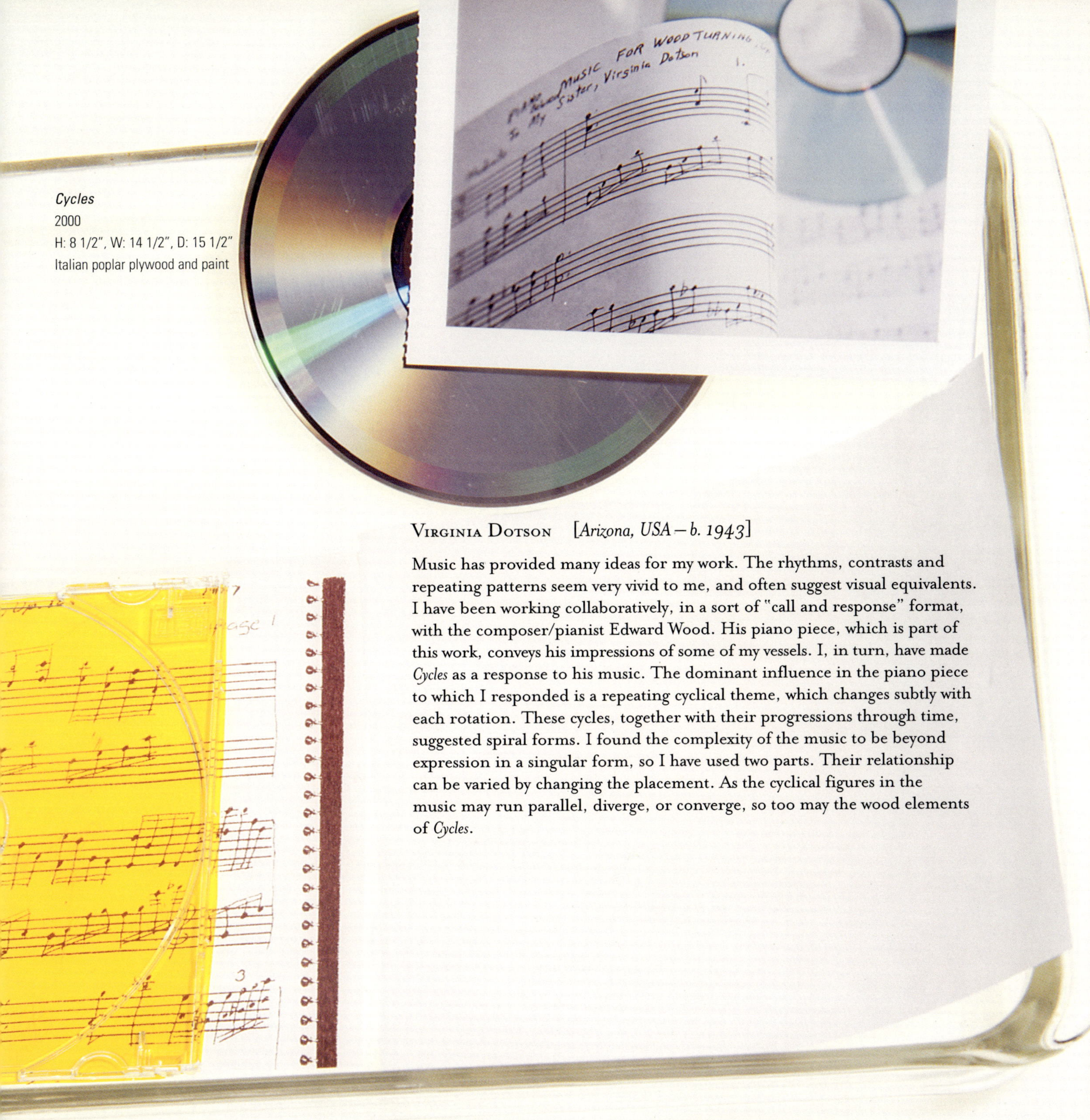


*Cycles*
2000
H: 8 1/2", W: 14 1/2", D: 15 1/2"
Italian poplar plywood and paint

## Virginia Dotson [*Arizona, USA – b. 1943*]

Music has provided many ideas for my work. The rhythms, contrasts and repeating patterns seem very vivid to me, and often suggest visual equivalents. I have been working collaboratively, in a sort of "call and response" format, with the composer/pianist Edward Wood. His piano piece, which is part of this work, conveys his impressions of some of my vessels. I, in turn, have made *Cycles* as a response to his music. The dominant influence in the piano piece to which I responded is a repeating cyclical theme, which changes subtly with each rotation. These cycles, together with their progressions through time, suggested spiral forms. I found the complexity of the music to be beyond expression in a singular form, so I have used two parts. Their relationship can be varied by changing the placement. As the cyclical figures in the music may run parallel, diverge, or converge, so too may the wood elements of *Cycles*.

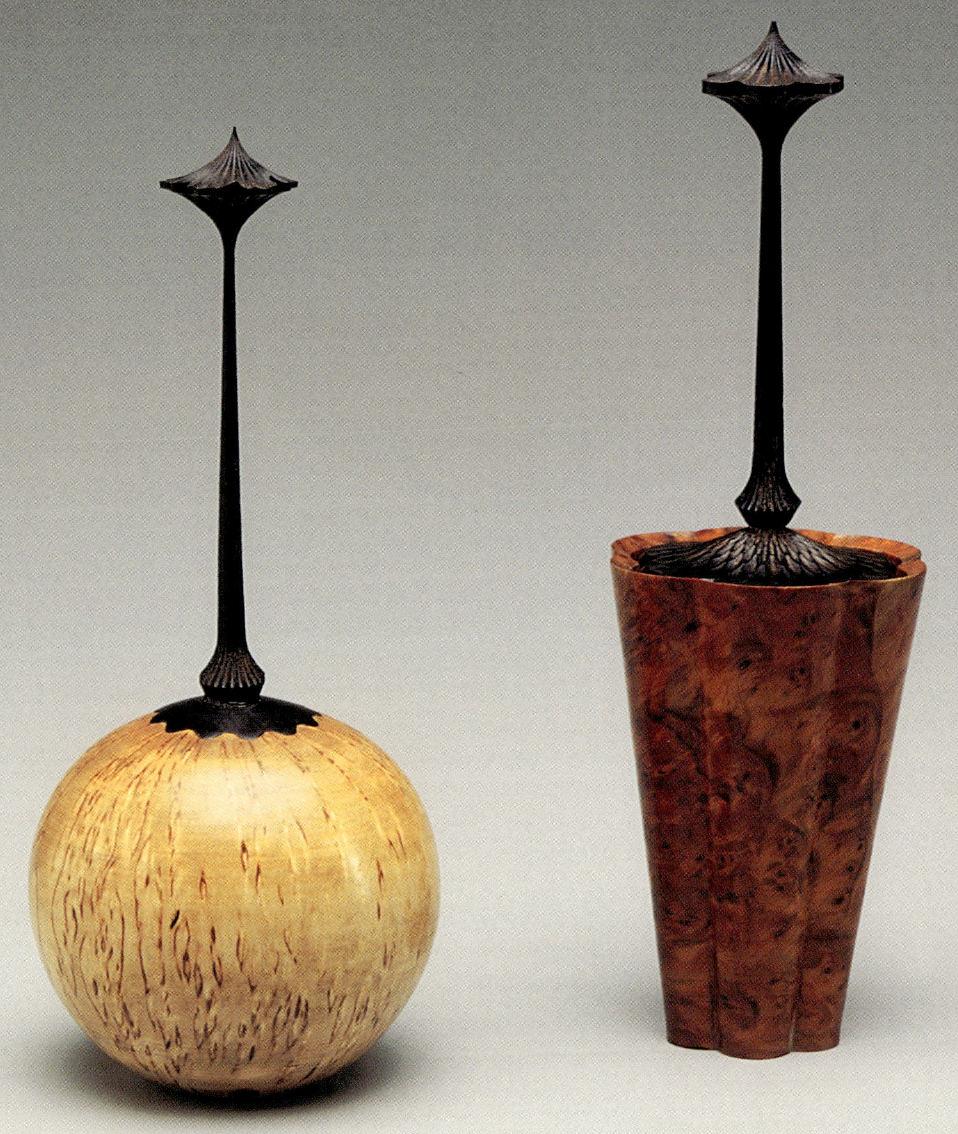

*Seattle Series (Variation)*
2000
H: 7 1/2", Diam: 3 1/2"
Masur birch and African blackwood

*Seattle Series (Variation)*
2000
H: 8 1/2", Diam: 2 5/8"
Paela burl and African blackwood

## Gorst du Plessis [*Louisiana, USA – b. 1938*]

I have been interested and involved in woodworking for 50 years — from whittling and duck carving, to making Queen Anne and Federal Style furniture. Approximately 16 years ago I was fortunate enough to acquire a Holtzapffel ornamental lathe (Circa 1842) and one of two Armbruster Rose Engine lathes.

Using exotic woods, precious metals and semi precious stones, I have been totally immersed in trying to master the intricacies of machines, materials and imagination. The only constants in my work are change and relying on my intuition from previous experience and exposure. I am a student of the history of turning. I turn every day, as it is the relaxation that I get in contrast to my "day job," the practice of medicine.

Regarding the inspiration for the boxes submitted, I have been experimenting with architectural motifs and these boxes are from my **Seattle Series** (i.e. the Space Needle) and explore the relationship of ornamental turned plain wood to highly figured wood.

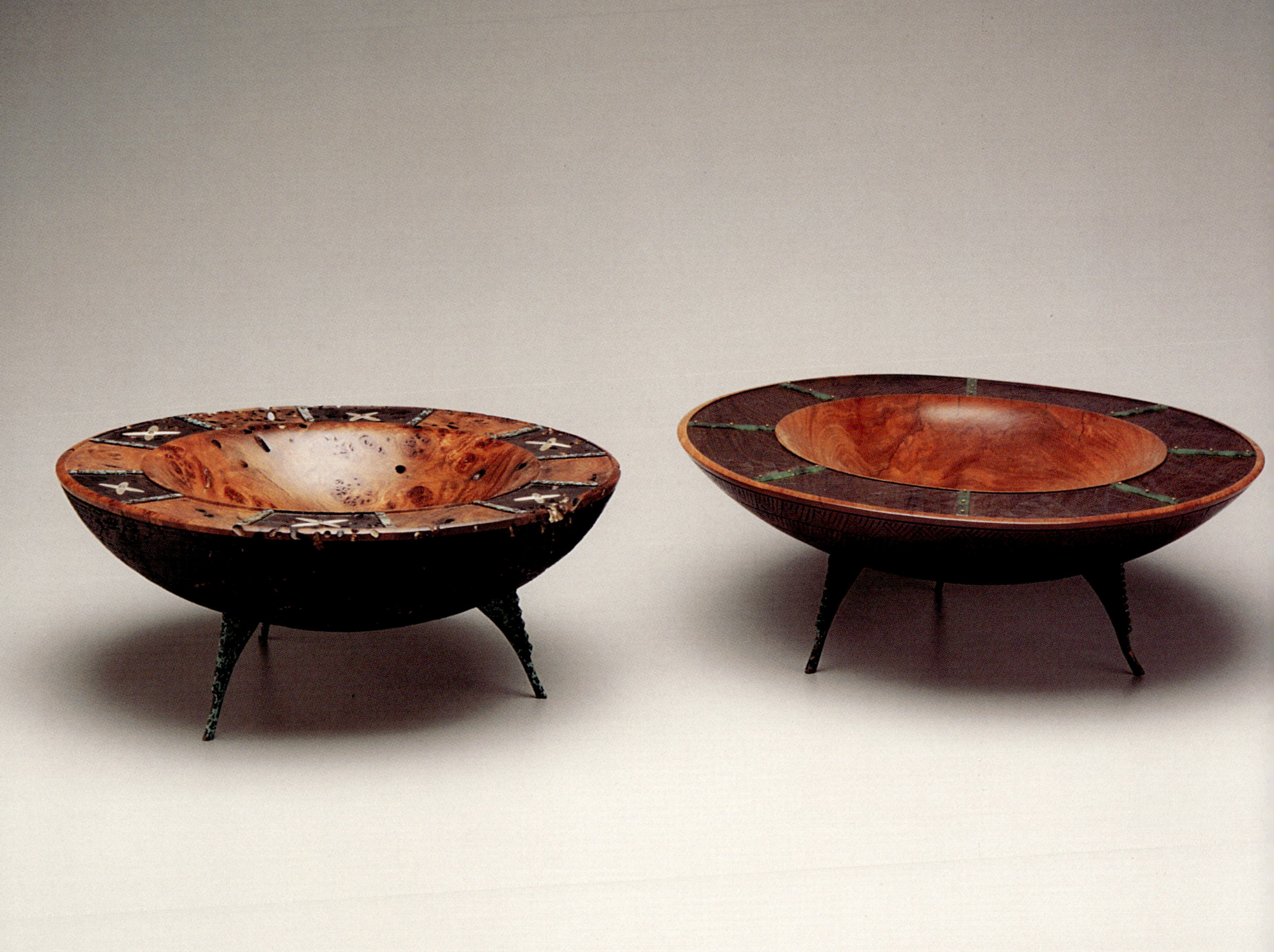

*Toledo Remnant Vessel*
2000
H: 6 3/4", Diam: 13 3/4"
Red beech burl, silver and patinated copper

*Pounamu Offering Vessel*
2000
H: 4 3/4", Diam: 17 1/2"
Pohutukawa, jade (pounamu), and patinated copper

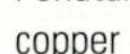

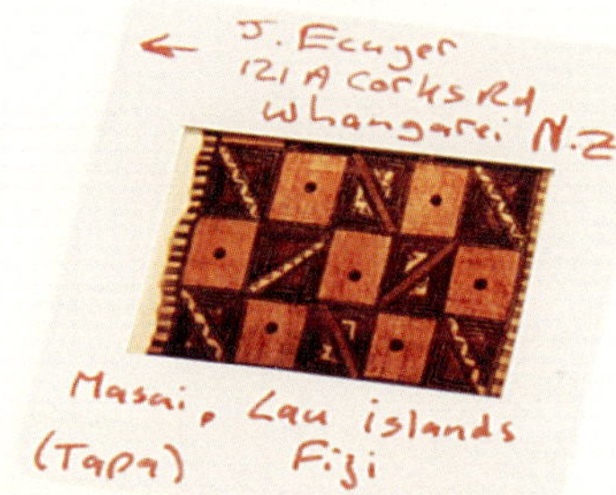


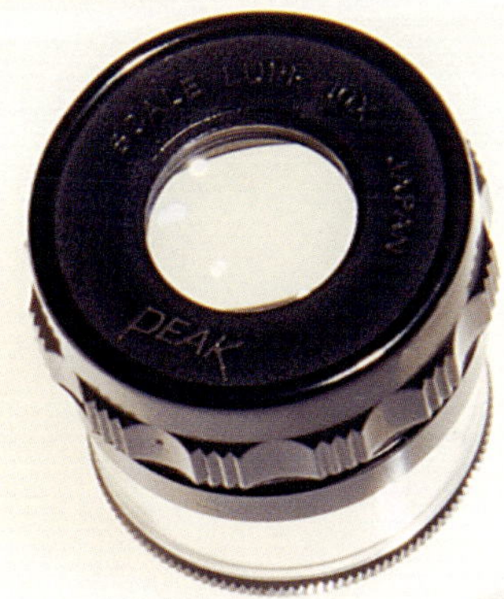


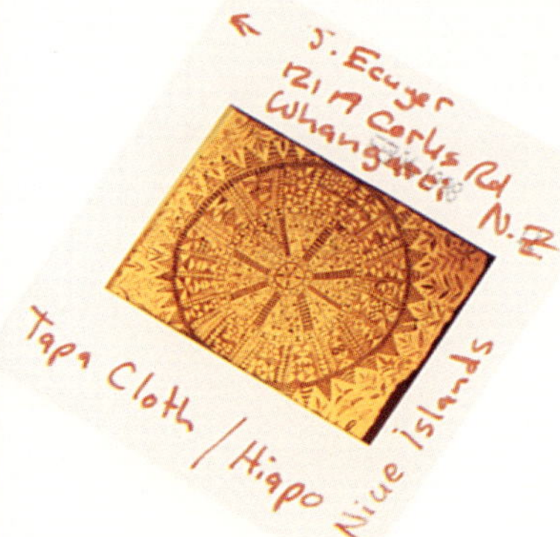


## John Ecuyer [*New Zealand – b. 1956*]

As a contemporary New Zealand wood turner, I have been influenced by the art and culture of the peoples who inhabit the South Pacific Islands. One of the most distinctive art forms for me has been the Pacific tapa cloth. These are made from the inner bark of certain trees, and their association with my basic material, wood, has been an inspiration to me.

I create wood turned vessels that are elevated on patinated copper legs. These vessels have wide rims which allow me to create repeating visual designs that are inspired by tapa cloth patterns. These repeating patterns are also divided into segments that allow for further infill designs. Often these divisions are in a bar form, which can be made from metal, shell or stone. The incised carving between is highlighted by black staining and often contains shell inlays.

The final pieces are elevated, legged vessel forms that speak of ceremony or offering. The visual surface designs are reminiscent of tapa cloth, and with the use of various other media, the piece takes on a multi-faceted appearance. Many of the materials I use reflect the South Pacific where I live, and give an expression to often-forgotten aspects of our modern lives.

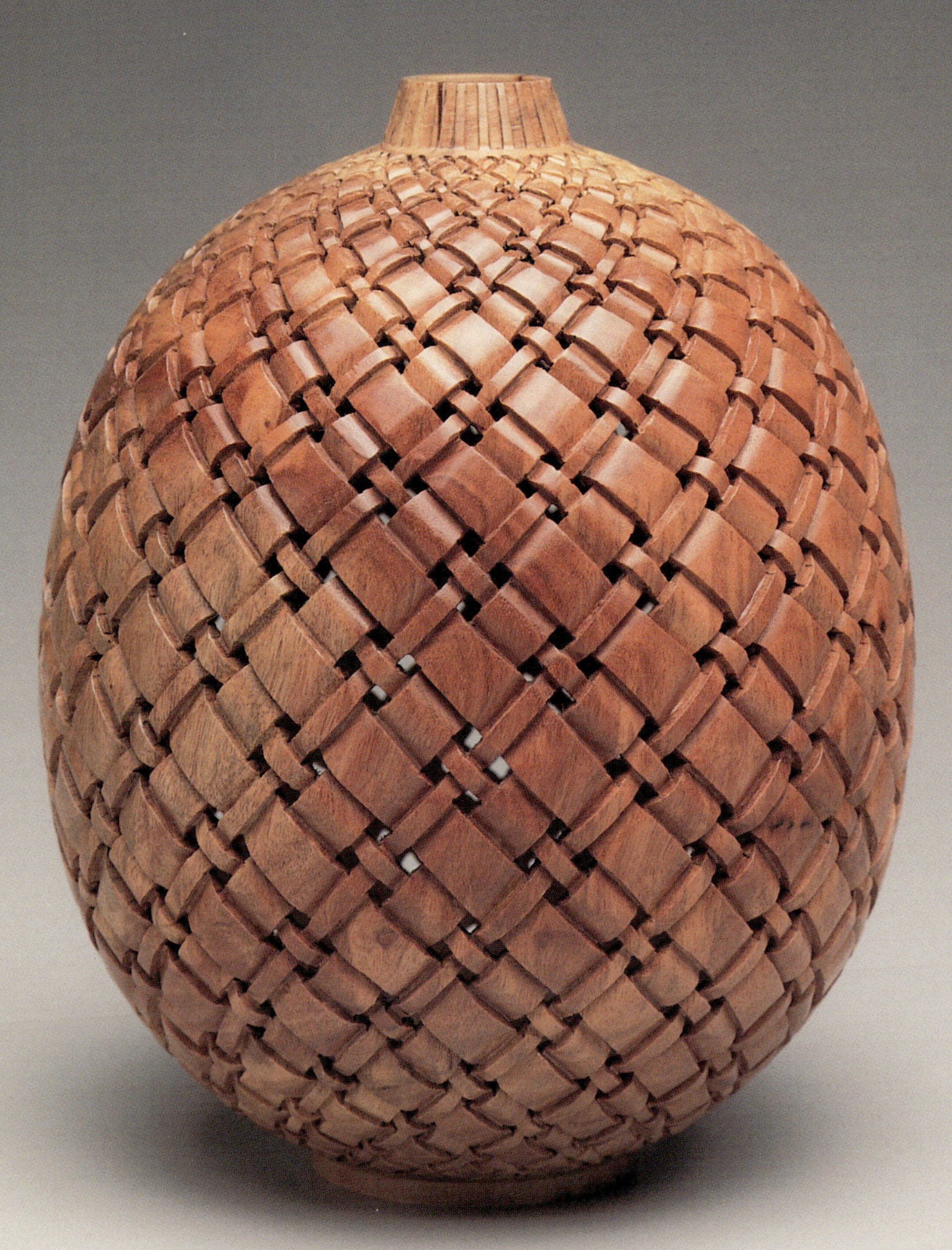

*Untitled*
2000
H: 10", Diam: 8"
Carob
(Collection of Marilyn Friedman, New York, N.Y.)

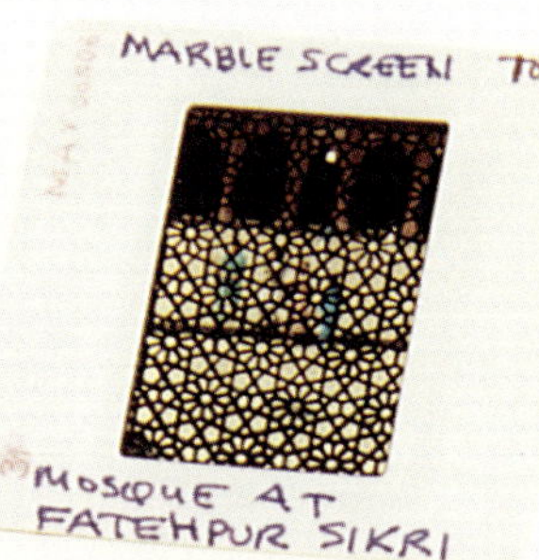


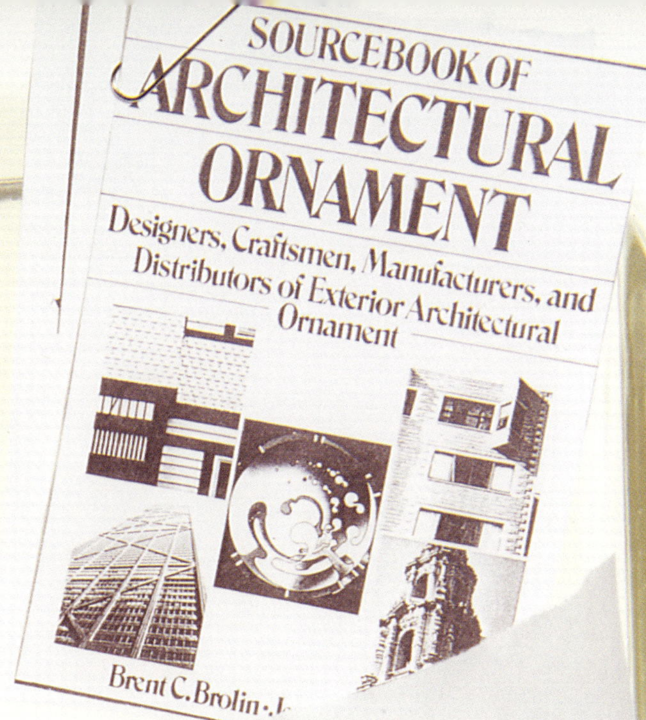


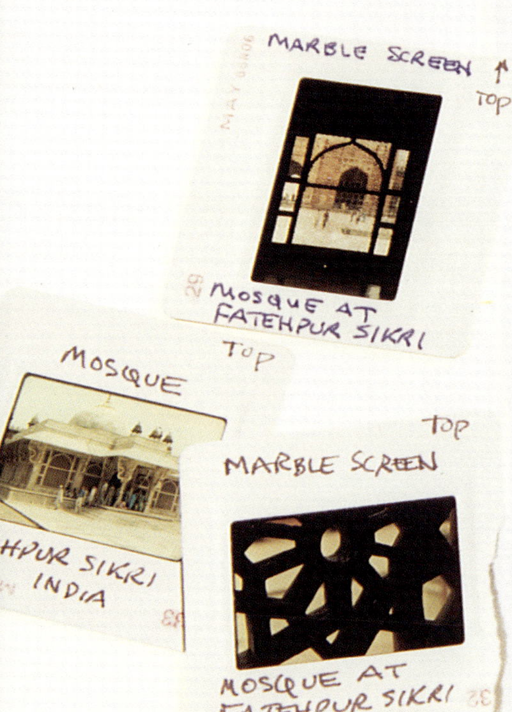


J. Paul Fennell [*Arizona, USA – b. 1938*]

My inspiration emanates from two distinct sources: first, a foreword composed by Eva Zeisel from the *Sourcebook of Architectural Ornament* which eloquently describes the basic human need for decoration. The second comes from a visit I took to the ancient city of Fatehpur Sikri in India, whereupon I became fascinated with the delicately pierced marble screens of the mosques, and was subsequently inspired to incorporate piercing in my own work.

My work has mainly focused upon the aesthetic of the hollow form vessel. To me, the vessel is a fundamental artifact of human civilization. Its ubiquity transcends time and cultural diversity. I have been intrigued by the similarity of pleasing forms and classical shapes that occur historically across a multitude of cultures.

My recent work, on the other hand, has much emphasis from designs found in architectural ornament and patterns abstracted from woven items of everyday use. Both sources identify with the idea of structure and enclosure, or containment. Their designs reflect uniquely with the culture from which they come.

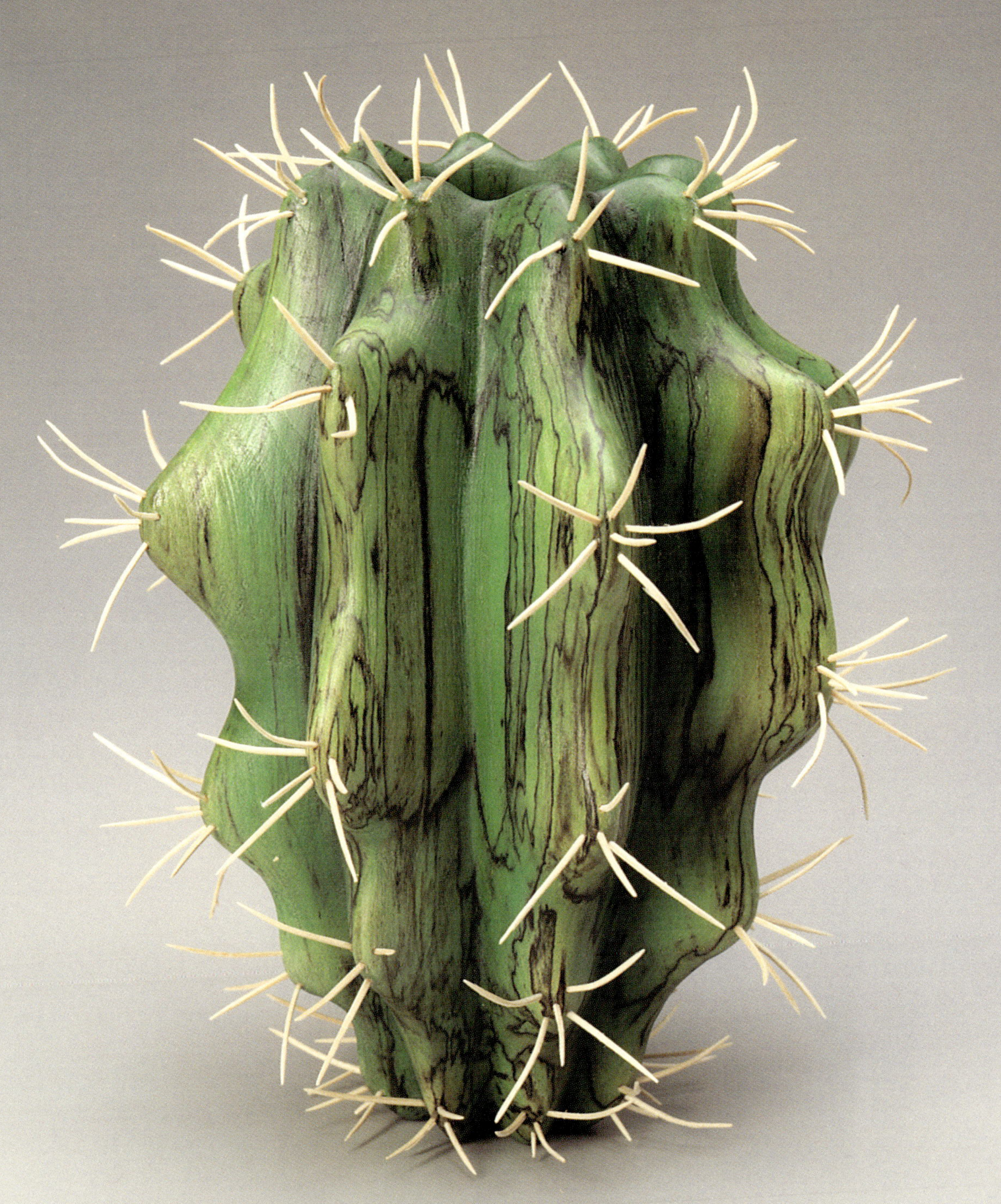

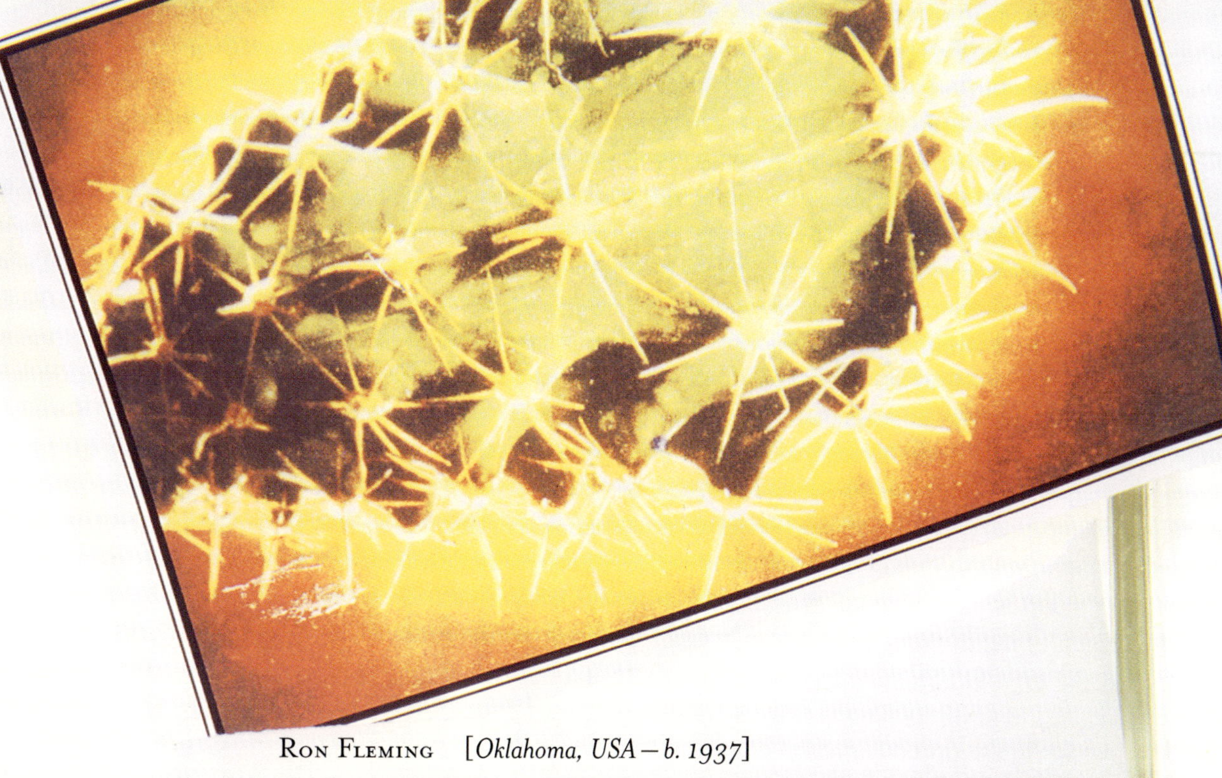

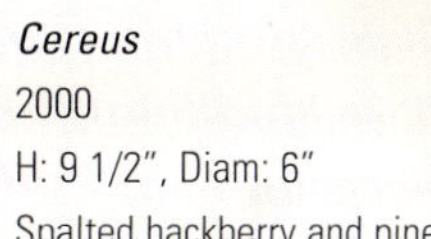

*Cereus*
2000
H: 9 1/2", Diam: 6"
Spalted hackberry and pine

Ron Fleming [*Oklahoma, USA – b. 1937*]

Cereus is a species of cactus. The idea was not to copy it exactly, but to give a stylized impression and still show that it is made from wood. I chose spalted hackberry so the strong spalting lines would show through the green color. The toothpicks were steamed and bent, then sanded to points and randomly placed on the vessel.

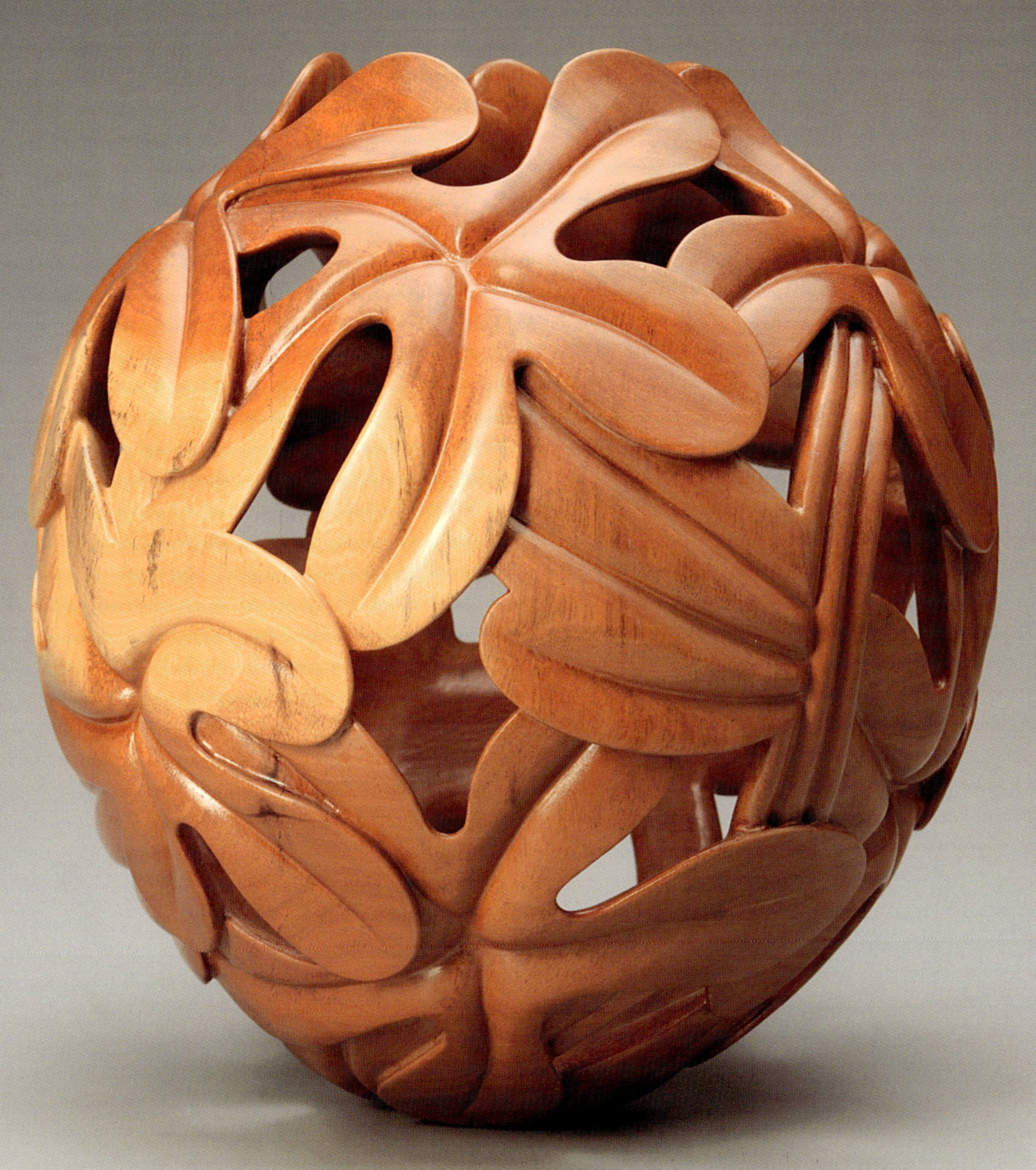

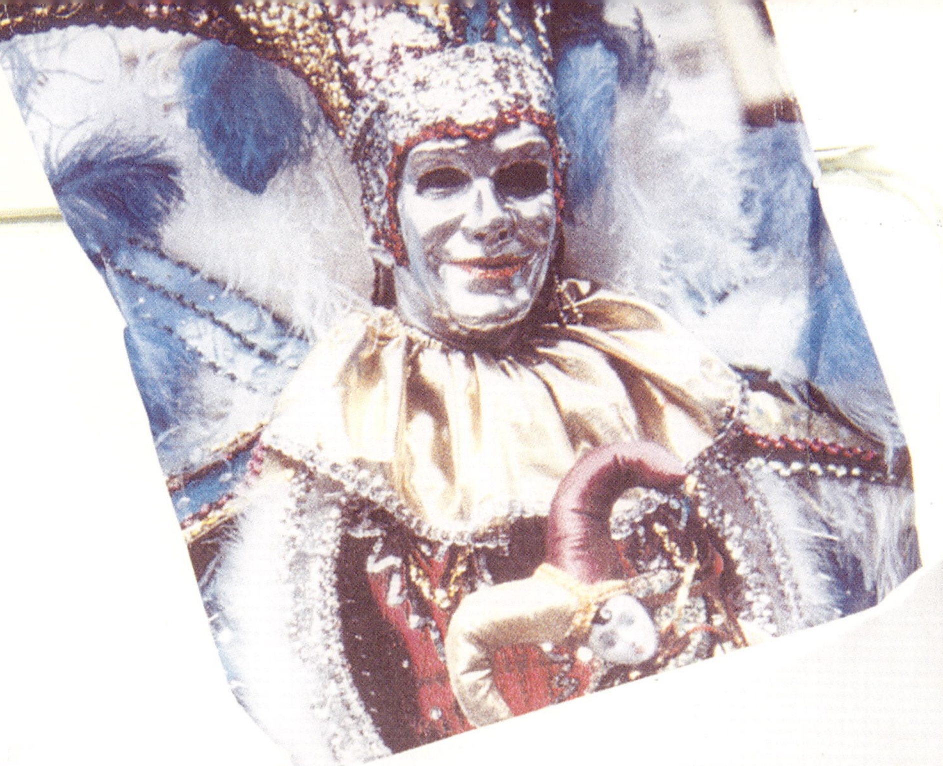

*Orpheus*
2000
H: 12", Diam: 10"
Brazilian mahogany

Ron Fleming [*Oklahoma, USA – b. 1937*]

As most ideas come from nature, the idea for this piece is no exception. Orpheus, in Greek mythology, was a musician whose skill on the lyre had a magic affect on beasts and even rocks and trees. My impression was to use foliage on the piece to represent the gaiety of the music. My intent was to convey a sense of rhythm and celebration as in Mardi Gras.

"ORPHEUS"

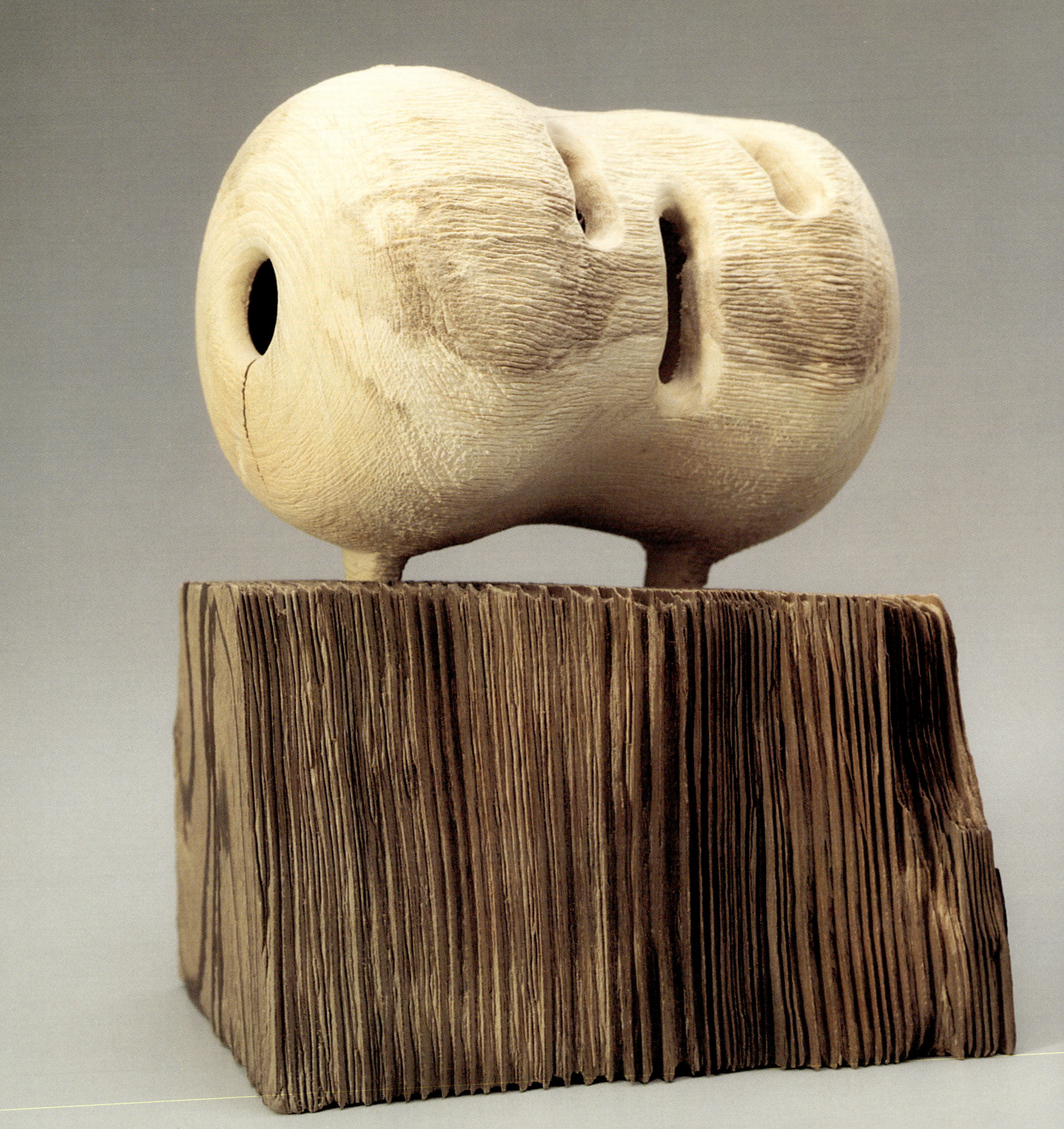

*Journey of Will*
2000
H: 6 3/4", W: 4 7/8", D: 3 1/2"
Cherry and lignitized cedar

## Satoshi Fujinuma [*Japan – b. 1962*]

For me, lathe turning exists at the core of my works. My source of inspiration is the rotating movement of the lathe. Rotating movement would bring out the potential of wood and elevate it towards a higher level. I believe that rotating movement can make me transcend the limits of my own capability.

I try to express in this work the journey from the unconscious to the self-conscious. The hole and windows are entrances to another world.

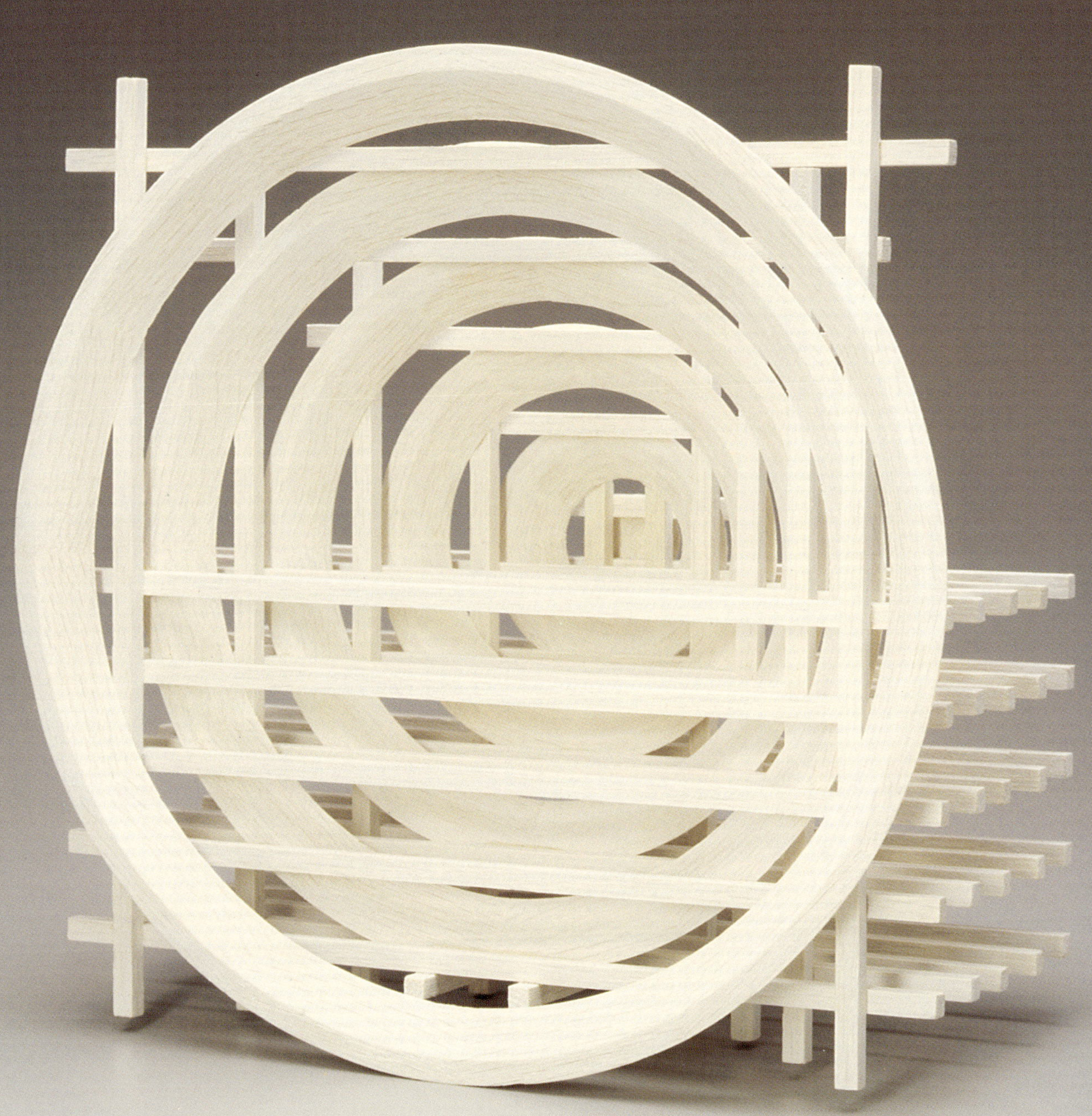

*Gridded Bowl*
2000
H: 5 1/2", W: 10 1/2", D: 10 1/2"
Oak (bleached)

Dewey Garrett [*California, USA – b. 1947*]

I occasionally pass a building under construction and find it interesting to observe the work and its day-to-day progress. I think the appeal is the transformation of the complexity and confusion into a purposeful construction. This work addresses an analogous complexity and transformation of a simple vessel form.

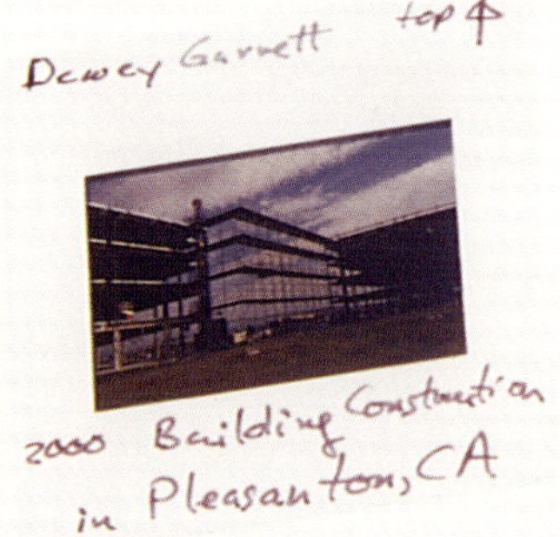


The source image for the piece is a photograph of a local building under construction. This building is now complete, and the complexity once so apparent in its formation, is now hidden within a modern, functioning office building.

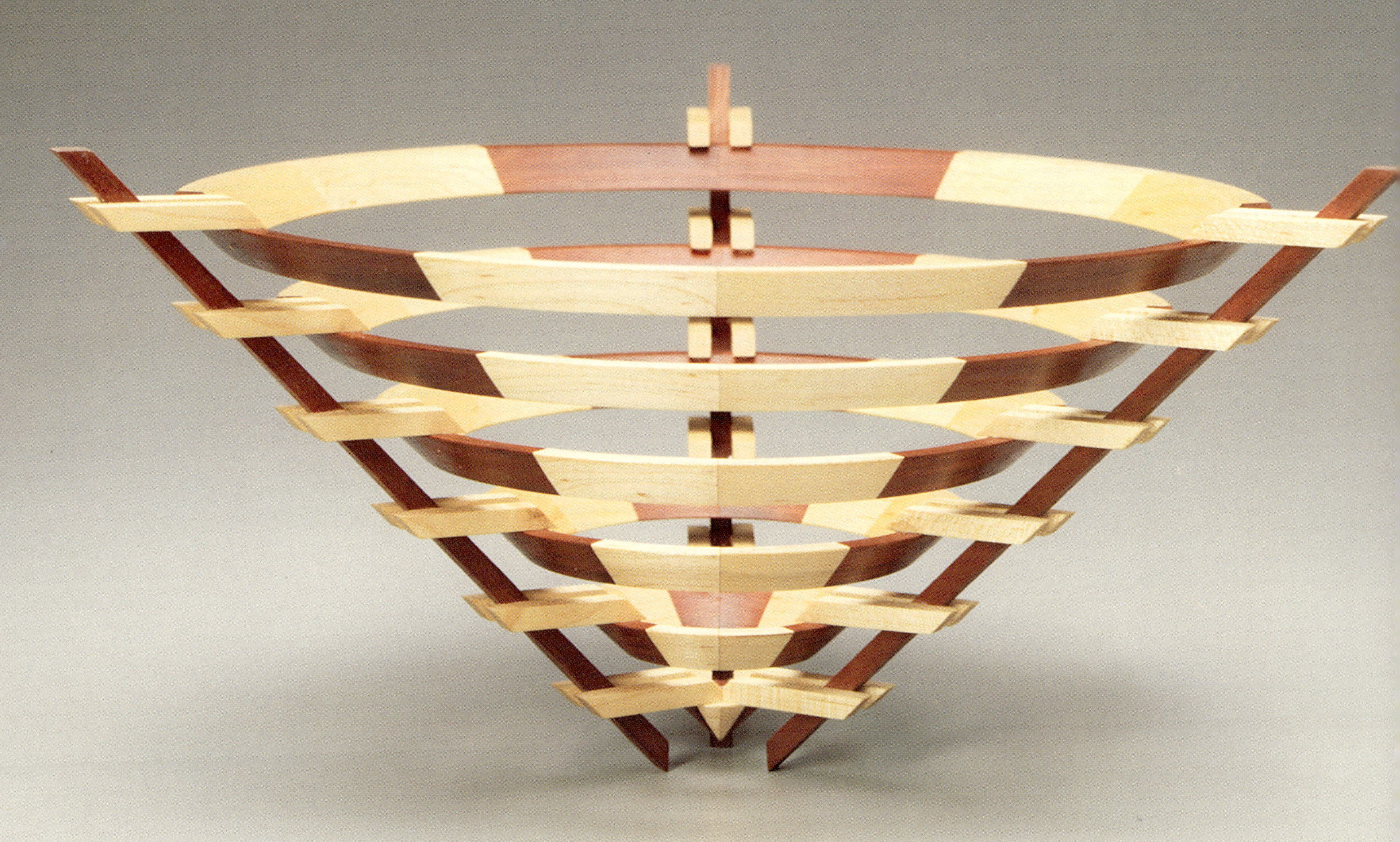

*Suspension #4*
2000
H: 6 1/2", W: 13", D: 13"
Chaktekok and maple

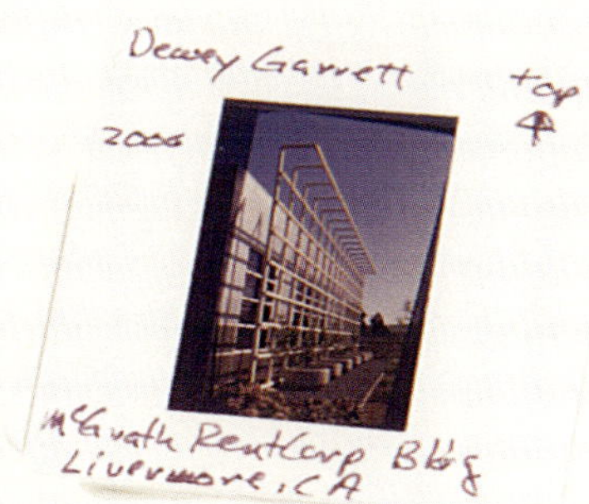


Dewey Garrett [*California, USA – b. 1947*]

I frequently make objects that are compositions of the sections of a simple form, which include the air or space about it. I saw a photo of a local building in a news article cited for an architectural award. The building had a distinctive light and airy look, made possible by an exo-skeleton that surrounded its plain exterior walls. The architects' design made an ordinary suburban office building different and interesting.

My challenge for this piece was to design a vessel incorporating a similar exo-skeleton. I chose a conical form for its straight sides and simplicity. Overall, I think the piece is an expression of architectural design elements that create open spaces with minimal intrusion of structure.

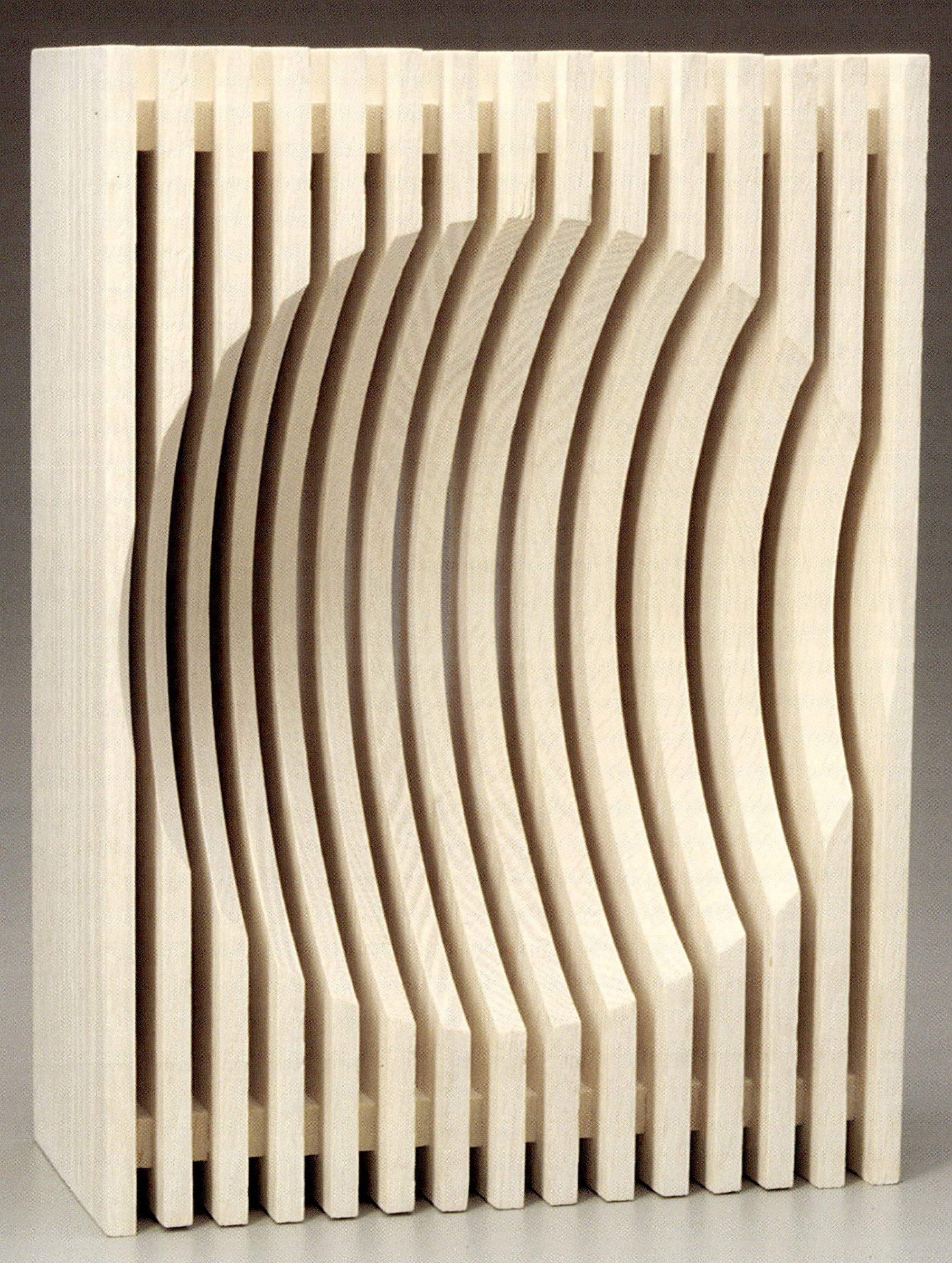

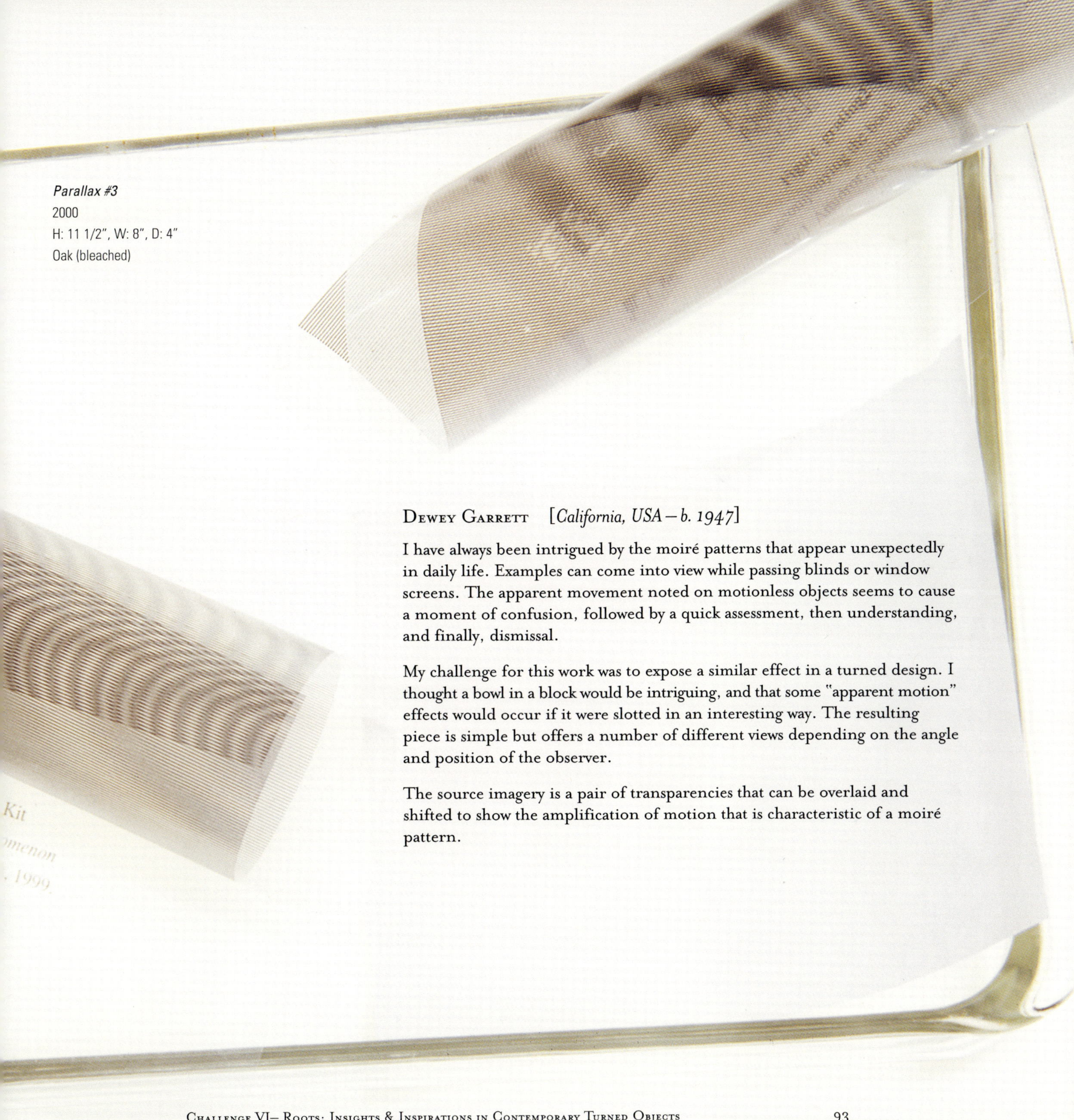

*Parallax #3*
2000
H: 11 1/2", W: 8", D: 4"
Oak (bleached)

Dewey Garrett [*California, USA – b. 1947*]

I have always been intrigued by the moiré patterns that appear unexpectedly in daily life. Examples can come into view while passing blinds or window screens. The apparent movement noted on motionless objects seems to cause a moment of confusion, followed by a quick assessment, then understanding, and finally, dismissal.

My challenge for this work was to expose a similar effect in a turned design. I thought a bowl in a block would be intriguing, and that some "apparent motion" effects would occur if it were slotted in an interesting way. The resulting piece is simple but offers a number of different views depending on the angle and position of the observer.

The source imagery is a pair of transparencies that can be overlaid and shifted to show the amplification of motion that is characteristic of a moiré pattern.

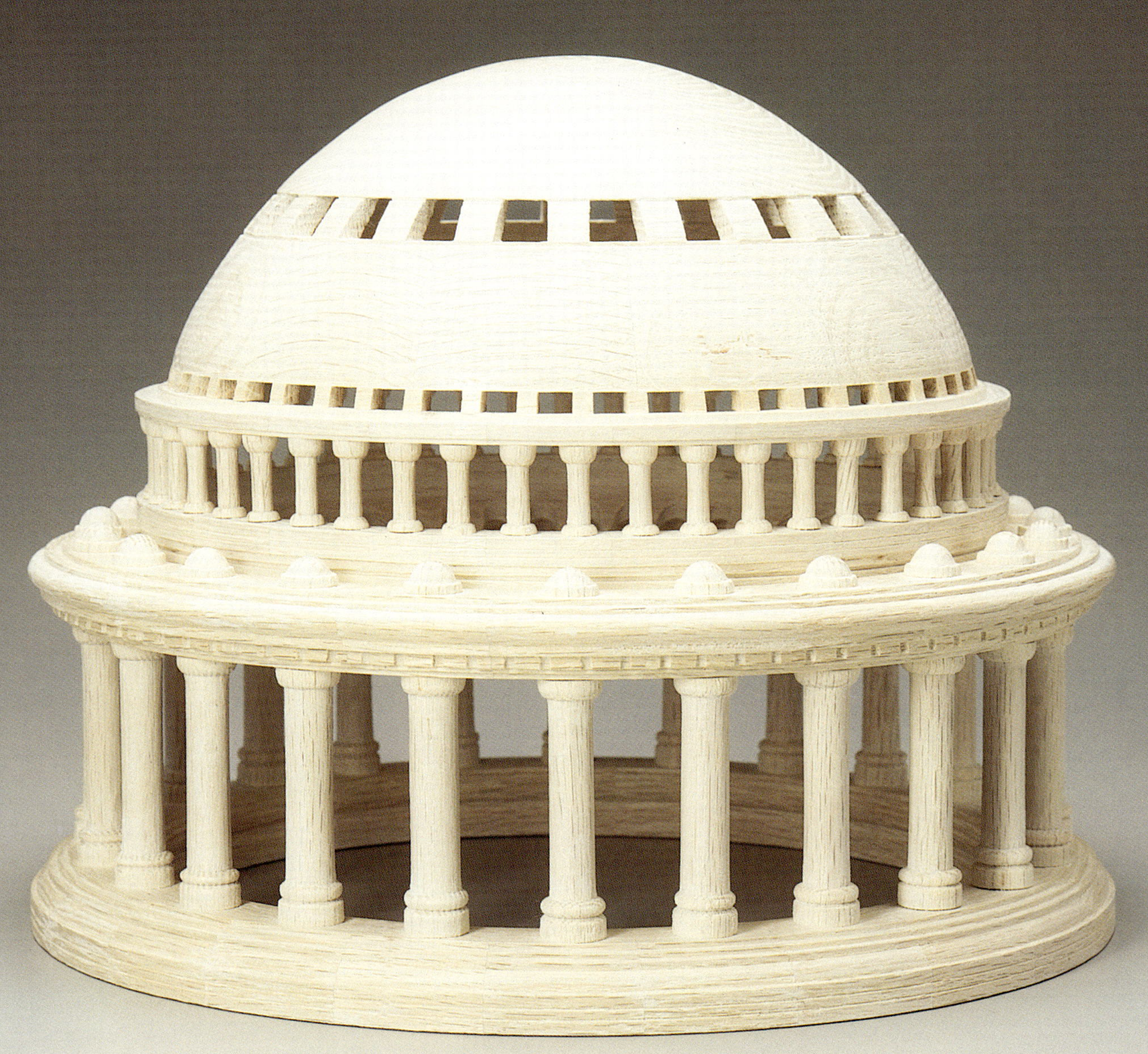

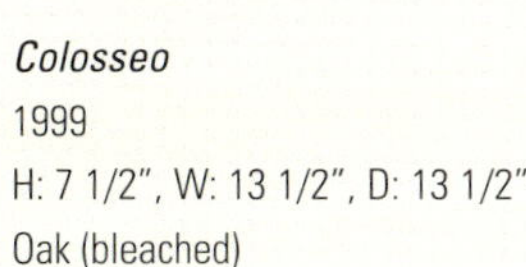

*Colosseo*
1999
H: 7 1/2", W: 13 1/2", D: 13 1/2"
Oak (bleached)

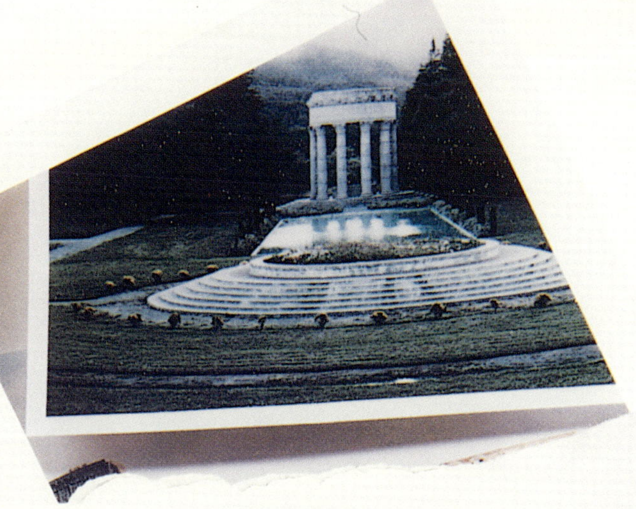

Dewey Garrett [*California, USA – b. 1947*]

I remember a long-ago trip and my first views of the ruins of the Coliseum in Rome. Walking through that structure was a humbling experience, as its scale, complexity and purpose echoed the achievements (and the horrors) of a forgotten time.

The challenge addressed in this work is to incorporate familiar, classical architectural elements within a vessel form. The design for the piece begins with a simple bowl supported by a "colonnaded" structure. The vessel is topped with a decorative awning and a columned celestory level. This design can be transformed into a domed structure by inverting the bowl.

The source item is a friend's vacation photograph of the Coliseum showing the ancient structure in its modern environment.

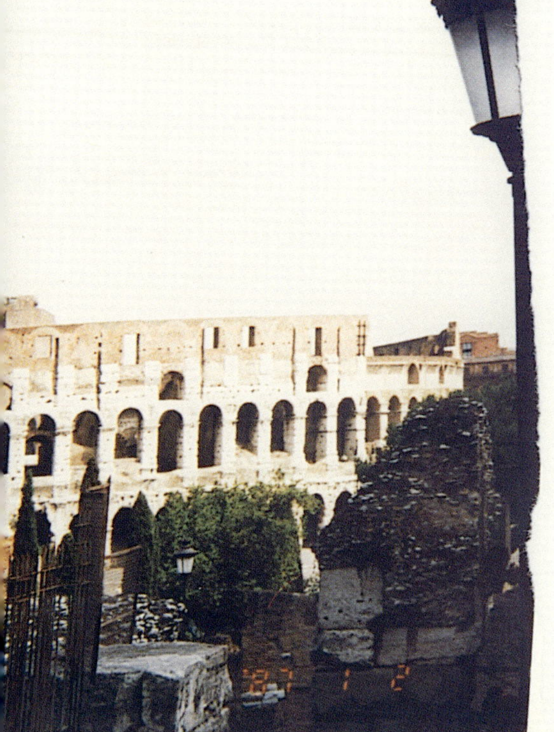

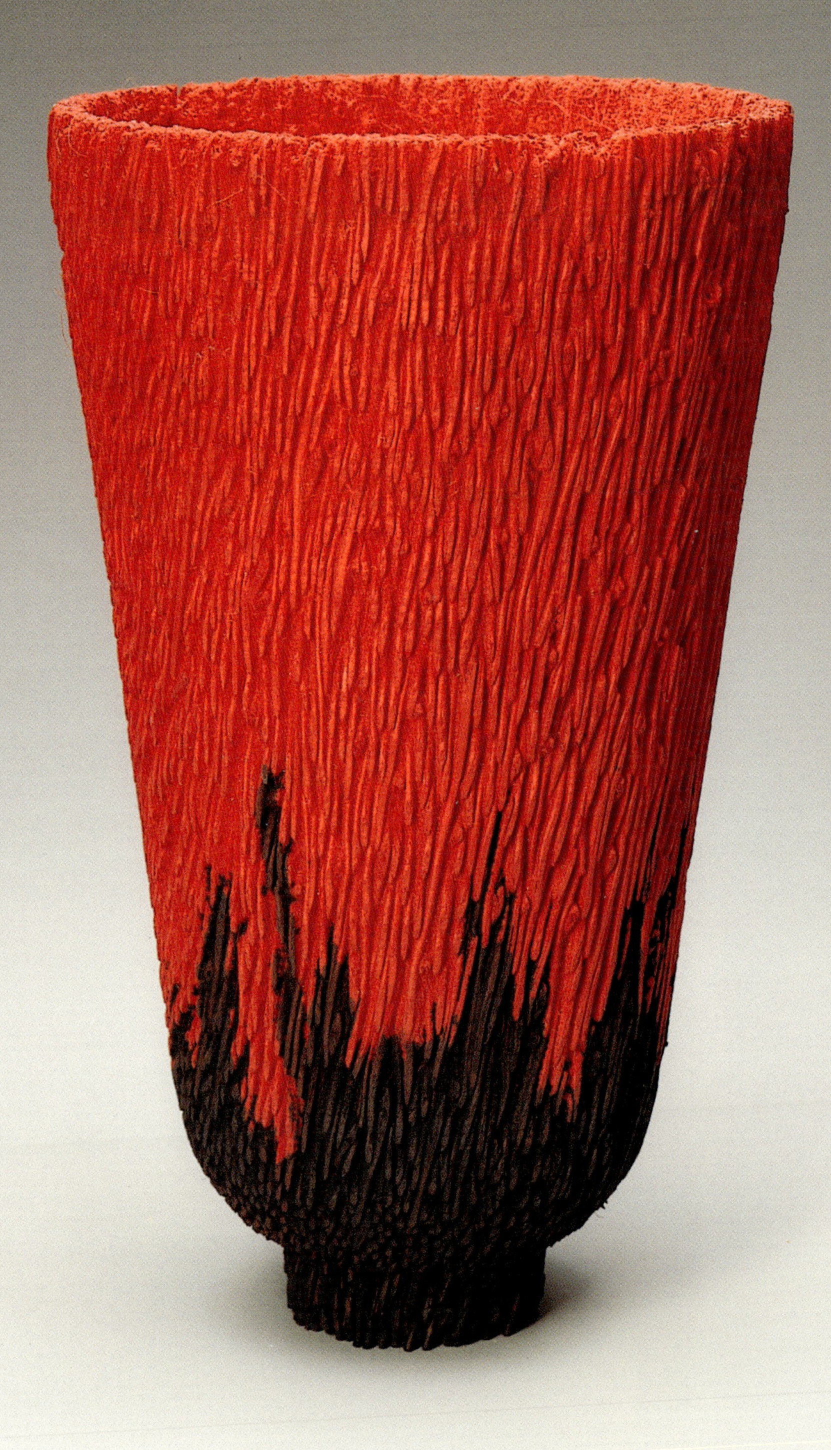

*Rouge et Noir*
1999
H: 12", W: 7", D: 7"
Palm, aniline dyes

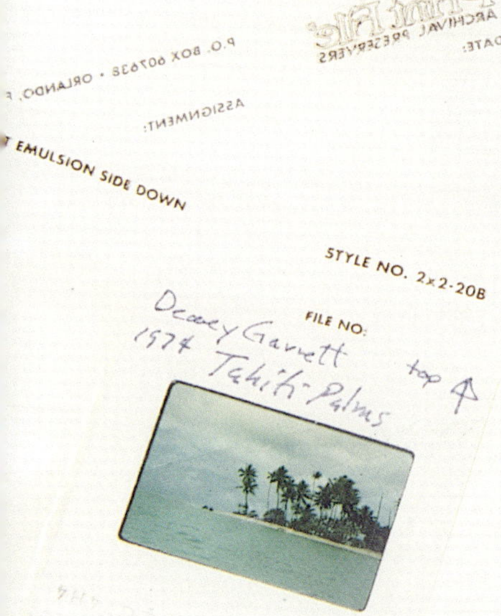


DEWEY GARRETT [*California, USA – b. 1947*]

Sometimes the inspiration for my work is based on the material available. Palms are common decorative trees in California, but they have always seemed exotic to me, since I was raised in the Midwest. I first saw this unusual wood when a friend challenged me to turn something from sections of palm removed in a street renovation project. Instead of the familiar rings and hard wood, fresh cut palm is composed of wet, spongy pith, dotted with many long, stringy fibers. After numerous attempts, I learned to chuck the wood with the grain along the turning axis, and was able to produce interesting shapes that exposed the long fibers in a vertical orientation. By experiment, I found that wire brushing emphasized the fibers, and bleaching removed discolorations that occurred in drying. Further experiments showed that the modified material was an excellent absorber of aniline dyes, and I learned to color them with vibrant stains and markings. The source photo is a palm-lined beach in Tahiti.

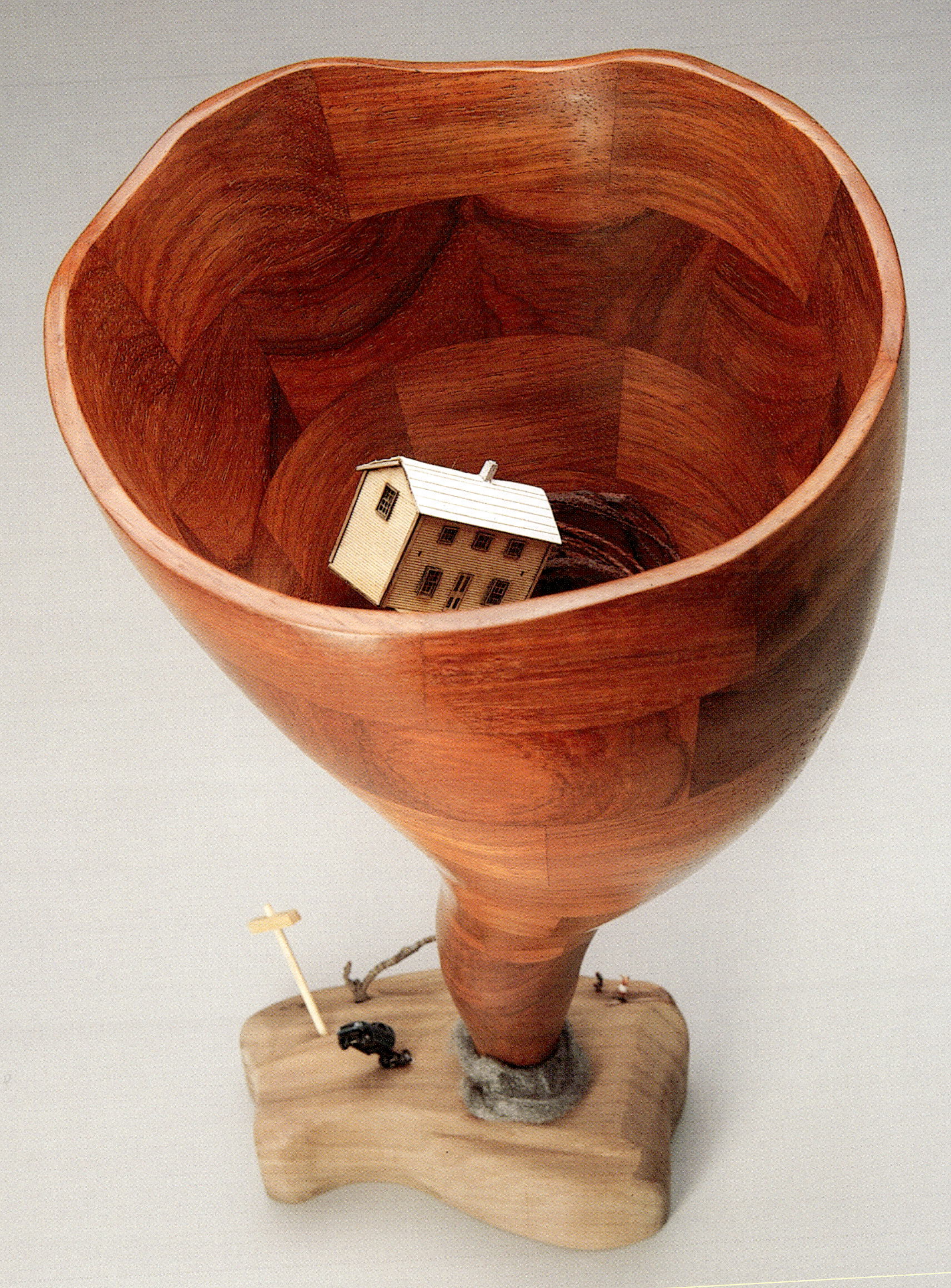

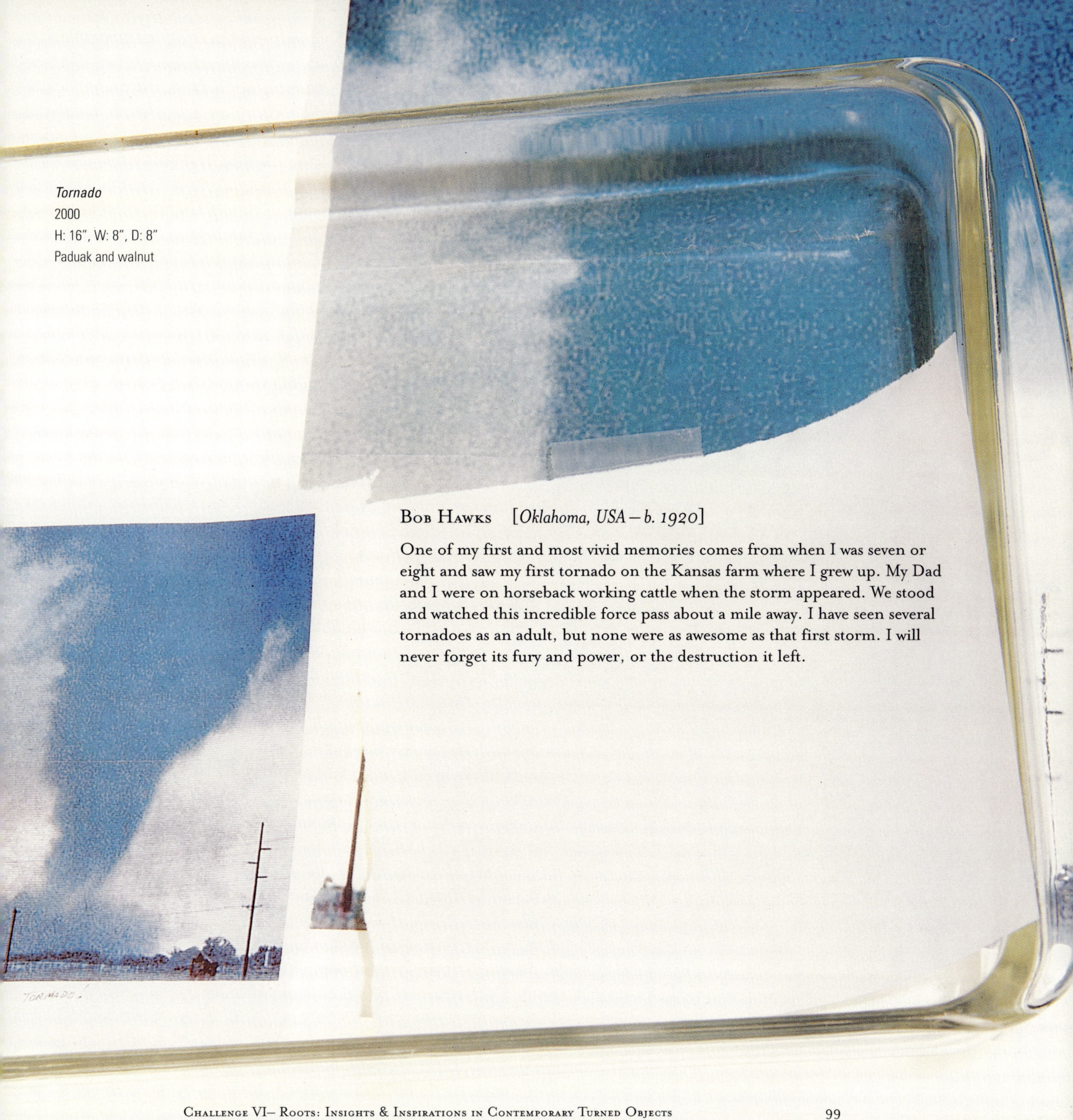


*Tornado*
2000
H: 16", W: 8", D: 8"
Paduak and walnut

Bob Hawks [*Oklahoma, USA – b. 1920*]

One of my first and most vivid memories comes from when I was seven or eight and saw my first tornado on the Kansas farm where I grew up. My Dad and I were on horseback working cattle when the storm appeared. We stood and watched this incredible force pass about a mile away. I have seen several tornadoes as an adult, but none were as awesome as that first storm. I will never forget its fury and power, or the destruction it left.

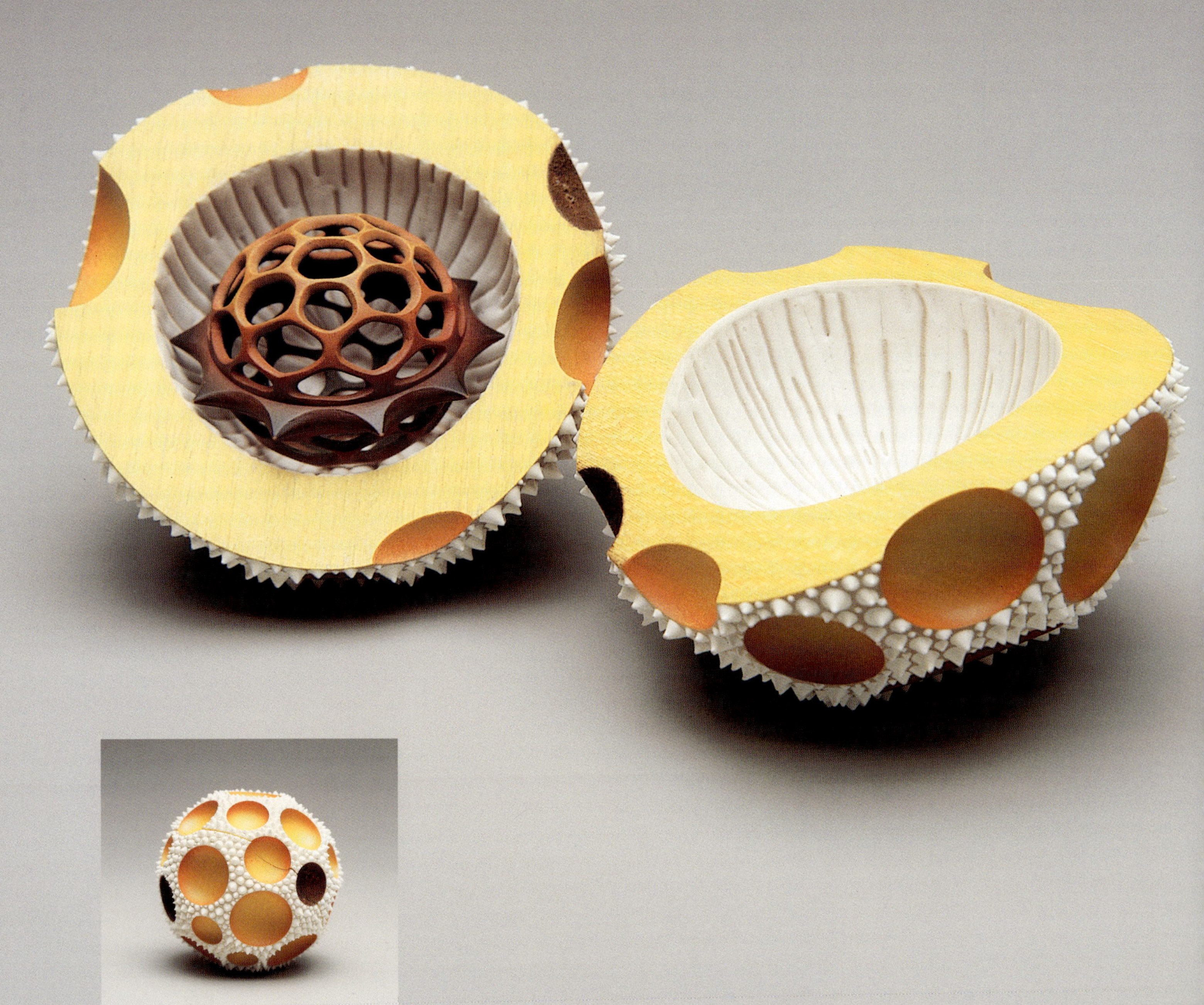

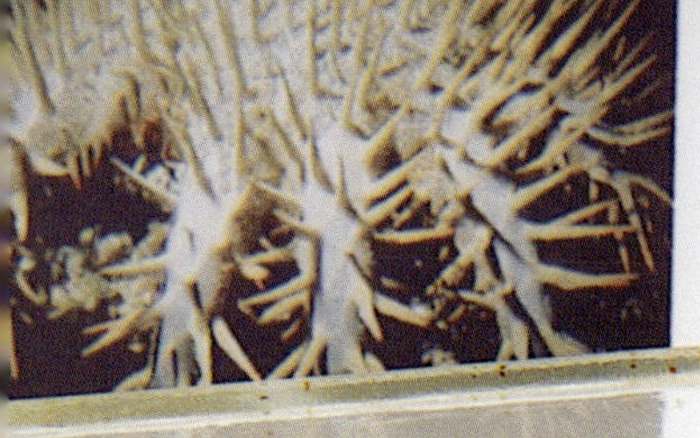

*Cinachyra Box*
2000
Diam: 4 1/4"
Sycamore, blackwood, polyester resin and acrylic ink.

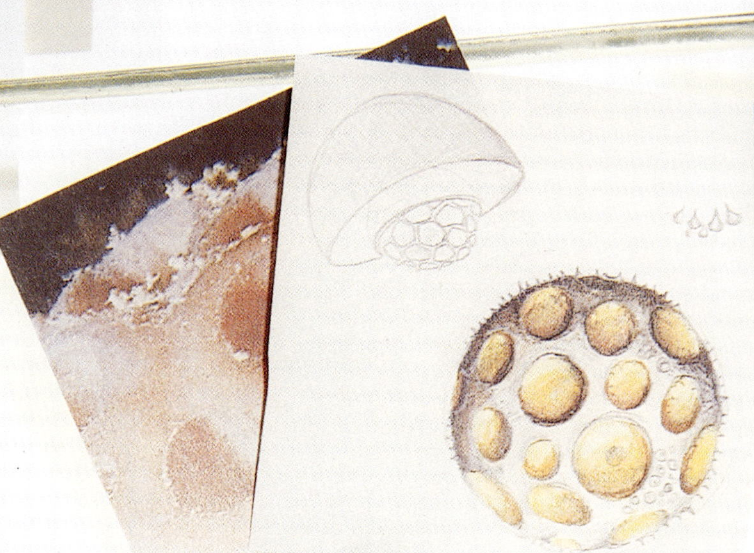

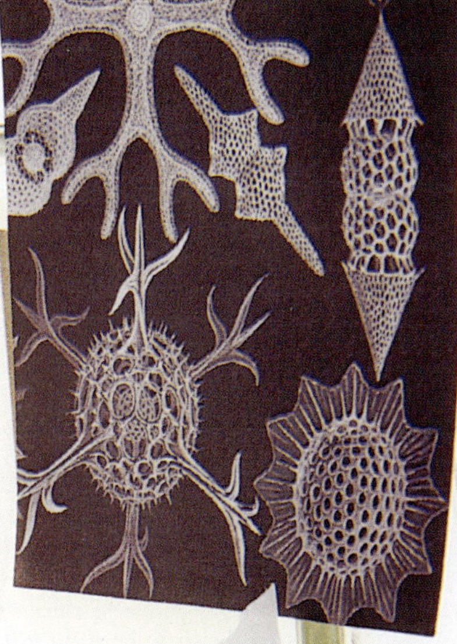

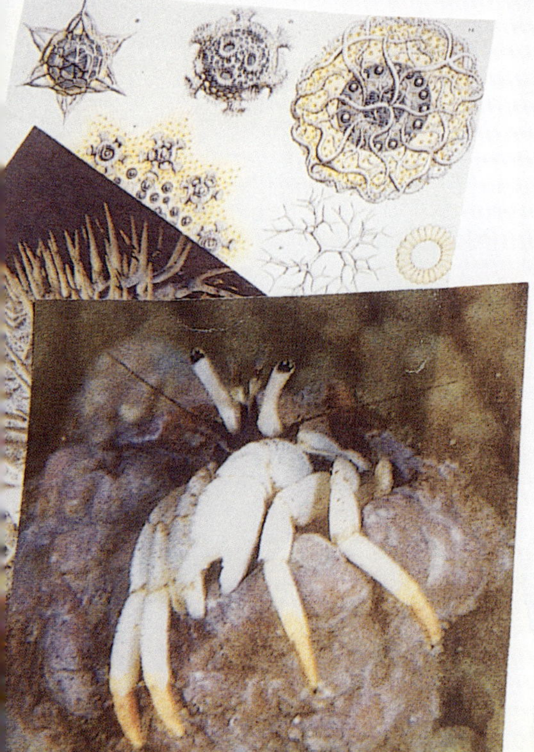

## Louise Hibbert [*Britain – b. 1972*]

This box, like many of my pieces, is an amalgamation of different creatures from the inexhaustible, wonderful world of marine life. The strong fascination that I have with strange forms, from microscopic organisms upwards is translated into three-dimensional sculptures. Like the artist/biologist Ernst Haeckal, I am drawn to the incredible beauty and organic symmetry of the radiolarians and echinoderms. His sumptuous illustrations, drawn in the nineteenth century, are constantly echoed in my work.

Many artists are inspired by natural forms because of their perfect balance and proportion. But of course, perfection can be impossible to improve upon. I often find that if I try to develop an idea away from its original inspiration, the elusive element that made the feature so attractive in the first place is lost. So, I focus in on a form, texture or color combination that I find particularly irresistible initially and combine it with others until I have my own "mythical" organism.

This particular one has characteristics that will help protect it for its journey – a hard, spiny exoskeleton, enclosing a delicate interior, to encourage careful handling.

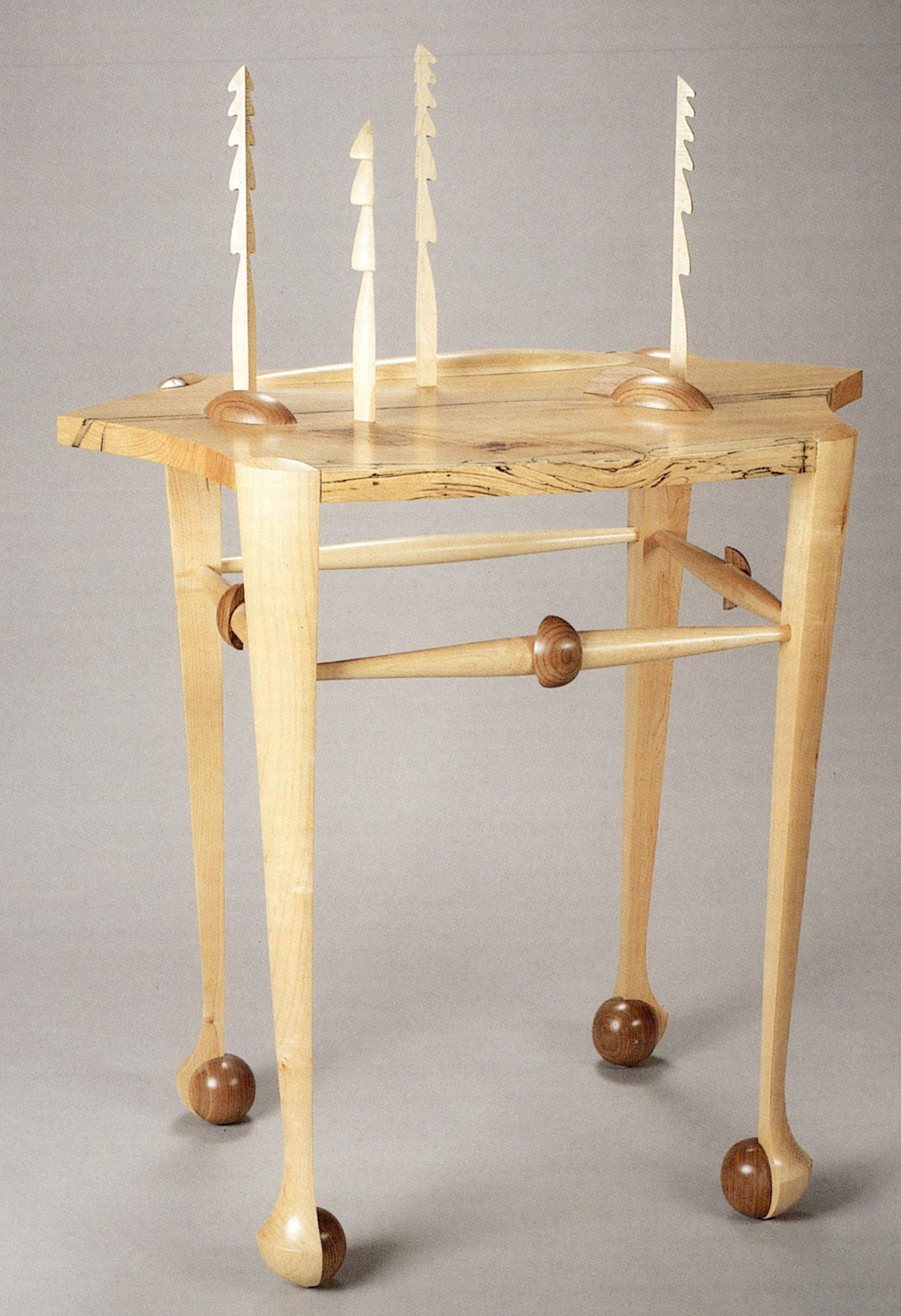

*Conversation through a Table*
2000
H: 48", W: 36", D: 21"
Beech, maple and walnut

Stephen Hogbin [*Canada – b.1942*]

The subtle change of meaning by altering two letters in conversation – conservation has held my interest for many years. The overriding idea for this landscape table stems from these words. This miniature landscape on which things may be placed functions as an entrance or side table. In the entrance we pass by laying down keys and letters or picking them up as we leave. The activity of exchange is like a conversation. In this conversation too many objects will spoil the image of the land by cluttering the space.

The maple wood came from the branch of a tree and the walnut was saved from a pile of firewood. Using more of the whole is something I can do for the tree while extending the conversation. Conversation and conservation are circular with interruptions of exchange that make for valued human experience.

The leg of the under-structure is reminiscent of the cabriole leg, the form arising probably from China where a dragon's claw grasped a pearl. *Cabriole* is a French term used in dancing derived from Italian and the goat's leap "capriola."

The legs for the table do not gesture with the double curve of the traditional cabriole leg or the leaping goat's leg and neither does the foot hold a pearl. However there is no escape from the references as they enrich the conversation in *Conversation through a Table*. The leg is strong, taut and appropriate for the dance while holding the earth as a pearl in space.

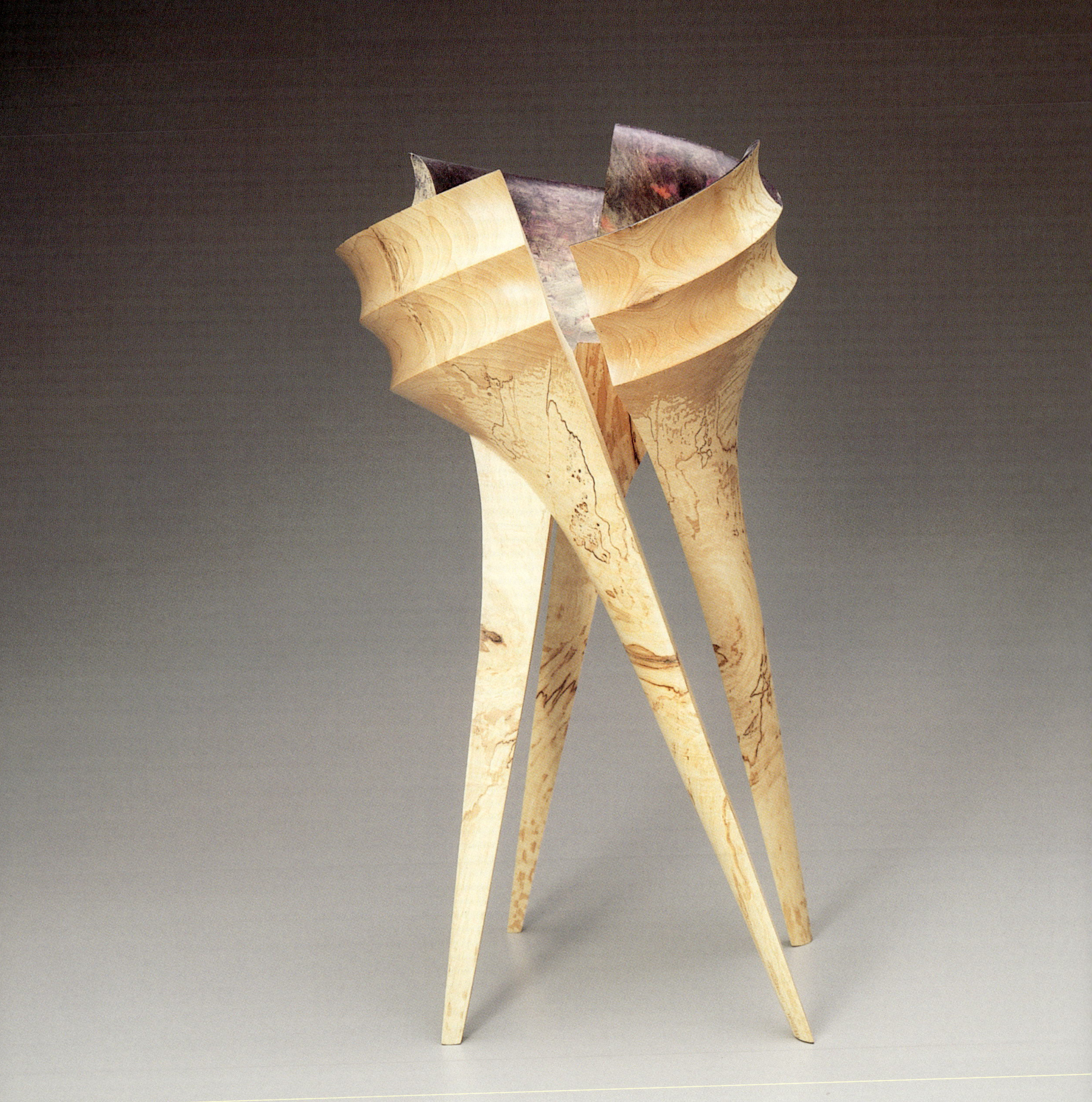

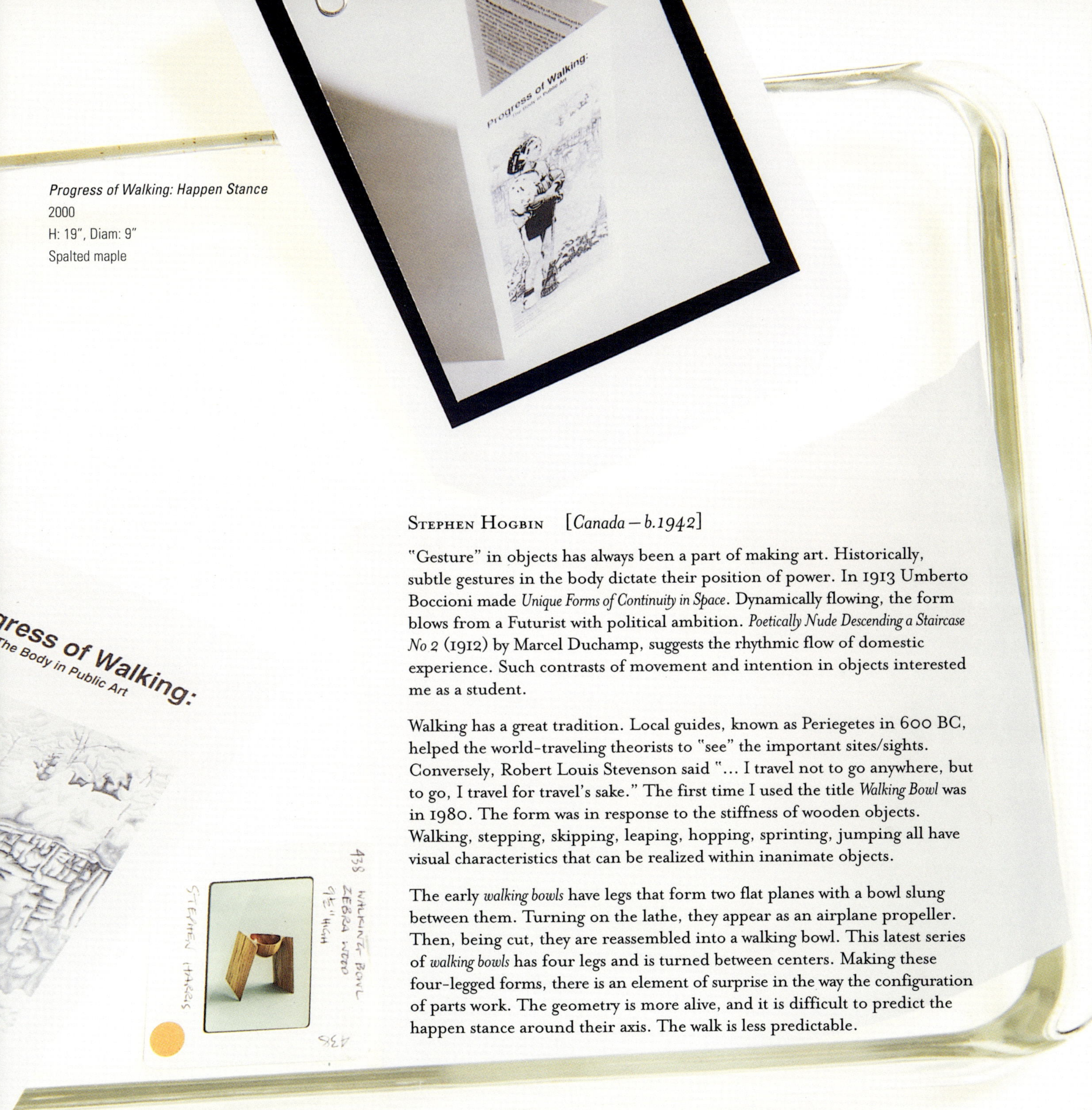


*Progress of Walking: Happen Stance*
2000
H: 19", Diam: 9"
Spalted maple

Stephen Hogbin [*Canada – b.1942*]

"Gesture" in objects has always been a part of making art. Historically, subtle gestures in the body dictate their position of power. In 1913 Umberto Boccioni made *Unique Forms of Continuity in Space*. Dynamically flowing, the form blows from a Futurist with political ambition. *Poetically Nude Descending a Staircase No 2* (1912) by Marcel Duchamp, suggests the rhythmic flow of domestic experience. Such contrasts of movement and intention in objects interested me as a student.

Walking has a great tradition. Local guides, known as Periegetes in 600 BC, helped the world-traveling theorists to "see" the important sites/sights. Conversely, Robert Louis Stevenson said "... I travel not to go anywhere, but to go, I travel for travel's sake." The first time I used the title *Walking Bowl* was in 1980. The form was in response to the stiffness of wooden objects. Walking, stepping, skipping, leaping, hopping, sprinting, jumping all have visual characteristics that can be realized within inanimate objects.

The early *walking bowls* have legs that form two flat planes with a bowl slung between them. Turning on the lathe, they appear as an airplane propeller. Then, being cut, they are reassembled into a walking bowl. This latest series of *walking bowls* has four legs and is turned between centers. Making these four-legged forms, there is an element of surprise in the way the configuration of parts work. The geometry is more alive, and it is difficult to predict the happen stance around their axis. The walk is less predictable.

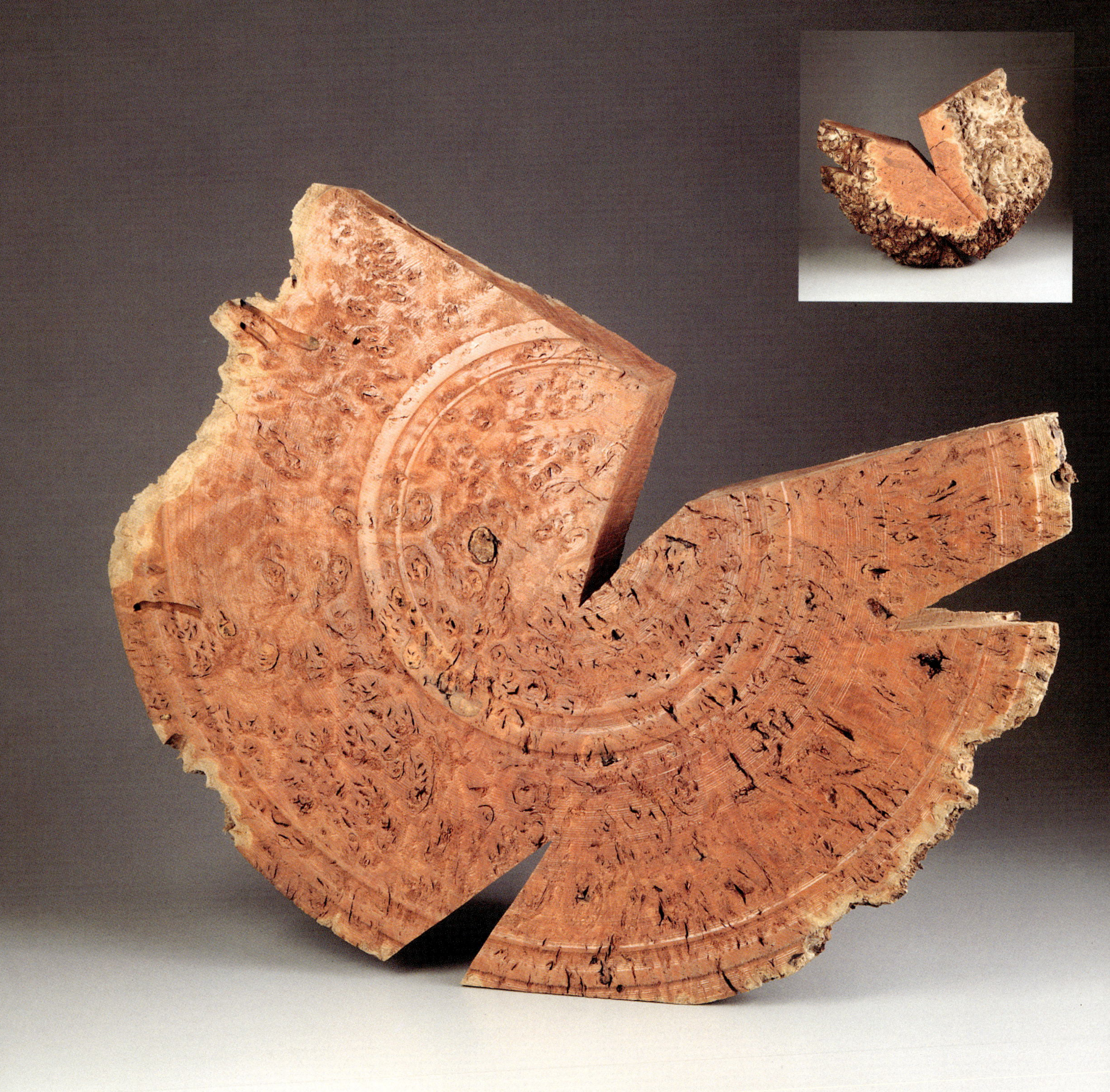

*Fractured Millstone*
2000
H: 24", W: 24", D: 7"
Jarrah burl

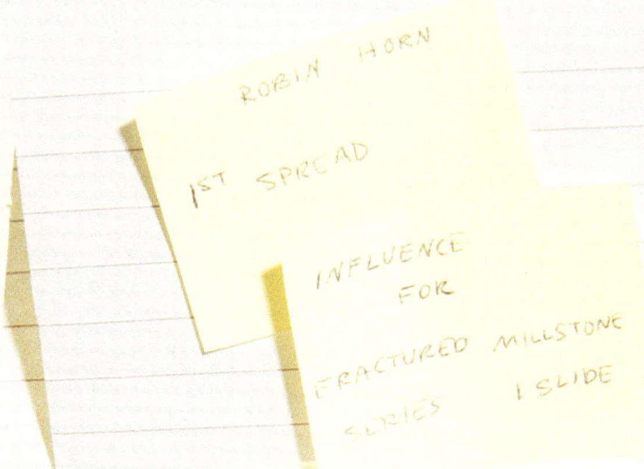


## Robyn Horn [*Arkansas, USA – b. 1951*]

My work has always had a reference to stones and their strong, solid shapes. The first series focused on geodes and the contrast of the smooth polished interior to the rough exterior. My next series was related to millstone shapes, dealing with the variety of geometric patterns and designs provided by the land and furrows dressed into the face of a millstone. My **Stepping Stones** series dealt with a negative space cut out at the bottom of a piece with a suspended component that suggests a foot reaching for its next step. This series is a continuation of the implied motion also evident in the **Geode** series. Works from the **Standing Stones** series have more of a sense of vertical strength to them. They have a feeling of energy, like sentinels from the past, guarding their posts with force and vigor. *Fractured Millstone* is a compilation of most of the previous series, but it is influenced most directly by the **Millstone** series. This series also has the negative space and suspended components of the **Stepping Stones**, and while they are relatively round in shape, they have an upright strength and the energy of the **Standing Stones** series.

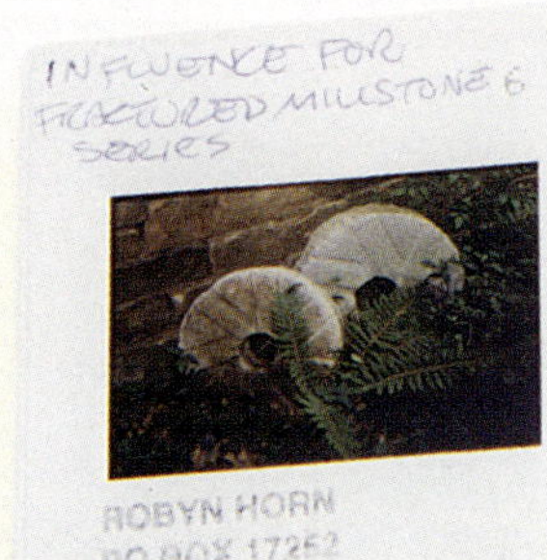

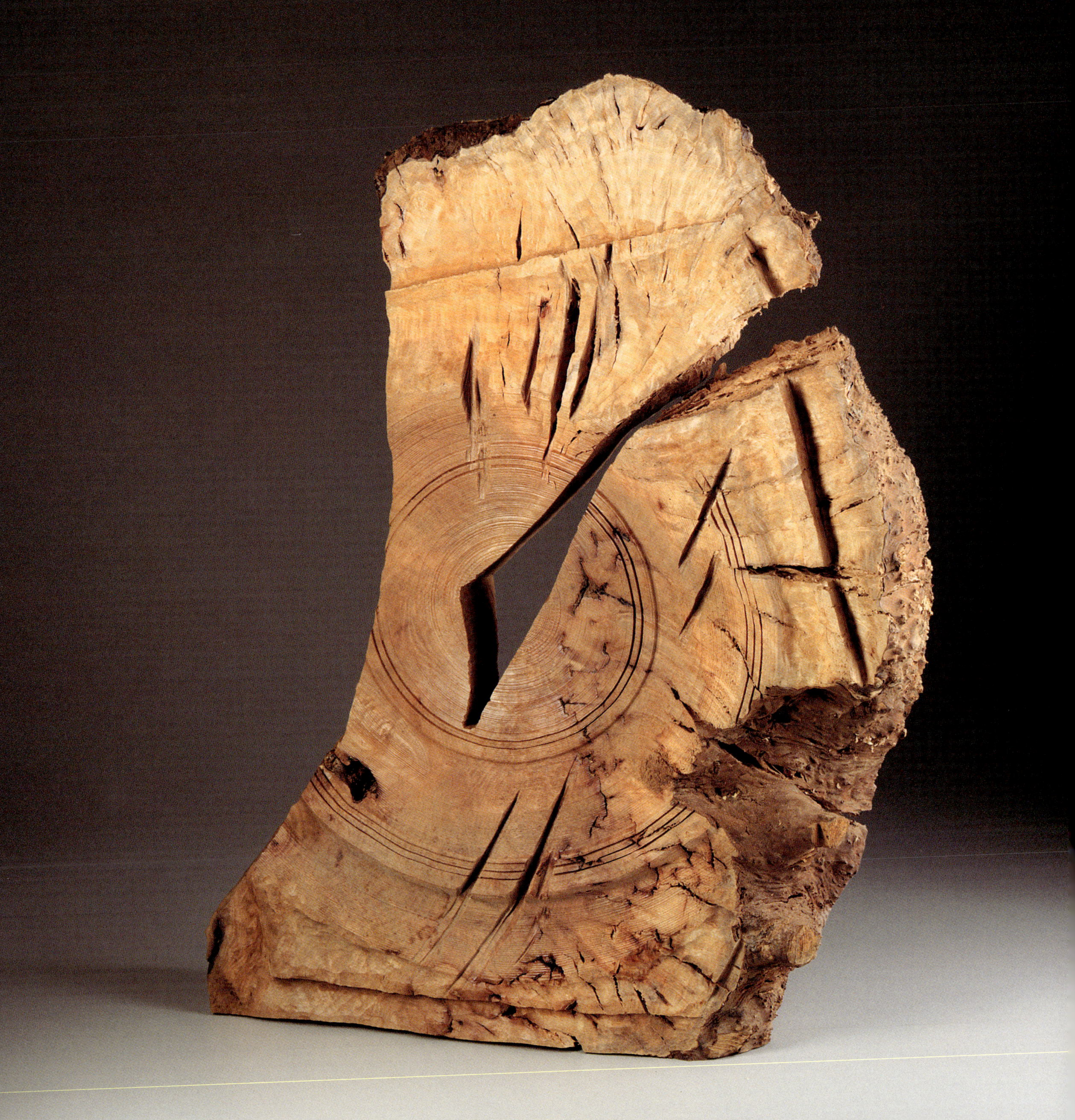

*Arched Stone*
2000
H: 27 1/2", W: 20", D: 4 1/2"
Madrone burl

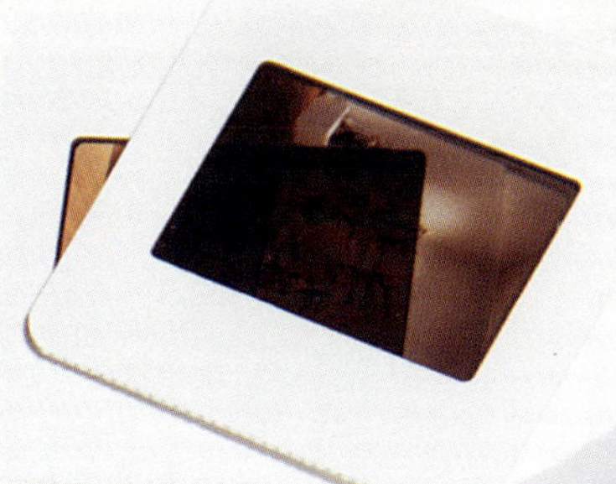

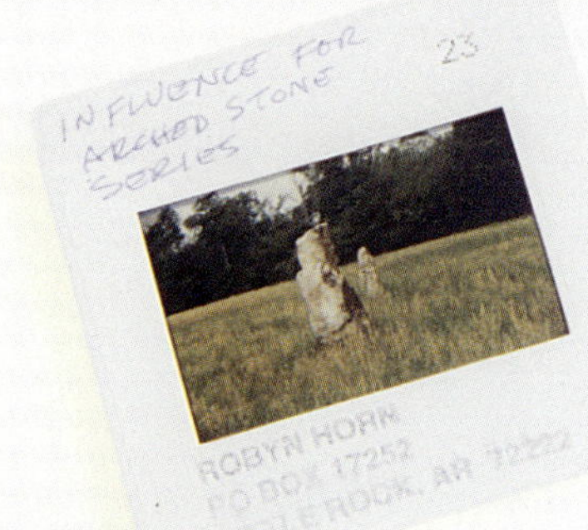


Robyn Horn [*Arkansas, USA – b. 1951*]

My work has always had a reference to stones and their strong, solid shapes. The first series focused on geodes and the contrast of the smooth polished interior to the rough exterior. My next series was related to millstone shapes, dealing with the variety of geometric patterns and designs provided by the land and furrows dressed into the face of a millstone. My **Stepping Stones** series dealt with a negative space cut out at the bottom of a piece with a suspended component that suggests a foot reaching for its next step. This series is a continuation of the implied motion also evident in the **Geode** series. Works from the **Standing Stones** series have more of a sense of vertical strength to them. They have a feeling of energy, like sentinels from the past, guarding their posts with force and vigor.

*Arched Stone* is more directly influenced by **Standing Stones**. Its vertical lines and leaning arch convey the movement of the **Stepping Stones**, and the negative space slashed through to the middle shows the strength of stones, but the livingness and cohesiveness of wood.

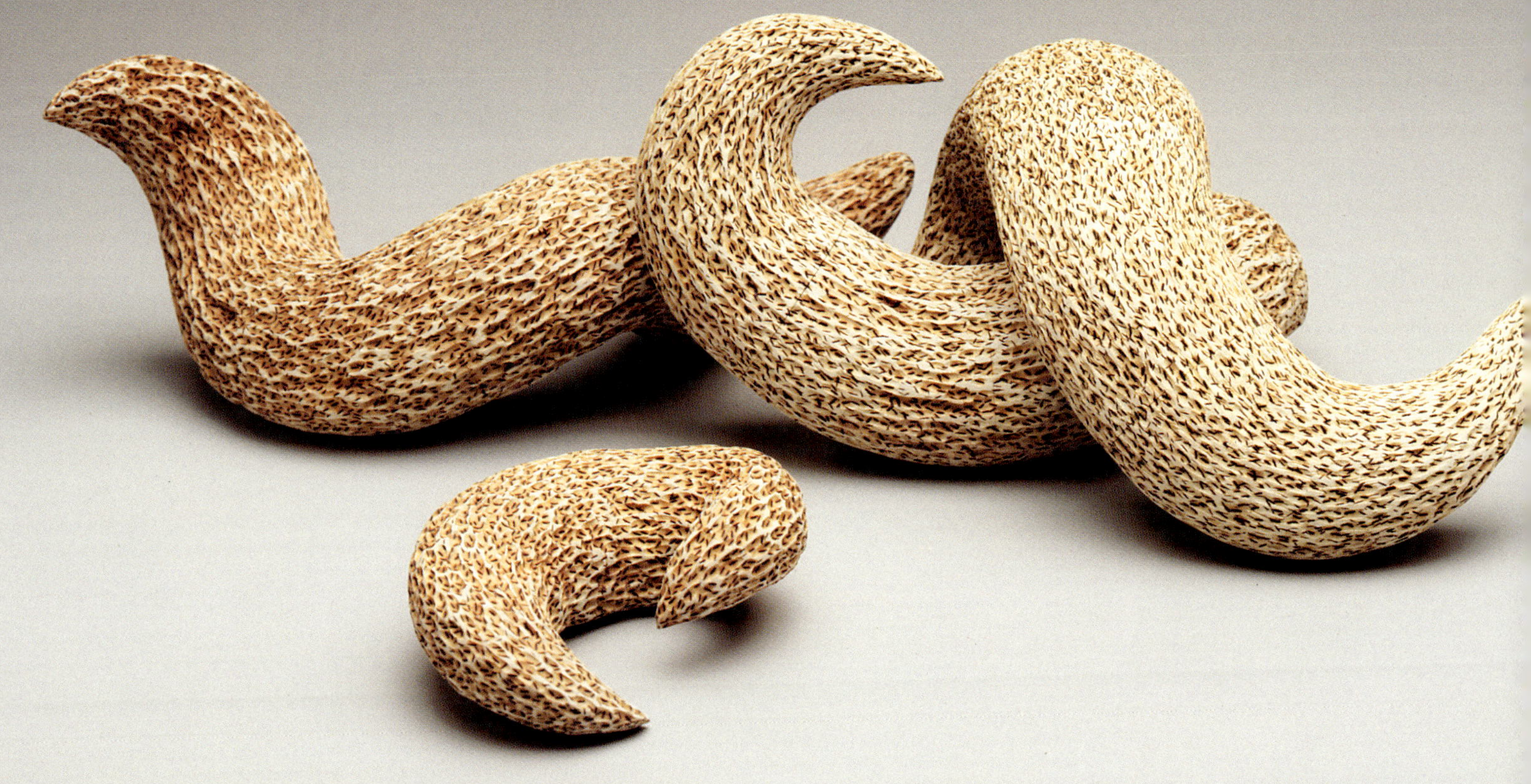

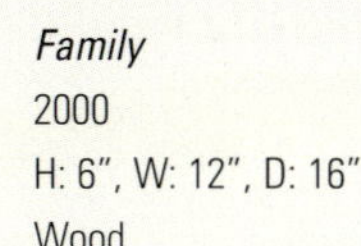

*Family*
2000
H: 6", W: 12", D: 16"
Wood

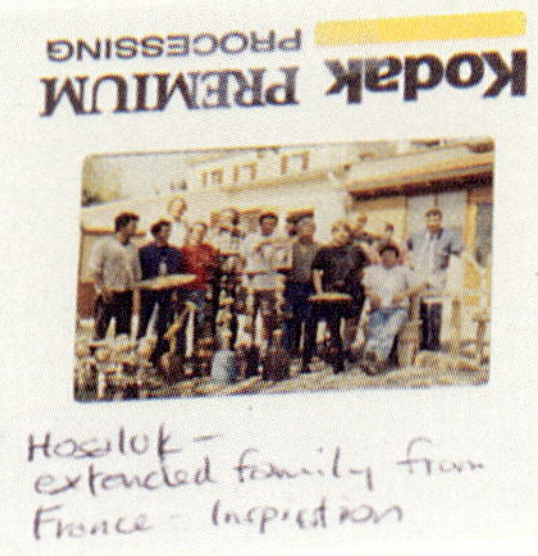


Michael Hosaluk [*Canada – b. 1954* ]

My work is my way of expressing ideas from my social and ideological life. The work *Family* was inspired from first my immediate family and the daily interaction and how it is always changing. Other thoughts of family are from the global "family" of friends and colleagues created from the field of wood turning that has inspired me to contribute to this movement. Nature also played a part in the creation of this series.

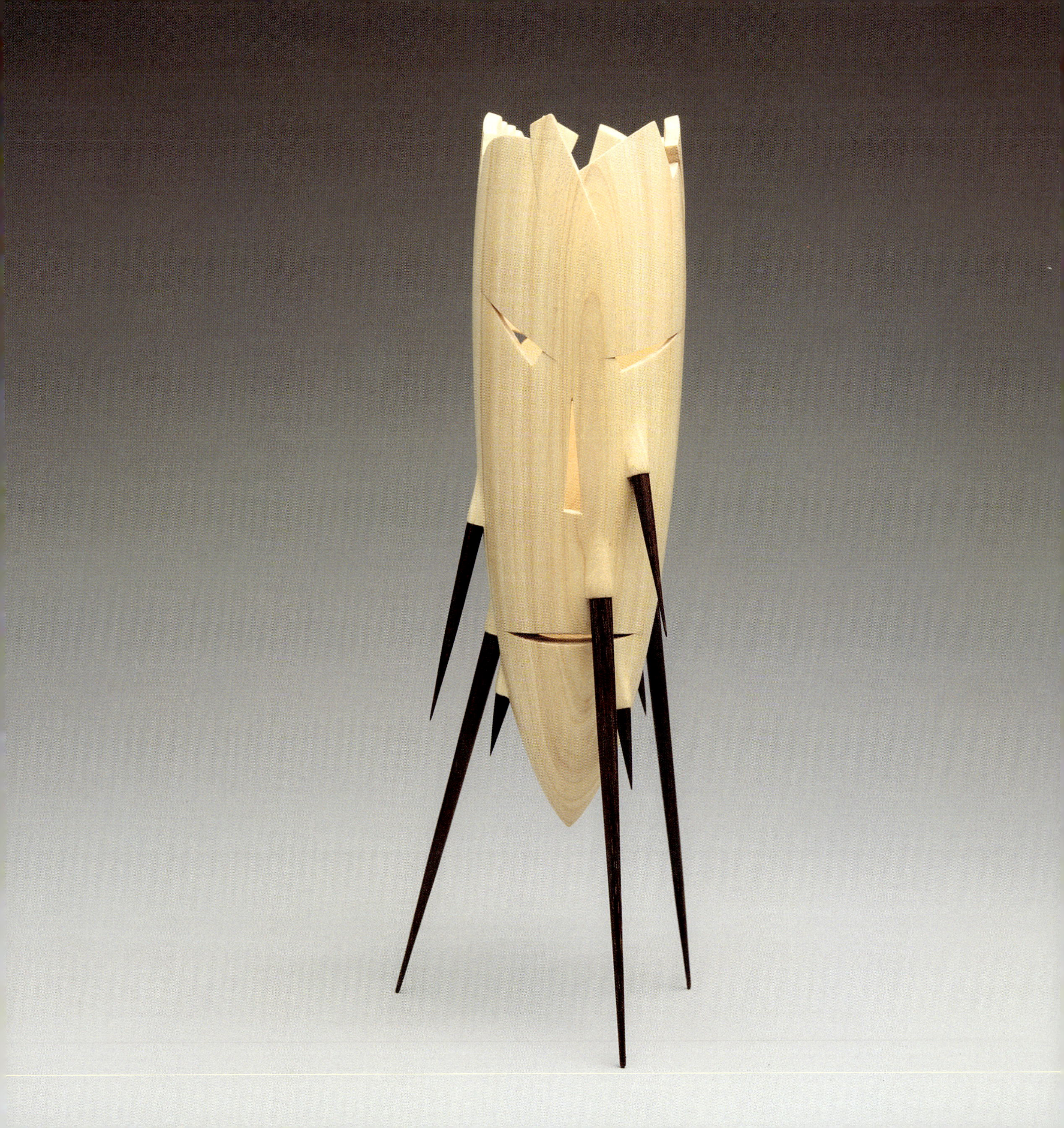

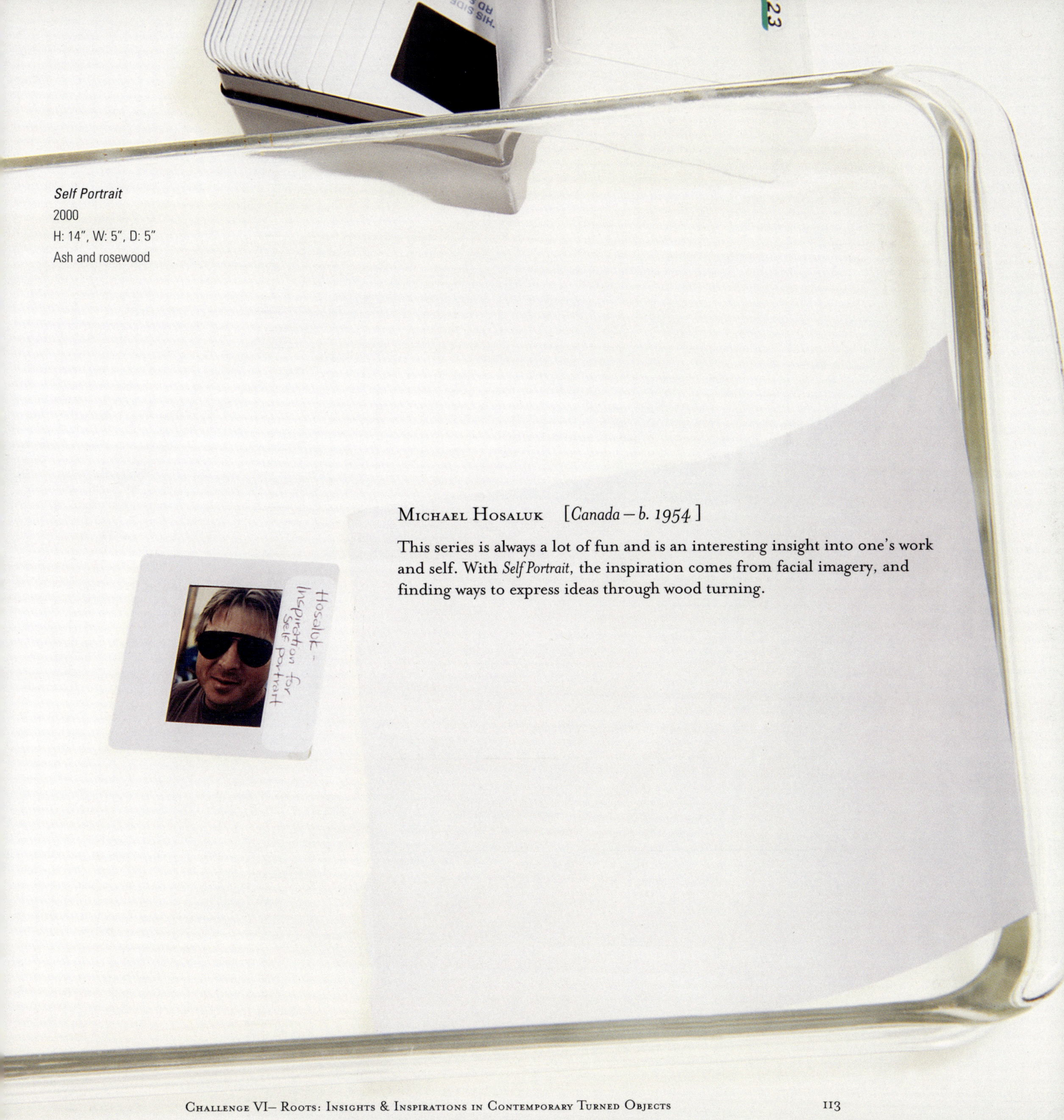


*Self Portrait*
2000
H: 14", W: 5", D: 5"
Ash and rosewood

Michael Hosaluk [*Canada – b. 1954*]

This series is always a lot of fun and is an interesting insight into one's work and self. With *Self Portrait*, the inspiration comes from facial imagery, and finding ways to express ideas through wood turning.

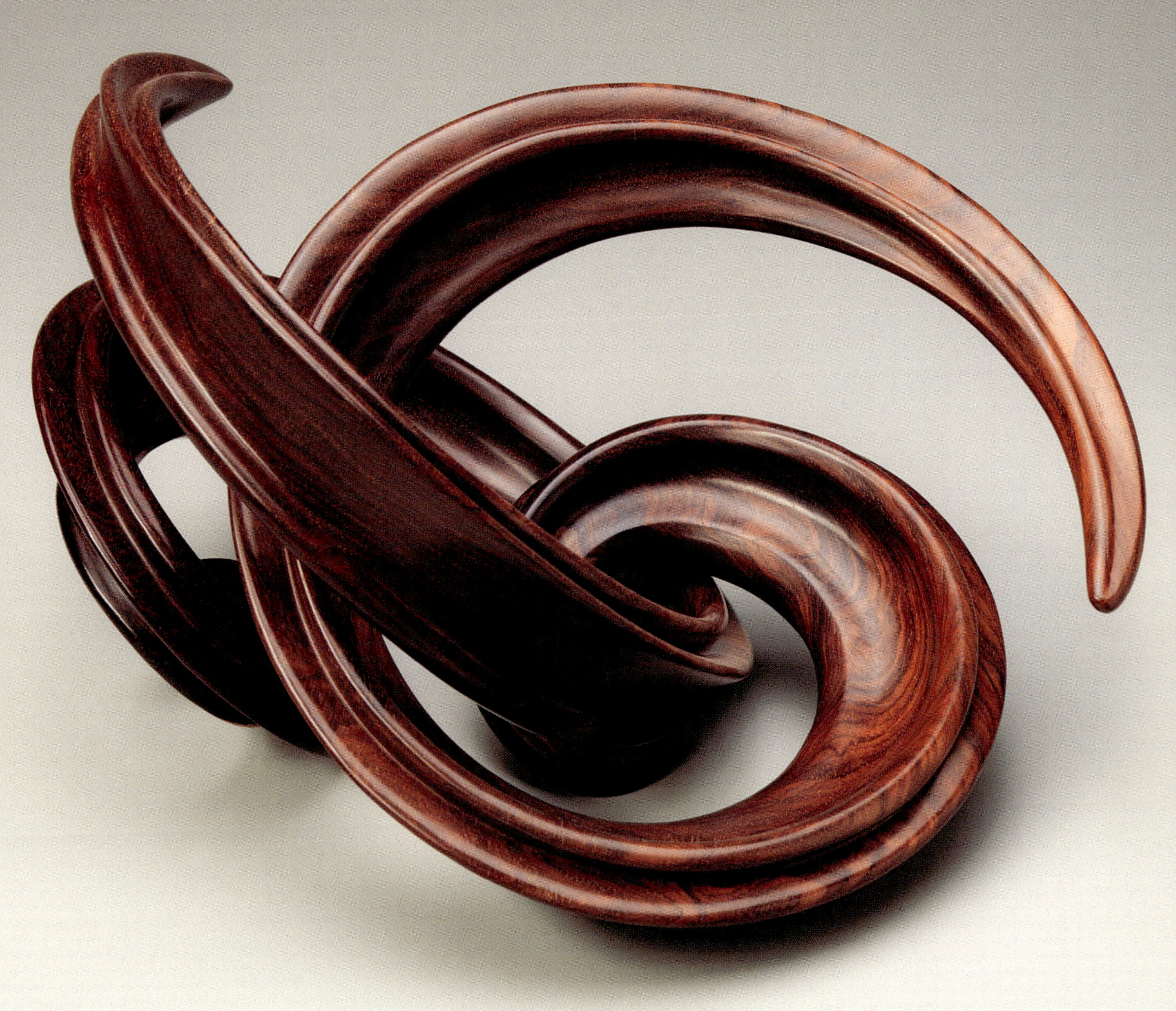

*Reciprocal Helix*
2000
H: 12", W: 12", D: 24"
Cocobolo rosewood

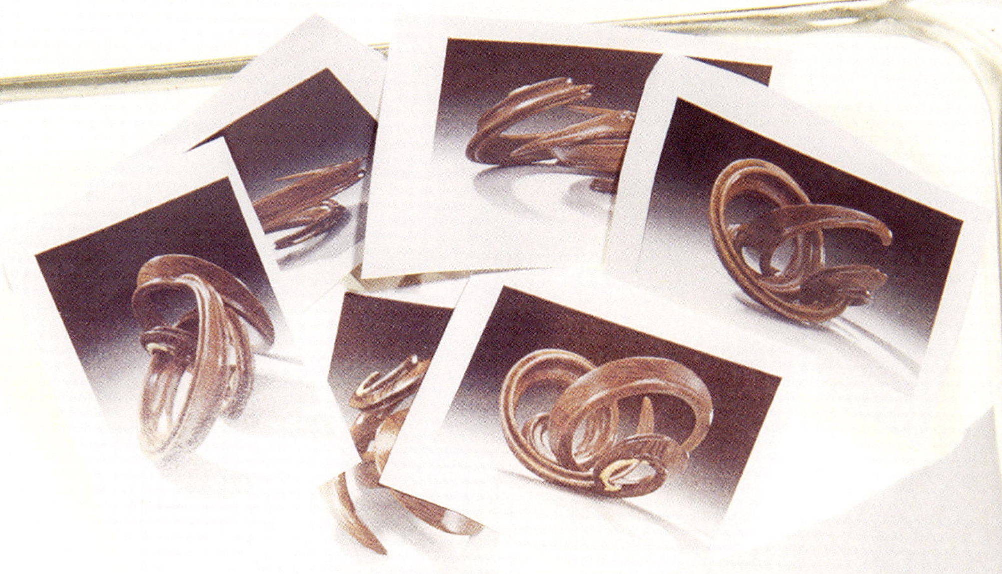

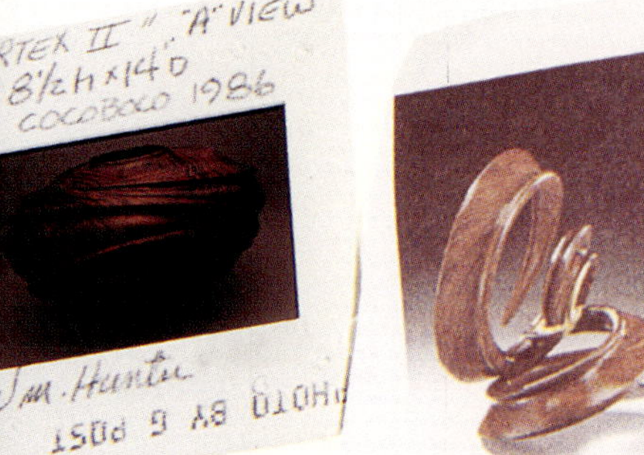


William Hunter [*California, USA – b. 1947*]

My work is the abstraction of my perceptions of beauty; of macro/microcosms from galaxies to DNA, expressed through sculpted rhythms, gestures, finessed proportion, light and shadow, and the material's reality juxtaposed by illusion. The inspiration for *Reciprocal Helix* is the evolution of my work. Using *Vortex II* (1986) for illustration, I'll briefly trace the 30-year journey to *Reciprocal Helix*.

In 1969, I began disc-sanding and texturing turned objects to create surface designs and motions — illusions intended to add implied narratives to pure forms using fluid and spiraling lines most natural to me. I began deeply sculpting the forms to make the carving appear naturally integral; developing control of energy and gesture through use of rhythms, patterns and line, thus accentuating the fluidity and dynamic tension. *Vortex II* arrived. In the '80s, I began cutting through vessels, releasing "voices" of abstract narratives expanded by a dialogue of disclosure/enclosure made geometrically more complex by relationships of mass, space and light, blurring reality with the metaphorical vessel.

The various partially cut series (i.e. *Phantom Vessels*), led to the completely released forms of *Reciprocal Helix* dissolving the vessel walls. This was an electrifying compounding of possibilities in interactive pieces. One form supports, rests within, encroaches upon or embraces the other. Configurations can seemingly defy gravity or wind into themselves as if in a process of transformation, speaking to a continual evolution. Space comes alive with the push/pull energy of mass/void.

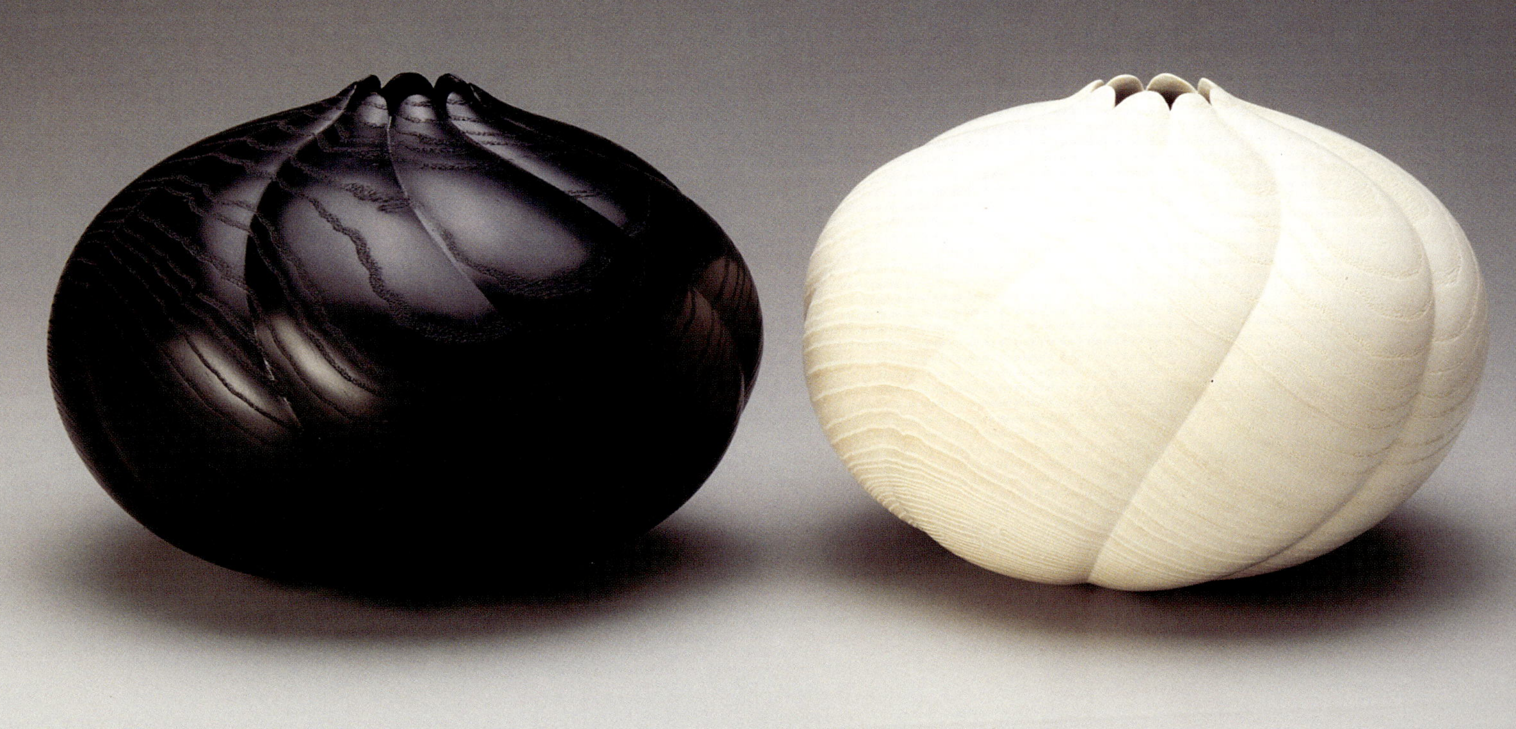

*Black/ White Pair*
2000
H: 7", W: 22", D: 9"
Ash

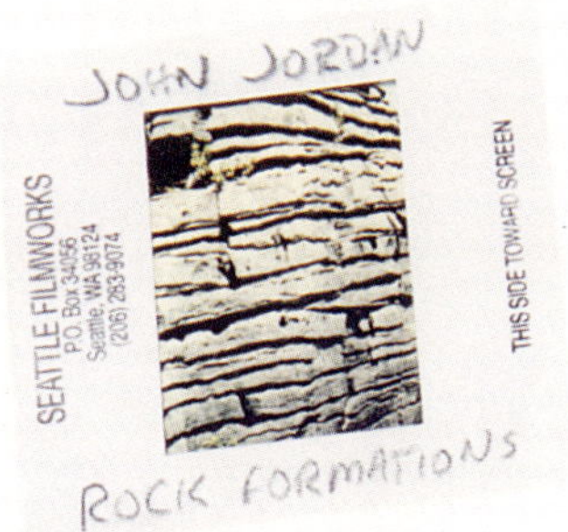


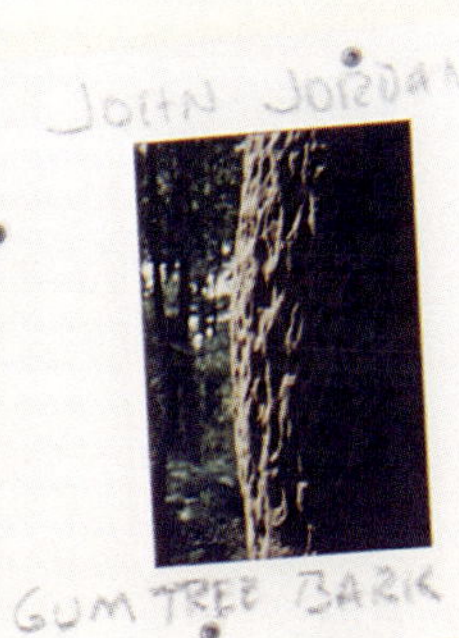


## John Jordan [*Tennessee, USA – b. 1950*]

My friend Clay Foster wrote a piece a couple of years ago in which he discussed the apparent ease with which some artists are able to demonstrate or produce work from ideas that they seem to pull out of their pocket. He pointed out that what may not be as apparent is that they have spent years, or a lifetime, filling their pockets. I like that analogy, and I can't think of a better way to explain my sources of inspiration. Surfaces and textures, patterns and repetitions, both natural and man-made, landscapes and architecture, contemporary as well as ancient and ethnic objects interest me greatly. The effects of music, of all sorts, and a comfortable, relaxing place to work certainly has an impact on what I produce. My emotional and physical states as well enter into my work. But, without question, the strongest and most direct influence and source of inspiration I have is the work that I am currently making. The second strongest influence/source of inspiration is the material that I use.

*Black/White Pair* was a clear vision in my mind from the beginning. A section of ash log was split to make the two pieces. The pair is about relationships — of the pieces having grown foot to foot, the opposing spirals and the black/white contrast. The grain patterns are very carefully balanced and wire brushed to emphasize those patterns.

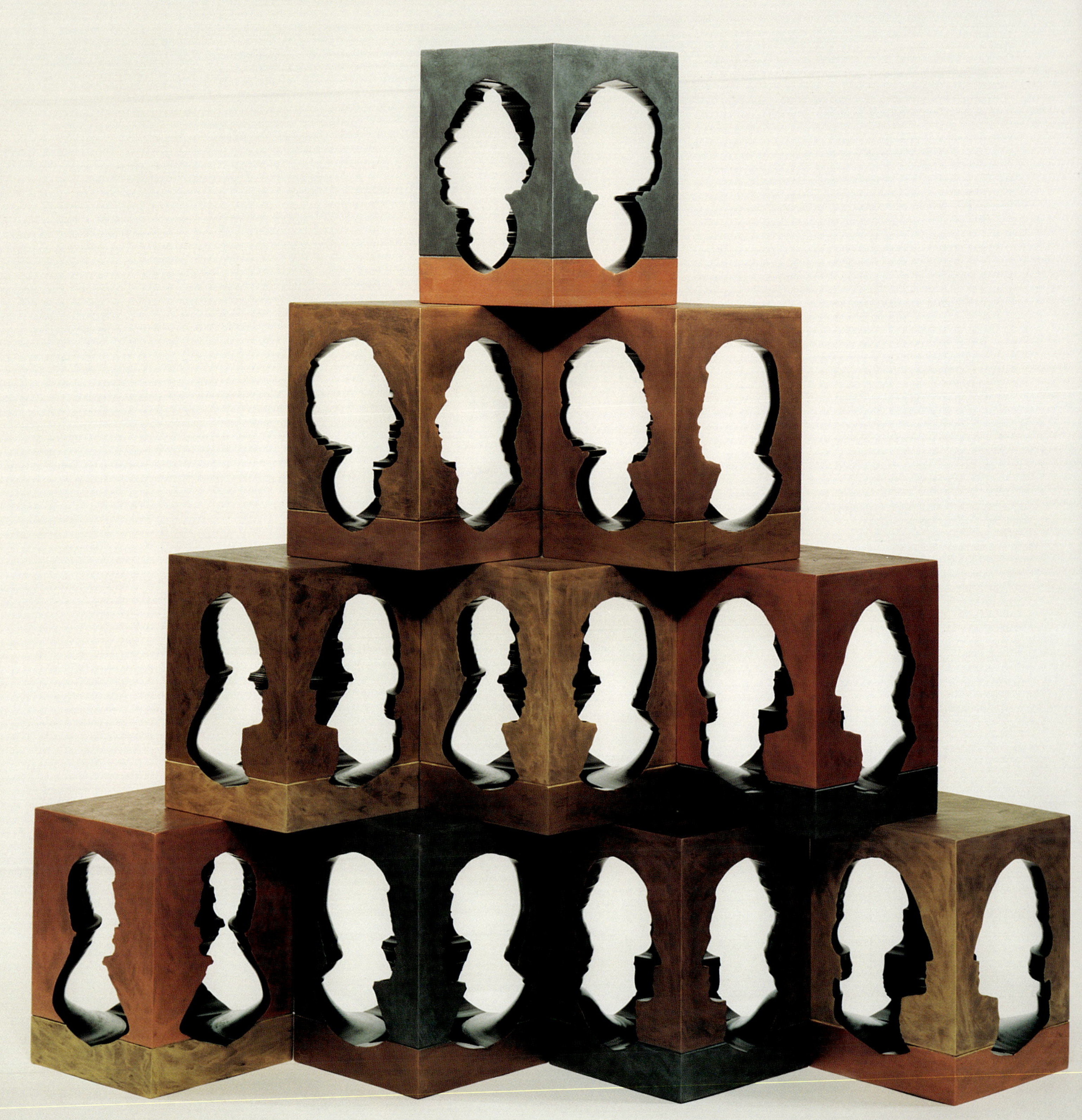

*Rushmore 2000*
2000
H: 64", W: 66", D: 16 1/2"
Painted poplar and basswood

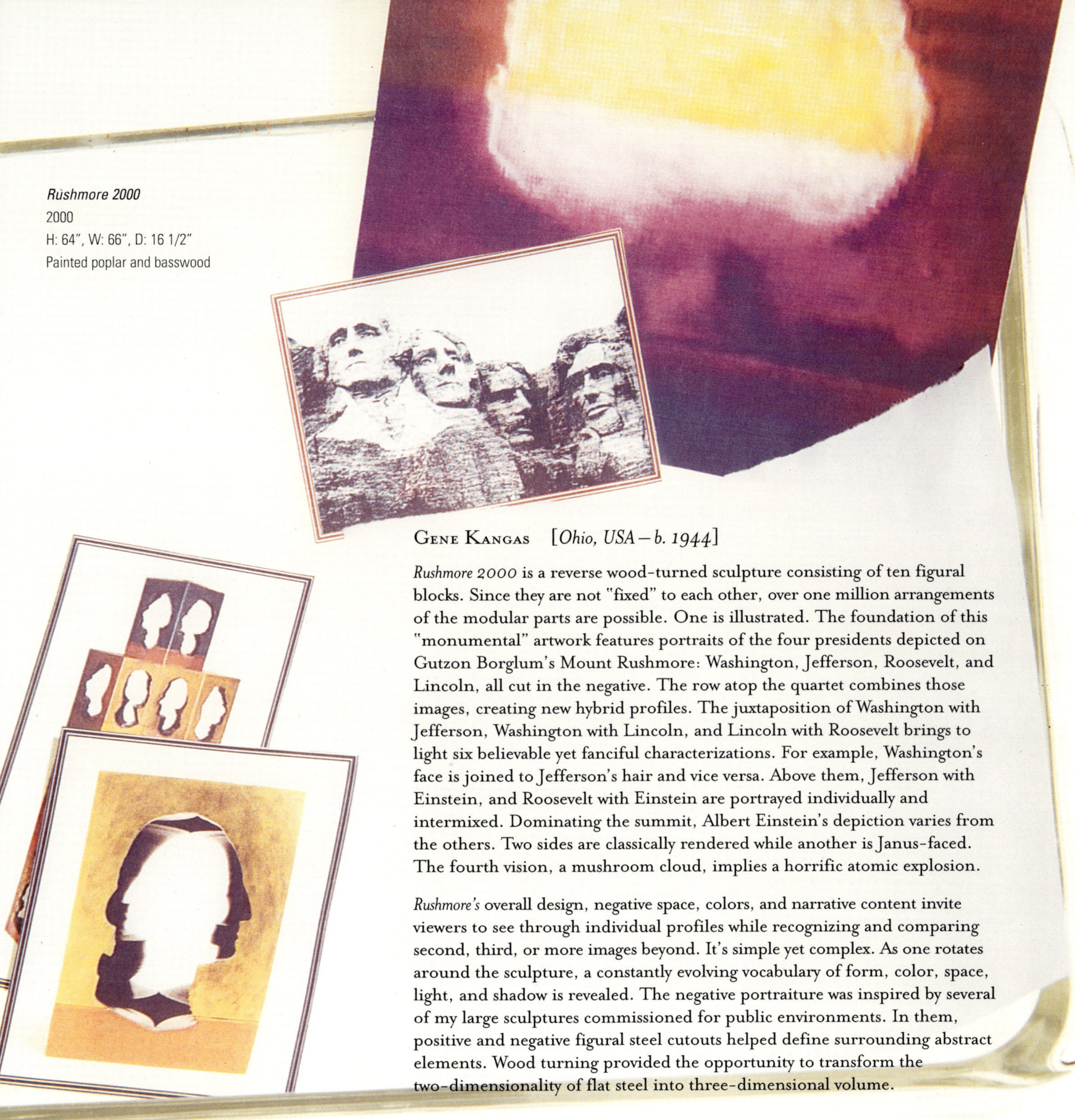

## Gene Kangas [*Ohio, USA – b. 1944*]

*Rushmore 2000* is a reverse wood-turned sculpture consisting of ten figural blocks. Since they are not "fixed" to each other, over one million arrangements of the modular parts are possible. One is illustrated. The foundation of this "monumental" artwork features portraits of the four presidents depicted on Gutzon Borglum's Mount Rushmore: Washington, Jefferson, Roosevelt, and Lincoln, all cut in the negative. The row atop the quartet combines those images, creating new hybrid profiles. The juxtaposition of Washington with Jefferson, Washington with Lincoln, and Lincoln with Roosevelt brings to light six believable yet fanciful characterizations. For example, Washington's face is joined to Jefferson's hair and vice versa. Above them, Jefferson with Einstein, and Roosevelt with Einstein are portrayed individually and intermixed. Dominating the summit, Albert Einstein's depiction varies from the others. Two sides are classically rendered while another is Janus-faced. The fourth vision, a mushroom cloud, implies a horrific atomic explosion.

*Rushmore's* overall design, negative space, colors, and narrative content invite viewers to see through individual profiles while recognizing and comparing second, third, or more images beyond. It's simple yet complex. As one rotates around the sculpture, a constantly evolving vocabulary of form, color, space, light, and shadow is revealed. The negative portraiture was inspired by several of my large sculptures commissioned for public environments. In them, positive and negative figural steel cutouts helped define surrounding abstract elements. Wood turning provided the opportunity to transform the two-dimensionality of flat steel into three-dimensional volume.

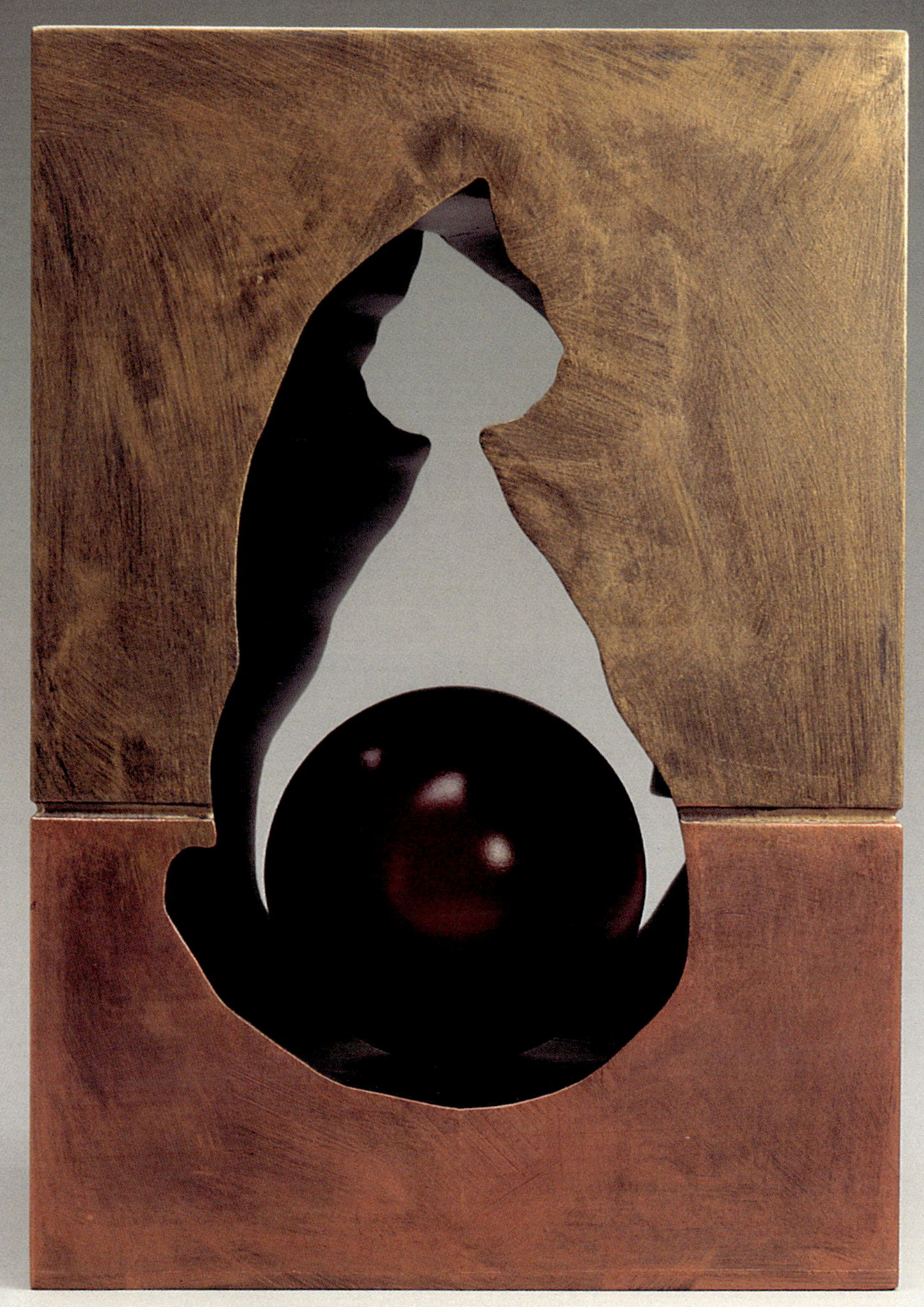

*Daisy Turns*
1999
H: 15", W: 10 1/2", D: 10 1/2"
Painted basswood and maple

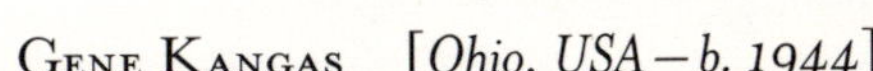

## Gene Kangas [*Ohio, USA – b. 1944*]

My friend Bernie lives in Canada. On a visit, I was introduced to his black and white cat Daisy. She's a bit overweight and likes to lie around; you could probably say she's lazy. She makes a great model. I kept a sketchbook handy, hoping to capture some of Daisy's many poses with the intention of using them later as reference materials for wood turning. It was interesting to notice subtle naturalistic shifts of her feline anatomy as she slowly changed from side to side.

*Daisy Turns* is one of four wood turned sculptures inspired by my friend's pet. As I worked on them, we e-mailed progress pictures and comments back and forth. At one point, Daisy jumped up on Bernie's computer table to see her digitized wooden counterpart displayed on the monitor. Sitting quietly, the movement of her tail indicated that she liked it.

Daisy is part of a recent series of negative-turned sculptures that concentrate on recognizable imagery. Inside this sculpture is a hollow "rattle ball" and it's Daisy's toy. Daisy's portrait is asymmetrical, meaning that her profile differs from each side of the centerline. This series continues my previous explorations into the sculptural applications of positive and negative figural space. The example illustrated features a steel cutout of a cat looking at a positive profile of a bird, both surrounded by tall grass. The cat's open body serves as a "frame" to simultaneously view both the feline and its surrounding environment.

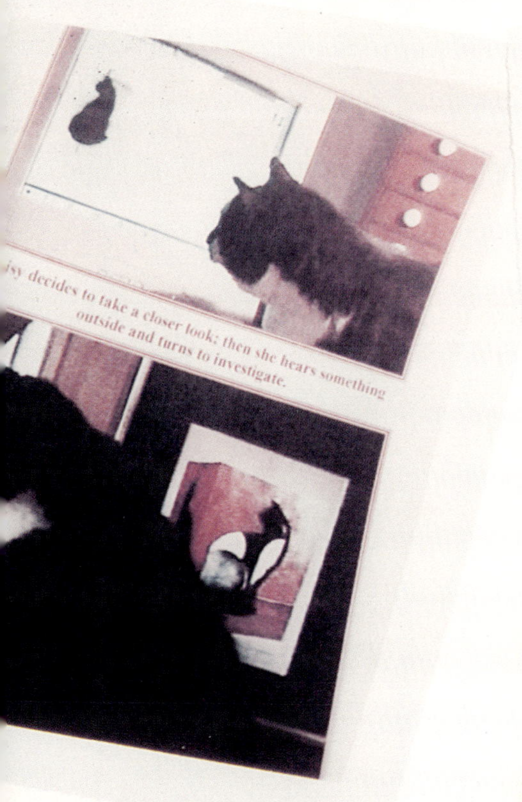

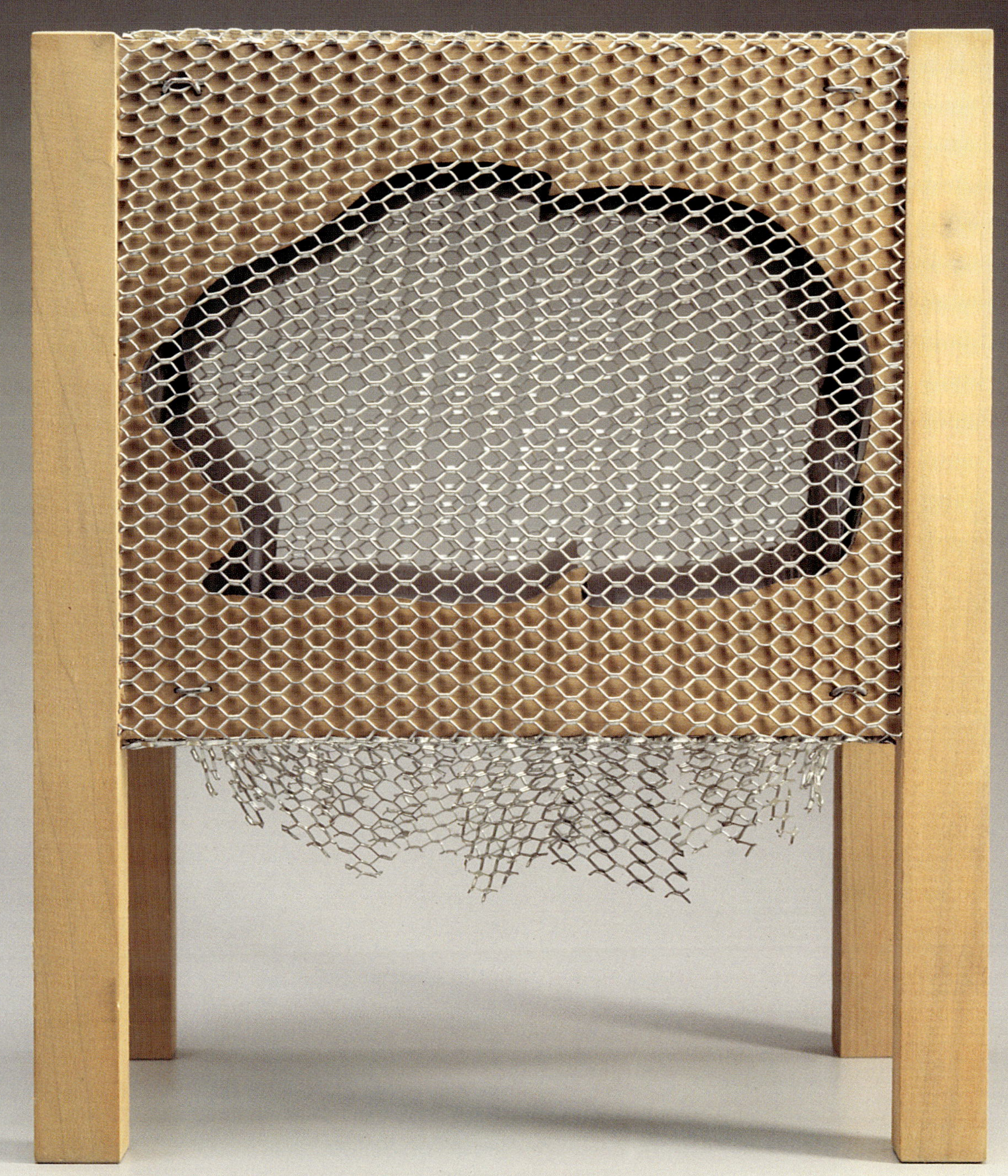

*Hutch*
2000
H: 17", W: 14 1/4", D: 10 1/2"
Poplar and wire screen

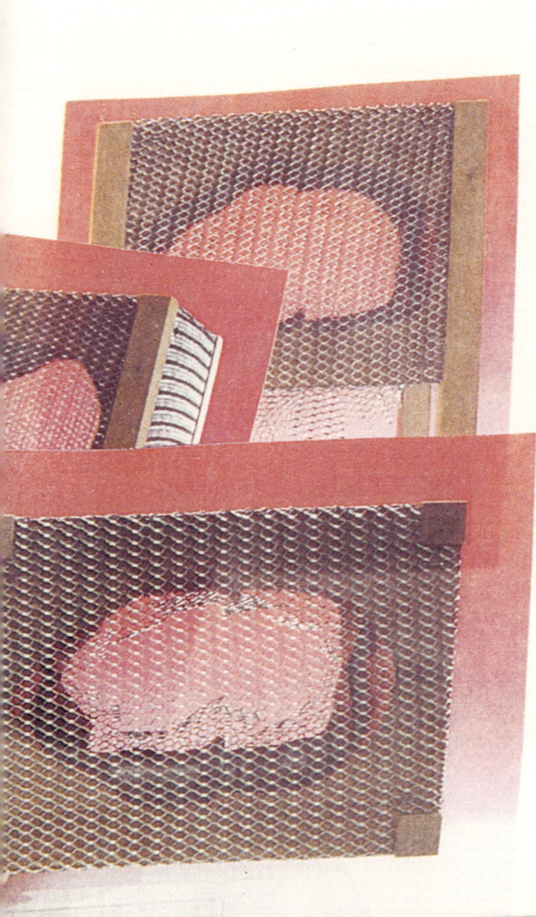

## Gene Kangas [*Ohio, USA – b. 1944*]

I have long admired Albrecht Dürer's watercolor rendering of a young hare. Accomplished in 1502, it remains a powerful, singular image. A rabbit hutch or cage seemed one way to pay homage to Dürer (1471-1528), a modern thinker who is considered Germany's greatest Renaissance artist. The format also helped me create a contemporary metaphor using the lathe. The wire-covered wooden hutch sits vacant; the rabbit is gone, perhaps escaped to freedom.

Each of the four turned elements was designed so that when studied from the front or back, the rabbit's side profiles become readily apparent. However, the arrangement also produces an actual "top view" and "bottom view" of the hare when seen from those vantage points. All sides are intentionally different, utilizing three-dimensionality. To discover the turnings and imagery, viewers are challenged to look through and around the containment barrier, a metal screen. Historically, wood turning has been confined by various restraints, yet the ripping open of the bottom is an indication of potential movement outward.

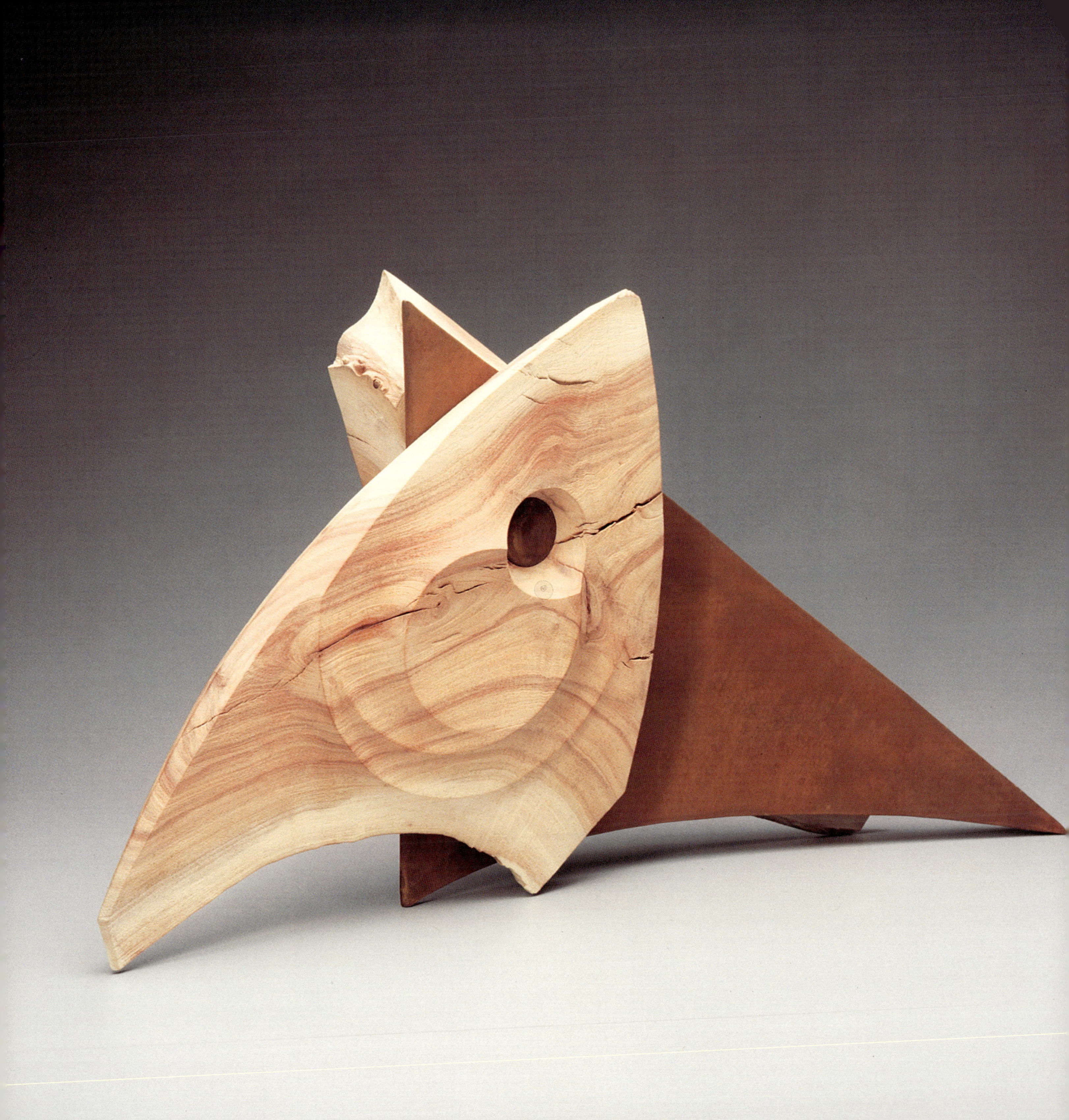

*Little Wing*
2000
H: 14", W: 33", D: 8"
Carob and steel

## Stoney Lamar [*North Carolina, USA – b. 1951*]

The ideas behind *Little Wing* began with an early **Avian** series. Since then I have dealt with avian forms and flight in many different ways. These latest winged forms are the culmination of almost 15 years of exploration into conceptually interpreting these notions in the abstract. Additionally, "Little Wing" by Jimi Hendrix, a song that is practically burned into my sub-conscious, is in both lyric and soaring melody about flight. I often name pieces in progress using music as a reference, which then informs the piece as it is being developed. My goal is to reflect the rhythm and narrative that is embodied in these musical selections.

The development and use of multiple axis techniques as a way of applying texture or sculpting asymmetrical forms on the lathe has allowed me to transcend the round object and to create a sense of image and movement that is suggestive of what I see while the object is being formed on the lathe.

The work also begins as a relationship I have established with a particular piece of wood, and how its characteristics interplay with my intentions and emerging technical and conceptual vocabulary. As I adjust the work's axis and continue turning, new challenges and possibilities are constantly presented, thereby allowing a subtractive process to become an intriguing way of constructing an object. The resulting figurative, architectural or abstract objects are an attempt to create balance and tension by juxtaposing asymmetrical and symmetrical elements.

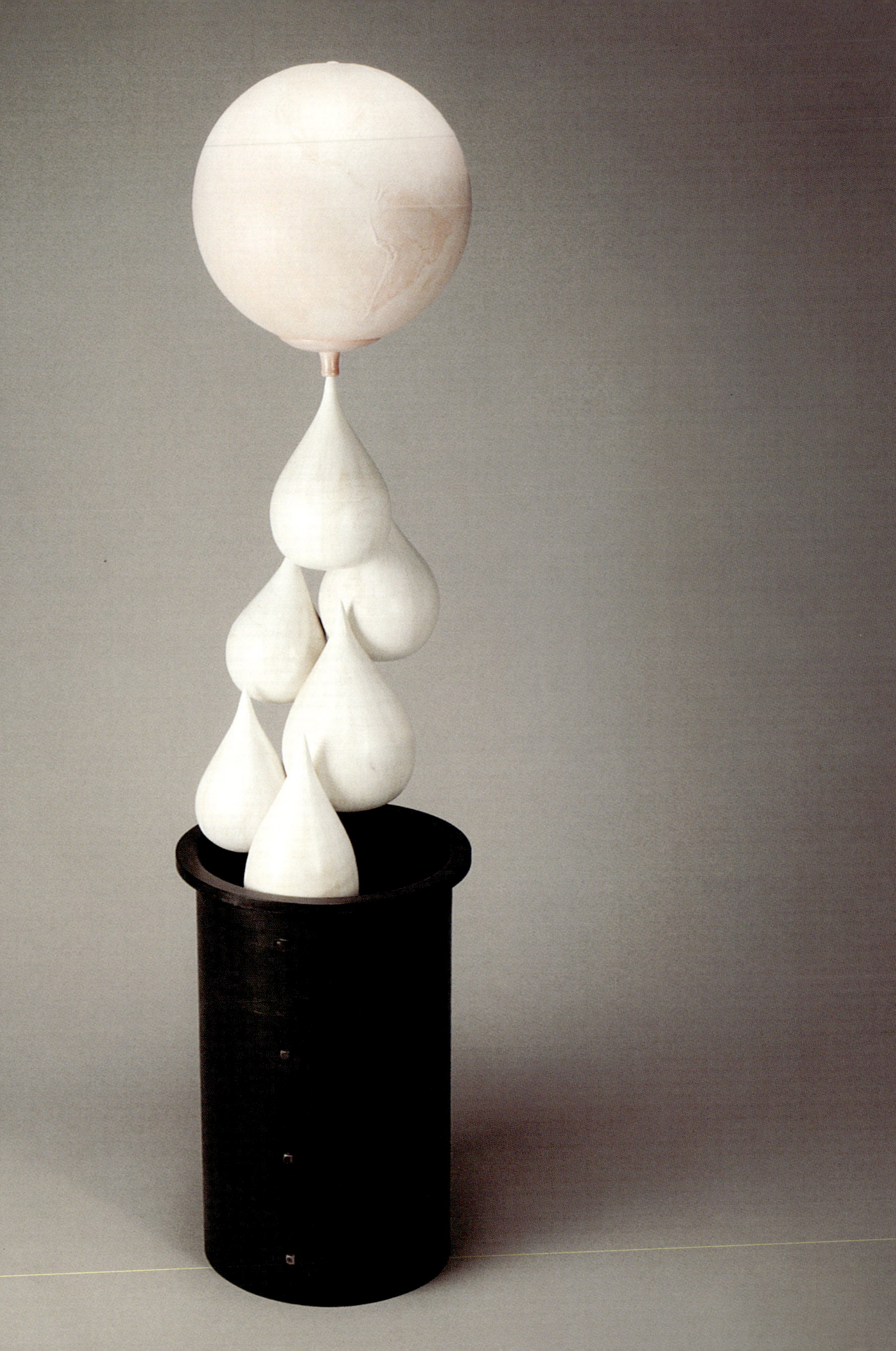

*Mom Loves Us, Even When We're Selfish*
2000
H: 75", Diam: 16"
Mixed woods, globe

Jack Larimore [*Pennsylvania, USA – b. 1950*]

This piece was commissioned by the Waterworks Restoration Committee of the Fairmount Park Commission for an exhibition of artwork inspired by the historic waterworks on the Schulkyll River.

The architecture at this site is eclectic and wonderful, but, as I spent time there, I was mostly drawn to the river itself. The inspiration for *Mom Loves Us...* is the power, vitality and endurance of the Schulkyll. The Waterworks becomes a counterpoint to the river, representing our prevailing attitude towards it and the rest of the environment, as only a resource for our use. Selfishly we suckle.

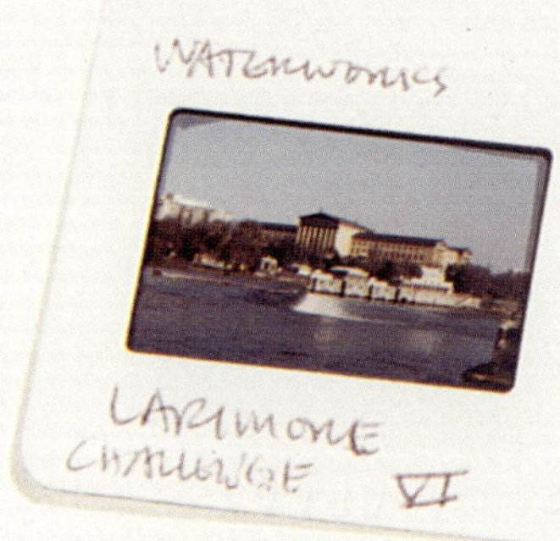

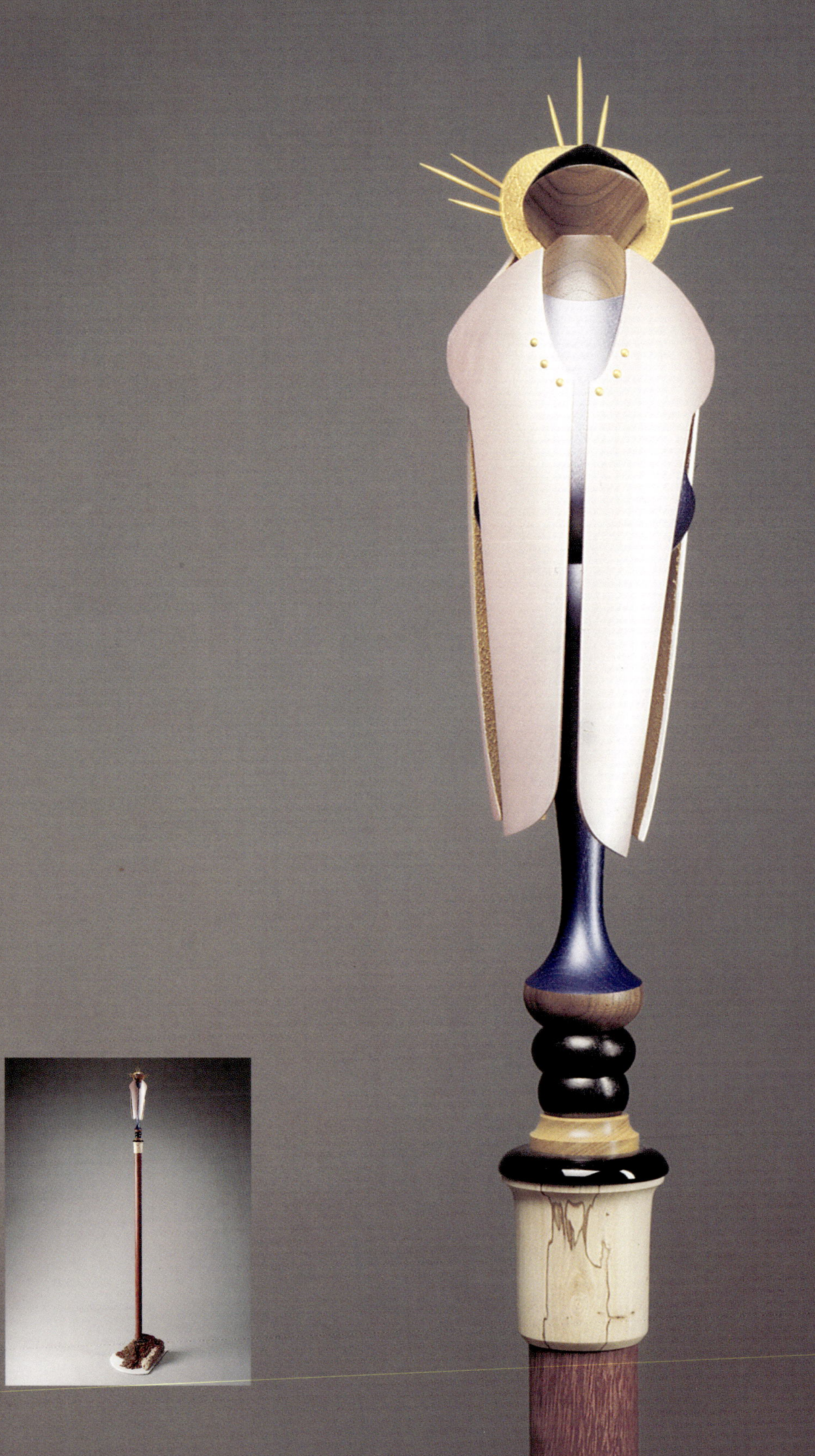

*Chartres Revisited*

Steve Loar, in collaboration with Mark Sfirri and Frank Sudol

2000

H: 85", W: 19", D: 14"

Walnut, walnut burl, birch, spalted elm, satinwood, Plexiglas, Corian and purpleheart veneered struct-tube

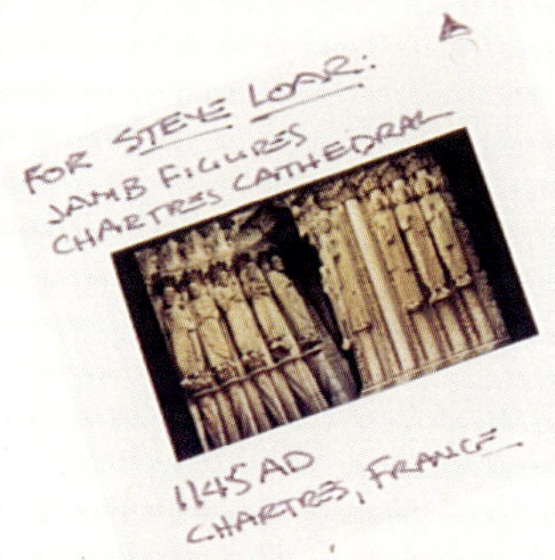


## Steve Loar [*New York, USA – b. 1949*]

The primary thematic reference for *Chartres Revisited* is the jamb figures of the West Royal Portal of Chartres Cathedral (1145 A.D., Chartres, France). The relationship that is created between these jamb figures and the viewer is quite unlike a pedestal in a modern gallery. Similarly, I wanted to place a sculptural craft object on a post to visually isolate it, while placing the viewer in an uncommon relationship with the object—intimate yet removed. I had been discussing the idea of forced relationships with my friends in the field for several years. Its application for my own work seemed opportune. This relationship of object and viewer was reinforced by an illustration by Lisbeth Zwerger for *The Wizard of Oz* that I have had pinned to my studio wall for several years. The particular image shows a wall lined with various head and face forms mounted atop high poles. I had been searching for a way to use this engaging idea without making copies of it or sinking to "fantasy totems."

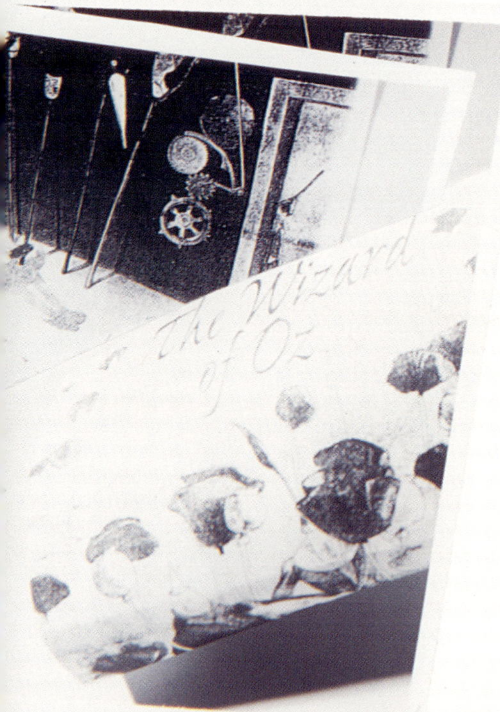

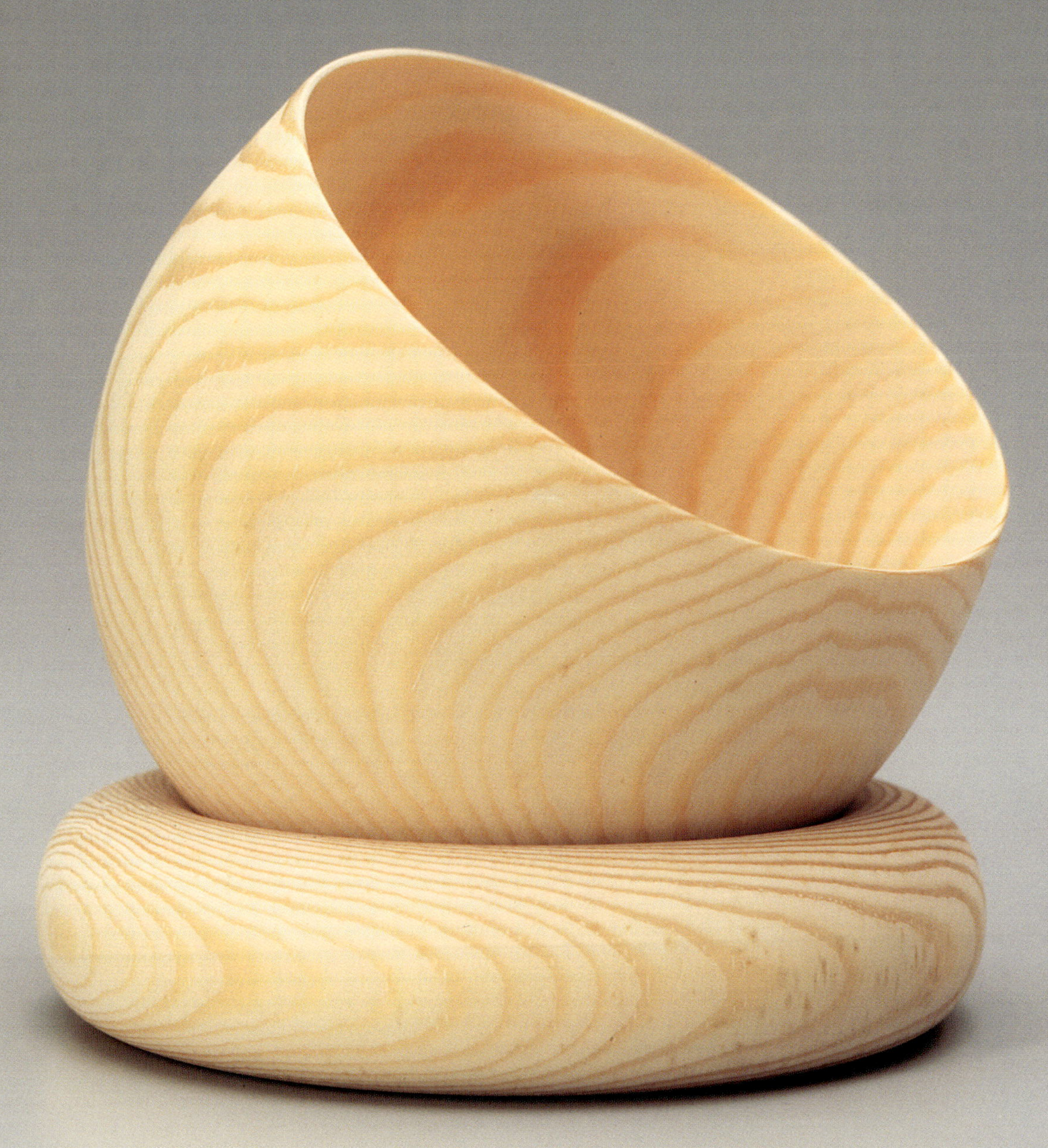

*Cup*
1999
H: 3 3/8", Diam: 3 3/8"
Pine

PETER LUISONI [*Germany – b. 1960*]

An egg turning between my fingers sitting on the table in the morning.

The quadration of a circle is successfully done. The realization in turning pine wood in its natural form, green and fresh, needs to give the object an imperishable form. By turning thin forms, I can avoid splitting. By not covering the surface with any chemical or natural lacquers or polishes, I can intensify the source of alp origin.

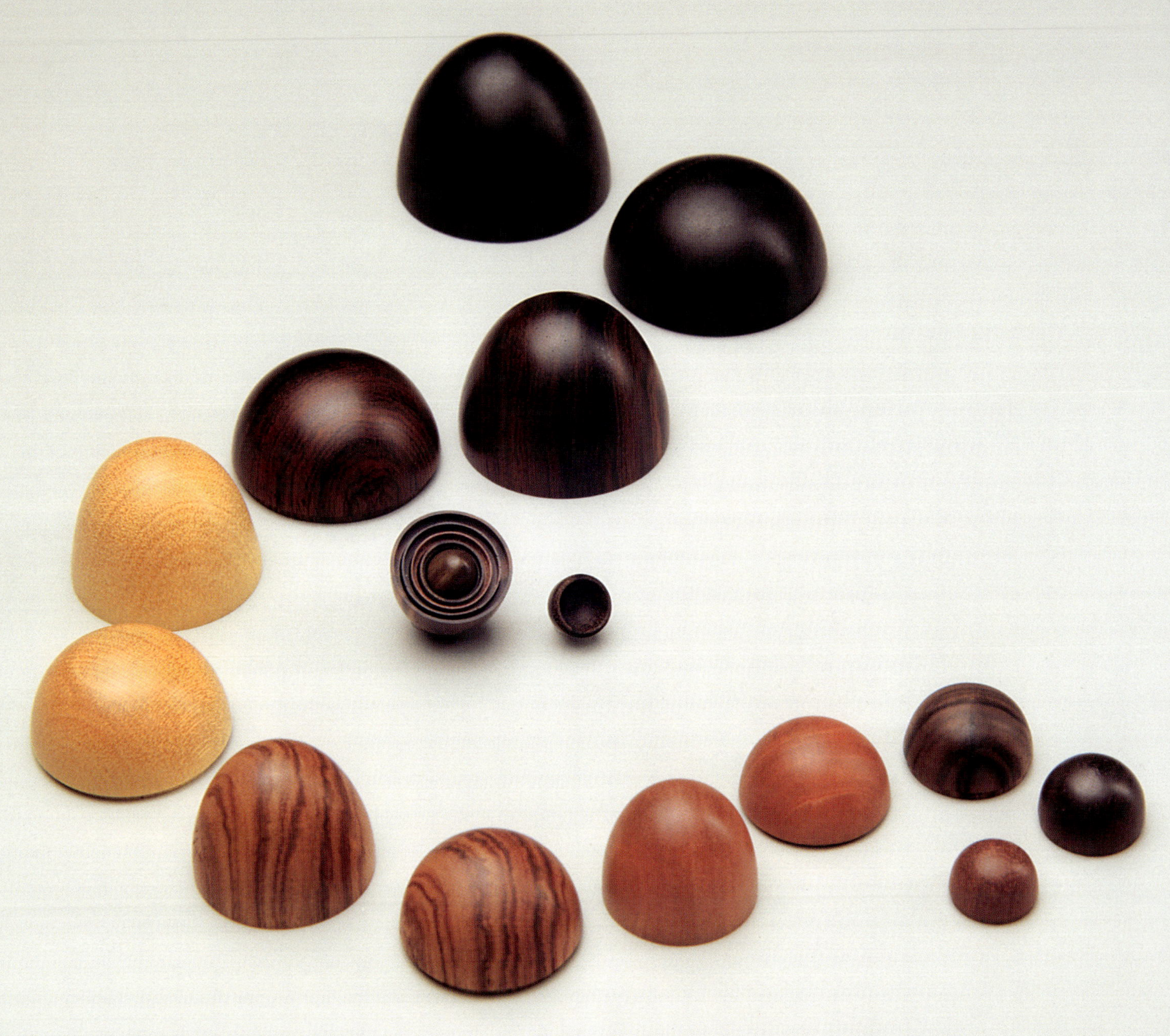

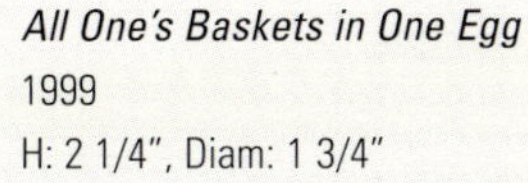

*All One's Baskets in One Egg*
1999
H: 2 1/4", Diam: 1 3/4"
Various hardwoods and 18k gold

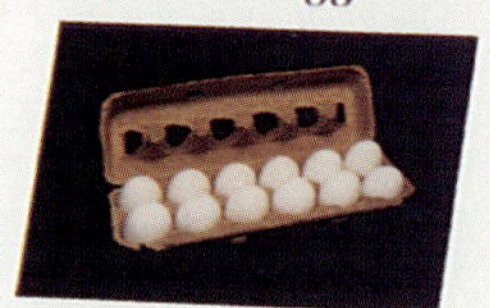


## Barry Macdonald [*Michigan, USA – b. 1945*]

Perhaps mankind's most ancient iconic symbol, the egg represents fertility, renewal, and rebirth. No other form, with the possible exception of the circle, has represented pure elegance and closure more so than the entrancing purity of the egg's blending of sphere and ellipse. The repeating layers of *All One's Baskets in One Egg* bring to mind everything from mystery unraveling (or deepening) to the innocent pleasure of a toy.

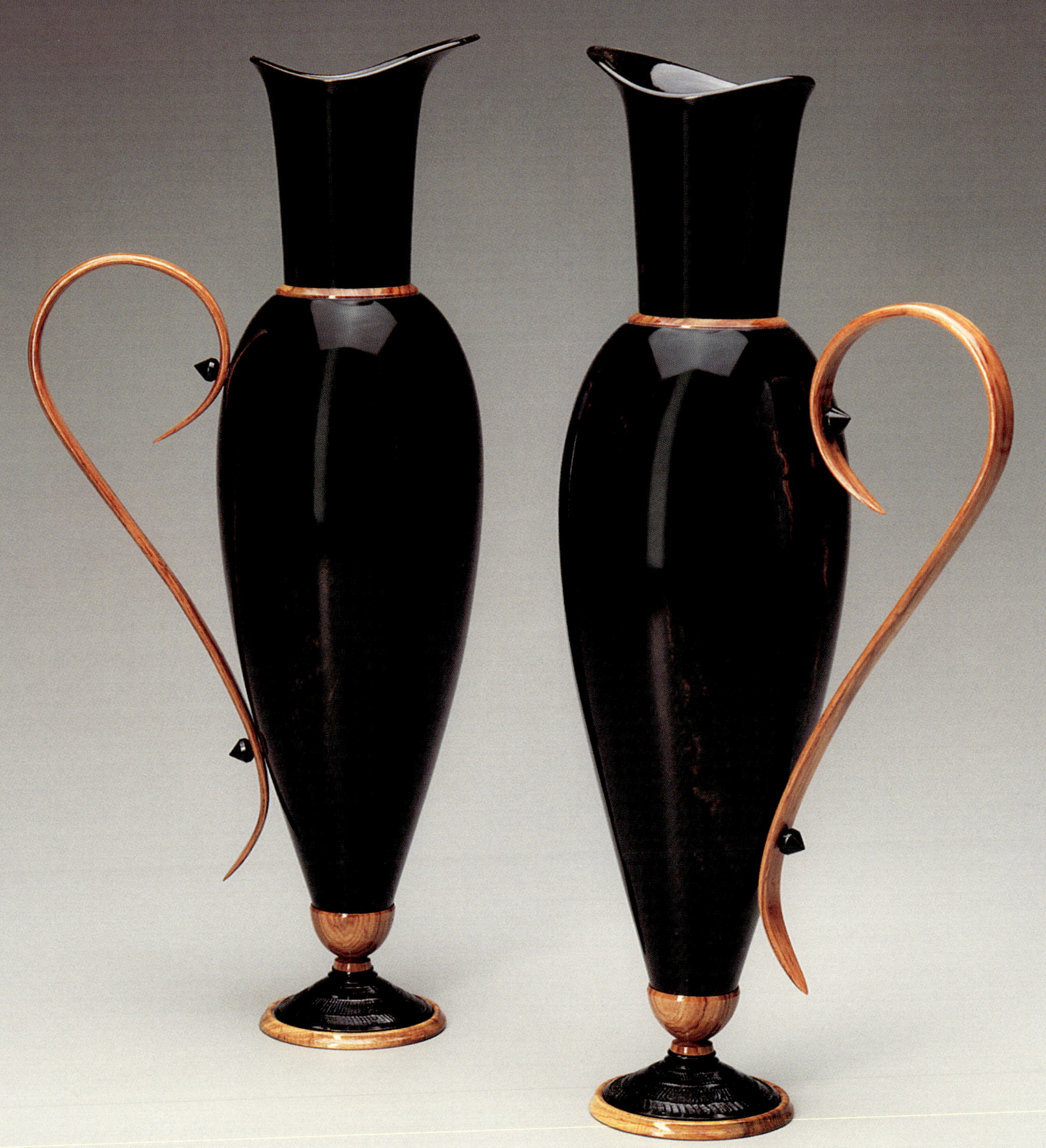

*Ewer Forms*
2000
H: 14 1/2", Diam: 6 1/2"
Ebony and tulipwood

Barry Macdonald [*Michigan, USA – b. 1945*]

Inspired by the classic Etruscan ewer, these pieces are my attempt to refine the dimensions of form by freeing it from the constraints of function: to achieve the perfect confluence of curves, to find the purest balance of proportion, to make color, texture, and detail essential and integral to the form. Pairs maintain symmetry, and by virtue of their anthropomorphic profile, introduce the themes of sharing, exchange, and the impulse to mate.

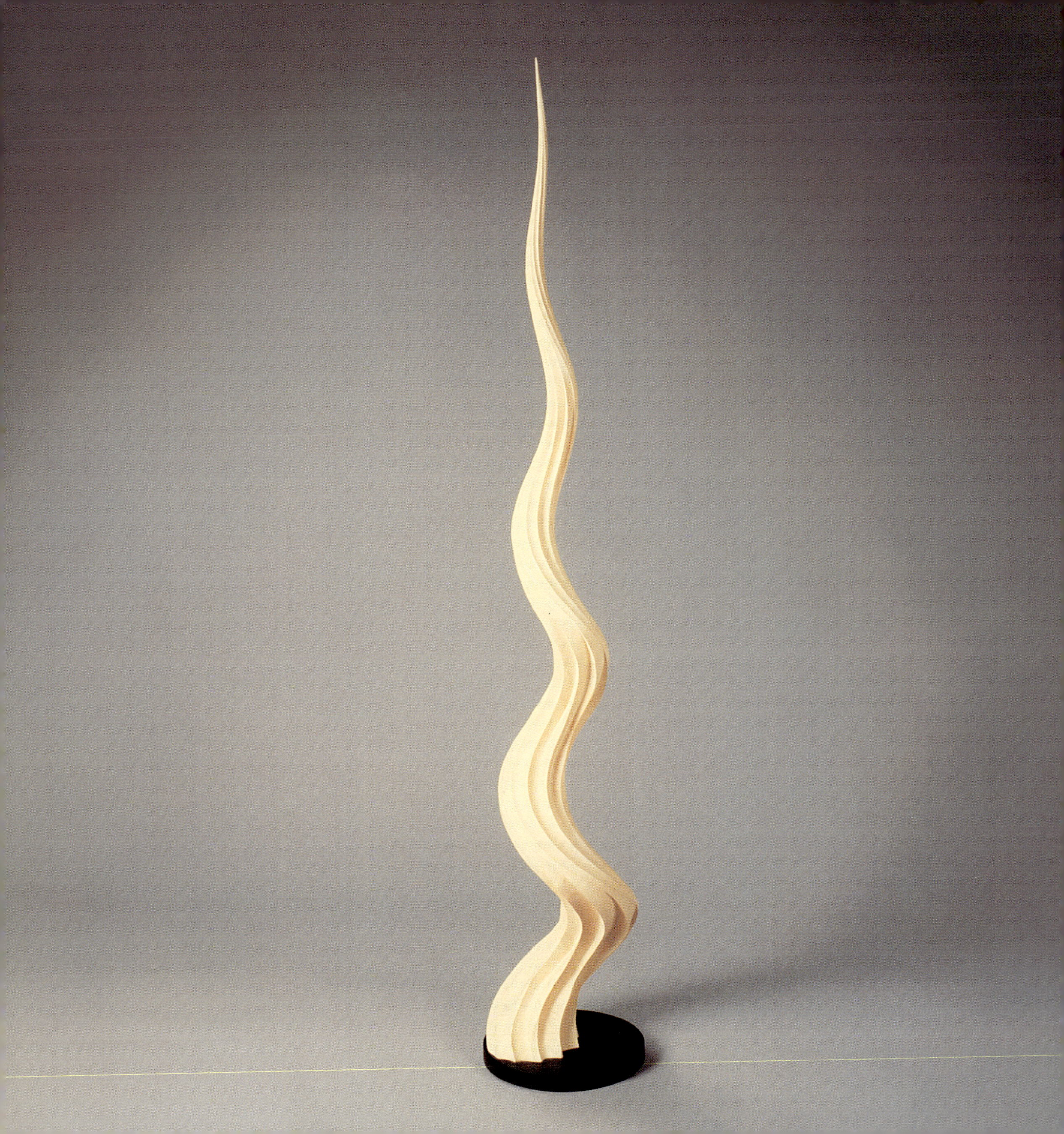

*Compound Conical Column #3*
2000
H: 66", W: 12", D: 12"
White pine and paint

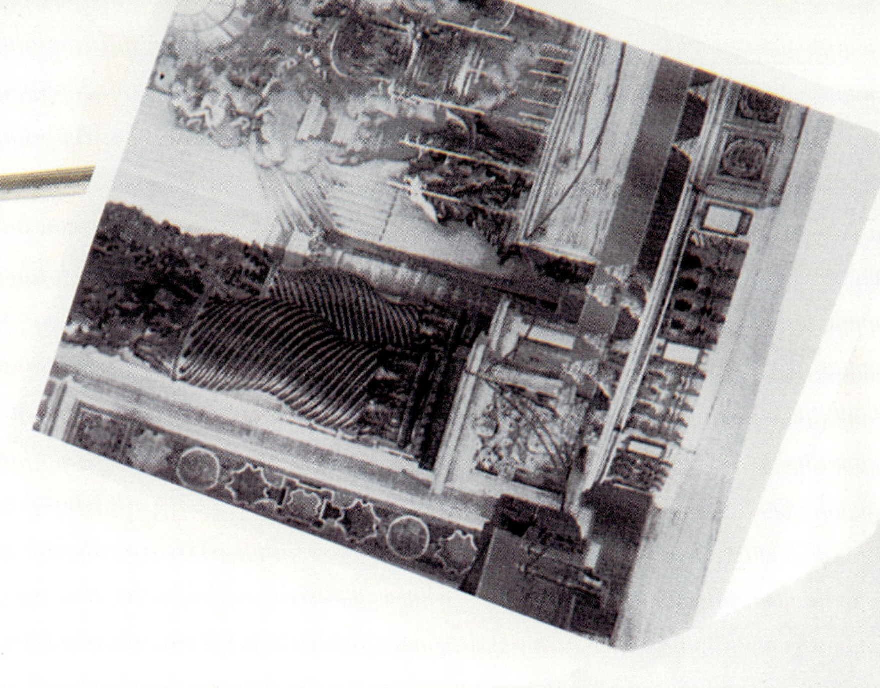

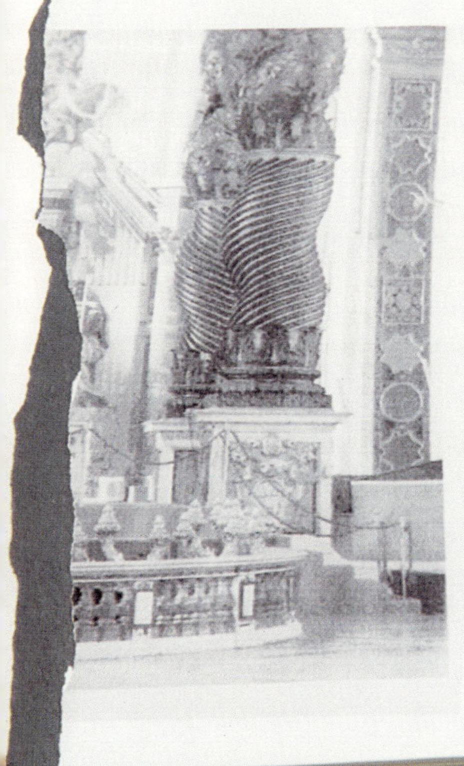

## John Macnab [*Canada – b. 1961*]

My recent projects are based on spindle turning, which is the earliest form of lathe work. Its origins may be traced to ancient Mesopotamia, where mathematics and mechanically determined form seem to have originated in tandem. I believe a line of descent may be drawn from this era to the extraordinary complexities of late industrial machine work. This is the tradition in which I locate myself and from which I draw inspiration.

My intention is to create a family of physical forms that have not heretofore been generated. I have inscribed or milled decaying mathematical functions onto elongated spiraling surfaces. On a cone, when spiraling lines of a constant pitch ascend, they also converge and diminish until at the top they approach a straight line. In this way one can describe infinity on a finite object. The resulting forms conjure many associations with familiar objects in our world and beyond. However, I do not set out to make shells, ferns, horns, or metaphysical sculpture. These and other worldly shapes and ideas inspire me in my practice, but only in an empirical sense.

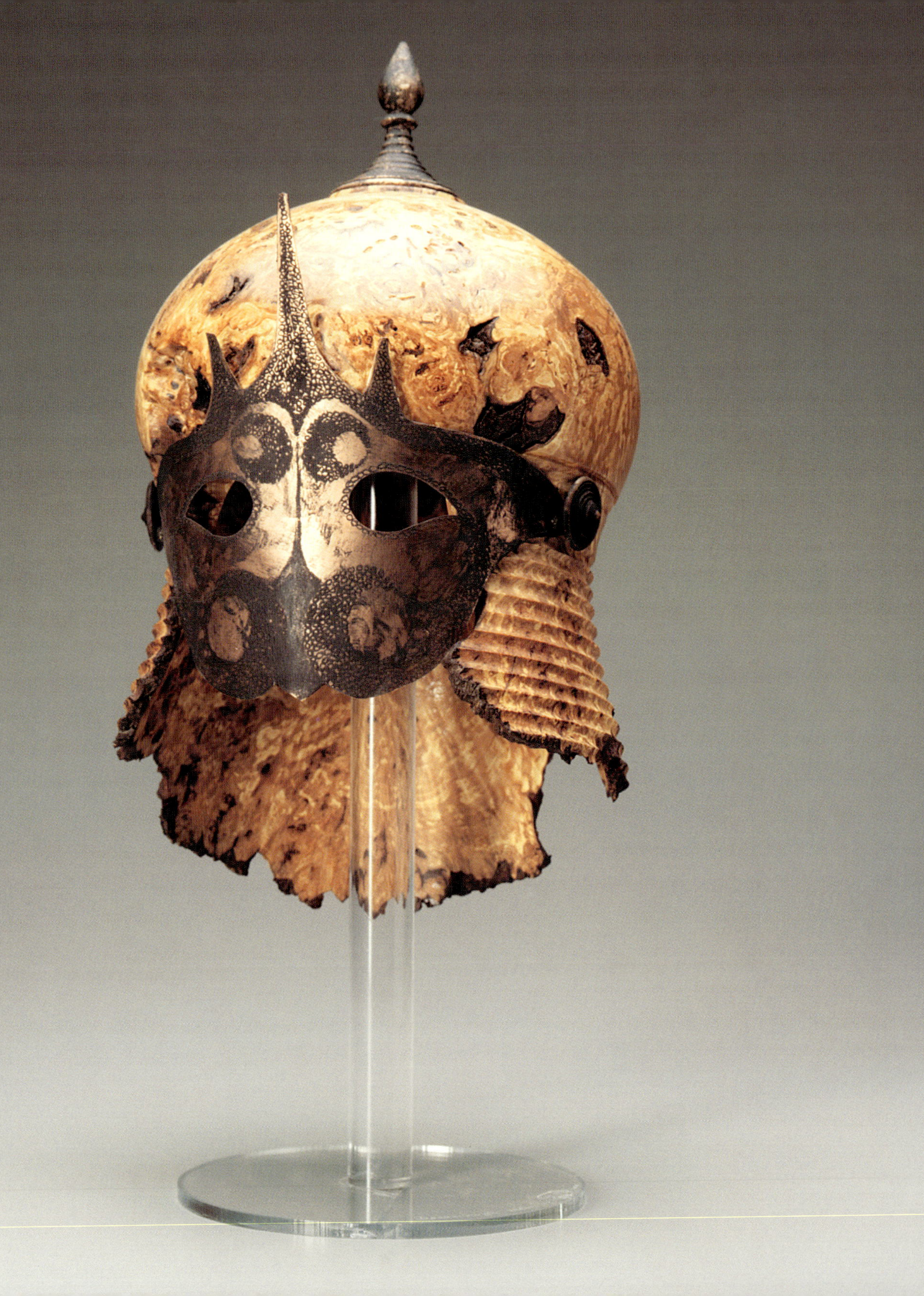

*Desborough Helm*
2000
H: 18", W: 8", D: 8"
Alder burl, copper and maple

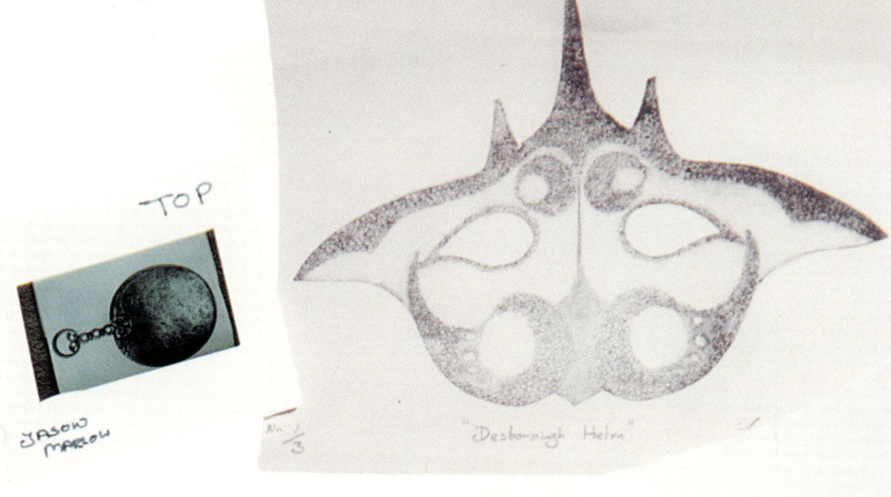


JASON MARLOW [*Canada – b. 1955*]

I have been exploring the idea of wooden helmets for some two years now. My father exposed my three brothers and me to as many art galleries, museums and churches as possible.

As a child, I remember listening to relatives talk about a Mirror and Desborough and Granpa Jesse. More than three decades later, I realized that the bronze Mirror I was admiring had been dug up by my great grandfather Jesse Marlow in 1908. The Mirror dates from the early first century A.D.

My first impressions of the Mirror were that of admiration and respect. I decided to try to incorporate some sense of this object, a mirror, into one of my helmets.

The alder burl, a local wood, was turned, textured and hollowed on the lathe. Exploiting the natural edges of the burl meant I had only to carve away a little for the facepiece. I wanted to be able to see into the Helmet.

The two small discs on the corners of the visor are called *phalarae*, normally used on horse harnesses or chariots. The Helmet's finial is made from maple and covered in copper leaf. The connection from Father to Great Grandfather to the Artist/Craftsman who made the Mirror spans over 900 years. It confirms in me the belief that with such strong foundations to build upon, the modern day artist/craftsperson can produce contemporary objects which celebrate the past yet still gaze forward into the future.

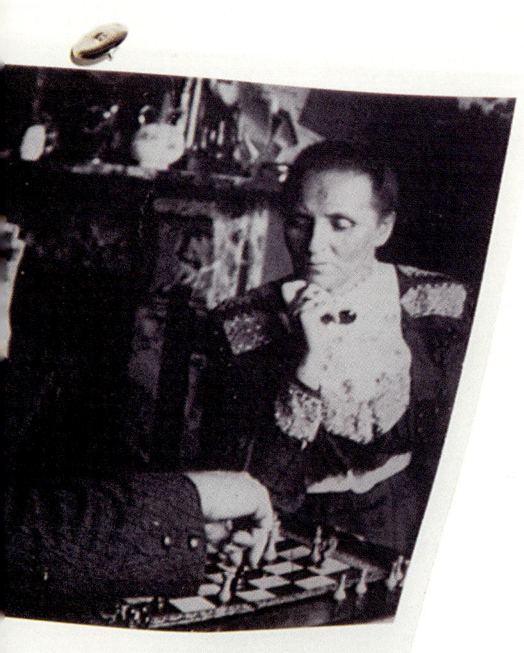

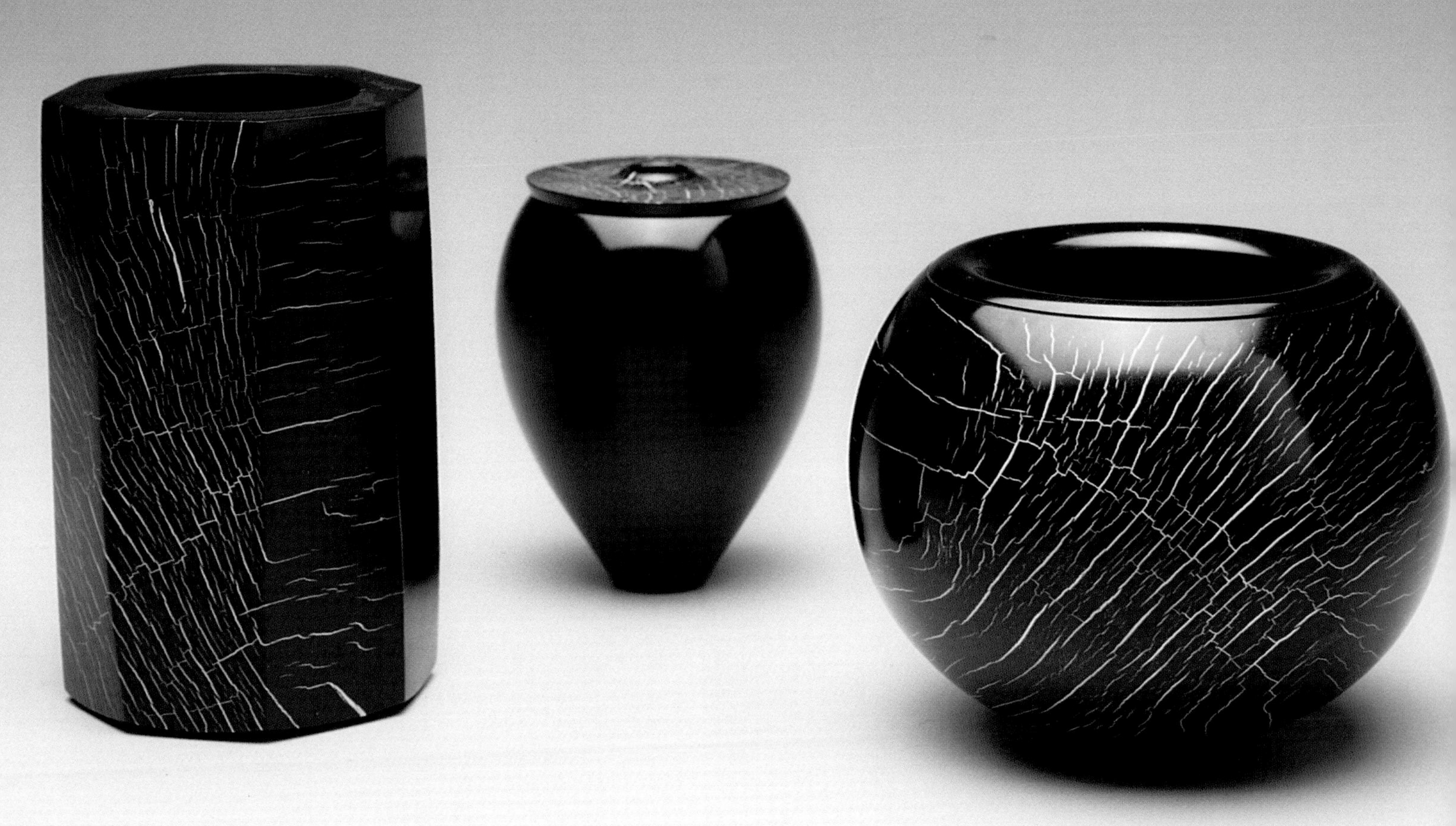

*Spider's Web*
H: 5 1/4", Diam: 6 1/4"
Ebony and silver alloy

*Ivy*
2000
H: 6 3/4", Diam: 4 1/4"
Ebony and silver alloy

*Poppy Fruit*
2000
H: 4 7/8", Diam: 4"
Ebony and silver alloy

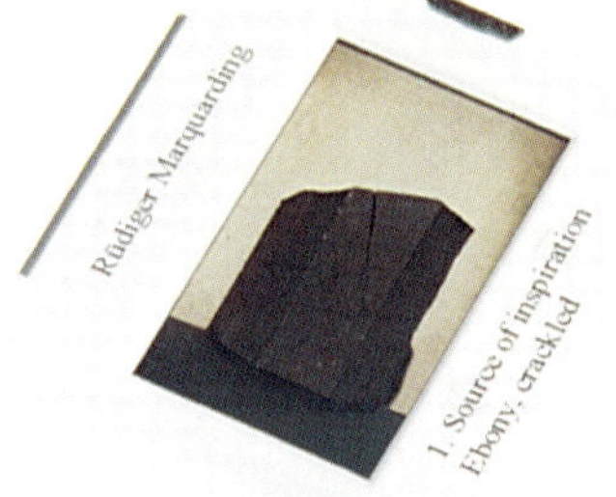


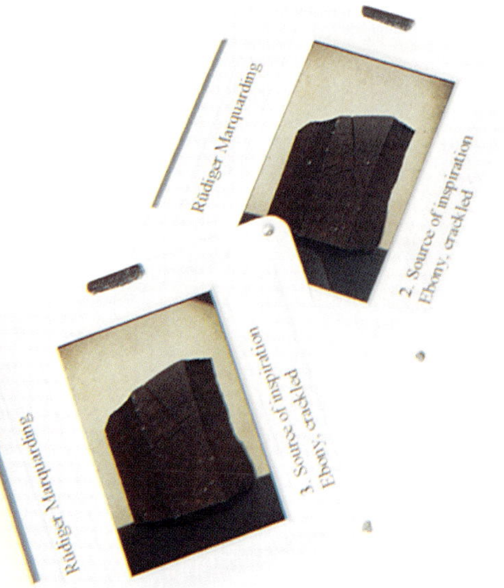


## Rüdiger Marquarding [*Germany – b. 1943*]

Explanation of the relationship between the sources and my creative reinterpretation: cracked wood — any wood turner's or carpenter's nightmare!

Wood showing cracks normally gets discarded — it's unusable. The occurrence of cracks or crackles during the entire process of manufacture or creation is more than annoying and bothersome.

Yet one man's horror is another one's delight. My interest in these crackles arose from my noticing their versatility and uniqueness—their free flowing lines and graphical patterns were fascinating. I then started looking for ways to utilize them as means of creation in jewelry, vessels, and sculptures.

Ever facing the problem of uncertainty, never really knowing the outcome, I was striving for the challenge of unpredictability — which crackles or patterns would emerge in the process of creation — positive and negative surprises await at any stage.

The exhibits — crackles in wood as a means of creative expression — are a result of my pioneering endeavors in this unusual sphere, which I believe is still in its infancy, and thus wide open to further artistic exploration.

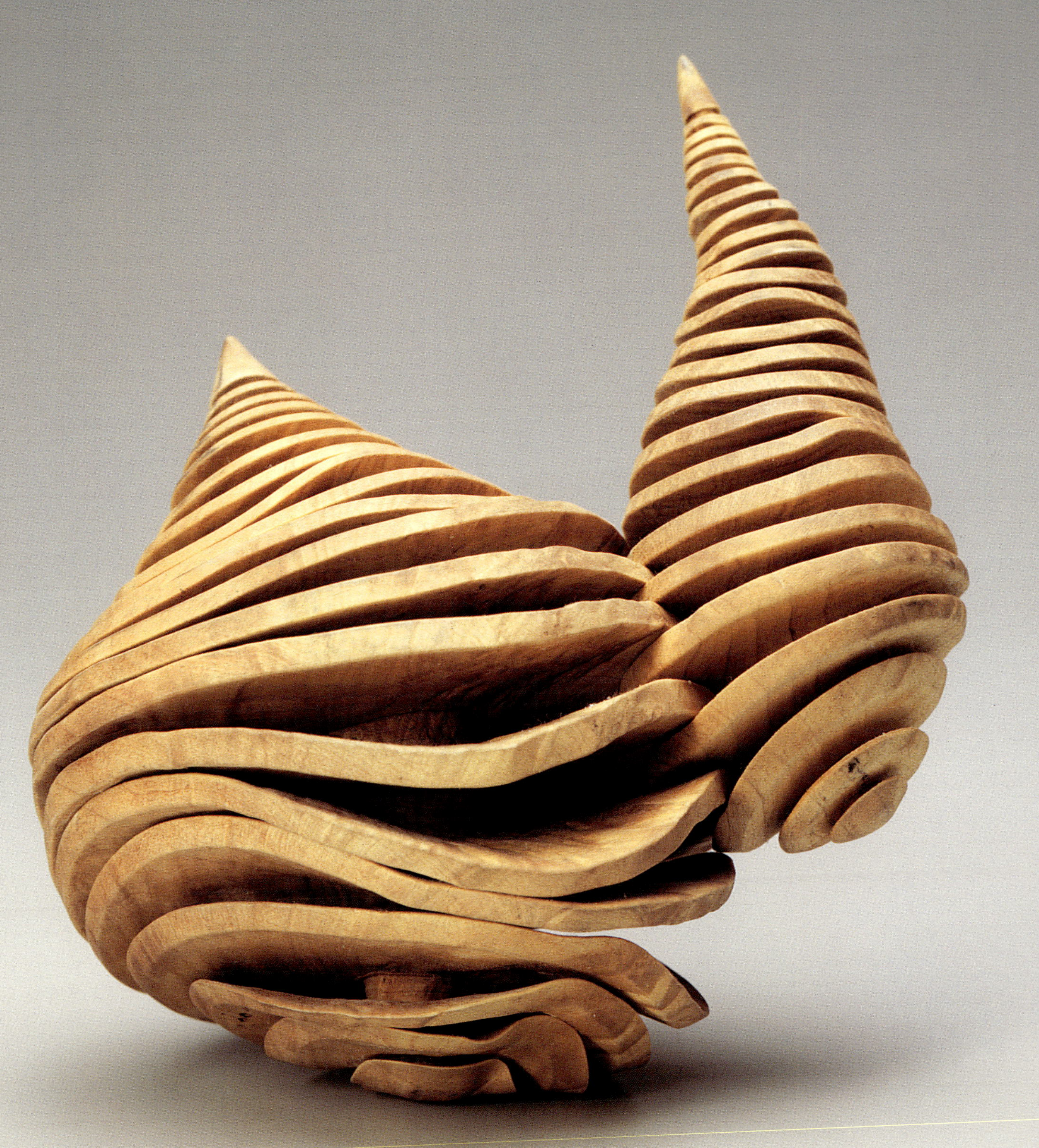

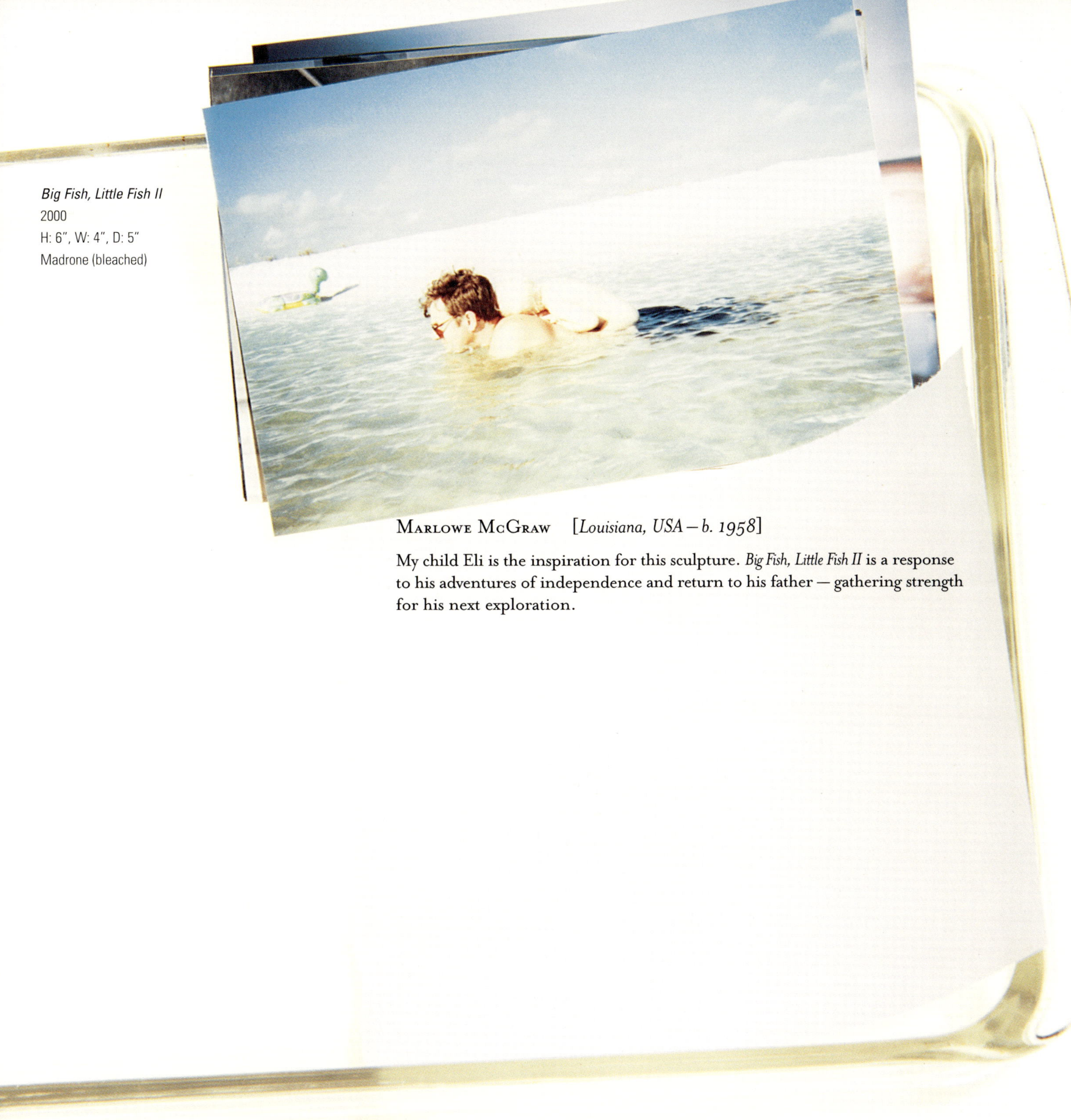

*Big Fish, Little Fish II*
2000
H: 6", W: 4", D: 5"
Madrone (bleached)

MARLOWE MCGRAW [*Louisiana, USA – b. 1958*]

My child Eli is the inspiration for this sculpture. *Big Fish, Little Fish II* is a response to his adventures of independence and return to his father — gathering strength for his next exploration.

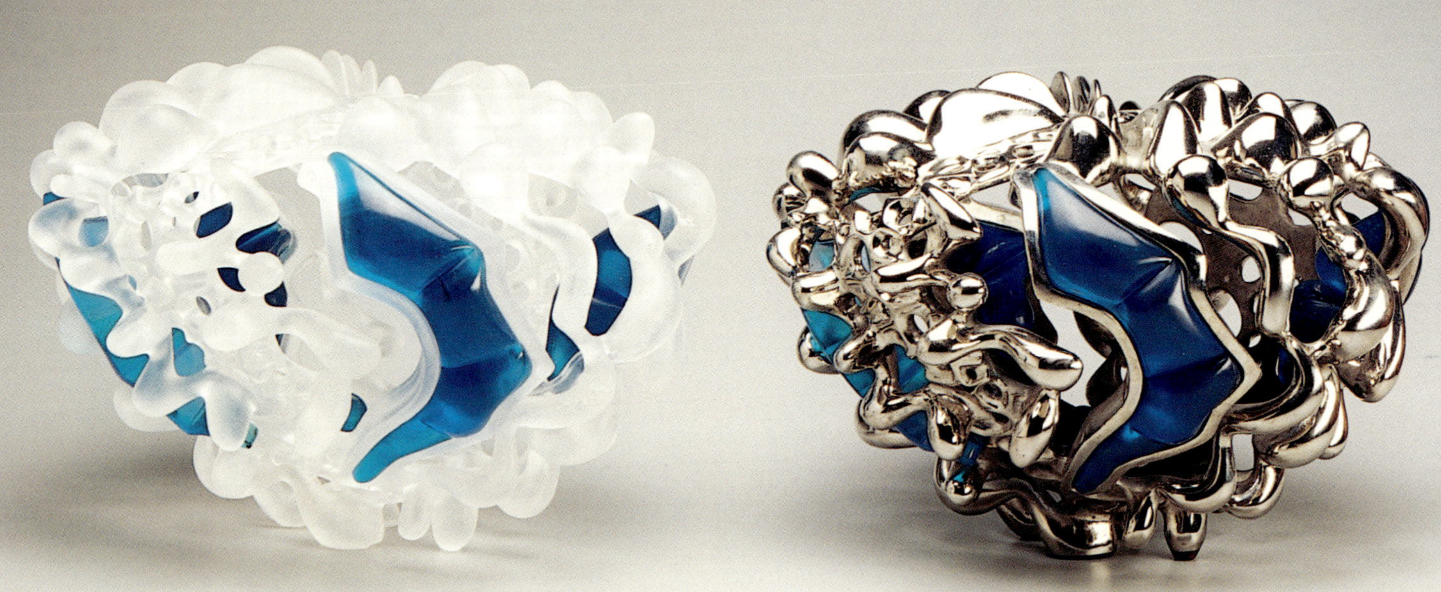

*Ruuach*
2000
H: 14", Diam: 18"
Cast leaded crystal

*Ruuach*
2001
H: 14", Diam: 18"
Nickel plated bronze and cast leaded crystal

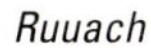

## Hugh McKay [*Oregon, USA – b. 1951*]

I don't have a preliminary sketch or even a source I can easily name for this piece. I did have a concept though. I had made an earlier piece with "strands of form" undulating from left to right around the outside of the vessel form. I wanted to have the strands undulate from right to left, and up and down in relationship to the center of the turning. I turned and hollowed the basic form leaving a 2 1/2-inch wall thickness. I then started "doodling" on the outside of the vessel form. As evidence of my doodling, I've submitted drawing #2, which I made during a long and uninteresting phone conversation. With some work, once I have a smooth turned form to draw on, I simply start sketching on that form with just basic ideas to guide me.

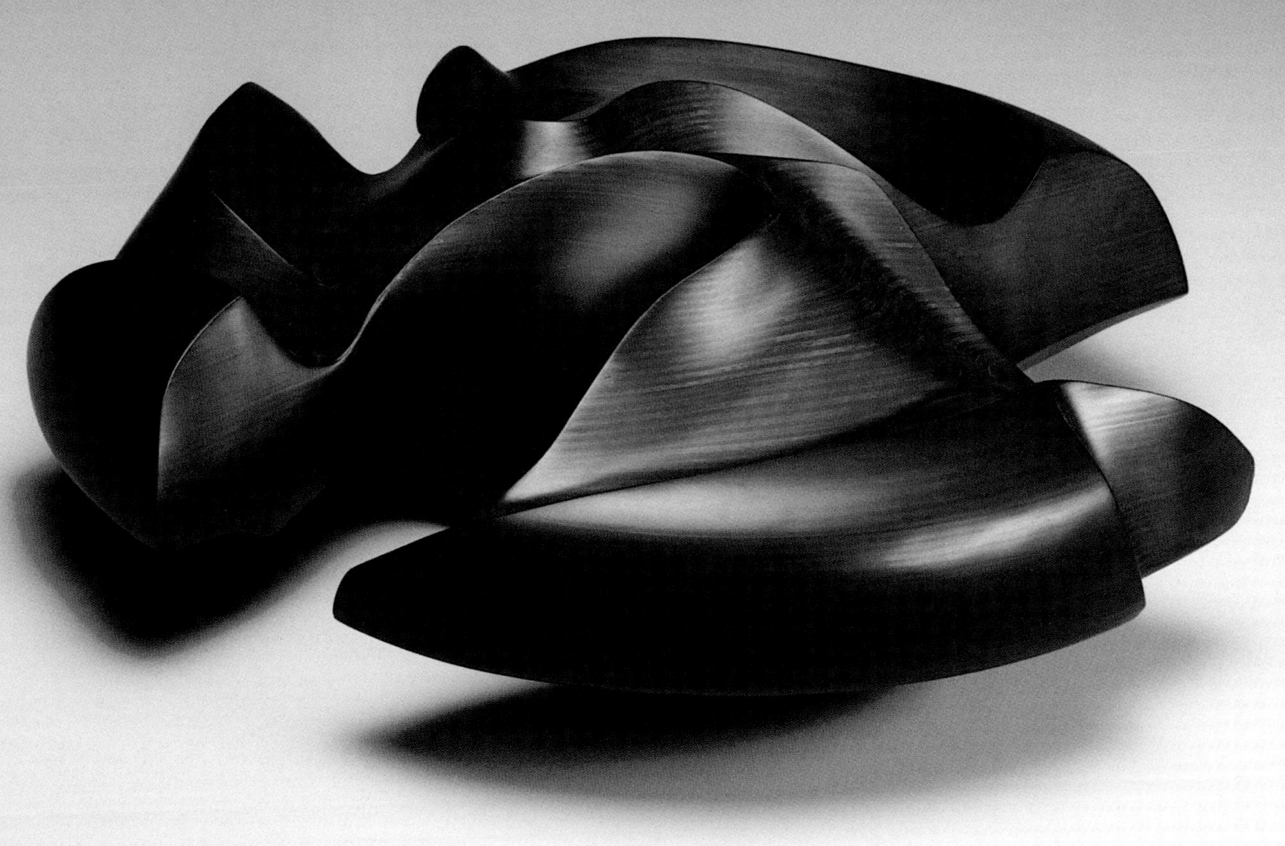

*Circle of Time-210 Blue Cliffs*
2000
H: 8", Diam: 22"
Plywood, acrylic and lacquer

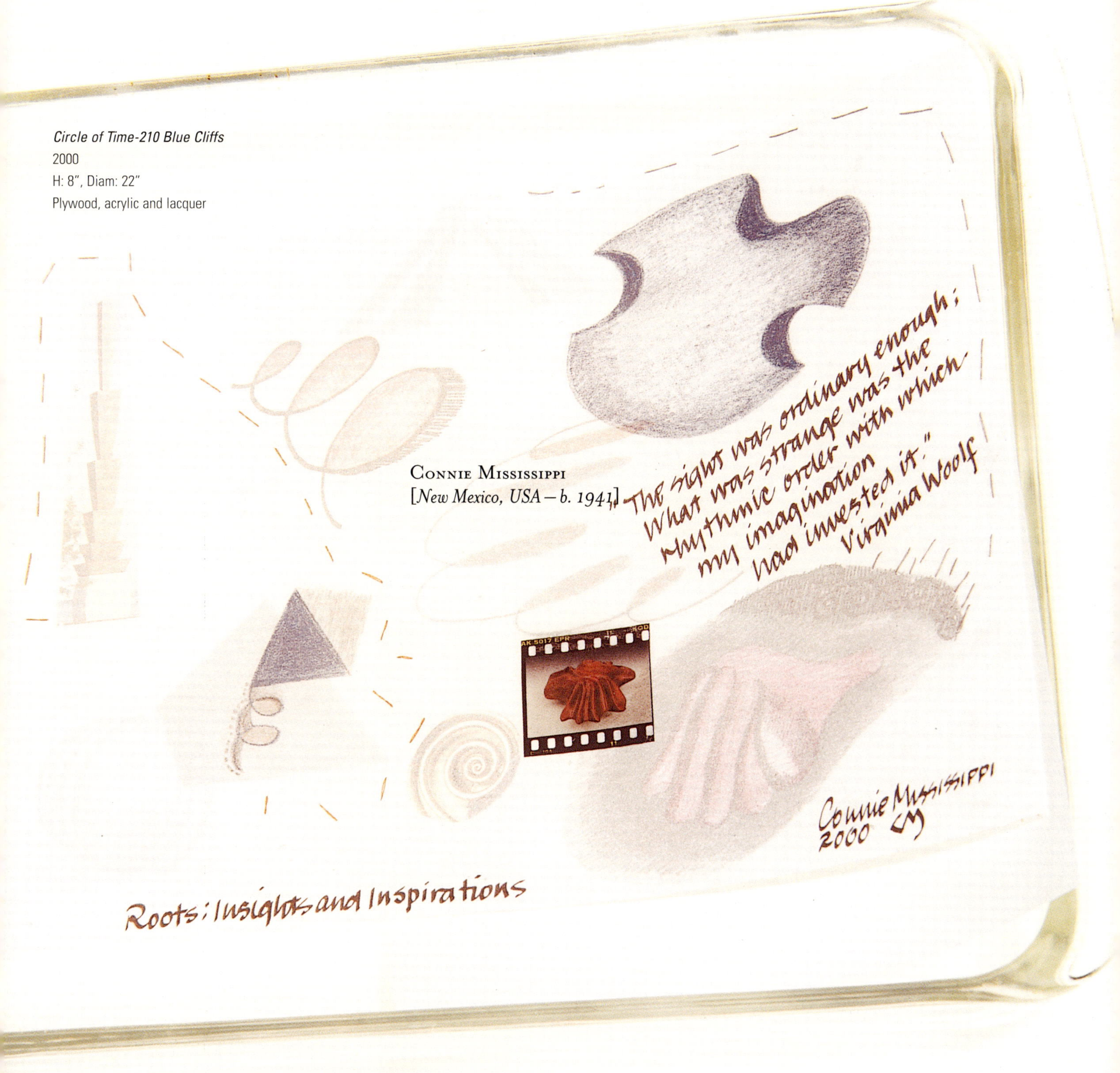

CONNIE MISSISSIPPI
[*New Mexico, USA – b. 1941*]

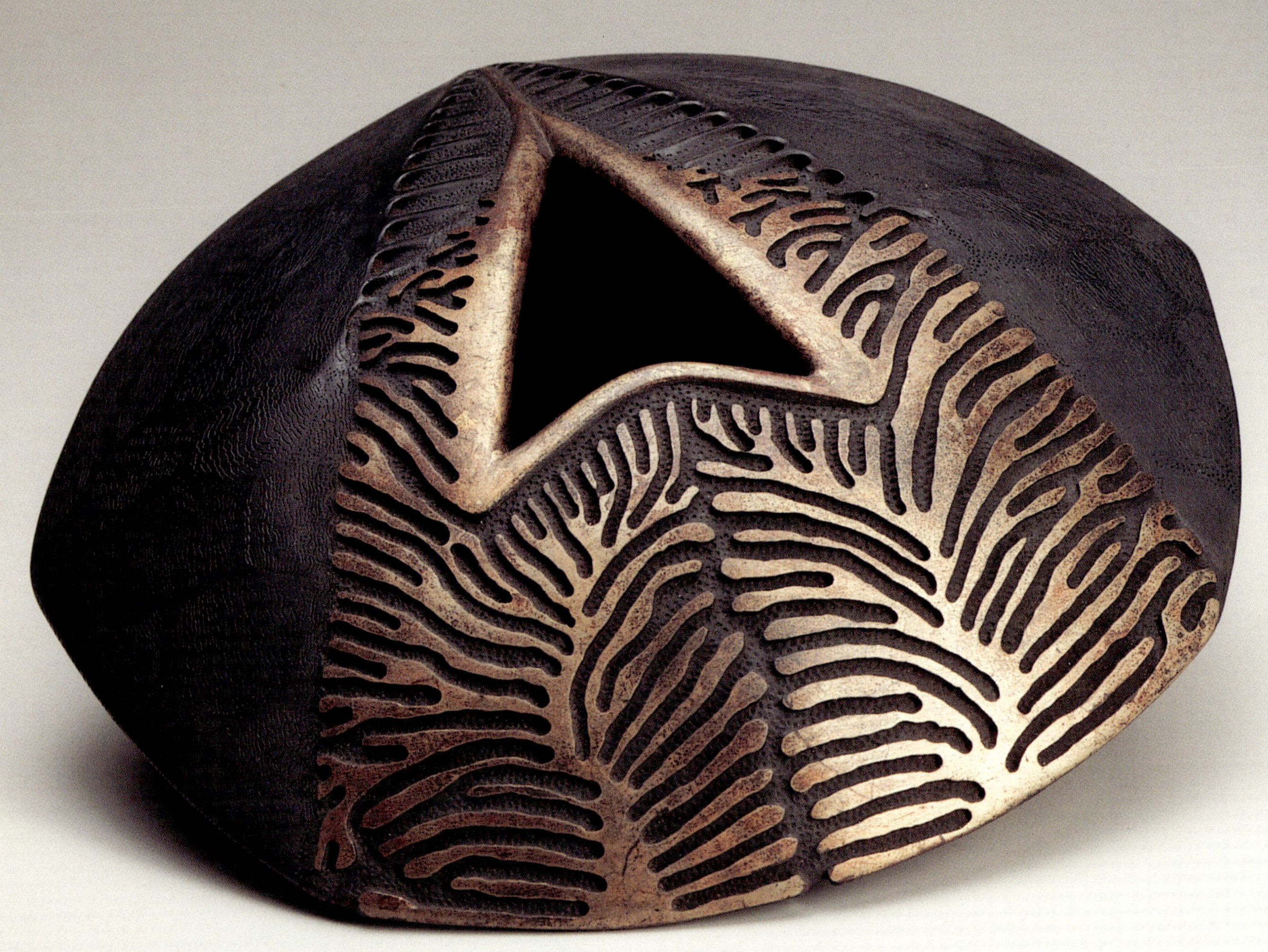

*Sea Biscuit Form II*
2000
Walnut, gold leaf and pigments
H: 3", Diam: 11"

## Rolly Munro [*New Zealand – b. 1954*]

This is a continuation of a series of hollow vessel forms based loosely on the shellfish family including sand dollars/sea biscuits. It is a branch from a previous series called **Shellform**, which focused on a visual tour from the exterior to the sculptures' inner voids.

In this series my attention has switched to the works' outer surfaces. The interior of the sea biscuit contains a maze of sinus-like cavities, which are a perfect balance of positive and negative mass. I have carved and overlaid with patinaed gold leaf a motif highly reminiscent of these passages on a portion of the work's surface. The fingerprint-like incisions on the remainder of the surface relate to the divisions and pores through which the organism breathes.

Through these shells I have sought to discover fresh visual material, while at the same time attempting to find a parallel or source of the finely manipulated surfaces of the wood art of Melanesia and Micronesia. While this work often doesn't attempt depiction of sea life, I have seen surface work that exhibits subtle scoring and perforations that appear to emulate the surface of shells.

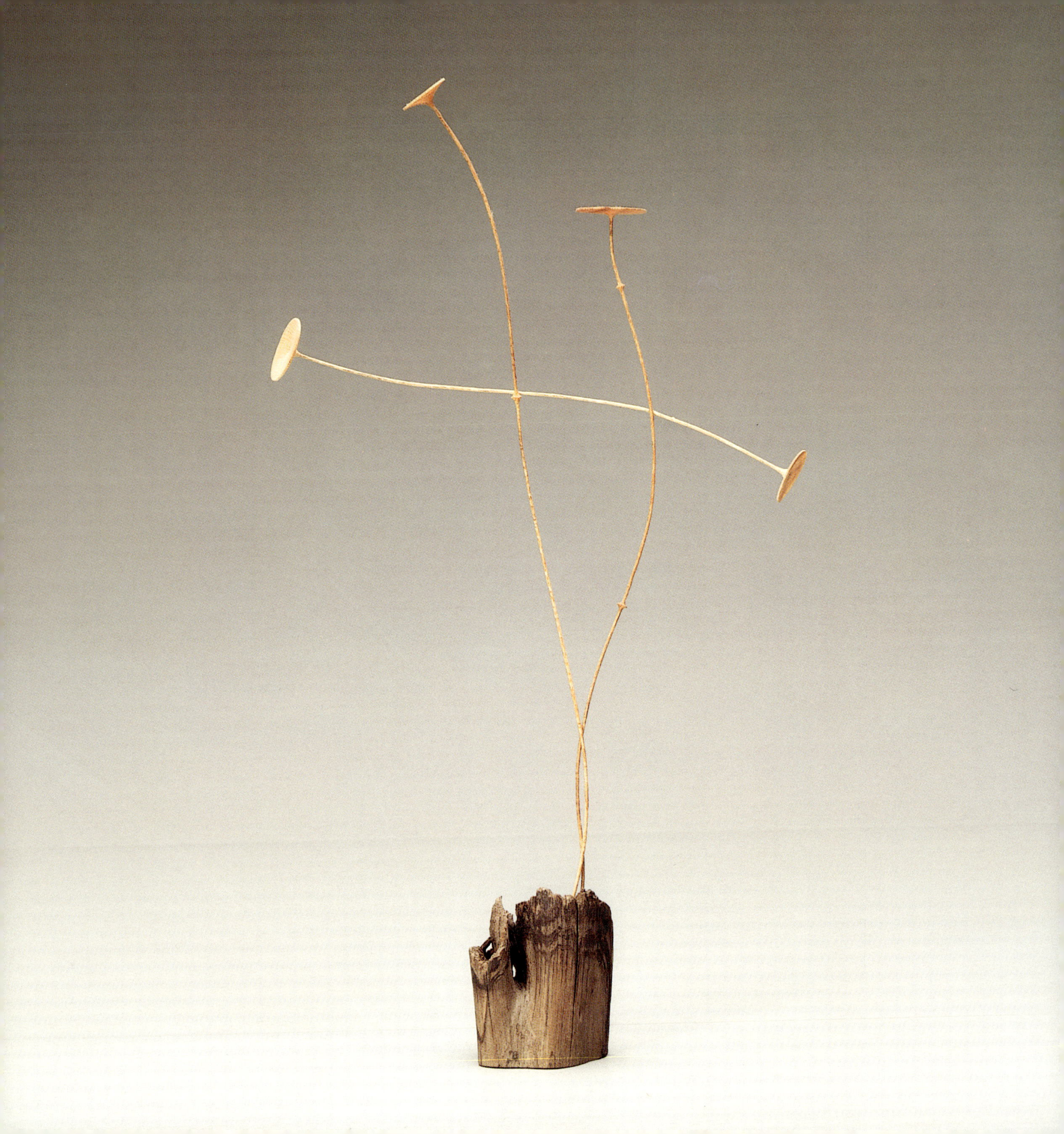

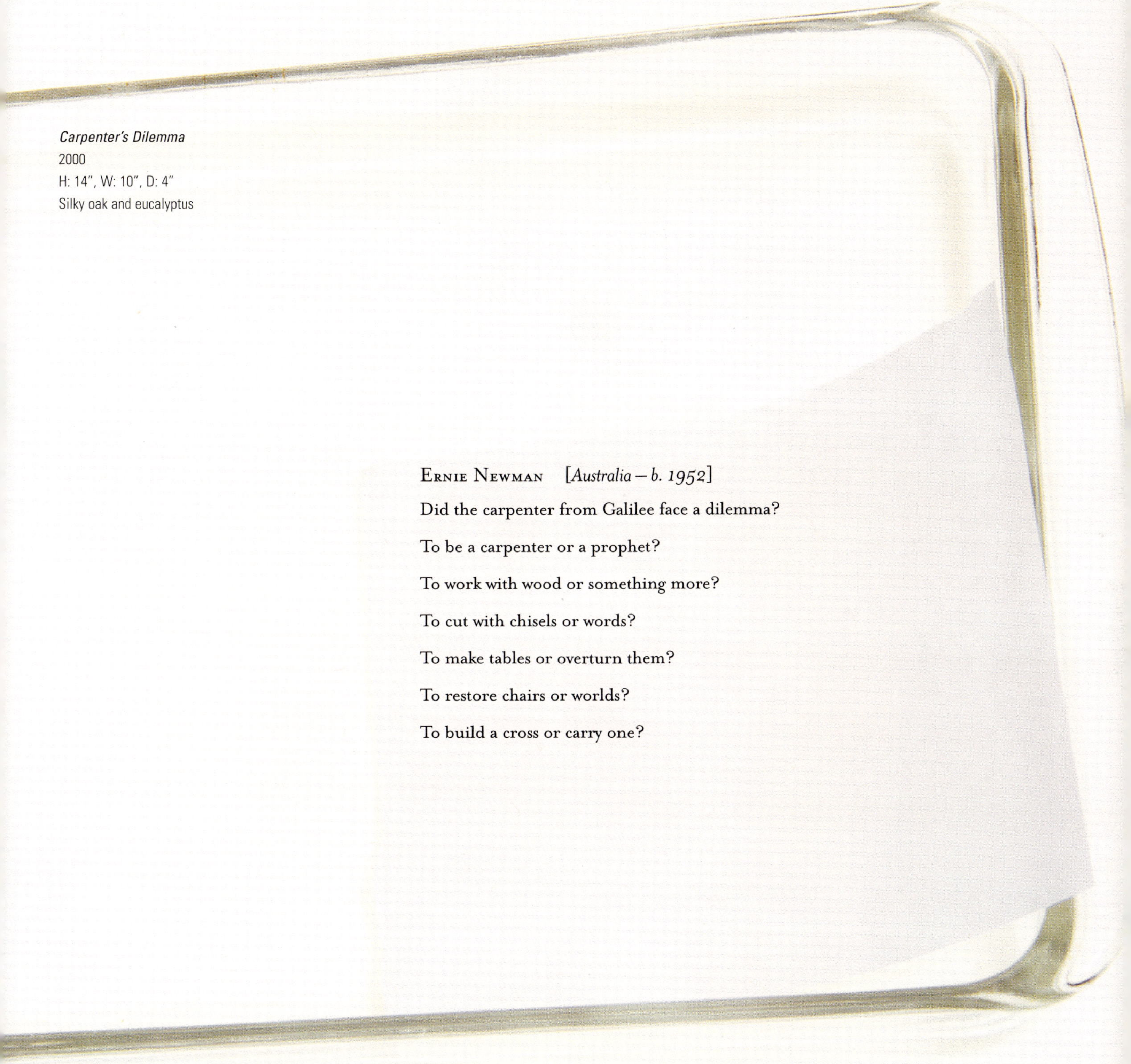

*Carpenter's Dilemma*
2000
H: 14", W: 10", D: 4"
Silky oak and eucalyptus

Ernie Newman [*Australia – b. 1952*]

Did the carpenter from Galilee face a dilemma?

To be a carpenter or a prophet?

To work with wood or something more?

To cut with chisels or words?

To make tables or overturn them?

To restore chairs or worlds?

To build a cross or carry one?

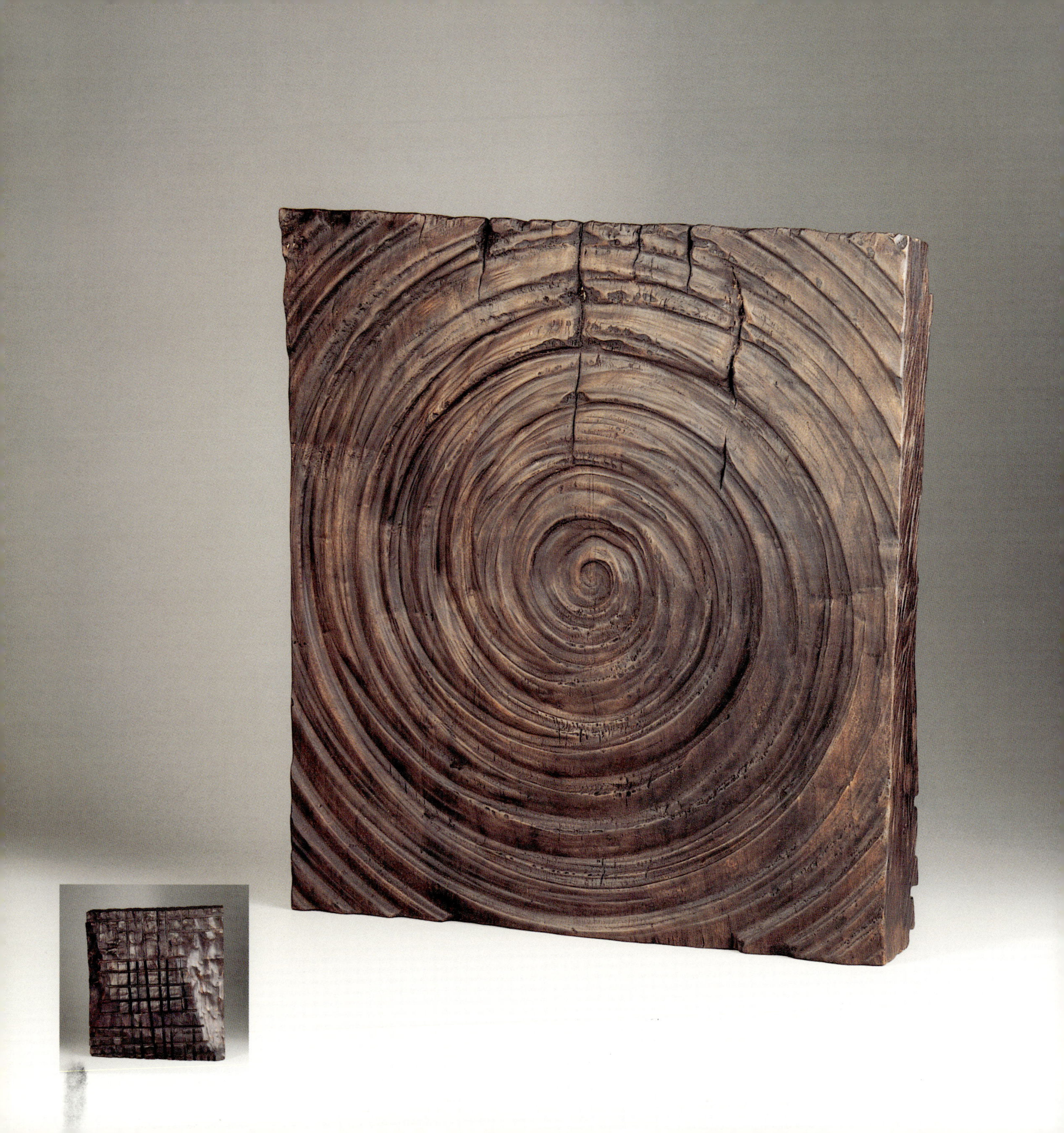

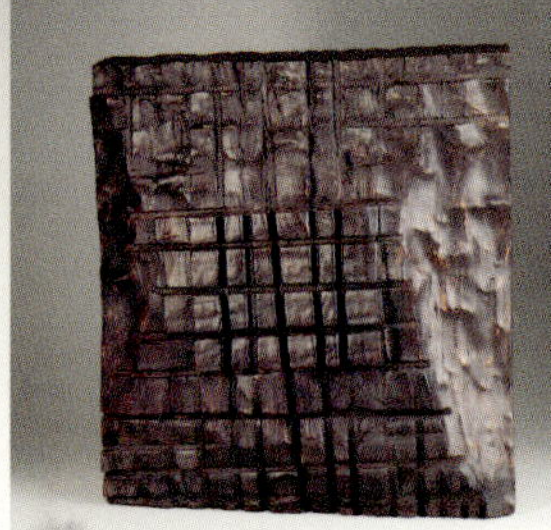

*Buddha's Mirror*
2000
H: 24", W: 21", D: 4"
Charred maple

"Sometimes.....when I make something, I put a little dent in it. I like to do something to make it really unique. Hit it with a hammer. Deliberately fuck it up. ...Machines can either liberate man or enslave 'im, because they're pretty neutral. It's man who has the bias to put the thing one place or another."

*Mike Lefevre, steelworker, talking about his work.*
*Studs Terkel, Working*

George Peterson [*North Carolina, USA – b. 1966*]

The most important element of inspiration in my work is simply the urge to make things, to play with the material and then stand back and look at it. My approach to making *Buddha's Mirror* was like my approach to any lathe-turned bowl. This piece has a front, a back, and a raised area that acts as a foot. Often, as I work the wood, I pay special attention to the marks left by my tools. The textural elements of this piece are inspired by the action of the tools themselves. In this case, I used a chainsaw, a lathe, a hammer and a blowtorch. Such fast acting tools allow me to work quickly in fluid, gestural movements. The scoring on the exterior is multi-purpose; it carves the wood to my desired shape, and by breaking off some of the protruding blocks, it leaves me with an interesting texture and a nice interplay of machined and natural surfaces. The spiral on the interior is made by letting the gouge ride along the surface of the wood, enlarging and intersecting the cuts with each pass. I don't attempt to control the cuts precisely; rather I hold the tool in a specific way and aim. The final surface is unique to the piece of wood and the travel of the gouge through the grain. By giving up some control, I am given something else. Elements of irregularity and spontaneity are added. The piece comes alive.

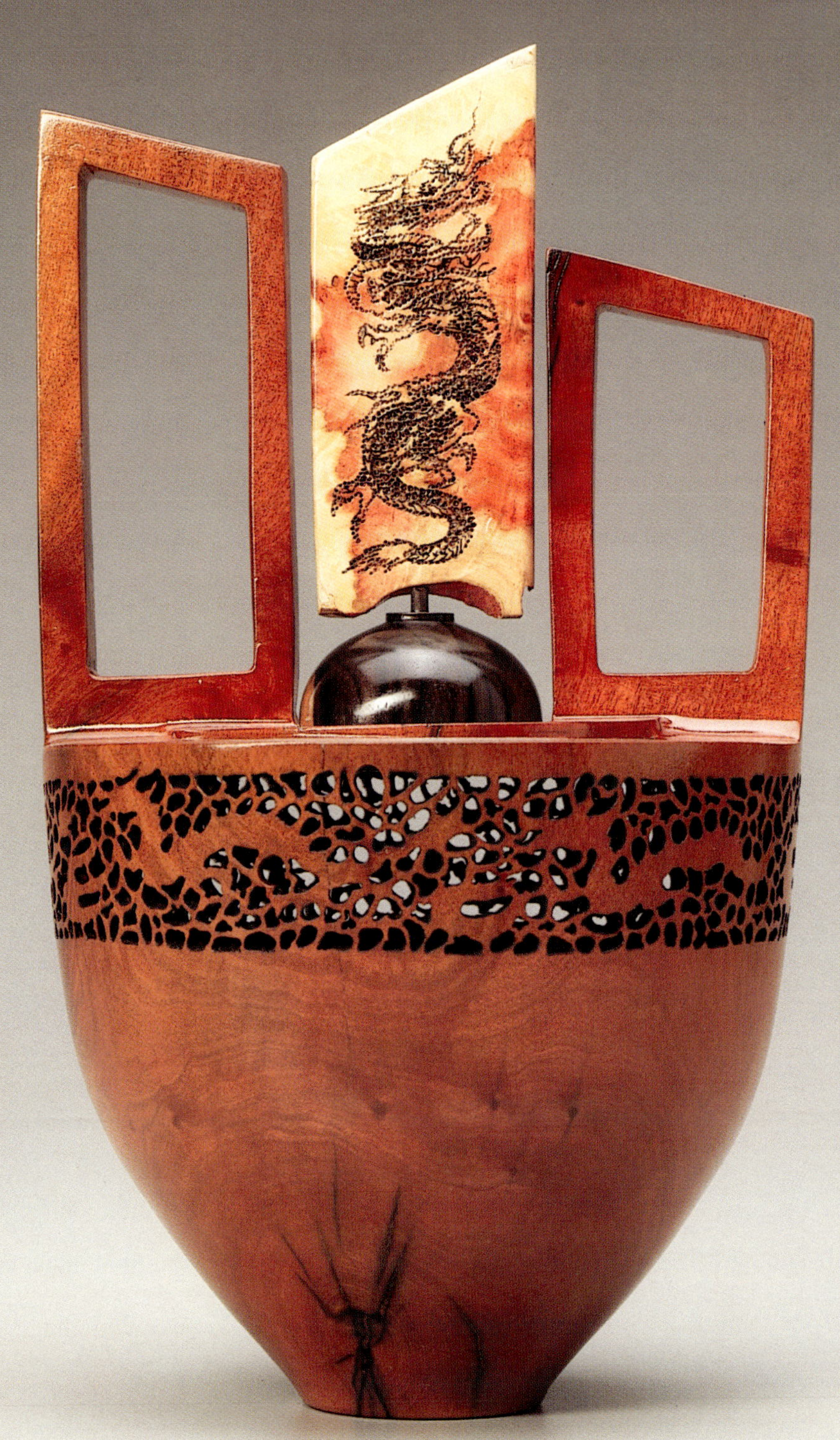

*Year of the Dragon*
2000
H: 9", Diam: 6"
Pink ivory, ebony and box elder burl

Binh Pho [*Illinois, USA – b. 1955*]

I design this vessel to co-celebrate the "Year of the Dragon" and the end of the millennium. The dragon is the only mythical animal of the twelve Zodiac signs, so strange things will happen this year. This event will happen once, so a one-of-a-kind vessel is required. The following "clip" is from the book, *Year of the Dragon, Legend & Lore*.

Chinese astrology is in practice far more subtle and complex than it first appears. The most curious thing to our eyes about the Zodiac is that, of the twelve signs, only one, the dragon, is what we consider a mythical beast. The presence of the dragon in the Zodiac shows how firmly the Chinese believe in the beast. To most of them the dragon is as real as other animals. It is unique only in being the one creature of their Zodiac credited with supernatural powers. So the Year of the Dragon, which recurs every twelve years, is considered particularly lucky, and children born in that year are to be blessed with health, wealth and a long life. It is also a good year for beginning new undertakings for everyone.

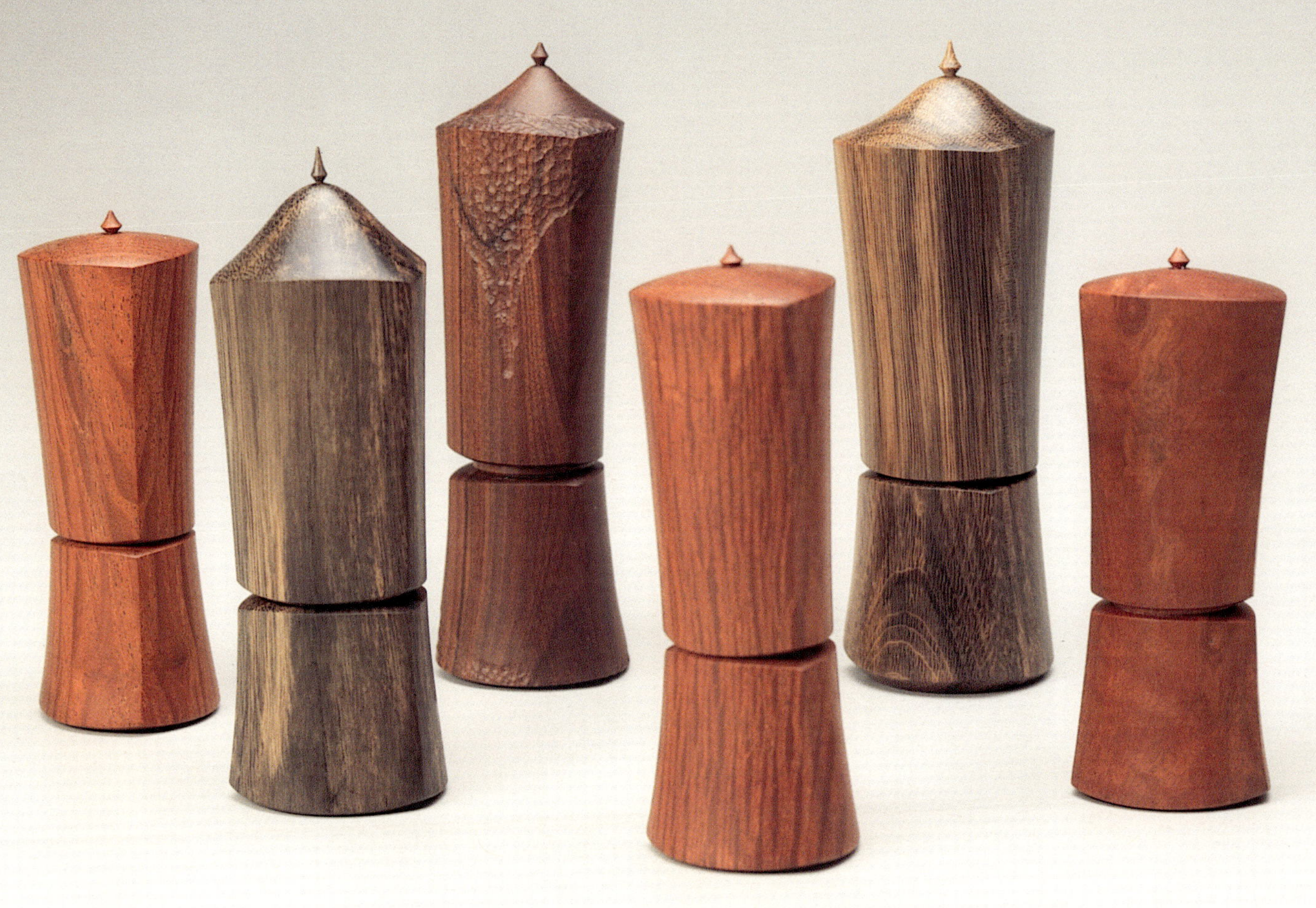

*Emperor Boxes*
2000
H: 4", W: 4 3/4", D: 1 3/4" each
She oak (casuarina fraseriana)
and red gum (eucalyptus camaldulensis)

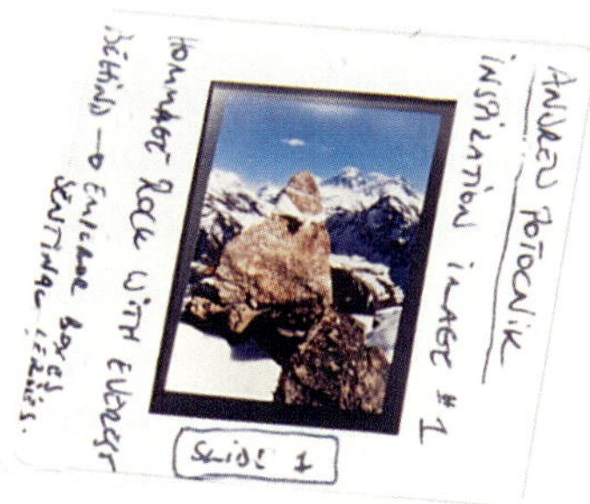


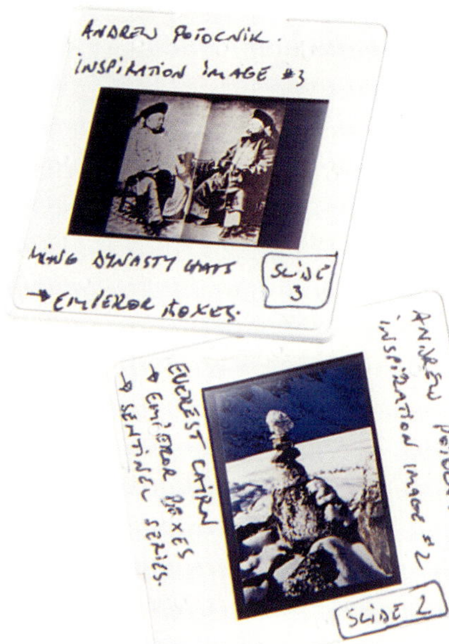


## Andrew Potocnik [*Australia – b. 1963*]

These pieces were inspired by homage rock formations and cairns from the Everest region of Nepal, and Ming Dynasty hats of China. Curves and points, typical of Ming hats, inspire the major form of these boxes; however, the stacked aspect of Buddhist cairns influenced the decision to define the "top" and "bottom" of the boxes.

Attracted to wood way back in high school, my fascination drew me to a teacher-training course where I could pursue my passion for wood at a tertiary level. During this period I began to specialize in turning and selling through outlets in Melbourne. Graduating, I quickly found work at a local secondary school and was able to establish a balance between teaching and developing my own work.

Still working from my core fascination for line and color, I draw inspiration and influence from a variety of cultures, most often observed first-hand during travels. Although my work rarely shows it, I am intrigued by textures, forms and decorative elements developed by indigenous peoples of the world.

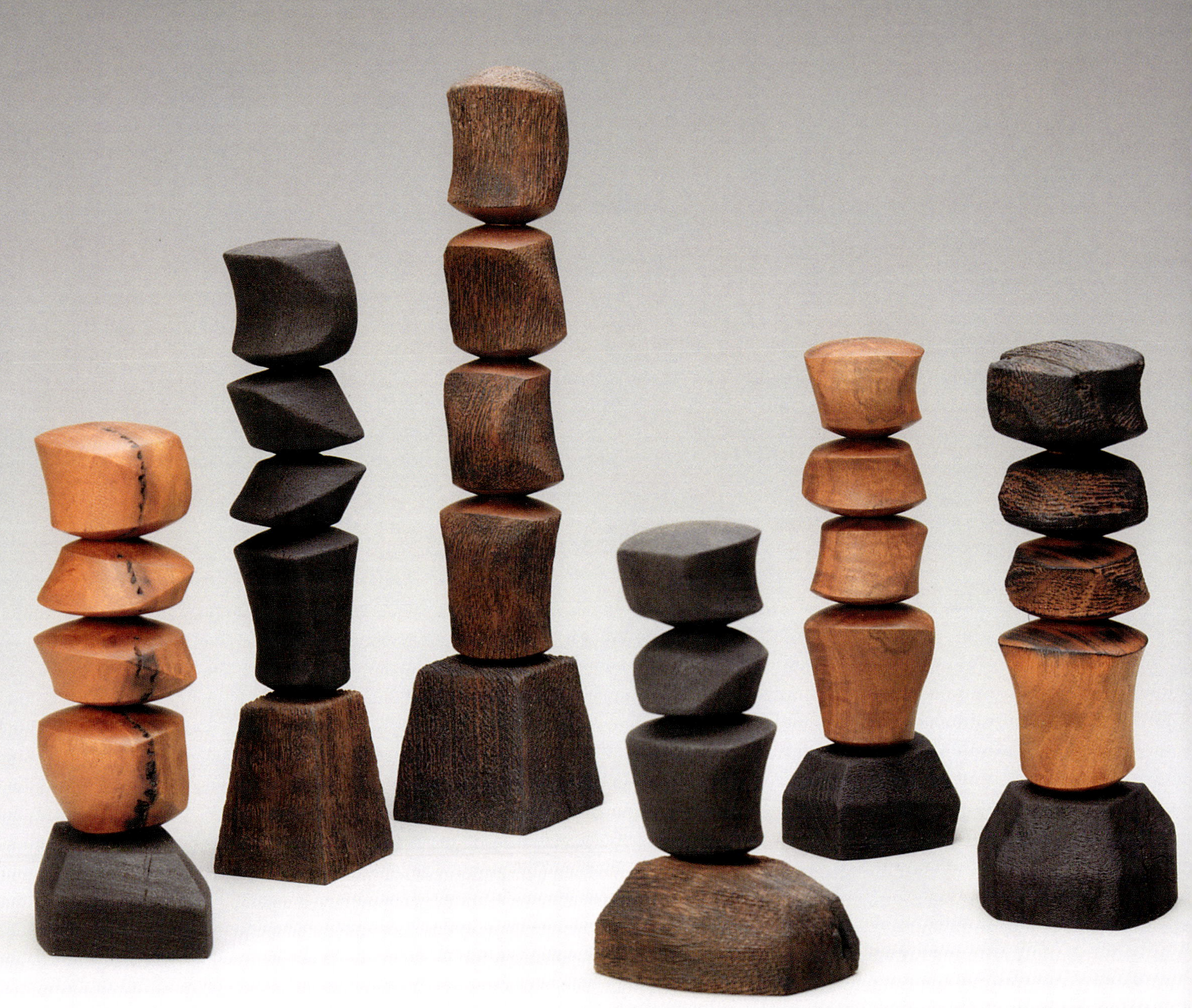

*Sentinel Series*
2000
H: 6", Diam: 2" tallest
Red gum (eucalyptus camaldulensis)

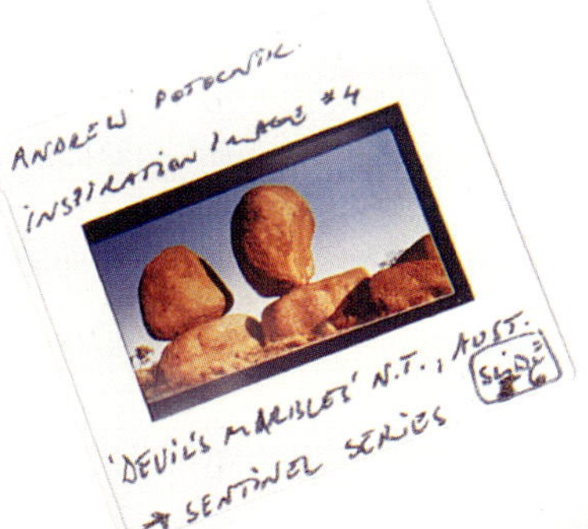


Andrew Potocnik [*Australia – b. 1963*]

This series of pieces was inspired mainly by rock formations I witnessed in Namibia, defying gravity, resting on tiny bases appearing ready to topple over. Similar formations exist in Central Australia, known as The Devil's Marbles. Other inspiration came from formations of rocks and cairns in the Everest region of Nepal where they serve as man's recognition of nature and a greater being.

Attracted to wood way back in high school, my fascination drew me to a teacher-training course where I could pursue my passion for wood at a tertiary level. During this period I began to specialize in turning and selling through outlets in Melbourne. Graduating, I quickly found work at a local secondary school and was able to establish a balance between teaching and developing my own work.

Still working from my core fascination for line and color, I draw inspiration and influence from a variety of cultures, most often observed first-hand during travels. Although my work rarely shows it, I am intrigued by textures, forms and decorative elements developed by indigenous peoples of the world.

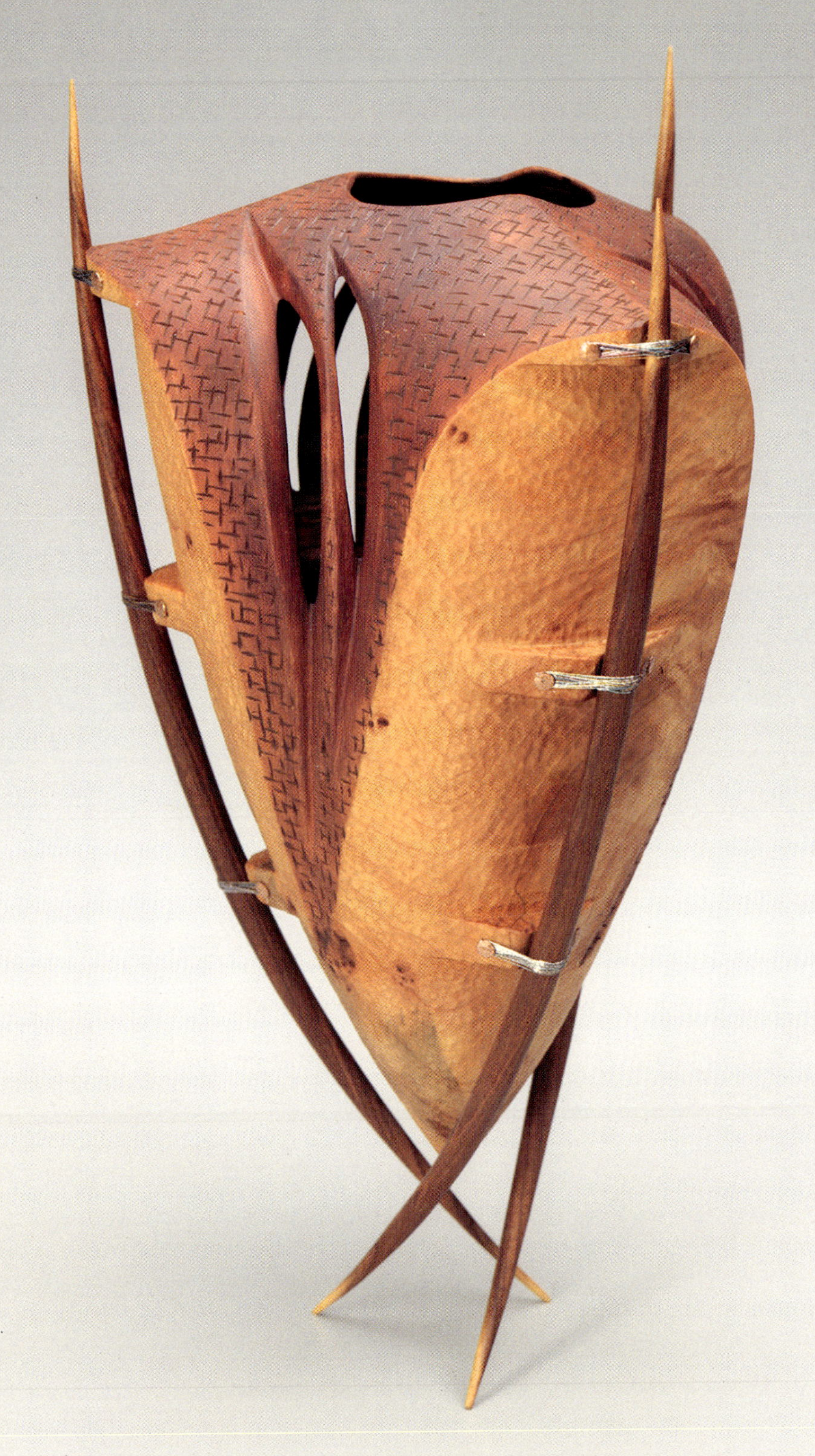

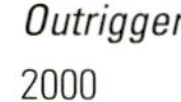

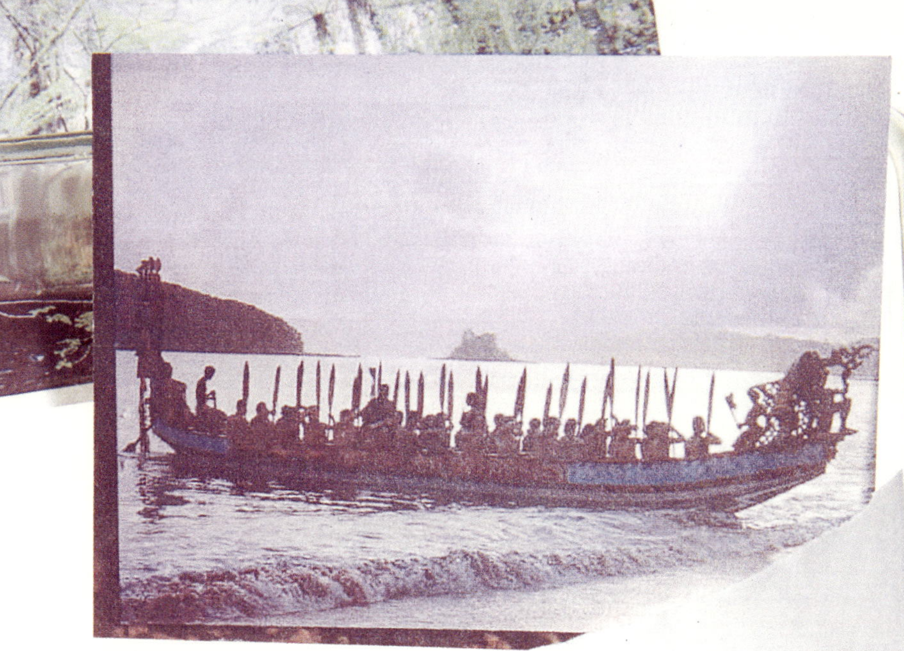

*Outrigger*
2000
H: 11", Diam: 5"
Macrocarpa, mulga, copper, metallic thread and acrylic paint

Graeme Priddle [*New Zealand – b. 1960*]

"Ka ngaro reoreo takata, kiki a manu, o atua, haruru tai ai."

(No human voice, only the voices of birds and gods, and the endless noise of the sea.) from "Homeplaces" by Ken Hulme

The patterns of the sea reflect patterns of the sky reflect patterns of the trees reflect patterns of life. The mighty Waka (canoe), carved from a single tree trunk with fire and stone adzes, fifty flashing paddles, and the warrior's chants send chills down the spine. Since I can remember, the sea has been my favorite place. Sailing, swimming, diving or just walking with the sand squeaking between my toes.

*Outrigger* is inspired by Polynesian outrigger canoe sails, which are triangular, woven and supported between two cantilevered spars. Other oceanic elements are represented by the textural effect on the natural wood, and the colored thread that lashes the vessel to the spars relates to the vivid colors of Paua shells that I find washed upon the beach. This piece is a progression of my **South Pacific Vessel** series which, like the ocean, its surroundings and inhabitants, is constantly evolving.

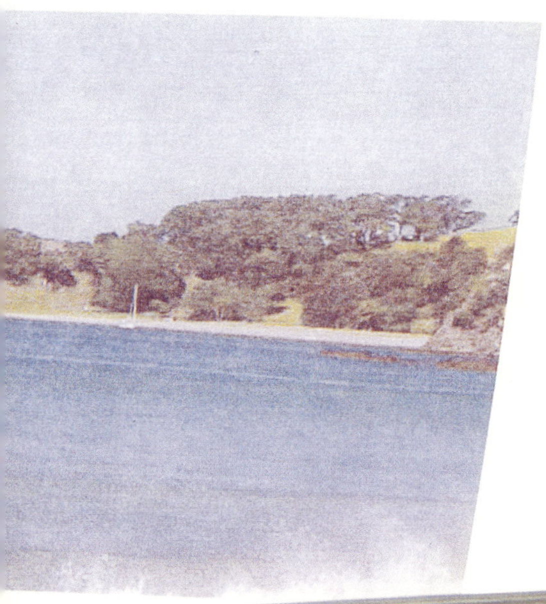

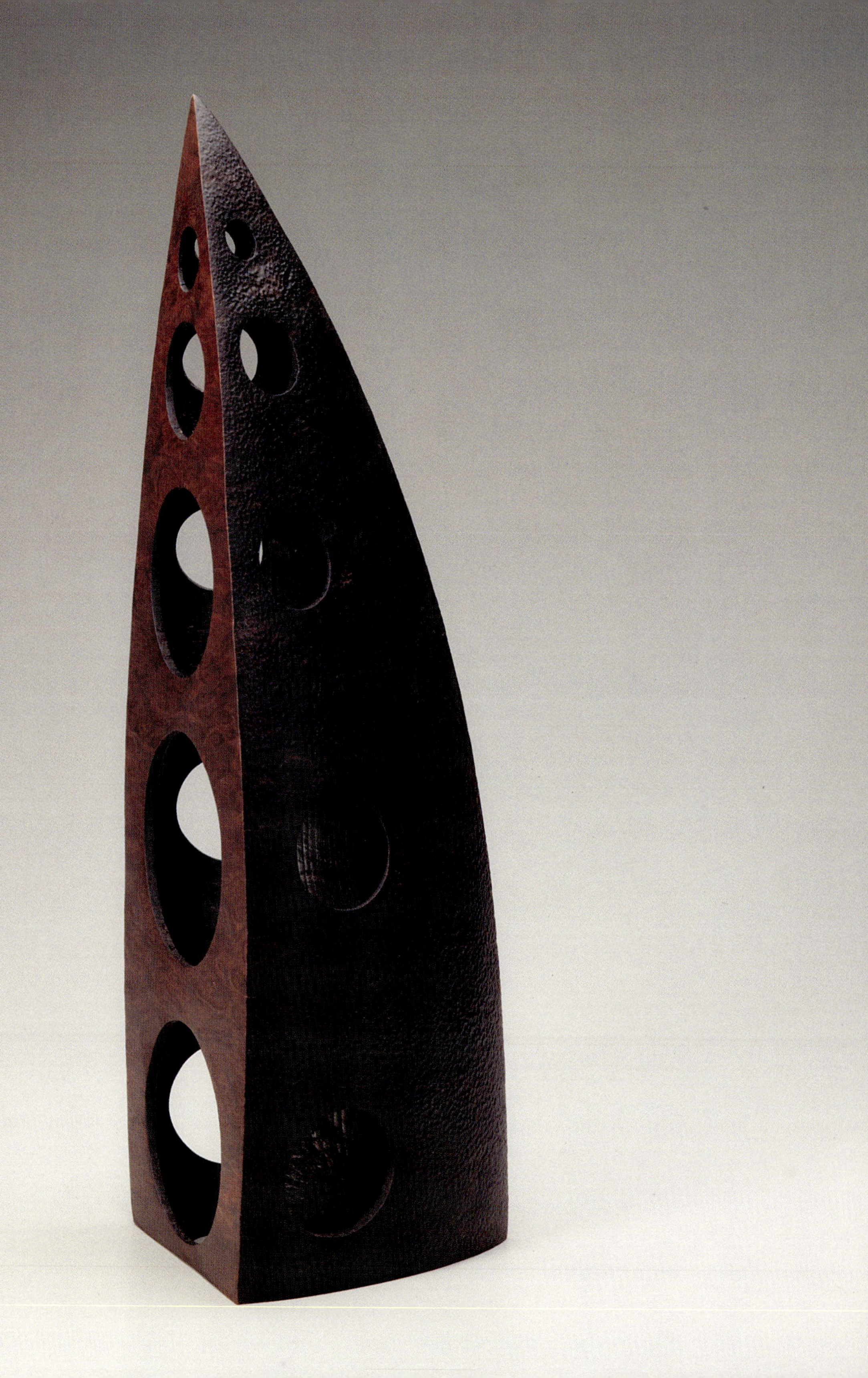

*Missing Home*
2000
H: 20", W: 6", D: 5"
Jarrah

## Graeme Priddle [*New Zealand – b. 1960*]

*Missing Home* is another new concept that emerged during the ITE program. While there is still the oceanic influence in the canoe form, the spaces inside the canoe conjure personal emotions, such as the homesickness I feel being separated from my family. The five spaces remind me of myself, my wife Maxine, and my three children, Jordan, Carly and Adrian. We are all very individual and in some ways independent, and allow each other the space for that. But at the same time, we are very close and our lives intersect and overlap in so many ways.

This piece also directly relates to me and my co-residents in the ITE program, who were my surrogate family for the duration of the program and the way our lives and work have interacted.

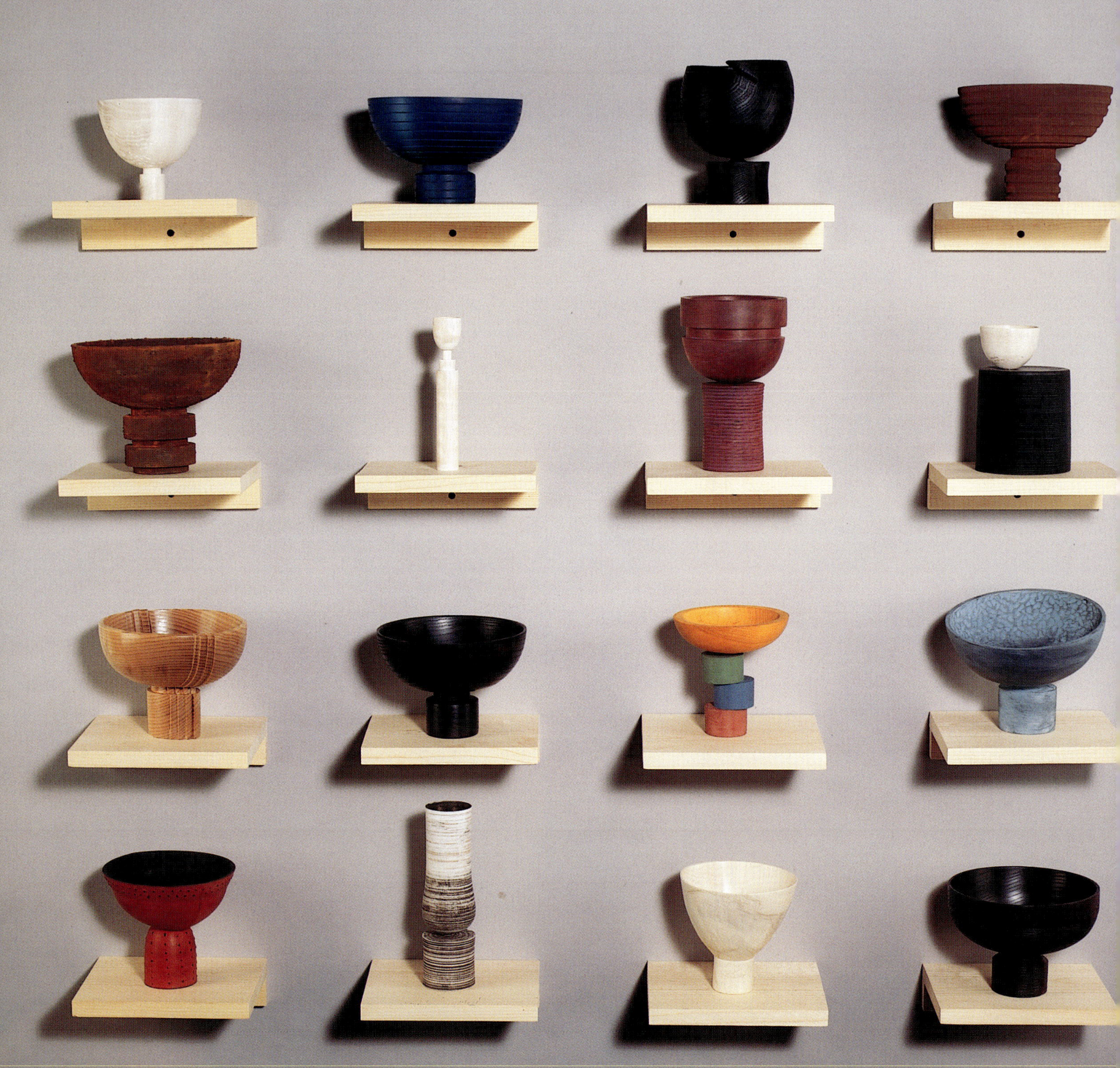

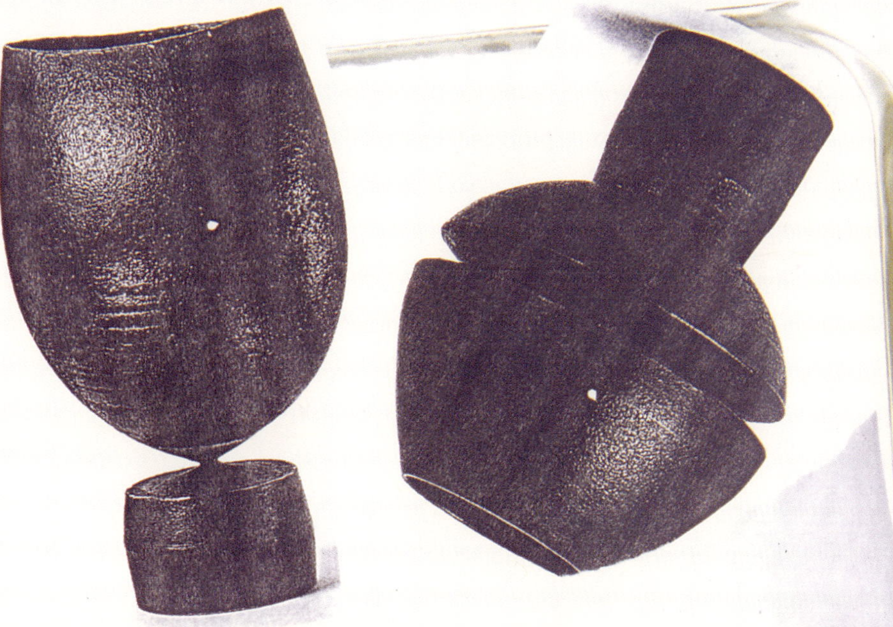

*Tribute: Hans Coper*
2000
H: 54", W: 47", D: 8"
Wood, paint and dye

Merryll Saylan [*California, USA – b. 1936*]

I saw a form of Hans Coper's that I thought was so interesting. Exploring form, changing some aspect of it, even a different base. Exploration of a form. I'd started working that way with the *Color Theory* pieces. The concept of clean, simple forms that change through color, surface, textural variations, and even with different species of wood.

Now I want to push these forms further. What would happen if the base dominated and there was only a teeny bowl on top, or the bowl was slipping off the base, or it was taller/shorter? I particularly like the juxtaposition when one piece is next to another so that a viewer is able to see these changes and explore the variety. Minimally, the installation would include 15 pieces with up to 20 pieces mounted. I give both figures because I don't really know how this exploration will completely go — 15 may just not be enough.

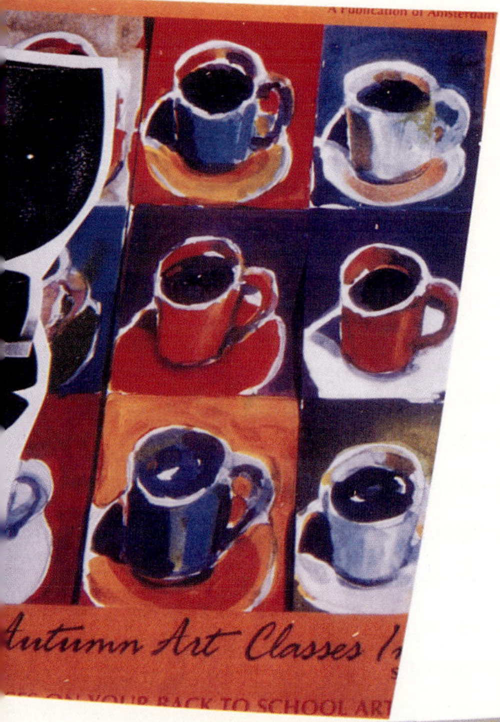


I have also included as reference a copy of a painting of teacups — I love those with their variety of colors. There is power in the number and the repetition of form. Morandi's work is another influence; his years of drawing and studying simple white forms — their shadows, their details, their differences.

I heard an interview recently with the young author of a book, *White Teeth*. She talked of sameness — of things and of people — yet within that is infinite variety. Somehow I thought of my bowls.

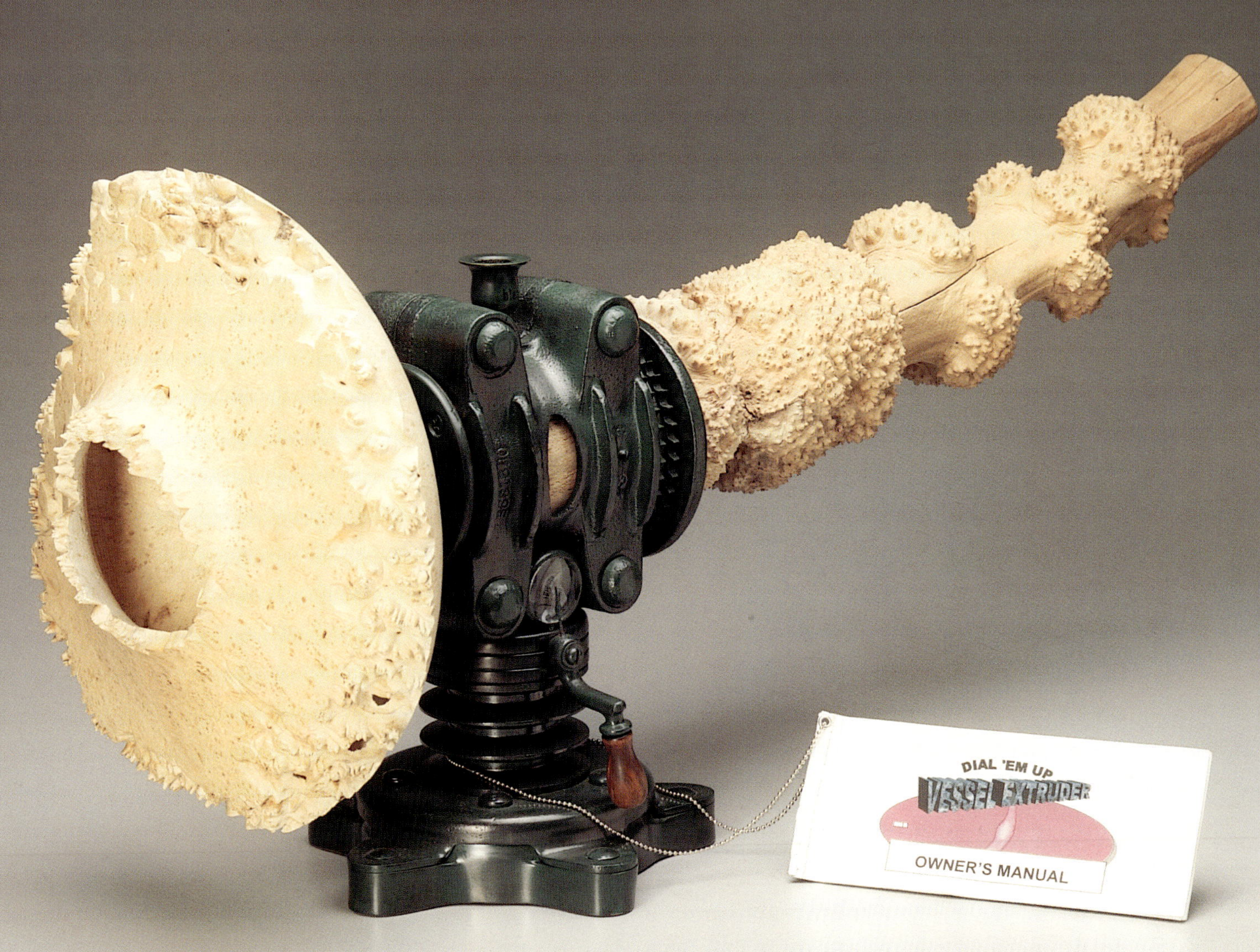
DIAL 'EM UP
VESSEL EXTRUDER
OWNER'S MANUAL

*Dial-em–up Vessel Extruder*
2000
H: 17", W: 34", D: 14"
Rhododendron burl, maple burl, steel and paper

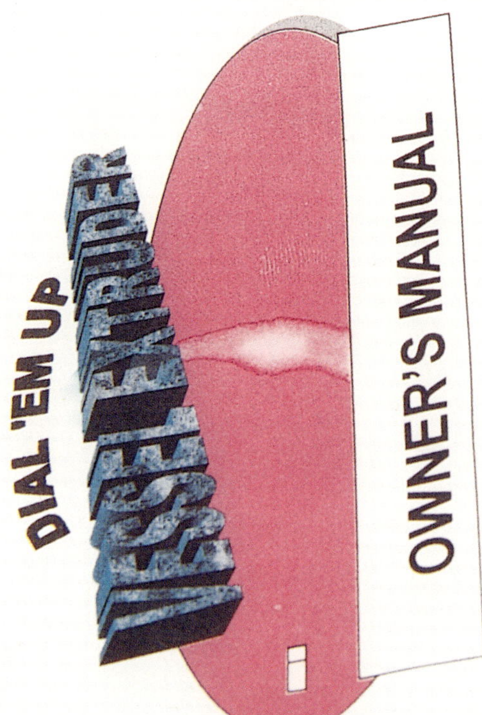


David Sengel [*North Carolina, USA – b. 1951*]

In the transformation of raw material into "art," the lathe has traditionally been the medium, in this field, through which form is created or altered. I fabricated from found metal a machine, a fantasy "lathe attachment," that automatically recreates the work of different wood turners at the change of a dial.

The inspiration for this conceptual piece is the woodturning movement itself and its progression from industrial/functional/multiple to include the artistic vessel and then the sculptural. Some issues involved in that progression include originality, style, imitation, esthetics, process and technology. I was able to have fun making this piece, especially with the ideas that came for the "Owner's Manual." The camaraderie among turners, collectors, gallery owners, the shared struggles of trying to make good work, and the ability to poke fun at ourselves are all the "subject" here. There is also a tongue-in-cheek reference to the industry that supplies the tools and materials we use, and to that portion of the public that has difficulty understanding what goes into making art.

*A note about what one cannot see in the picture: Both wood pieces are on bearings and do turn. The dial can be set to various well-known names in woodturning. The owner's manual includes spoof endorsements by Jordan, Sfirri and Ellsworth, as well as various optional attachments, warnings, instructions, etc.

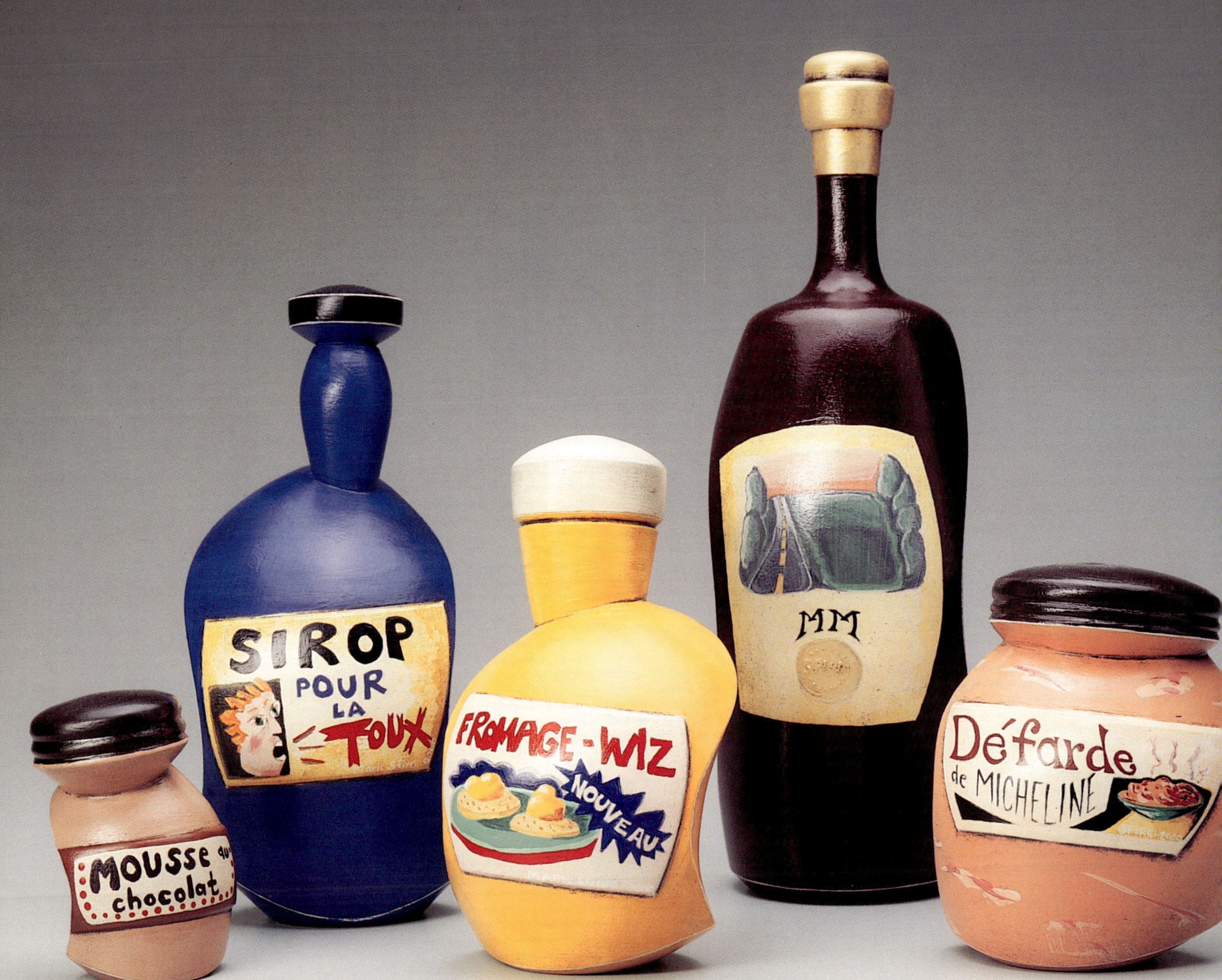
MOUSSE au
chocolat
SIROP
POUR
LA
TOUX
FROMAGE-WIZ
NOUVEAU
MM
Défarde
de MICHELINE

*French Vessel Series*
2000
H: 13 1/2", W: 26", D: 6"
Poplar and paint

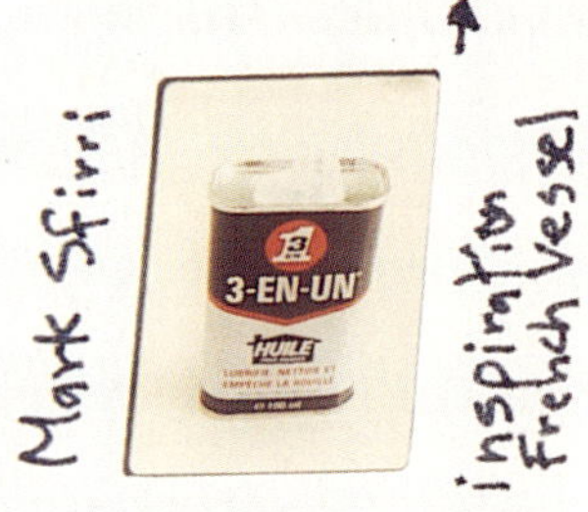


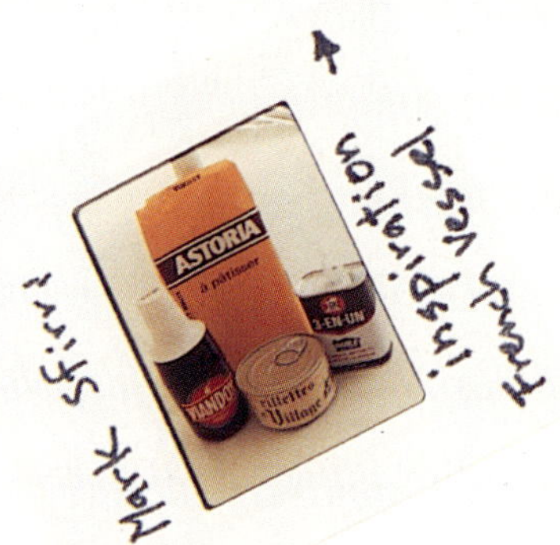


MARK SFIRRI [*Pennsylvania, USA – b. 1952*]

I have been intrigued when traveling by many aspects of different cultures: the architecture, the landscape, the language, the food, the customs. Wherever I go, the grocery store is a highlight. I see rows of things for sale and have only a bit of an idea what is in the colorful packages and I am challenged. I start by looking at how things are grouped and trying to pick out key words. The colors, the graphics, and the contents are often different from what I'm accustomed to in the United States. My *French Vessel Series* grew out of this fascination with unfamiliar groceries. They are a continuation of my experimentation with multi-axis turning but incorporate my interest in graphics, and are my first venture into the "vessel" form. I am inspired by the everyday vessels of industrialized culture: the bottle, the jar, and the can.

This series is also sort of a social commentary. In the unlikely event that the United States should ever succeed in the French food market, I'm sure the makers of Cheez Wiz® would be delighted to offer "Fromage-Wiz" to French consumers. This is a foreigner's perspective, meant with the utmost respect for the French food culture and with somewhat less respect for American food culture.

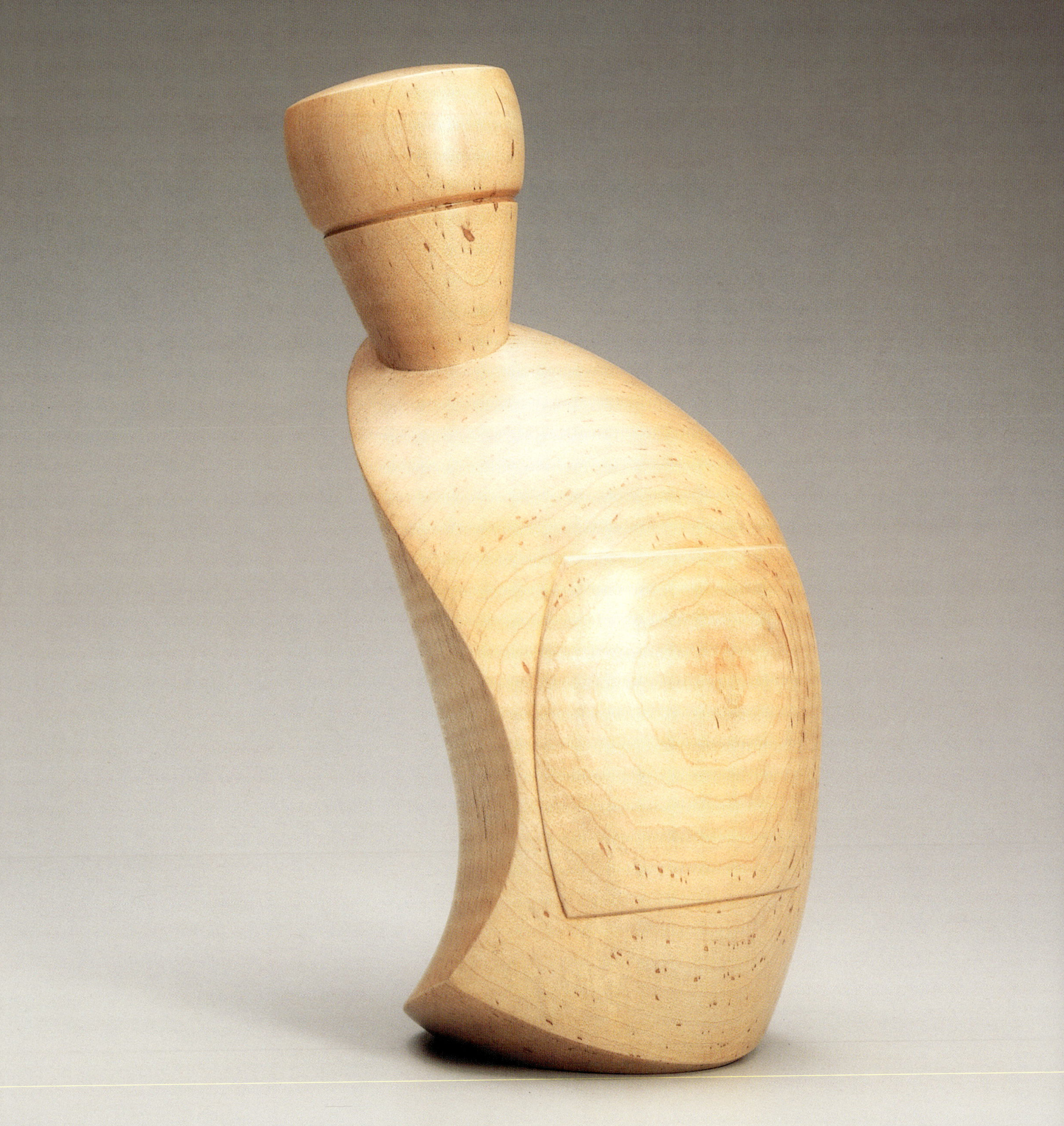

*The Natural Vessel Series*
2000
H: 11 3/4", W: 6", D: 5"
Curly maple

MARK SFIRRI [*Pennsylvania, USA – b. 1952*]

My new **Vessel** series is a continuation of my experimentation with multi-axis turning, achieved by calculating the axes mathematically, and it is my first venture into the vessel form. I was again inspired by the everyday vessels of industrialized culture: the bottle, the jar, and the can. This "vessel" is an outgrowth of my painted *French Vessel Series*, rendered this time as a natural wood object. I chose to raise the label to give importance to the form. This general sense of a bottle is intended to be a contradiction within itself. It is an interpretation of an everyday, throwaway object, but it is made of one of the most precious woods on earth. I had the piece of wood from which the vessel was made for over twenty years, and this bottle seemed like the perfect form to bring out in it

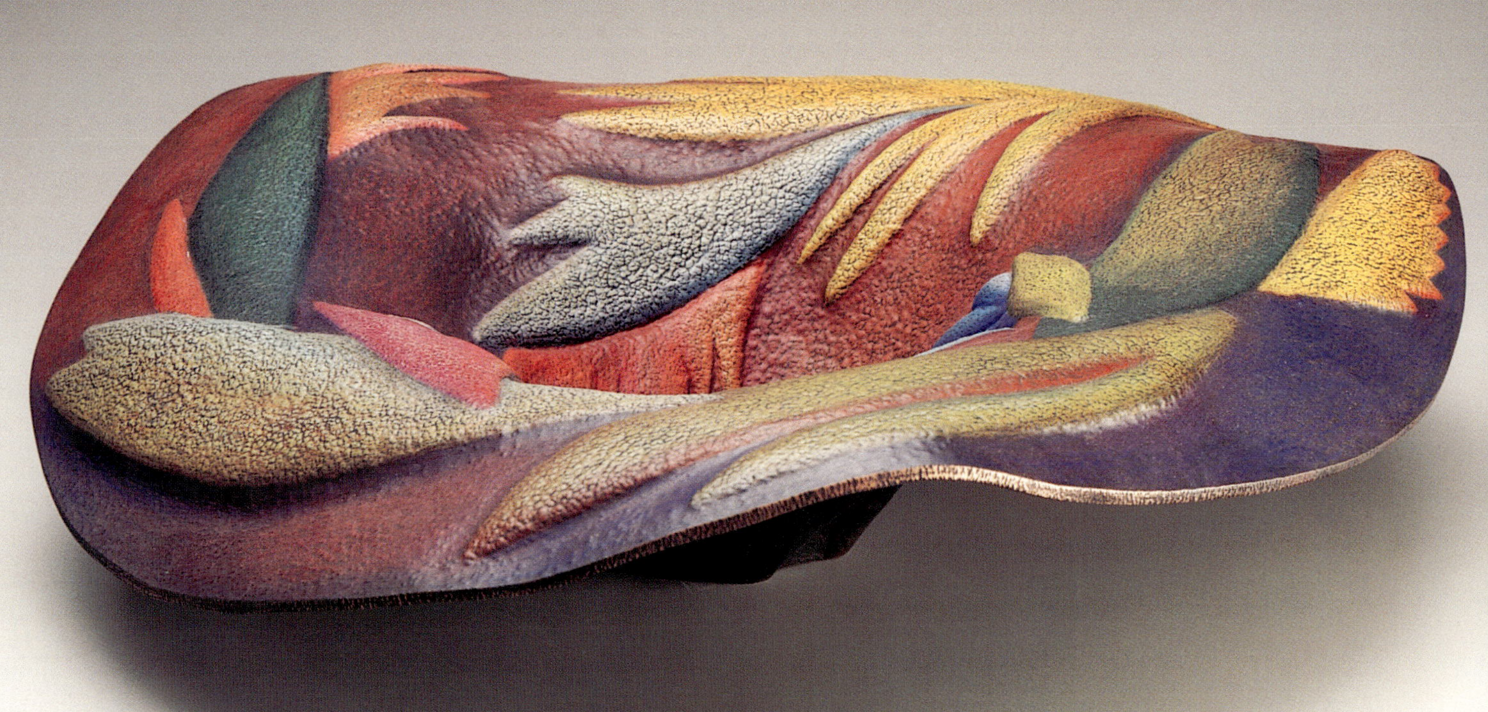

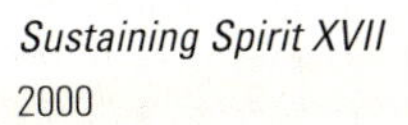

*Sustaining Spirit XVII*
2000
H: 6″, Diam: 23″
Copper, patina and Prismacolor pencils

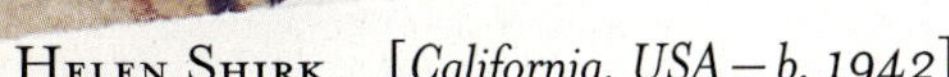

## Helen Shirk [*California, USA – b. 1942*]

Landscape has strongly influenced my hollowware for the last 14 years. The diversity of the natural habitat and vegetation around my home in southern California provides a rich resource from which to draw inspiration and meaning for my work. My interest in brilliantly colored and textured forms reflects the lasting impact of time spent in Western Australia; one of the richest and most varied wildflower areas on the world. The unusual structure and color of the bird of paradise flower in my backyard was the inspiration for this piece. With it, I tried to create an environment of mystery and vitality. The large circular scale of the piece allows the viewer to enter it more completely and explore its sensuousness, strangeness, and intimate details.

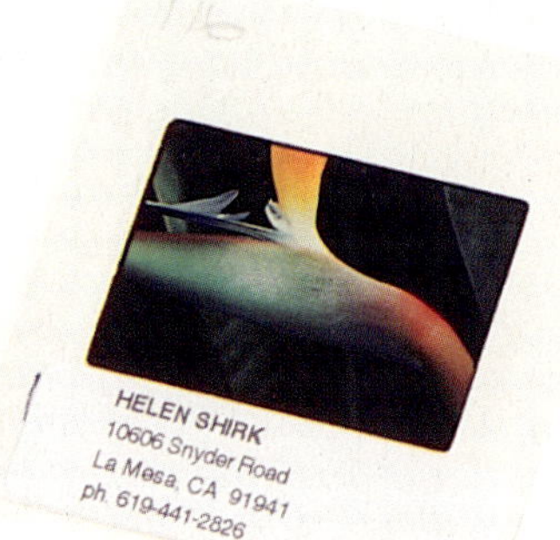

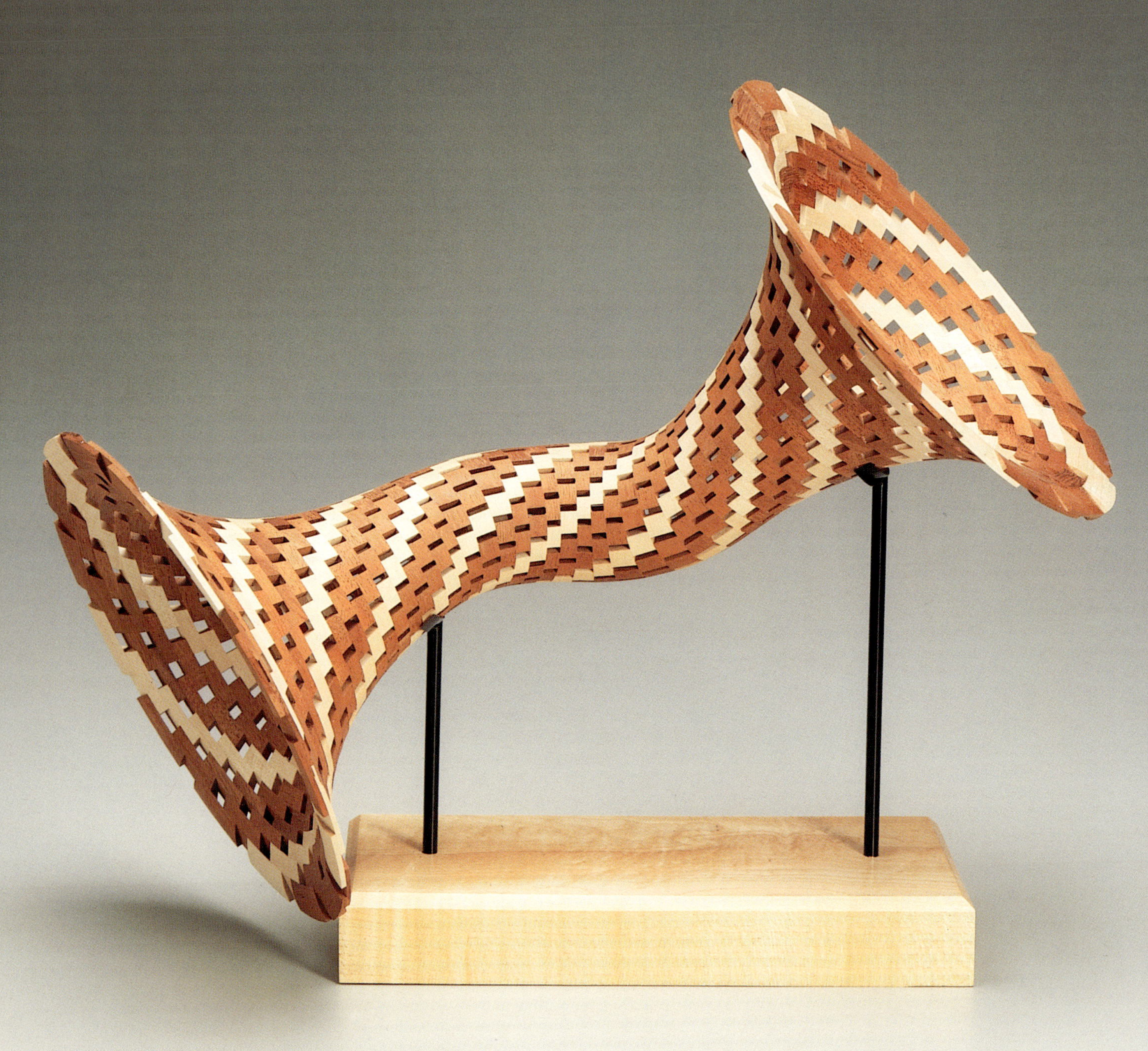

*Down the Rabbit Hole*
2000
H: 13", W: 16", D: 9"
Mahogany, maple and brass

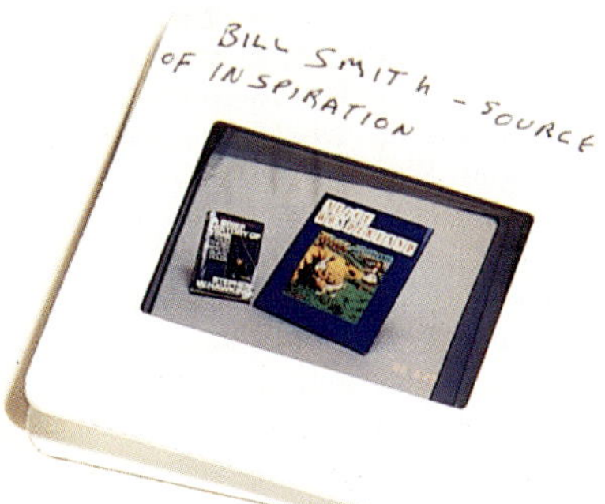


WILLIAM SMITH [*Pennsylvania, USA – b. 1947*]

My work often provides for many hours of contemplation during the glue-up stage. This quiet and mentally uncluttered time allows my mind to wander and create associations between the developing piece and my "mind's eye view" of mythical places and imaginary things. As this piece developed, my thoughts drifted to my daughter's book *Alice In Wonderland*. Alice started in a normal, sane universe but as she traveled down her rabbit hole she found a distorted and impossible reality. Similarly, my rabbit hole begins with a normal turning that evolves into a meandering convoluted turning impossibility.

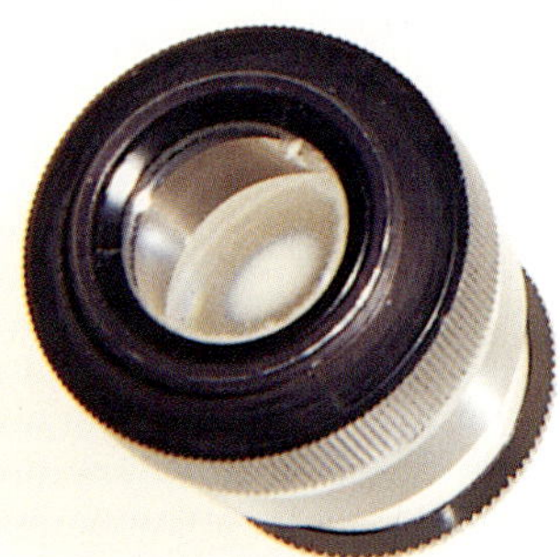

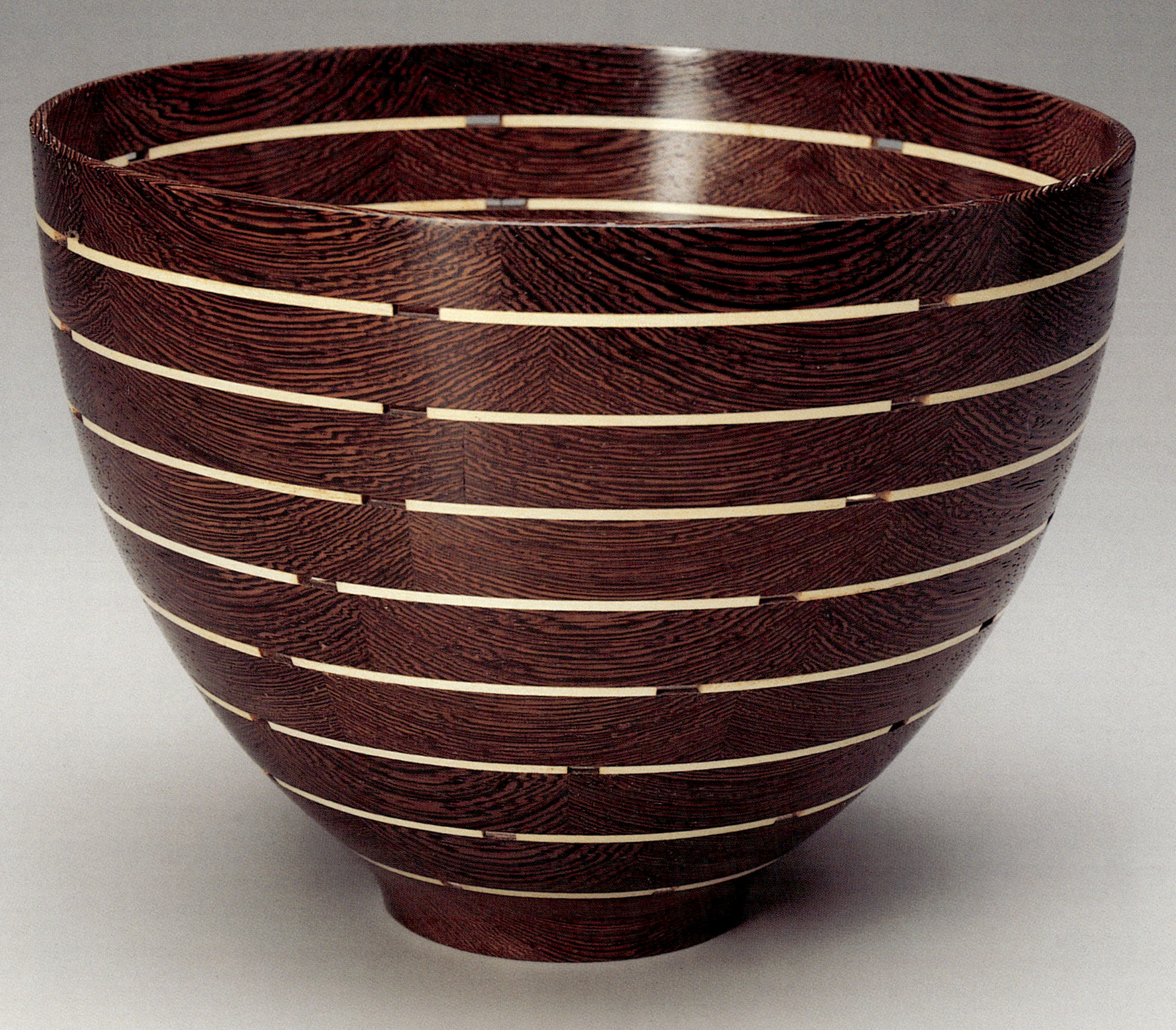

*Untitled*
1999
H: 7 1/4", Diam: 9 7/8"
Wenge and holly

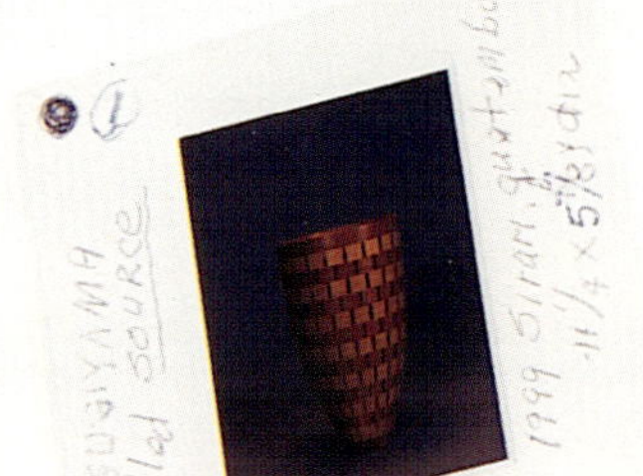


Yosh Sugiyama [*California, USA – b. 1932*]

I first started making turnings with open segmentation a little over twelve years ago. The inspiration for making turnings in this manner came after seeing a concrete decorative wall where each concrete block was separated by an open space giving it a trellis-like appearance. Since then, I have used this technique for making objects in a wide variety of shapes and forms. About a year ago, I began experimenting with designs by combining open segmentation with the traditional method of making segmented turnings; where the segments are assembled tightly one against the other.

A vase I made of sirari and guatambu was the precursor of the wenge and holly vessel. Wide bands of contrasting wood with open segmentation forms the primary design element. In the wenge and holly vessel, the segments of wenge were glued tightly together as in traditional segmented turning. A thin layer of open segmented holly separates each layer of wenge. Although the wenge dominates the piece with its dark color and strong grain pattern, the eye is nevertheless drawn to the open spaces in the holly that spiral around the vessel.

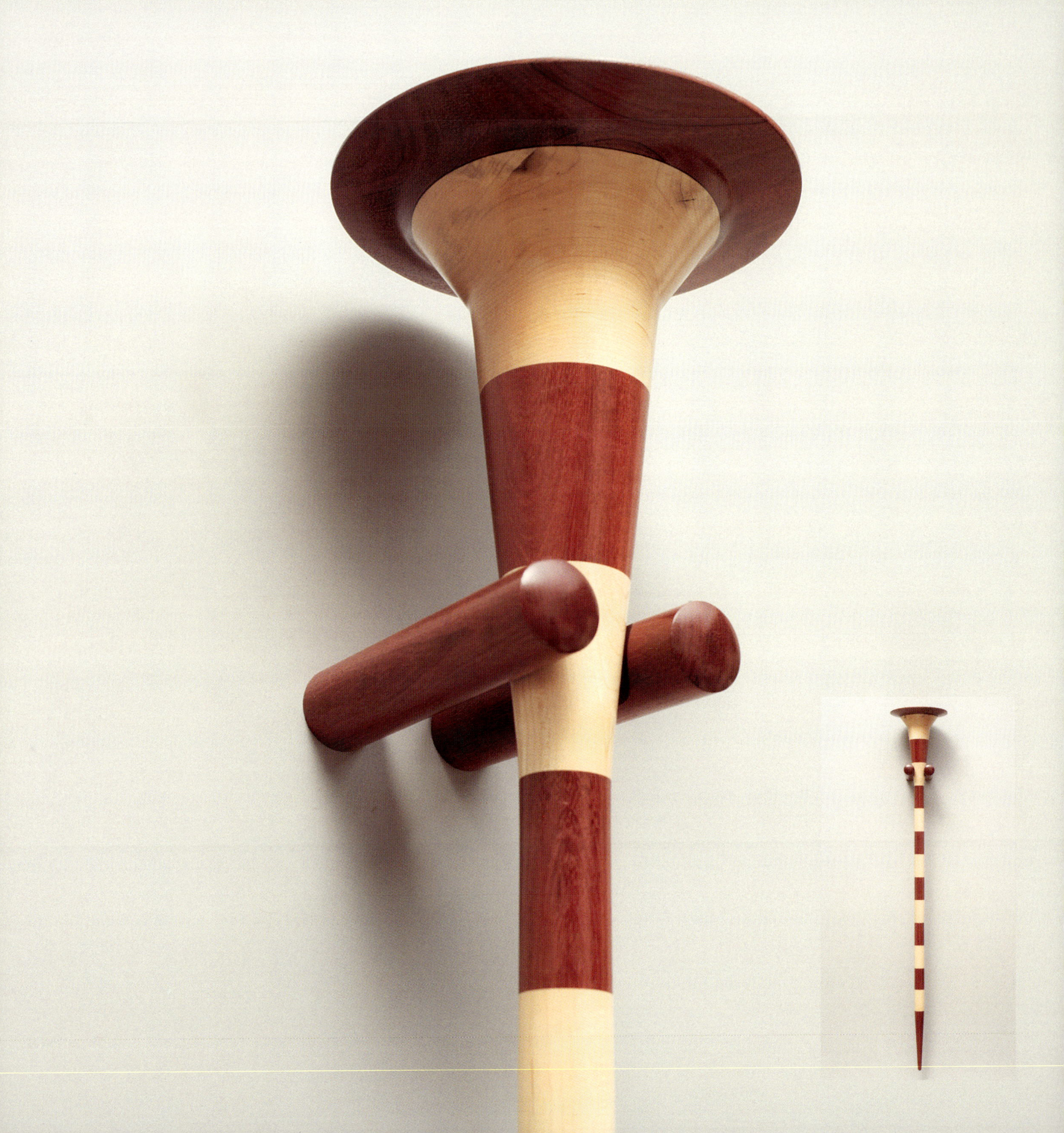

*Liar's Poker*
1999
H: 61", W: 9 3/4", D: 10"
Maple, purple heart and veneer ebony

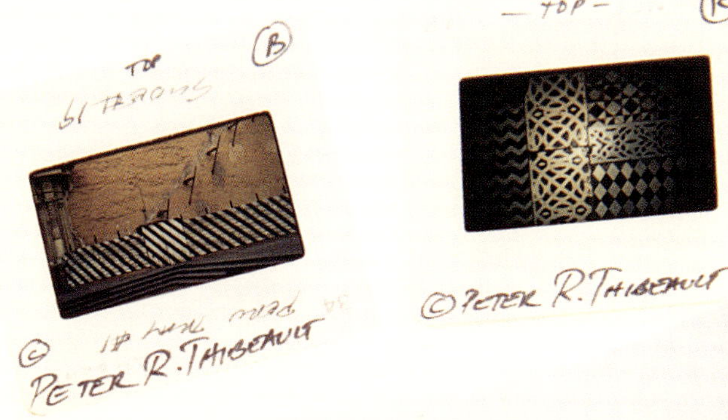


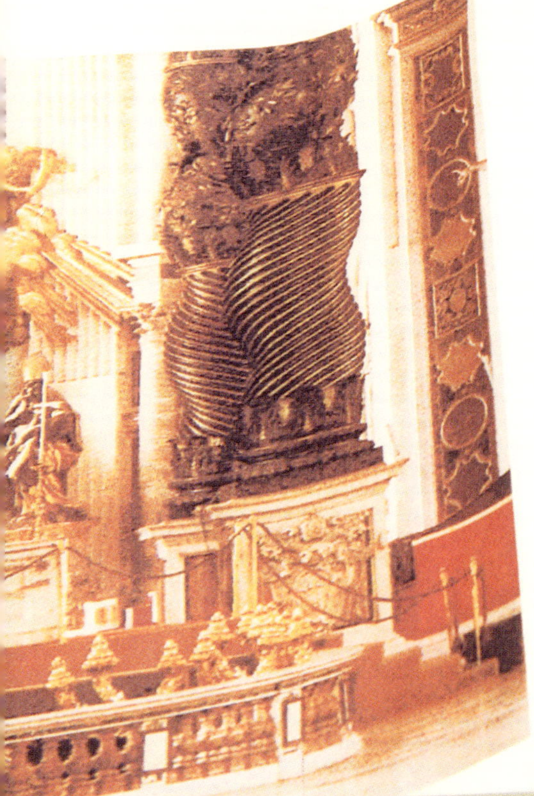

Peter R. Thibeault [*Massachusetts, USA – b. 1947*]

This piece grew out of a need to explore form development that reflected my life-long preoccupation with towers, elongated forms and vivid graphic contrasts. I have traveled extensively, always with a camera in hand. My intention has always been to explore and drink in the travel experience without preconceived ideas. What seems to come out over and over as I pore over the slides that I have taken is a consistent recording of color juxtapositions, simple structures and architectural details.

A few years ago, in reaction to an extensive period of commission production, I found myself longing to explore a more simplified form "vocabulary" and to combine it with my love of a strong graphic "read." This is one of the first major pieces to come from this exploration. It started with a glued-up bowl blank that had been kicking around my shop for years. It reminded me of a jester's mace, thus the title.

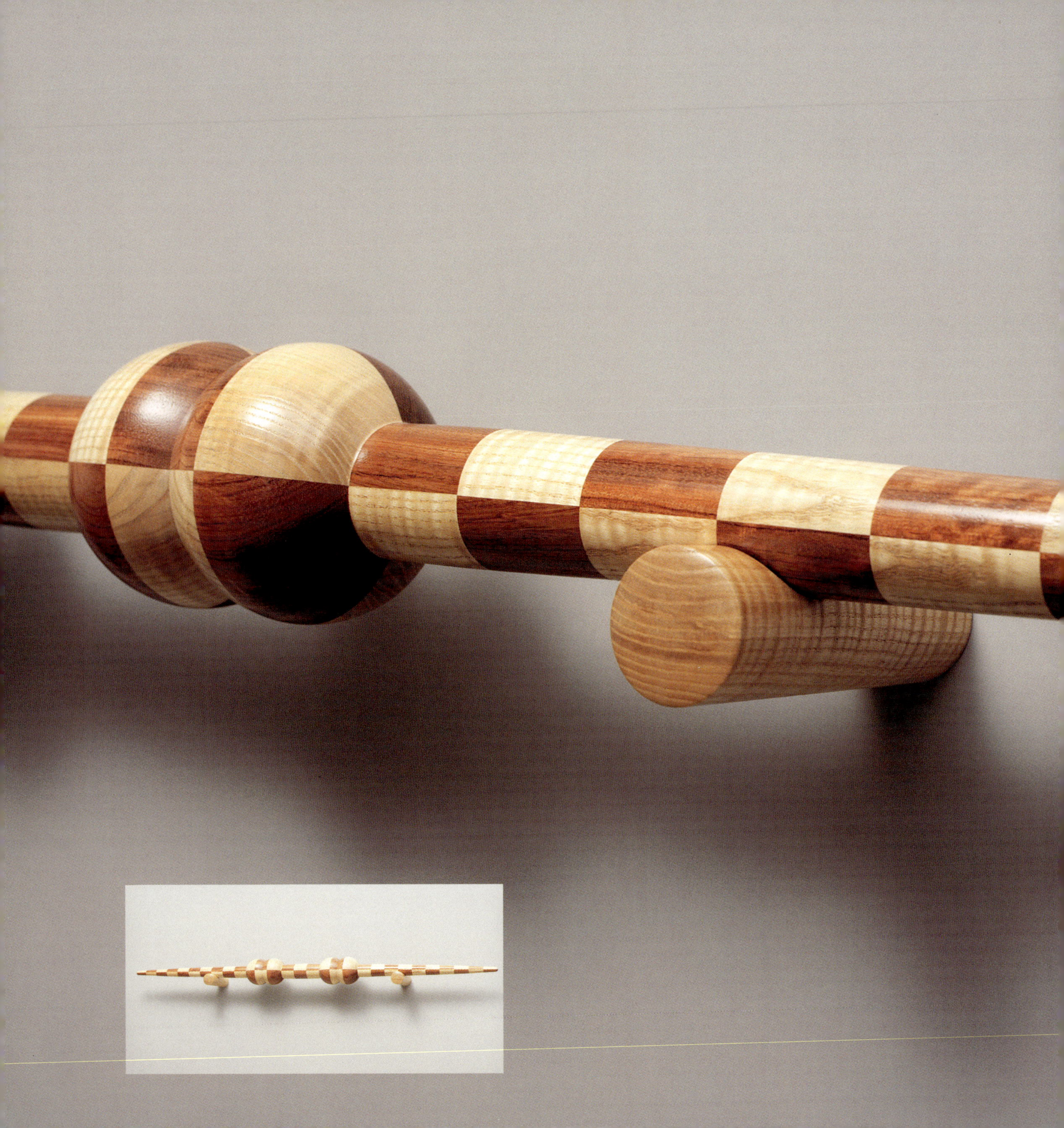

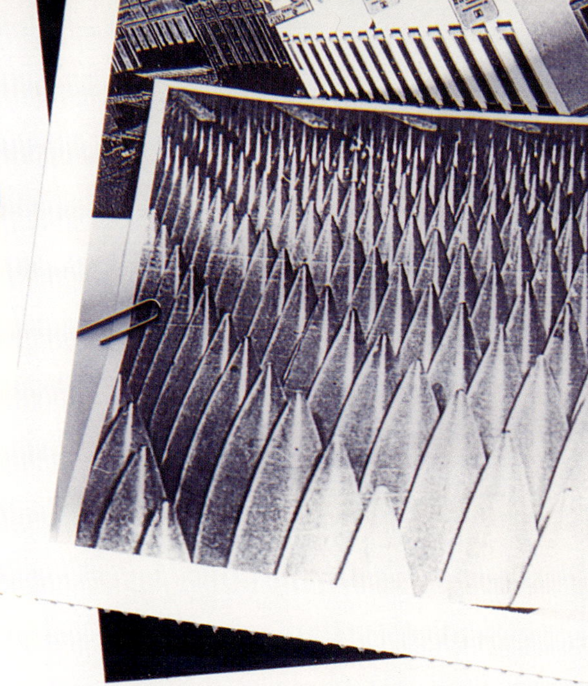

*Recumbant Monolith*
1999
H: 5 3/4", W: 79 1/2", D: 13 1/2"
Curly ash and bubinga

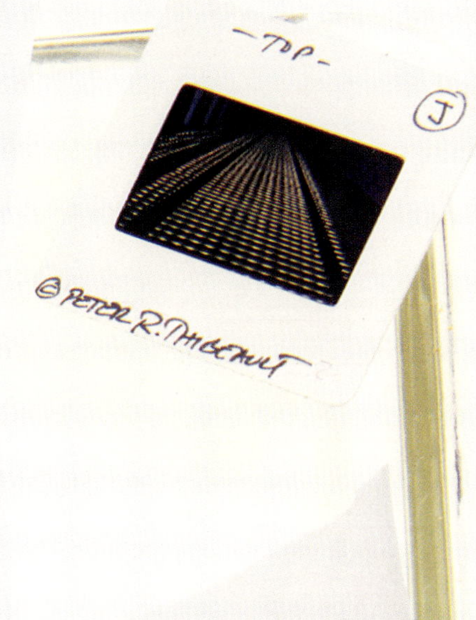


Peter R. Thibeault [*Massachusetts, USA – b. 1947*]

This piece was inspired by one of my favorite architects, Joze Plecnik, a Slovenian architect who died in 1957. He also was intrigued with the simple geometry of long thin forms. The title and horizontal configuration are lifted from his granite Slavata monument in the Rampart Garden of Prague Castle in Czechoslovakia. It is one of many destinations I have yet to visit.

The mounting for this piece was originally from the top of a pedestal. It was only after this and the other two pieces in the show were built that I devised the wall-mounted posts. (*Liar's Poker* was originally to be placed horizontally like this one but when it was to be exhibited in a previous show, the wall wasn't long enough.) The graphics are reminiscent of missiles, aircraft and the type of markings seen on crash test vehicles. It also reminds me of several olives speared by a toothpick.

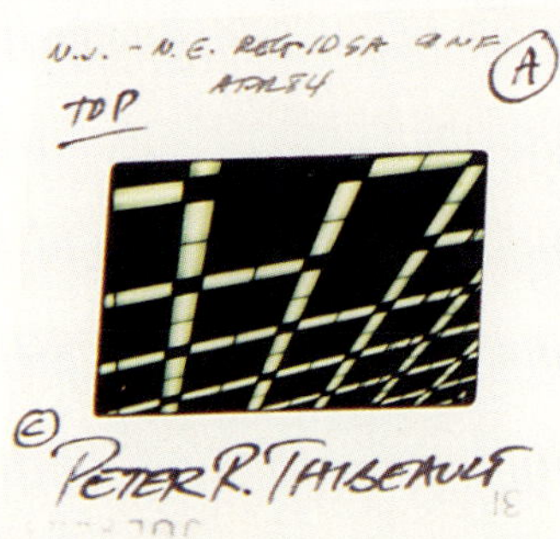

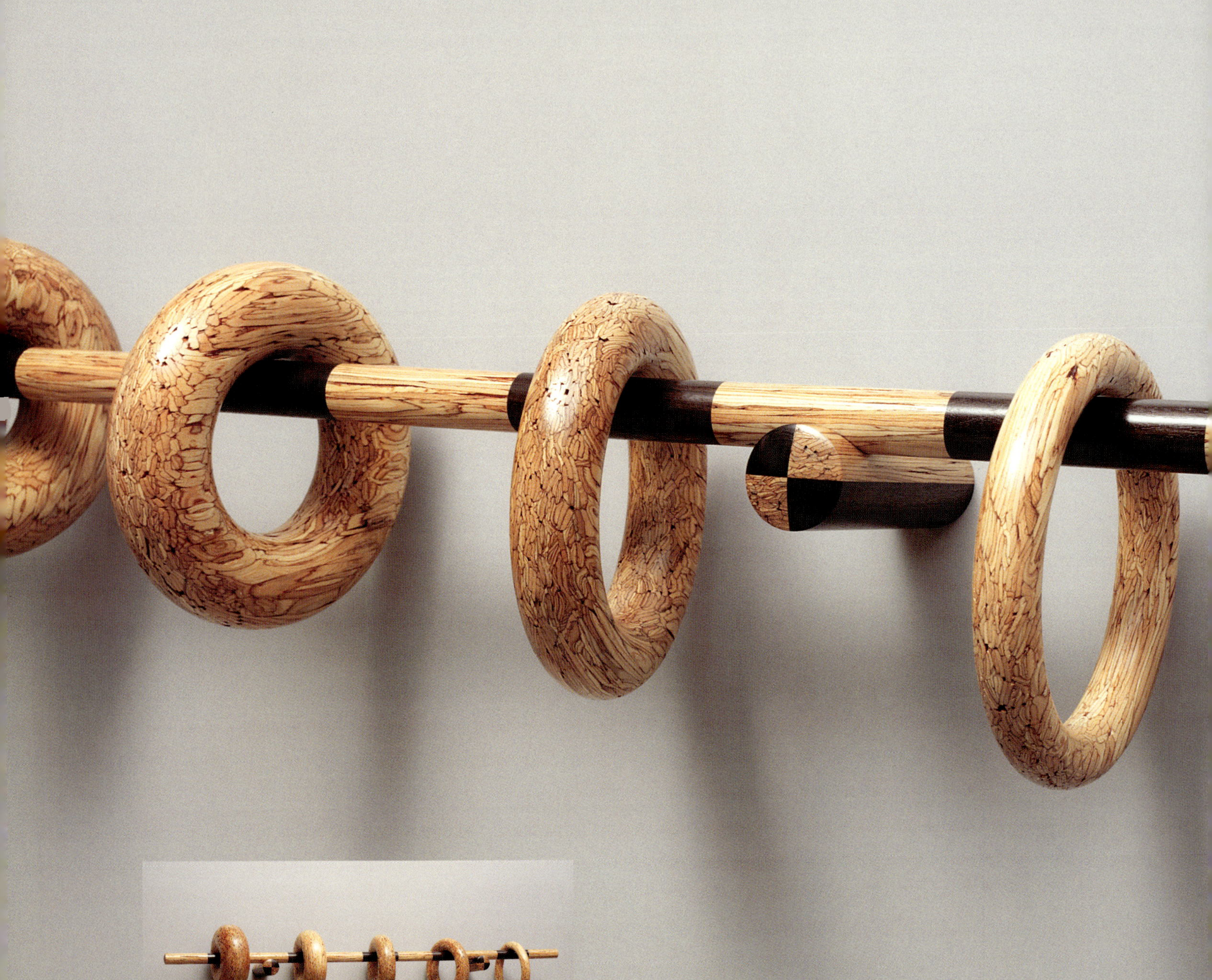

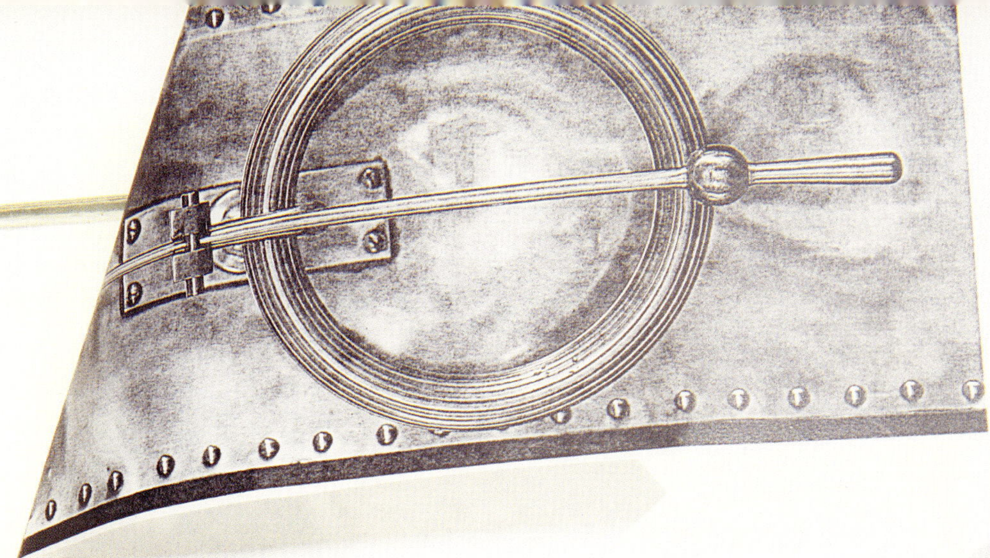

*Toroidal Entropy*
1999
H: 15 1/2", W: 76 1/4", D: 13 1/2"
Ebonized walnut and engineered lumber

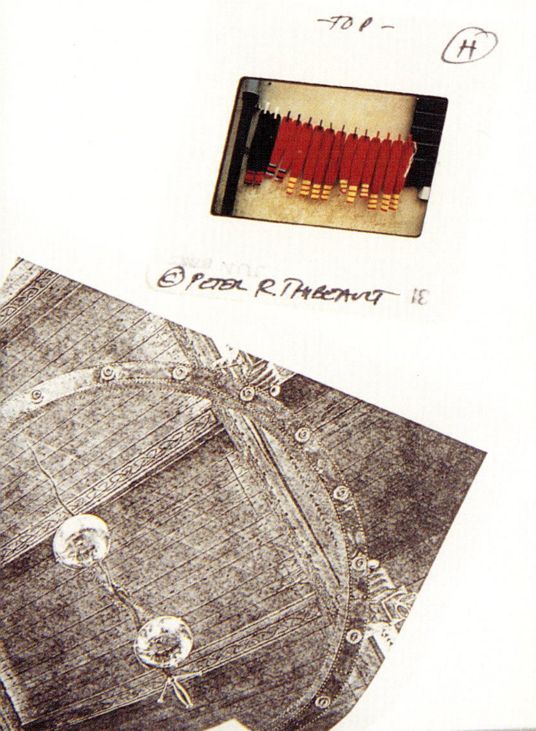


Peter R. Thibeault [*Massachusetts, USA – b. 1947*]

This piece combines my interest in graphics, geometry and curious new materials. The donut shapes are turned from segments of an engineered beam called parallel strand lumber. It was created to replace old-growth timber.

The darker portions of the piece are of a material called "Ebonex." This was created by dyeing walnut with a proprietary process that turned it black throughout. It was created in the wake of waning supplies of ebony. I enjoy finding new and interesting materials and seeking simple forms that enhance their natural properties. The "donuts" started out as a series that was to be stacked on a vertical cone. When they were all turned, the rod hangings configuration came to me after I envisioned them to be a series of "Life Savers®" slowly dissolving in my mouth.

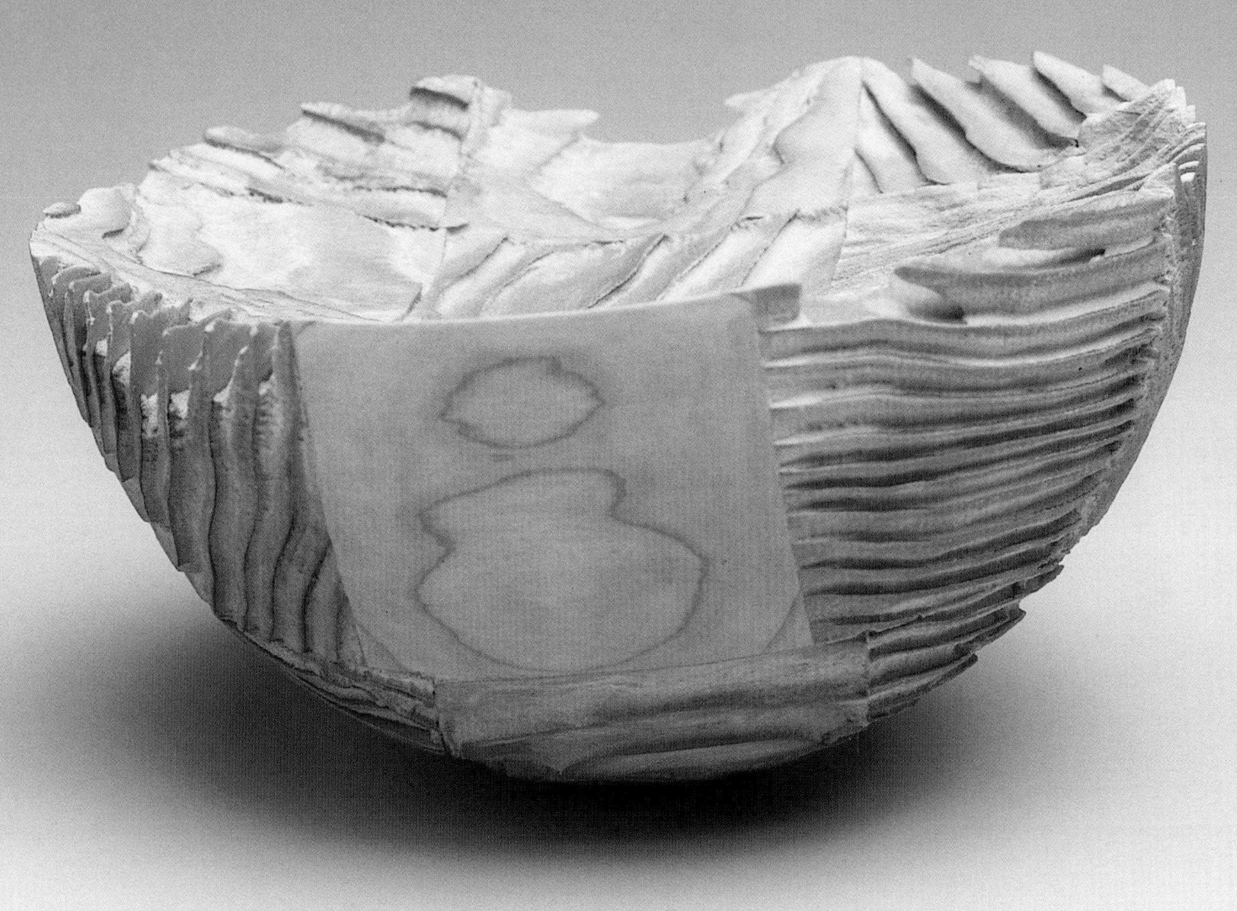

*Boolean Ia*
2000
H: 5", Diam: 8"
Laminated fir

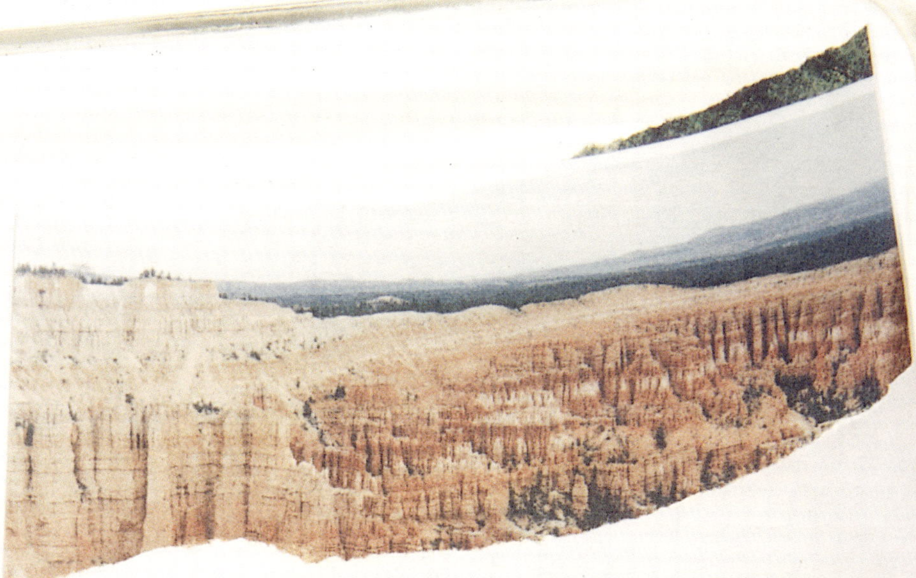

James Thurman [*Pennsylvania, USA – b. 1971*]

This current body of work explores the development of objects based primarily on rotational processes. The pieces are created employing a variety of materials and means of production. Whether the work is made of pine turned on a wood lathe, copper spun on a spinning lathe or machined steel, I find the resulting work similar in its use of an aesthetic founded in its rotational origin. I look to the center of the work where there exists something elusive yet fundamentally captivating.

Within this body of work, I am interested in exploring the relationship between materials and processes. I have just begun to mine the potential that exists in the juxtaposition of various woods and metals. The manner in which different processes such as sandblasting and beadblasting affect the materials is also of primary import.

Specifically, *Boolean Ia* is the manifestation of inspiration drawn from the geological strata of our planet. Just as the elements erode the ground and expose the layers within, lathe turning and sandblasting have been used to reveal the structure of the wood grain and lamination pattern. One section of the piece was masked to further emphasize the affect of the sandblasting on the form and material. The combination of the spherical form and eroded surface is representative of the natural forces that surround us and mankind's role within them.

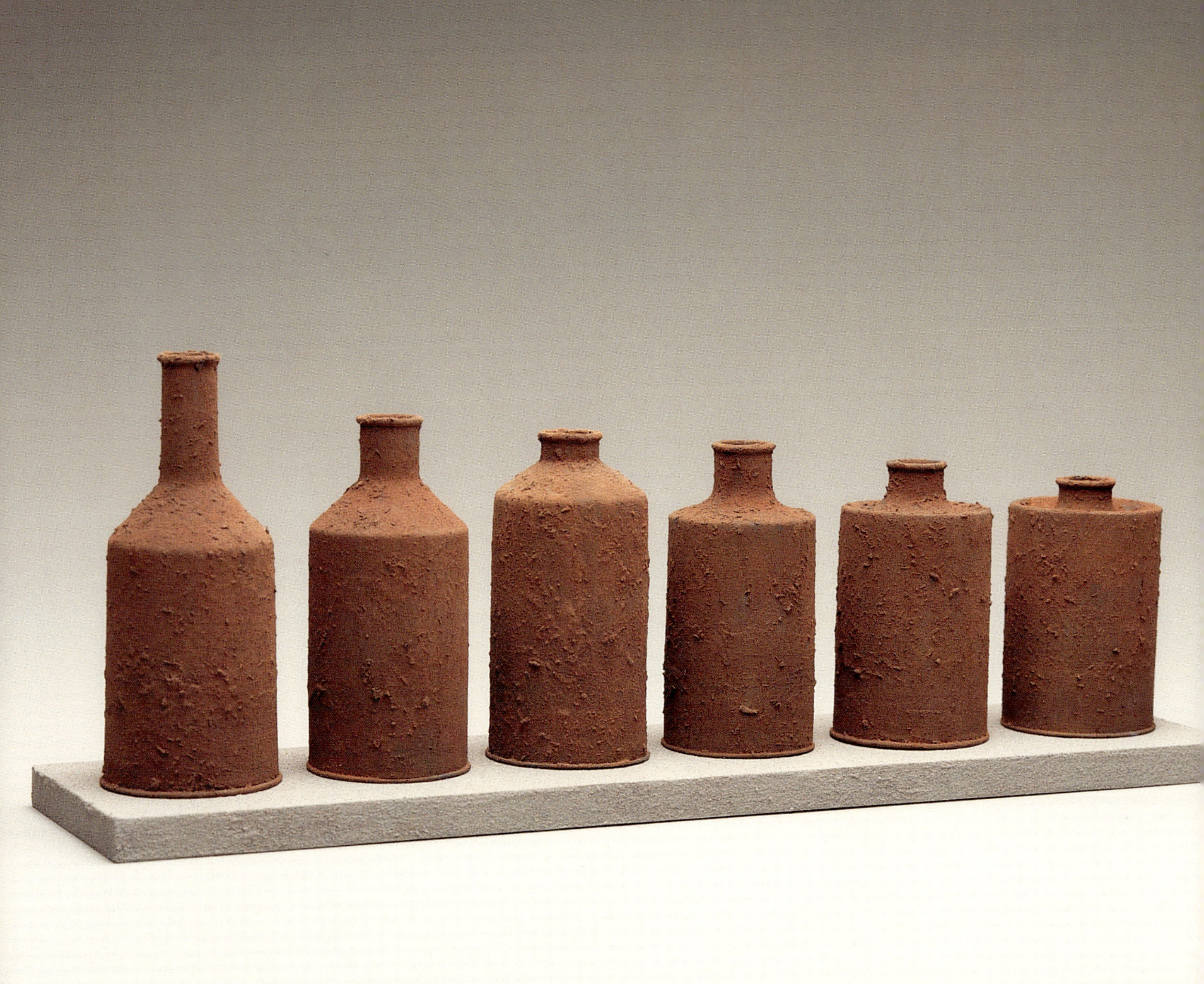

*Pop-A-Top*
(From The Junk Can Series)
2000
H: 7 1/4", W: 18 5/8", D: 4 1/2"
Oak, iron oxides, MDF and acrylics

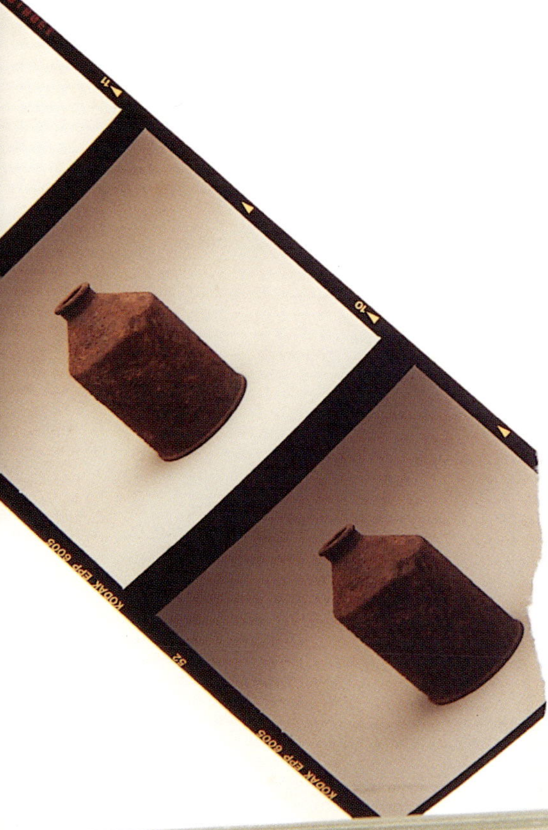

Richard E. Tuttle [*Pennsylvania, USA – b. 1942*]

Another in my series of **Junk Cans**, *Pop-A-Top* explores further the concept of "visual rhythm." The "visual rhythm" of a picket fence can be interrupted when a few slats are missing or when the pattern or silhouette of the pickets changes. In the case of *Pop-A-Top*, I have attempted to make the change in shape then rhythm. I also envisioned a hypothetical experiment using firecrackers of increasing power and lighting them from inside the five "cans." If the walls and bottoms of the cans were strong enough to contain the blasts without distortion, but the tops were not, what would happen to the shapes? Provided the firecrackers were properly sized, the resulting distortion of the tops would create the progressive "visual rhythm" effect of *Pop-A-Top*.

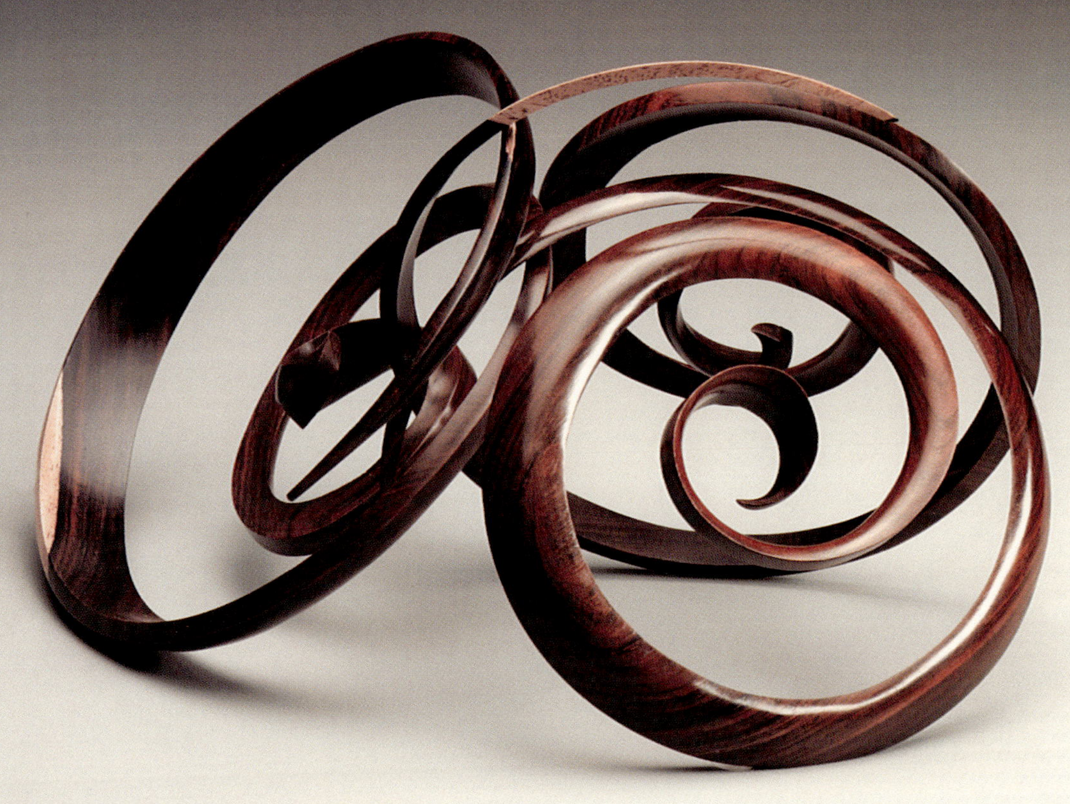

#6: 'Music To My Ears'

A more complex helix form that illustrates the complexity that can be obtained by manipulating the turned form. In this case the original form was similar to that of a bundt pan. These forms can be attractive as a table piece but take on a totally different personality if suspended as a mobile.

Material: Cocoblo
Size: 10" X 10"

*Music to My Ears*
2000
H: 6 1/4", W: 14", D: 11"
Cocobolo
(Collection of Susan and Neil Kaye, Wilmington, DE)

PHILLIP WALL [*Pennsylvania, USA. – b. 1935*]

Much of my carved work is inspired by that of William Hunter. Long fluid spiral images seem to appeal to us both. These helix forms are but an adaptation of his work and I did them because the line and form were simply pleasing to me. Then, I received a most unexpected surprise; people who saw them were reacting emotionally. The first time this occurred, I had asked a friend, who is a devotee of English country dance, to assemble a three part piece in a way that she found interesting. She did so and her immediate response was, "Wow, that's how I *feel* when I dance!"

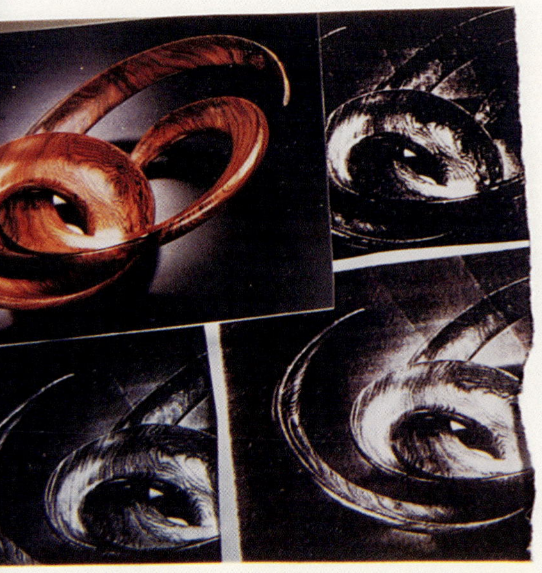

It was then I realized that something magical had occurred. Instead of creating static form "as pleasing to the hand as to the eye," the result was a living entity that also touched the heart. Interestingly, each piece has a unique personality. Each has its own balance and dimension. Because of this it accepts guidance but resists any attempt to make it conform, eventually developing its "self."

The result is a well balanced composition that is better than any that could be imposed by outside influence. An interesting metaphor to the human experience.

I have come to understand that these forms involve not only the Creator of the material, the "soul of the tree" and the creativity of the artist, but also engage the hand and the imagination of the recipient, thus forming an inseparable bond that encompasses all.

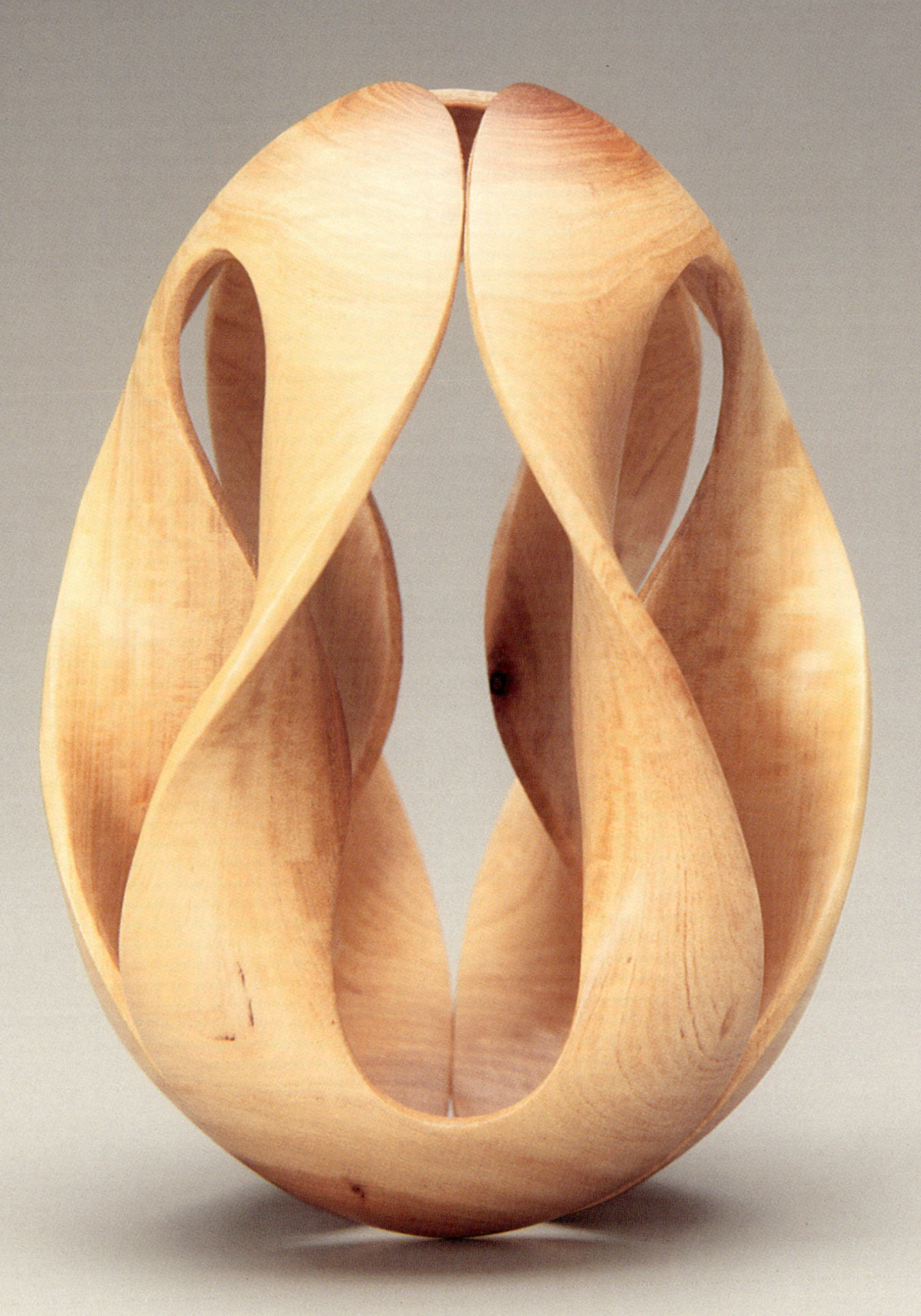

*Egg Infinitum*
2000
H: 6", Diam: 4 1/2"
Quandong

## Gordon Ward [*Australia – b. 1937*]

While in New Zealand recently, I picked up a gift of jade (Greenstone) for my partner. It was the Maori symbol for eternity, which took the form of an endless knot. The profile suggested an egg form to me.

The egg usually signifies a beginning, so combining the continuous knot with an egg form was my next logical step. The form lacked excitement so I looked at other mobius forms. The next progression was from seeing the logo of our national broadcaster, the ABC.

When each of the crossovers was given a mobius twist and then transposed into an egg profile the final form was arrived at.

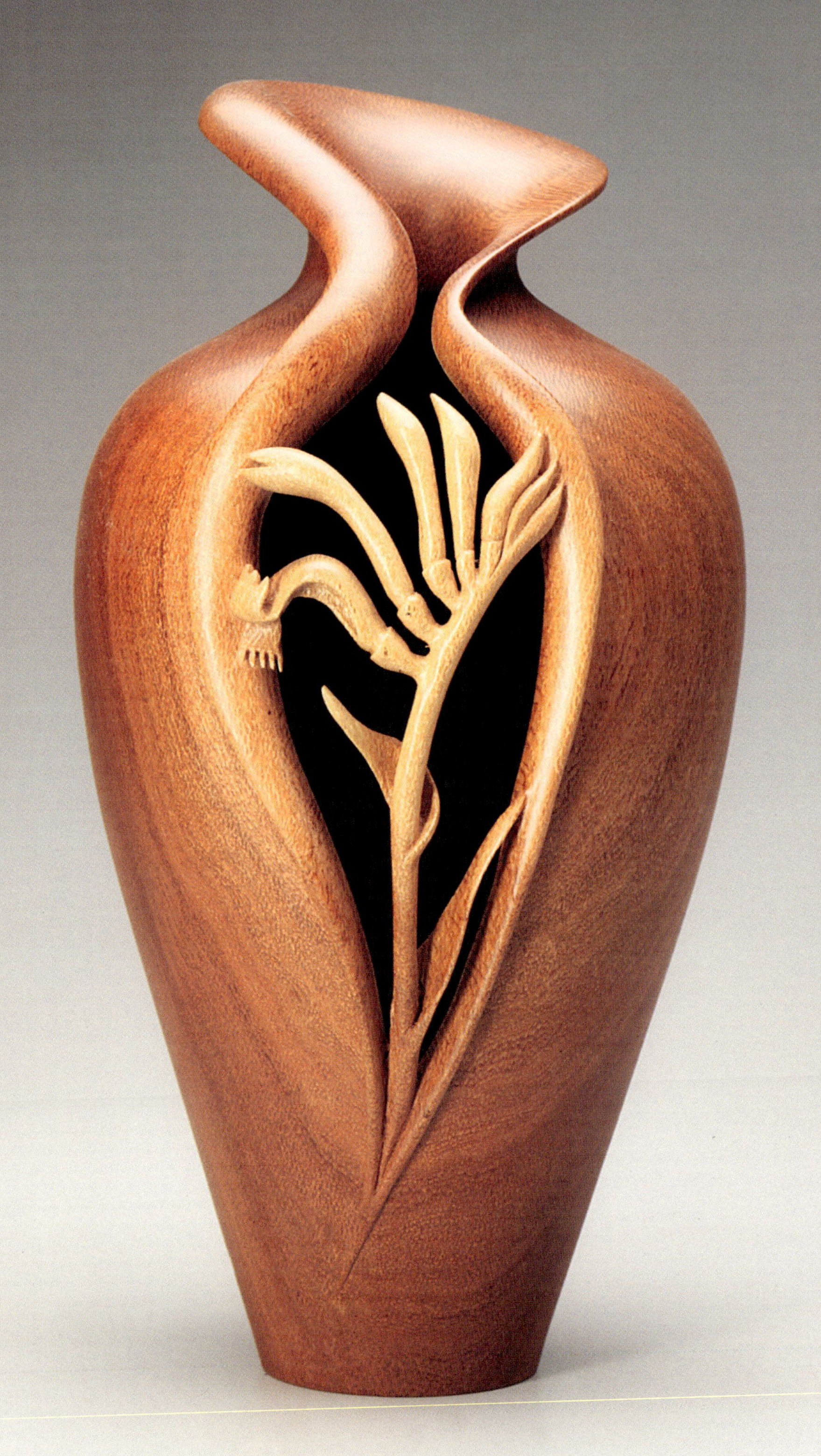

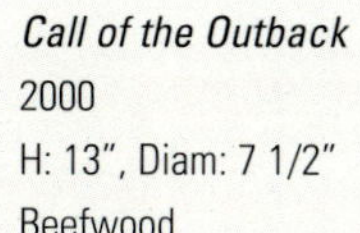

*Call of the Outback*
2000
H: 13", Diam: 7 1/2"
Beefwood

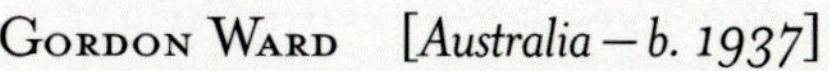

## Gordon Ward [*Australia – b. 1937*]

The inspiration for this form came from my need to find a different treatment for the Gum leaf vases I have developed.

The inspiration was in the form of the national symbol of Western Australia, namely the Red Kangaroo Paw.

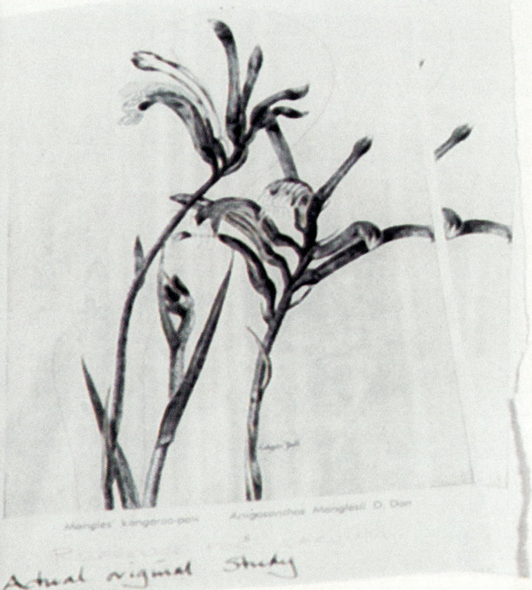

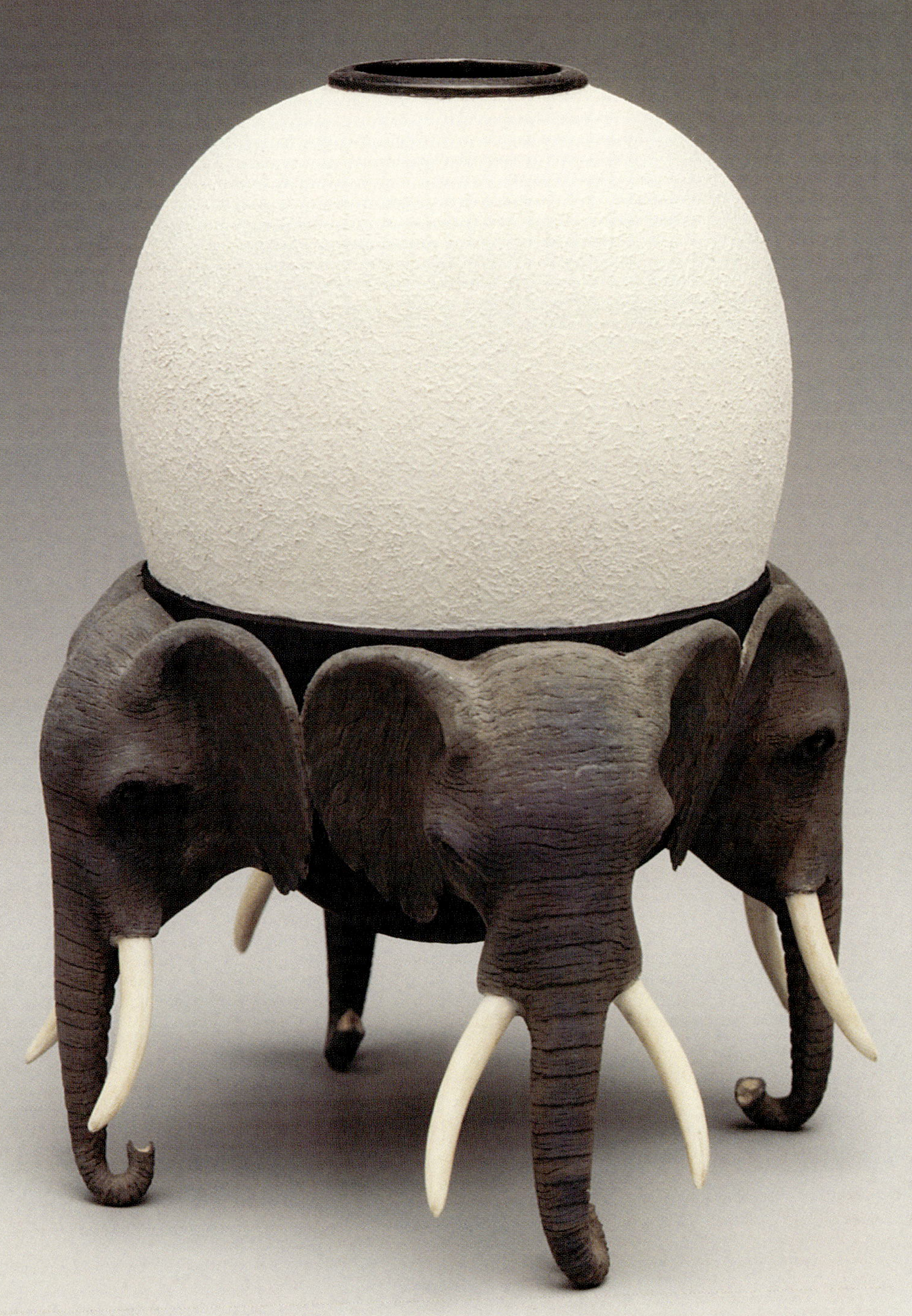

*Bachelor Herd*
2000
H: 9 1/2", Diam: 7 1/2"
Linden

Douglas Weidman [*Pennsylvania, USA – b. 1944*]

This piece came from an idea that I felt was a challenge, incorporating both my turning and carving abilities. I had discussed my vision with a veteran turner who encouraged me to bring this unique idea to full term. I chose linden wood for the ease of its carving properties. The wood has no grain and lacks character, but I found it much more accessible in the application of detailed carving. The turning of this piece required much manipulation in order to achieve my desired goal. I chose to use acrylic paint on the elephants, and finished the globe with textured paint. I find these turnings with carving to be very rewarding.

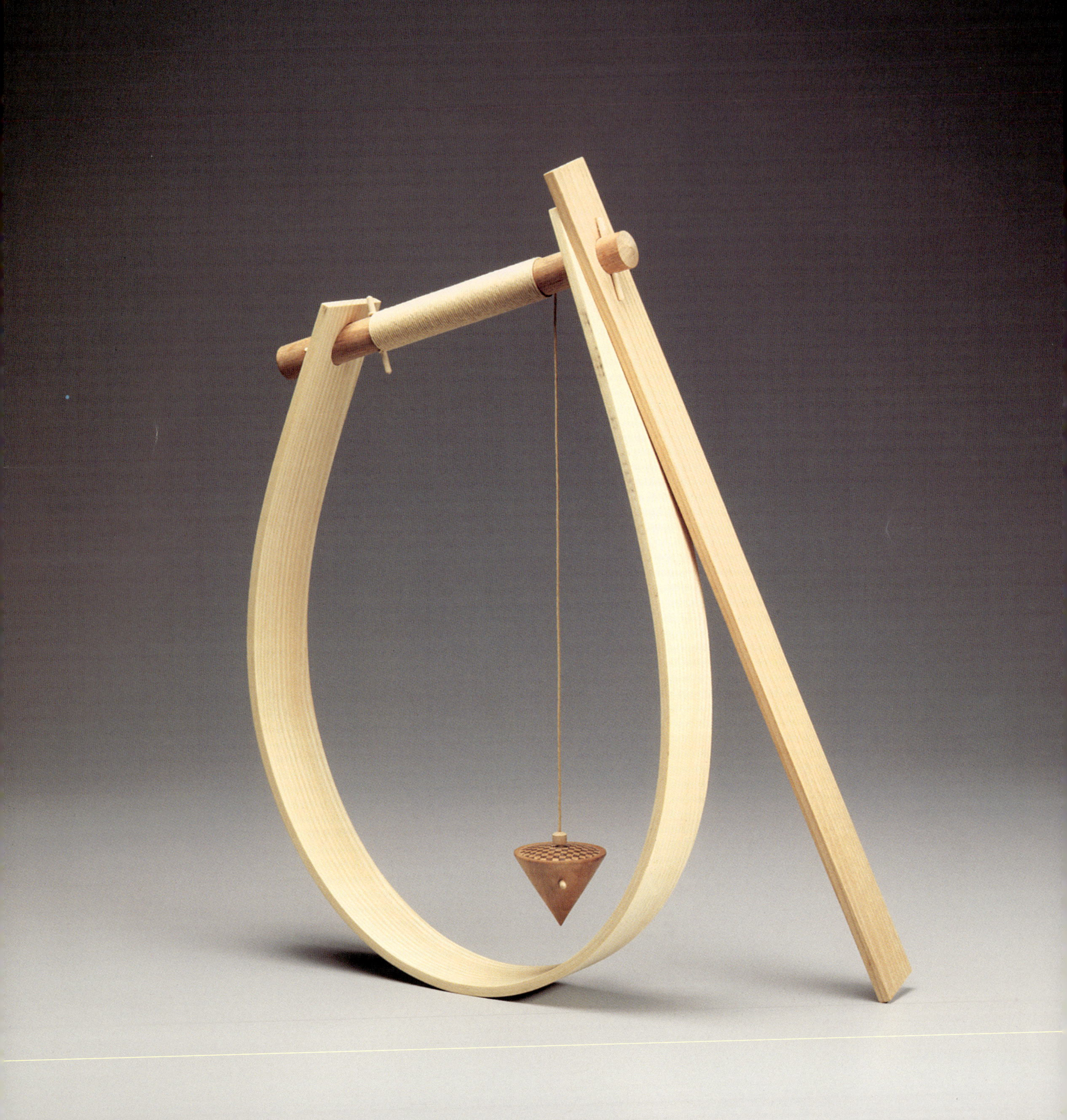

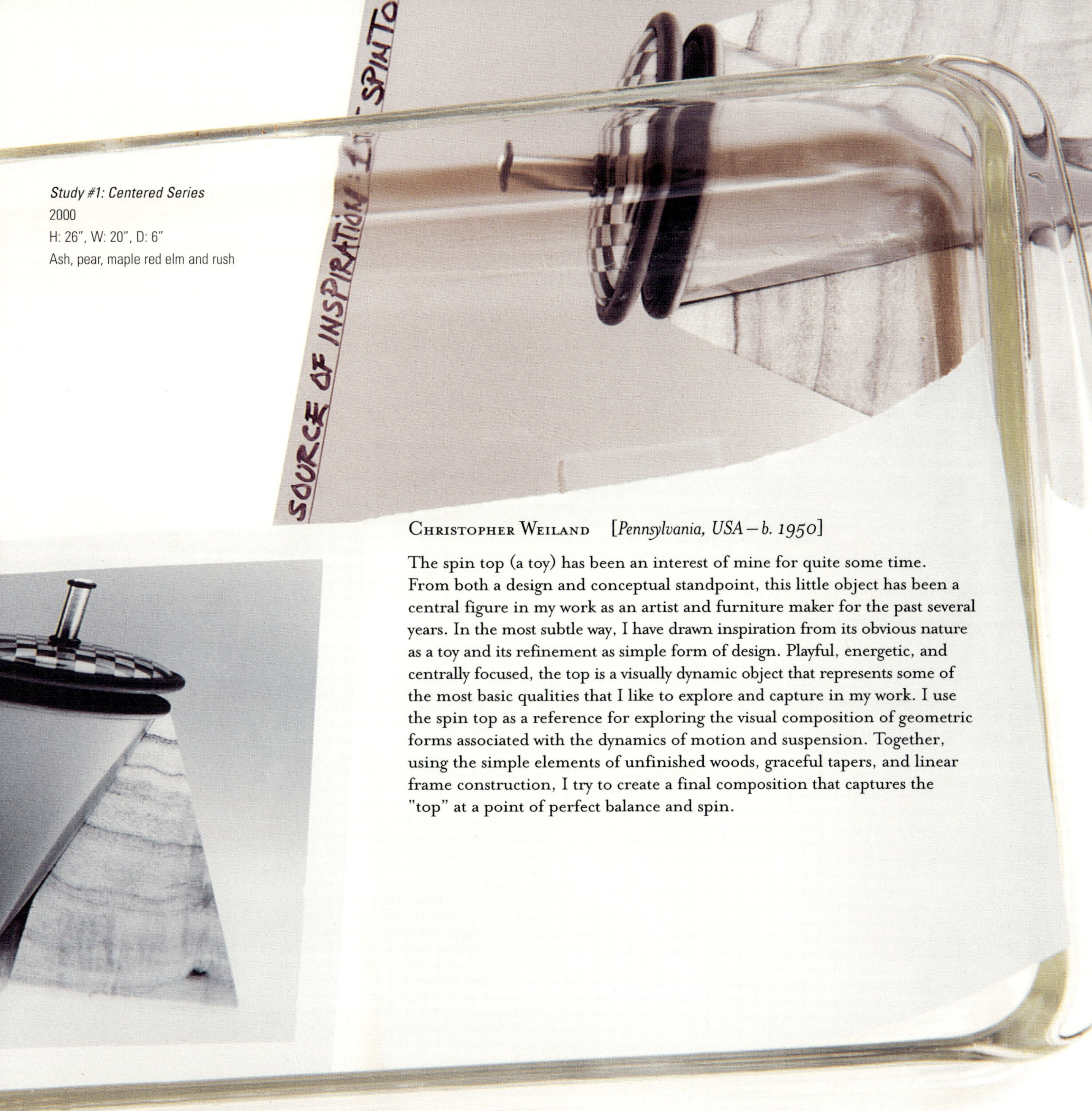


*Study #1: Centered Series*
2000
H: 26", W: 20", D: 6"
Ash, pear, maple red elm and rush

Christopher Weiland [*Pennsylvania, USA – b. 1950*]

The spin top (a toy) has been an interest of mine for quite some time. From both a design and conceptual standpoint, this little object has been a central figure in my work as an artist and furniture maker for the past several years. In the most subtle way, I have drawn inspiration from its obvious nature as a toy and its refinement as simple form of design. Playful, energetic, and centrally focused, the top is a visually dynamic object that represents some of the most basic qualities that I like to explore and capture in my work. I use the spin top as a reference for exploring the visual composition of geometric forms associated with the dynamics of motion and suspension. Together, using the simple elements of unfinished woods, graceful tapers, and linear frame construction, I try to create a final composition that captures the "top" at a point of perfect balance and spin.

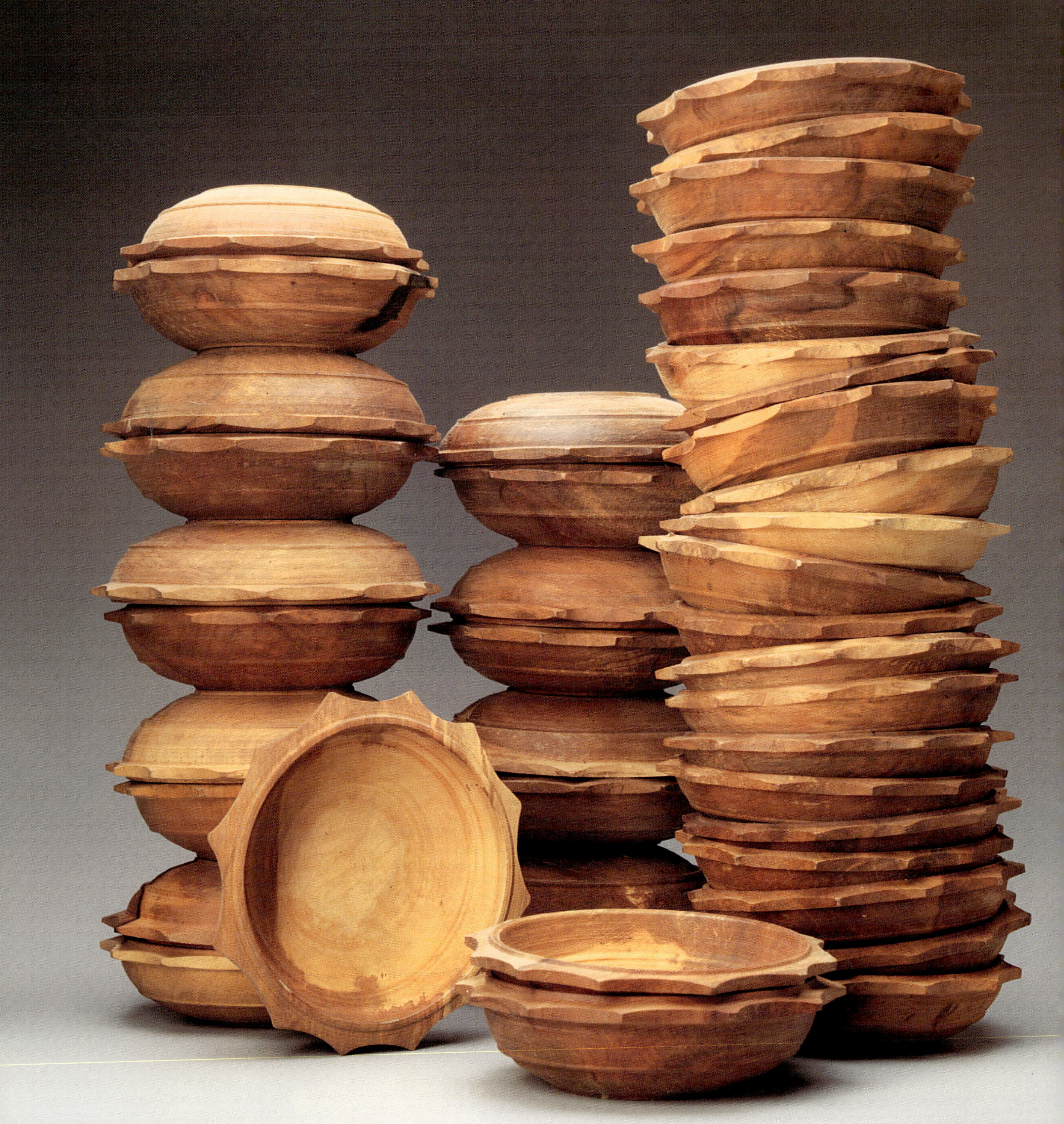

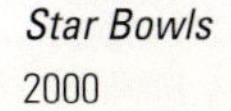


*Star Bowls*
2000
H: 2 1/2", Diam: 8" each
Pear wood

## Robin Wood [*England – b. 1965*]

The inspiration for this work is a fifteenth-century bowl from Braunschweig, Germany. I am deeply interested in the roots of woodturning and the humble wooden bowl is as much a part of our cultural identity as ceramics are for the Chinese.

Over the last five years I have handled thousands of medieval wooden bowls and have developed a deep respect for the turners who made them. This work is an homage to those turners, and I hope it will bring knowledge of their skills to a wider audience.

I find this design very satisfying; I could easily have changed and developed the form in order to make it my own but felt no need. I could remake this bowl a thousand times and still no two would be the same. The fifty-one bowls here appear similar but look closely, pick them up, feel the marks of the tools, feel where the weight lies. To me subtle differences in balance and form make one bowl sing whilst another doesn't. Like fine wine, it is often the barely perceivable that makes the difference and like fine wine, it is the variation that makes them interesting. I turn and carve them by eye. I use only the tools used five hundred years ago: the pole lathe, the axe, the knife, not out of some nostalgic vision, but because they work efficiently and give the variation in texture and form which I desire.

# A Fruitful Balance Between Influence and Originality

*by Robin Rice*

An artist, writer, teacher and curator, Robin Rice is the senior art critic for the *Philadelphia City Paper.* She regularly contributes to the scholarly publication, *Woman's Art Journal,* and other periodicals including *Sculpture* magazine, the *New Art Examiner, ARTnews,* and *American Craft.*

Ms. Rice received a BFA in painting from Ohio Wesleyan University and an MA in Drawing and Ceramics from the University of Missouri, where she later taught studio art for two years.

Her interest in the social implications of the arts, and in painting as a living tradition, is reflected in numerous essays about Philadelphia's mural arts program, most recently the catalogue essay for *Wall Power* (2000), a project of the Institute of Contemporary Art, Fleisher Art Memorial and Philadelphia Mural Arts Program. As an Assistant Adjunct Professor at the University of the Arts, Ms. Rice teaches Modernism, Crafts History, and graduate seminars in Criticism and Art & Society.

Aleksandr Pushkin's poem addressed *To the Poet* is sometimes cited as a concise definition of the Romantic artist, the prototypical modern artist, a persona that retains its power even in the postmodern era. "Poet! Do not prize the love of the crowd," the young writer admonishes. "The praise of enthusiasts will pass — a momentary hubbub.... You are Tsar. Live alone./Travel the open road where your unfettered intellect draws you./Cultivate the fruits of cherished thoughts,/ not demanding rewards for your noble work.... You, yourself, are your highest tribunal."[1]

Pushkin's ideal artist, therefore, is not concerned with others' estimations of his (or her) work. More important, Pushkin seems to suggest, the true artist exercises absolute freedom, freedom to "cultivate... cherished thoughts" without considering rules prescribed by others (perhaps even Pushkin's rules!). In a concluding stanza, Pushkin casually allocates possession of the tripod seat of the chief priestess of Apollo, the god of poetry, to the artist, himself. It's a poetic conceit, but a meaningful one.[2]

This notion of art as being intimately connected to the individuality and free will of the maker is implicit in the premise of *Challenge VI– Roots: Insights & Inspirations in Contemporary Turned Objects* , but so is a complementary principle: constraint. Certain constraints are intrinsic to the materials, techniques, and traditions of every art form. Others are devised or chosen by the artist: self-imposed limits. A dynamic tension between freedom and restraint nourishes art, but absolute freedom is purposeless, non-communicative: a vacuum where nothing can grow.

Though he does not articulate it directly, Pushkin's message *To the Poet* is more complex and complete than it first appears. For one thing, Pushkin did not follow his own command to poetic anarchy. In numerous ways, he acknowledges the aesthetic achievements and traditions of the past and of his craft. Not only does he evoke the sacred rites of classical antiquity as a primary metaphor for the creative act, Pushkin chooses a familiar vessel for his work. *To the Poet* is a sonnet, one which in every way conforms to the "rules" of an

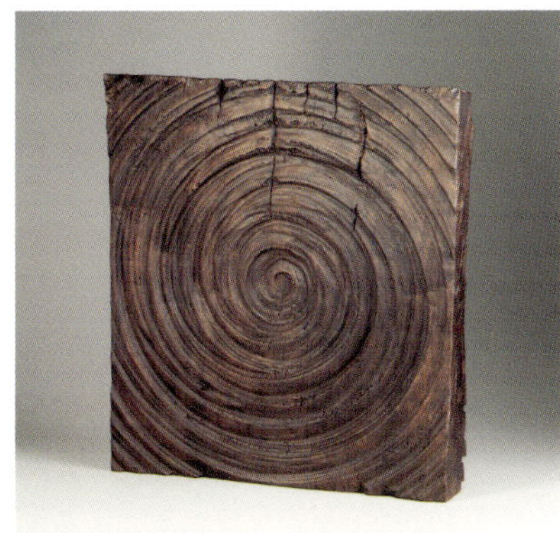

1
George Peterson
*Buddha's Mirror,* 2000
H: 24", W: 21", D: 4"
Charred maple
lent by the artist

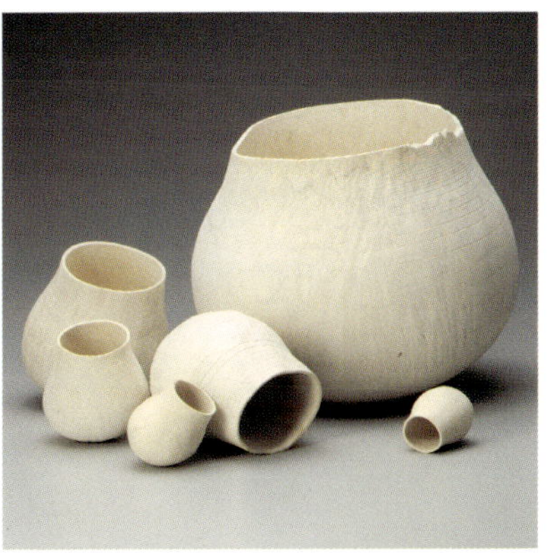

2
Christian Burchard
*Gourds,* 1999
H: 13", W: 2" to 16" x 18" x 13"
(approx. 5 pieces)
Bleached madrone burl
lent by the artist

established sonnet form: in the structure of ideas, line length, meter, and rhyme scheme. On an even more basic level, Pushkin is able to speak to us across nearly two centuries because he followed the rules of a *grapholect*: a known, historic, written language. A grapholect may be the most definitively recognized kind of language, but language of a sort — visual, written, auditory, or kinetic — is necessary to the communicative function of art, even when the artist chooses to manipulate it in surprising ways.

Art is personal, expressive, and exploratory, a Romantic facet of life. It appropriates authority to itself. Yet because it involves the material world and language, art exists in a context of conventions and established processes. Like Pushkin's poem, art sometimes acknowledges rules by attacking them—just as George Peterson's scorched turnings of unrefined chunks of wood [1] draw attention to the nature of the turning process and to the primal character of wood by presenting both in a fashion which in other circumstances might be seen as a grotesque mistake. By violating ordinary rules, Peterson reveals a new and unexpected beauty. He records his process as an interactive dance of energy and resistance in which something of discord plays a leading role. Controlled danger and power are intrinsic to turning and, therefore, implicit in even the most refined turned objects. By rejecting pre-ordained form and absolute control, Peterson makes process an explicit part of the content of his work. The work, though, is not simply about turning, it suggests a context in which approximations, accidents, and irregularity have a positive meaning, a world which rewards boldness and simplicity.

Although all lathe-turners might be said to be revolutionary (pun alert!), *Challenge VI* does not set out to shock the art community with a roster of iconoclastic firebrands. Still, a great many of the works selected by curators Michelle Holzapfel and Chris Tyler gently or decisively nudge the envelope of possibilities.

For example, the curving forms of Christian Burchard's family of vessels [2] have the timeless completeness suggested by the Roman Emperor Marcus

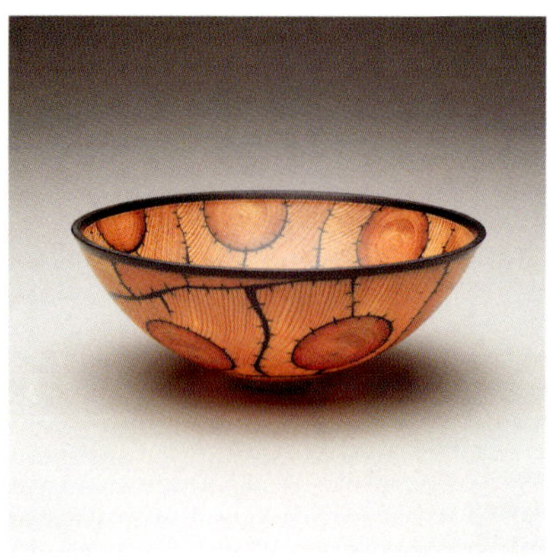

4
Gianfranco Angelino
*Pine, Pine Branch Bowl*, 1999
H: 3 1/2", Diam: 9"
Pine and pine branch
lent by the artist

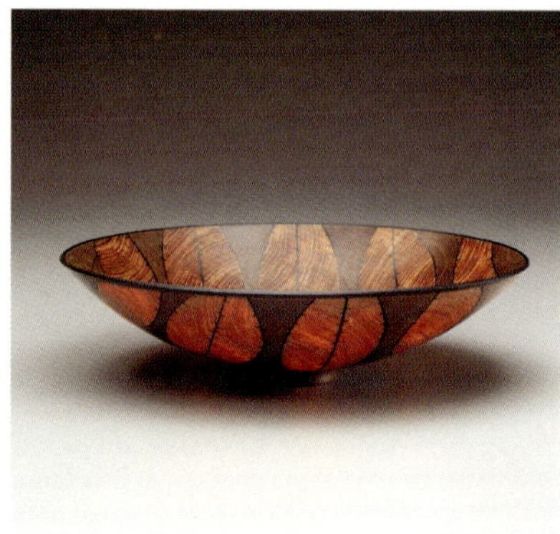

5
Gianfranco Angelino
*Walnut Pitch Pine Bowl*, 1999
H: 4", Diam: 13 1/2"
Walnut, pitch pine, epoxy resin and cotton yarn
lent by the artist

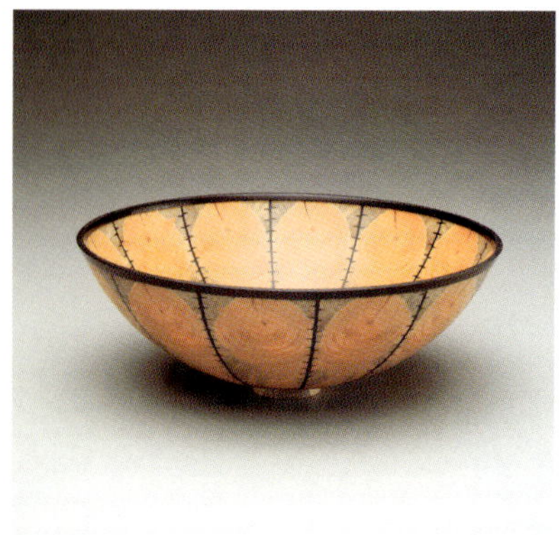

3
Gianfranco Angelino
*Pine Branch Bowl*, 1999
H: 4 1/2", Diam: 11 1/4"
Pine branch, epoxy resin and cotton yarn
lent by the artist

Aurelius's meditation on perfection: "The soul attains her perfectly rounded form when she is neither straining out after something nor shrinking back into herself; neither disseminating herself piecemeal nor yet sinking down in collapse; but is bathed in radiance which reveals her to the world and herself in their true colours."[3] Partly because the artist has eliminated a flat foot or base, each of Burchard's turnings seems designed for the hand, an epitome of utility. There is a softness and a living quality in the skin — like slightly rippling surfaces that accords well with the perfection of the circle. Yet for all his classicism, Burchard is a rule-challenger of sorts. By working with wood when it is still wet, he voluntarily relinquishes some control to the material itself — to chance. How will it age? How will it change? And by accepting the limitations of the material, he animates it.

After her first year of teaching at Pratt, the great ceramic artist and designer Eva Zeisel "came to the conclusion that what was called limits...was just the opposite; it was very unlimiting. I set my students this project," she recalls. "I said, 'Please sit down and do the most beautiful thing you can imagine. You must have been thinking a lot about it.' And they were sitting around totally frustrated, without the slightest idea of how to fulfill their dream. Then I gave them limitations — 'Make something this high, with this function' — and suddenly they were all sitting there working like beavers."[4] A group of researchers at Hebrew University in Jerusalem recently arrived at a similar conclusion, experimentally. "To suspend criticism and think any idea is possible or good may ultimately be destructive to creativity," one researcher said, when explaining how they program computers to develop advertising ideas which are more imaginative than those thought up by humans.[5]

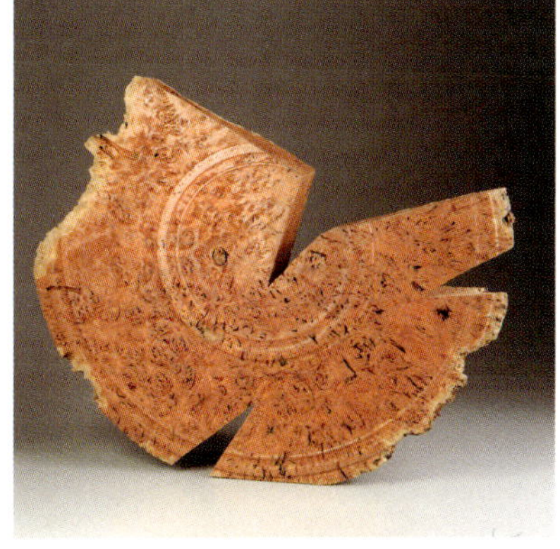

6
Robyn Horn
*Fractured Millstone*, 2000
H: 24", W: 24", D:7"
Jarrah burl
lent by the artist

**Celebrating the Limits of Nature**

The notion of "Roots" suggests a hidden branching from a central taproot, dividing and fanning out into an infinitesimal web of capillaries each stretching into perhaps subtly different types of soil, nurturing the visible art work with diverse sustenance. Although the *Challenge VI* artists collectively cite myriad antecedents of "Insight & Inspiration," thank goodness not one attempted a truly exhaustive list of all the sources — the tiny capillaries that feed into a single work of art! Instead each artist chose one or two or three important things that bear strongly on a specific result. The maker set up a situation or problem, or perhaps the situation was imposed by a material or other circumstance; however it happened, the completed work triumphs by 'solving' the situation.

Respect and reverence for materials were implicit in almost every entry in this exhibition, whether it was included in the show or not. Even when looking for more than the obvious inspiration of wood, it is impossible to ignore its importance as a source. The word "insight" from the exhibition title so perfectly describes Gianfranco Angelino's *Bowls* [3, 4 & 5]. Careful observation revealed to Angelino wood's unexpected potential for translucence. But the wafer-thin material is fragile. Angelino had to devise a way to uncover this "concealed beauty" and, by using epoxy resin and cotton yarn, ensure its durability. The heavenly splendor of stained glass, a source he acknowledges, inhabits his radiant and radiating forms, and is brought to earth by the homeliness of quilting suggested by stitch-like joins and familiar wood grain patterns.

Robyn Horn's large burl pieces are also inescapably and intentionally about wood as wood and as metaphor. It is the physicality, the craggy heft and mass that she honors when the naturally broken circle of a tree trunk becomes a *Fractured Millstone* [6], in which the history of human production (grinding grain and the slower grinding down the millstone) is conflated with the years recorded in the wood itself. In earlier work, Horn focused on wood's interior

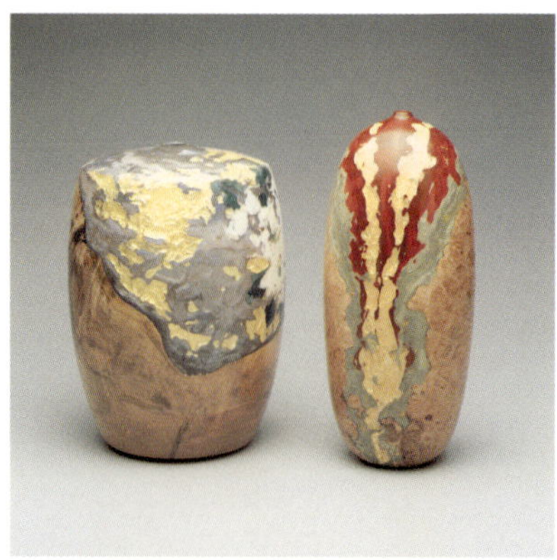

8
Robert Chatelain
*Dogwood*, 2000, *Wrapt*, 1999
H: 12 1/2", Diam: 8 1/2";
H: 14", Diam: 5 1/4"
Red maple burl, big leaf maple burl, epoxy resin, powdered pigments, mica and gold leaf
lent by the artist

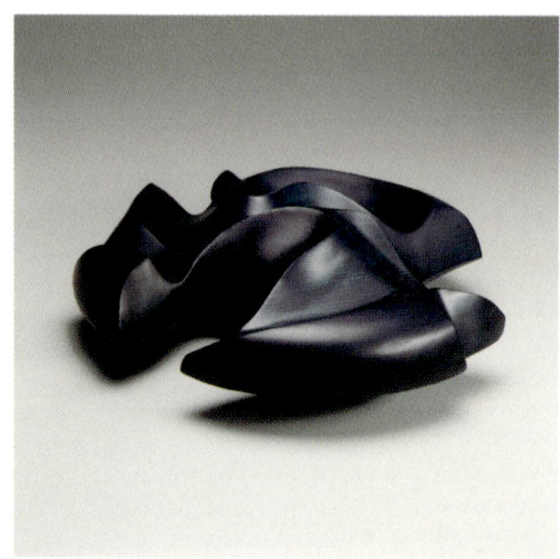

9
Connie Mississippi
*Circle of Time- 210 Blue Cliffs*, 2000
H: 8", Diam: 22"
Plywood, acrylic and lacquer
lent by the artist

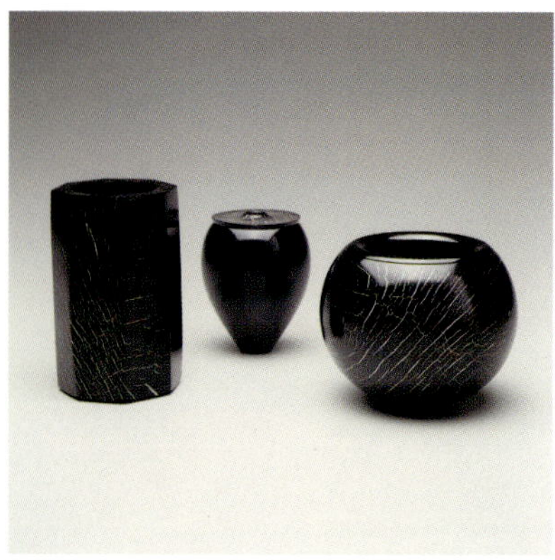

7
Rudiger Marquarding
*Ivy*, 2000, *Poppy Fruit*, 2000, *Spider's Web*, 2000
H: 6 3/4", Diam: 4 1/4";
H: 4 7/8", Diam: 4";
H: 5 1/4", Diam: 6 1/4"
Ebony and silver alloy
lent by the artist

visual richness, likening elaborate knotted whorls of grain to geodes, whose coarse plain exteriors reveal complex glittering interior facets.

How vastly different from Horn's and Angelino's wood-analogies are Rüdiger Marquarding's quintessentially refined exterior surfaces of ebony threaded with silver [7]! Nevertheless, Marquarding's engagement with a particular material leads him to find opportunity where others might see flaws. He fills naturally occurring cracks with silver, a shimmering contrast to the ebony's glossy slight translucence. His technique recalls the practice of old tea masters in Japan who repaired valuable broken tea bowls with thin veins of gold, thus enhancing their beauty.

Interestingly, Robert Chatelain, who restores the wholeness to burl by filling gaps with brilliant-colored pigmented epoxy and gold leaf [8], is indebted to the tie-died Japanese kimonos of Itchiku Kubota. Chatelain's sumptuous, painterly yet refined treatment differs in mood from Marquarding's cool reserve, yet both emphasize surface by choosing sleek, simple, closed forms.

The Transcendental attitude toward nature in art has become increasingly self-conscious in today's world. In his encyclopaedic discussion of *Landscape and Memory*, Simon Schama suggests that just as culture defined and shaped the apparently "unspoiled" landscapes, like the Grand Canyon or the redwood forest, that we revere, our understanding of landscape is socially constructed. Ralph Waldo Emerson's vision of art as "an abstract or epitome of the world" should perhaps be reversed to suggest that our vision of nature is a projection of our understanding of ourselves. Connie Mississippi depicts a mass of eroded land as if seen from an airplane [9], adding a sense of distance or objectivity to her metaphor for human aging. Her approach to geology recalls John Ruskin's provocative notion that no matter how angular they appear, mountains weather into attractive curving forms. He wrote in a passage that might well describe Mississippi's *Blue Cliffs*, "'Growth,' [Nature] seems to say, 'is not essential to my work, nor concealment, nor softness; but curvature is and if I must produce my forms by breaking them, the fracture itself shall be

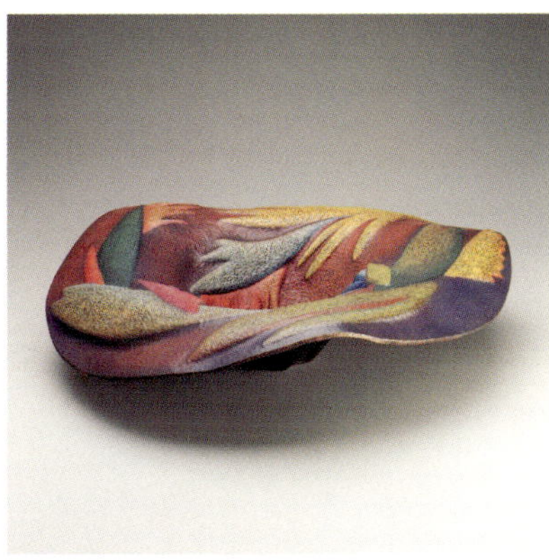

10
Helen Shirk
*Sustaining Spirit XVII*, 2000
H: 6", Diam: 23"
Copper, patina and Prismacolor pencils
lent by the artist

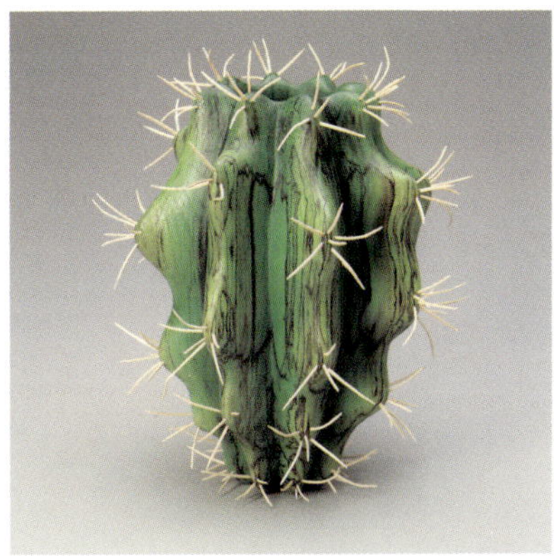

11
Ron Fleming
*Cereus*, 2000
H: 9 1/2", Diam: 6"
Spalted hackberry and pine
lent by the artist

in curves.'" Mississippi's quirky worn cliffs dissolve into curves. Ruskin, though, might wonder at her choice of a distinctive blue pigment.

Photographer Ansel Adams echoed Emerson when he spoke of a "deep personal distillation of spirit and concept which moulds these earthly facts into some transcendental emotion and spiritual experience," words which could easily be applied to Helen Shirk's marvelously intimate copper landscape [10] with its abstracted bird of paradise flowering, elaborately textured and pigmented surface. But Shirk's sense of harmony has a self-consciousness, a fragmentation that is subtly removed from the Transcendentalist vision.[6]

Much of the nature-based work in this exhibition also incorporates post Pop, postmodern sensibilities. It's about culture as much as it's about nature. Ron Fleming's little green cactus *Cereus* [11], with its delicate toothpick needles, is most realistic and yet partakes of a light-hearted kitsch sensibility. And Jack Larimore's tribute to the Schuylkill River [12], with its basketball-size globe and gigantic droplets of opaque white-painted water eschews the too-harmonious, melting gesture which would suggest nature triumphant over human folly. Even Larimore's title *Mother Loves Us, Even When We're Selfish* underlines the knowledge that we can't fool Mother Nature for a moment.

Curiously, "natural" Emersonian harmony in this show seems more powerfully suggested by the act of turning than by representation. On the one hand, this reflects the power of the circle as an enduring motif in all art disciplines, a theme that was addressed in depth by *Challenge V* essayist and juror Maria van Kesteren who wrote, "[A]ll forms that one wants to express derive from and lead back to the circle."[7] On the other hand, it mirrors the cadenced, rhythmic movements of a turner. Turning is a reductive process. There is an hypnotic fascination in the way a shape is exposed, evolved and refined. This fascination surely leads every turner at one time or another to go too far, and to destroy what has been created.

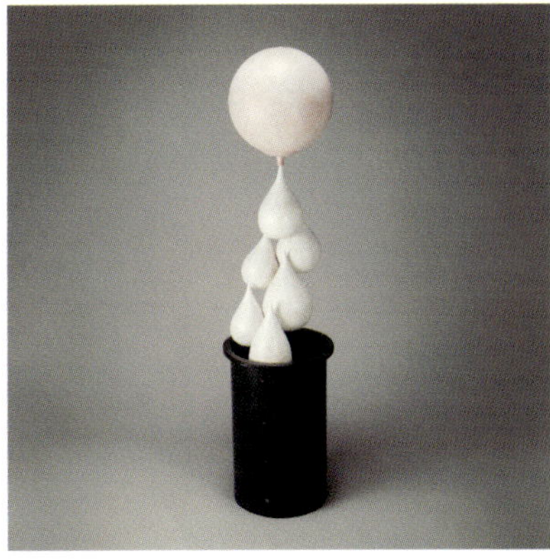

12
Jack Larimore
*Mom Loves Us, Even When We're Selfish*, 2000
H: 75", Diam: 16"
Mixed woods and globe
lent by the artist

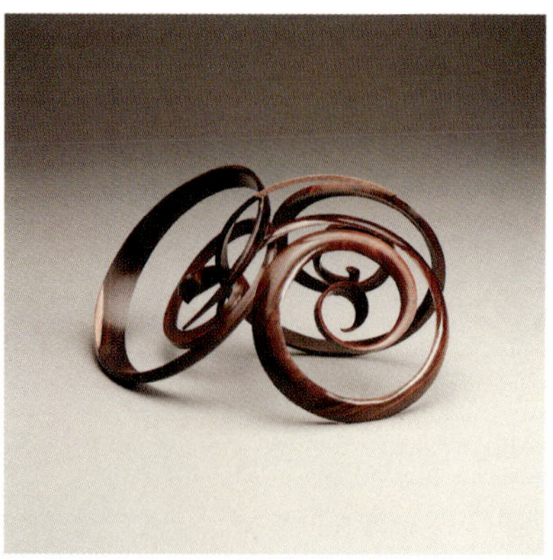

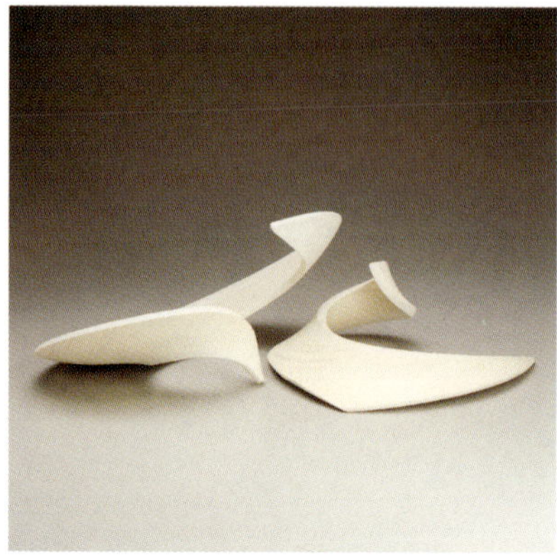

15
Virginia Dotson
*Cycles*, 2000
H: 8 1/2", W: 14 1/2", D: 15 1/2"
Italian poplar plywood and paint
lent by the artist

14
Phillip Wall
*Music to My Ears*, 2000
H: 6 1/4", W: 14", D: 11"
Cocobolo
Collection of Susan and Neil Kaye, Wilmington, DE

William Hunter's extended exploration of the vessel produced celebrated works composed of astonishing contrary-wise spooling ribs [13]. Hunter took a risk when he moved from that epitome of craft to a sort of *reductio ad absurdum* dissolution of the walls of the vessel. But the result was not absurd; it was a new way of envisioning form in a newly constructed or deconstructed sense of space. Hunter's interpenetrating, almost knotted spirals function as an abstract of energy. This is the sort of daring open-ended, individual exploration rooted in craft and history which Pushkin lauds and which *Challenge VI* hoped to encourage.

The work of a couple of other artists in the show looks like Hunter's at first glance, but their journeys were not the same. On the other hand, they are indebted to Hunter's example. Phil Wall, who gratefully acknowledges Hunter as an encouraging mentor, has a light lyrical touch in his suspended work [14], while Virginia Dotson's two-part piece of pale Italian poplar curves in a serene, shell-like classicism [15]. *Cycles*, with its subtle bands of white and grey, was developed with Dotson's frequent collaborator, the composer/pianist felicitously named Edward Wood.

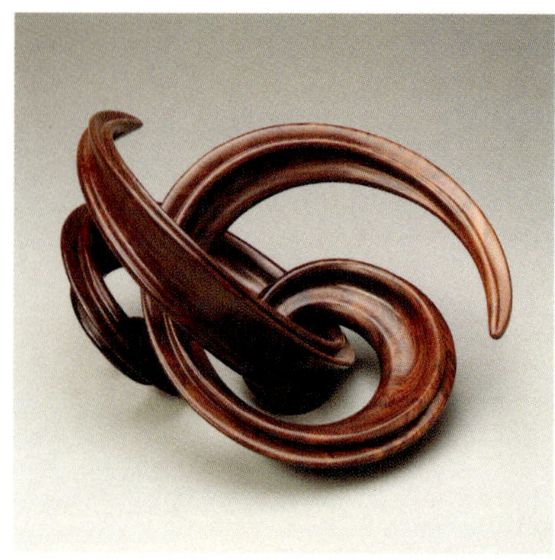

13
William Hunter
*Reciprocal Helix*, 2000
H: 12", W: 12", D: 24"
Cocobolo rosewood
lent by the artist

### The Past

Originality is a mysterious quality, one that is not necessarily based in the search for absolute uniqueness. Art is a regenerative, cyclical process. Each new generation of artists must claim its history and transform it. In a sense, the artist always works with two materials: a physical material (wood) and the past that is recorded in that material. The experience of countless generations of woodworkers produced a wealth of wisdom and technique, as well as centuries of vessels. Most of the really ancient ones are lost, but their shapes, surfaces and purposes survive in familiar forms. These ancient roots fuel contemporary action. Some of the most traditional objects in our exhibition are among the most satisfying.

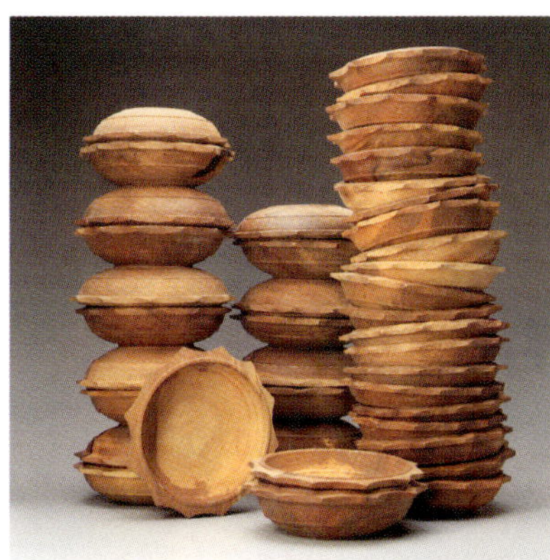

16
Robin Wood
***Star Bowls***, 2000
Each H: 2 1/2", Diam: 8"
(fifty-one bowls)
Pear wood
lent by the artist

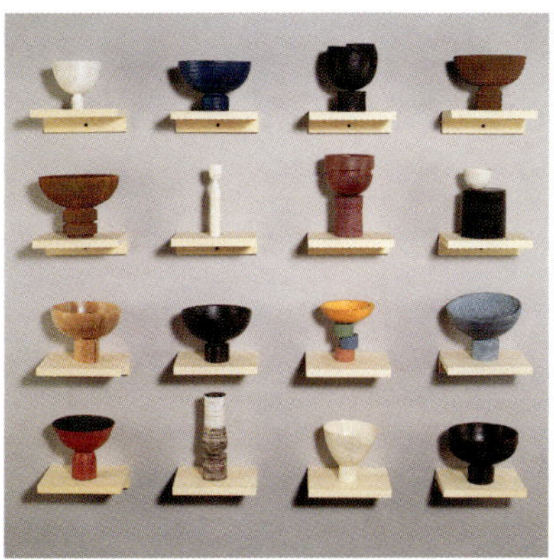

17
Merryll Saylan
***Tribute: Hans Coper***, 2000
H: 54", W: 47", D: 8"
Wood, paint and dye
lent by the artist

In his homage to the medieval turner, Robin Wood's rigorously faithful "approximations" (a term he prefers to replicas) of fifteenth century German *Star Bowls* [16] are made with tools identical to those used five hundred years ago. The proportions of Wood's twelve-pointed, round-bottomed bowl is quite similar to that of an eight-pointed, footed Roman pewter cup from the fourth century A.D., found in the British Museum. The raised lip and flared rim are almost identical, though the metal vessel has a short narrow stem and small foot. In his statement, Wood celebrates the uniqueness of each bowl he makes. He writes, "[L]ike fine wine, it is the variation that makes them interesting." An observation that recalls Brian Eno's remark, "Repetition is a form of change."

Another series, Merryll Saylan's *Tribute: to Hans Coper* [17], explores variation and evolution as corollaries of repetition. Saylan applied her exquisite sensitivity to the formal subtleties of ordinary objects, by analyzing a simple bowl and cylindrical base form suggested by Coper's ceramic goblets. A series of variations in color and texture led to dramatic changes in the proportions of the form as well. Mounted on the wall, these works acquire a dynamic, didactic, almost archetypal character, and a distinctive musical quality.

The invention of lathe turning facilitated the production of nearly identical vessels. Now, artists use the process as a way of commenting on repeated forms, either handmade or industrial. Richard Tuttle's critique of mass-produced objects, a row of rust-colored *Pop-A-Top* bottles [18], was inspired by finding a rusty discarded can (a rare positive outcome of littering). Even though his target was the boring products of industry, Tuttle could not resist the temptation to make each of his bottles different in color and proportion, giving each one a slightly individual personality.

Mark Sfirri's spoofs on the industrial container [19] break many rules. They're not alike; they're not symmetrical, and they aren't even containers. They even break an unwritten but fairly consistent rule of commercial production — They're not ugly! In their handsome and witty finish, they follow the rules of high craft.

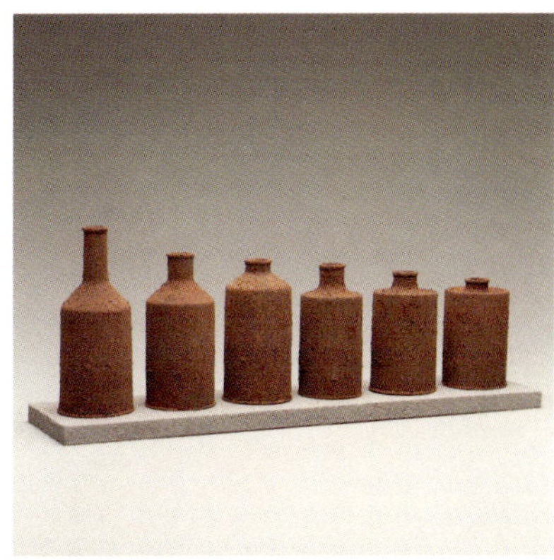

18
Richard Tuttle
***Pop-A-Top* (From the Junk Can Series)**, 2000
H: 7 1/4", W: 18 5/8", D: 4 1/2"
Oak, iron oxides, MDF and acrylics
lent by the artist

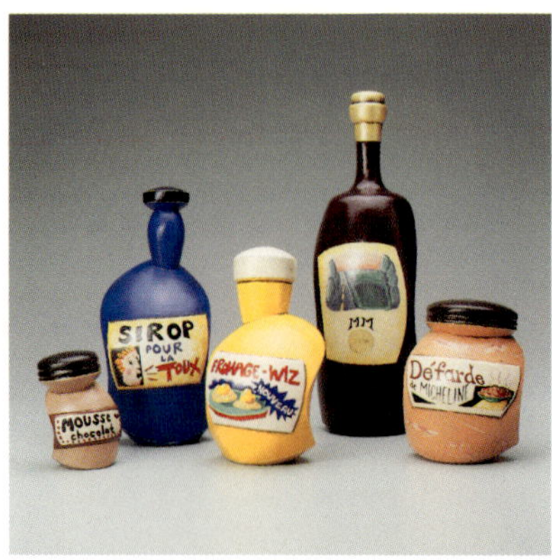


19
Mark Sfirri
*French Vessel Series*, 2000
H: 13 1/2", W: 26", D: 6"
Poplar and paint
lent by the artist

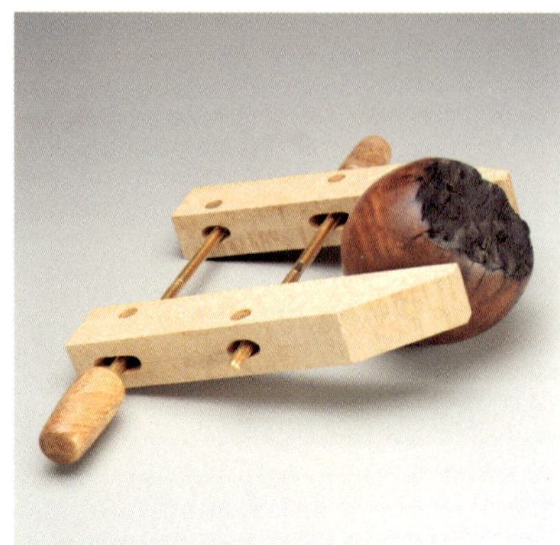

20
Steve Bishop
*Portrait of an Artist as a Middle Aged Man...*, 2000
H: 5 1/2", W: 19", D: 3 1/2"
Birdseye maple, redwood, maple burl and 24k gold-plated hardware
lent by the artist

**It's A Wonderful Life?**

It's axiomatic that all art is political. At the same time, it is autobiography, whether encrypted or obvious. The modern artist — the Romantic whom Pushkin describes — was deliberately self-referential — the hero or heroine of the "story." The postmodern artist sometimes treats personal or autobiographical material in an ironic manner—sometimes not—but he or she has no desire to withdraw into the anonymous craft worker role of the past. Steve Bishop chooses a witty but painful metaphor for the life of the contemporary man (himself): a clamp [20]. For a wood-worker, the clamp holding a sphere is an especially apt symbol. In addition, *Portrait of the Artist as a Middle-Aged Man (with a stressful job, a wife, two kids, a house, two mortgages, two cars, five cats and a neurotic dog)* is a conceptual work: the viewer must at least read Bishop's title to "get" it. His accompanying reproduction of a 1954 "American Dream" illustration adds another level of meaning. The work is a self-portrait, but Bishop informs us that his situation is not merely common, it has a complex social history. The care with which the artist constructed the clamp and sphere, and the fine materials he chose ironically echo the pristine perfection of the house and family in his picture. In addition, each material element of the work bears a metonymic relationship to his personal situation.

Irony is also a factor in Bob Hawks' representation of a *Tornado* [21] remembered from childhood. Like Bishop's clamp, Hawks' central subject is quite serious, though at first glance, the model-like sculpture with its tiny human figures and an almost silly tangle of string inside the walnut funnel cloud might seem to trivialize the ferocity of a tornado. A second consideration, however, suggests that a tornado is so cataclysmic that Hawks acknowledges human inadequacy in representing it. He's chosen the alternative of turning it and its destructive power into a kind of emblem or cartoon tornado, but one whose destructive power is illustrated.

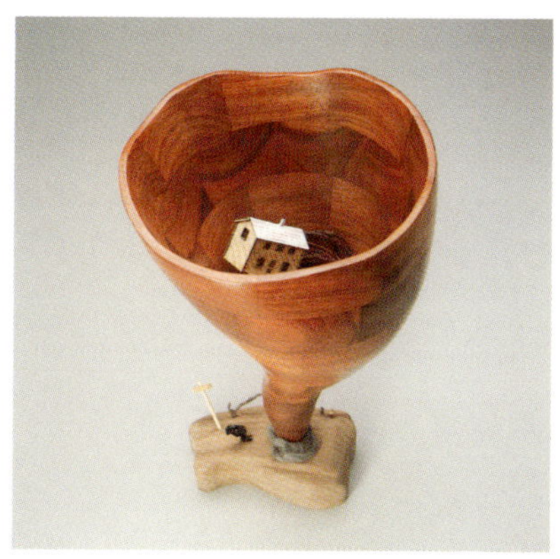

21
Bob Hawks
*Tornado*, 2000
H: 16", W: 8", D: 8"
Paduak and walnut
lent by the artist

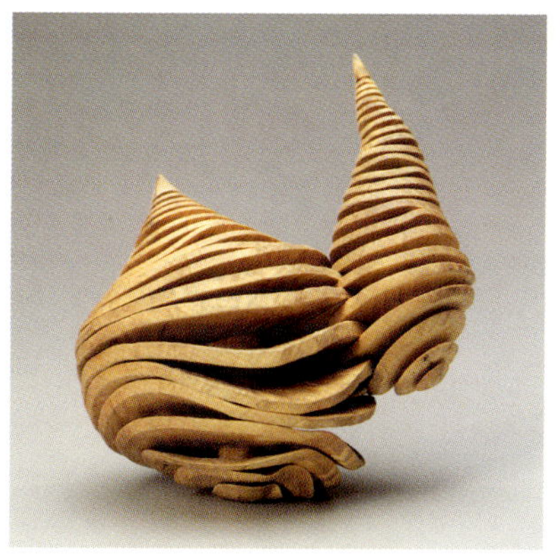

22
Marlowe McGraw
***Big Fish, Little Fish***, 2000
H: 6", W: 4", D: 5"
Madrone (bleached)
lent by the artist

Marlowe McGraw explores the parent-child bond in *Big Fish, Little Fish II* [22]. It's an abstraction in which the smaller pointed/rounded child-shape echoes the larger and more stable parent-shape. McGraw turned the deeply grooved pieces individually from green wood and then interwove their layers which aged into a permanent bond. In a literal sense, nature has joined the two generations permanently. Yet, like a good father, McGraw has depicted the "Little Fish" as if it is swimming away from the parental form, into independent growth.

Functional objects define our lives. This is especially true of a piece that celebrates an important family event. Michael Brolly's *Cradle* [23] was made for his newborn child, but it is descended from a cradle he made for his sister's child, a project that he says "led me to woodworking and the lathe." In his statement, Brolly also mentions that one reason he tackled the first cradle was the fact that his father said he couldn't do it: obviously a crucial parental challenge! The new cradle is an elaborated pod shape, an apt container for new life. Its brown exterior is protectively studded with individually turned, twisty spikes, and the interior is lined with fluffy white sheepskin like the silk inside a milkweed pod.

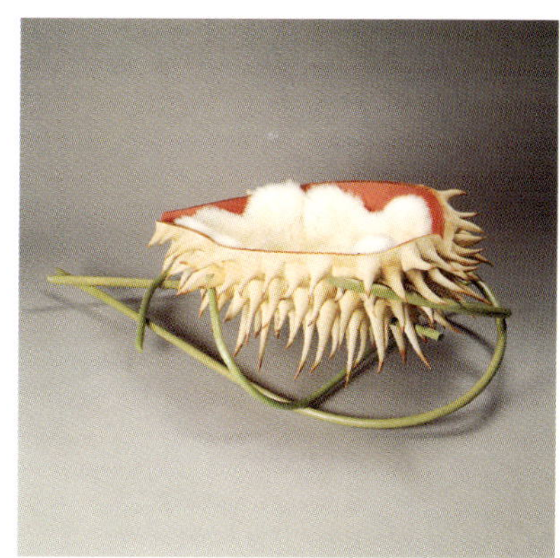

23
Michael Brolly
***Cradle***, 2000
H: 36", W: 24", D: 20"
Mahogany, paint and ash
lent by the artist

**Being and Nothingness**

Clay is molded to make a pot,
but it is in the space where there is nothing
that the usefulness of the clay pot lies.
Cut out doors and windows to make a room,
but it is in the spaces where there is nothing
that the usefulness of the room lies.
Therefore,
Benefit may be derived from something,
but it is in nothing that we find usefulness.

Attributed to Lao Tzu [8]

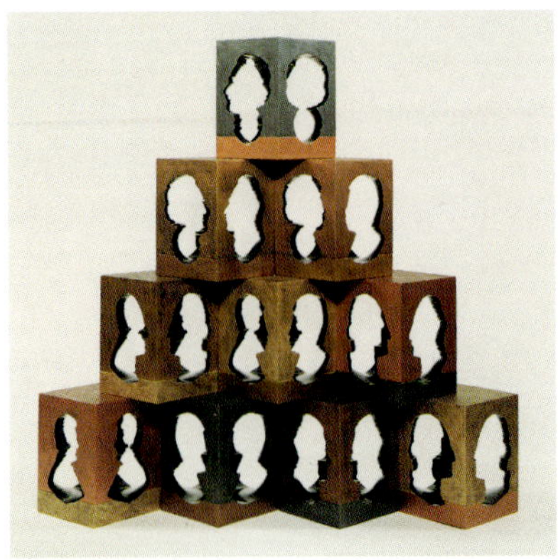

25
Gene Kangas
*Rushmore*, 2000
H: 64", W: 66", D: 16 1/2";
Panted poplar and basswood
lent by the artist

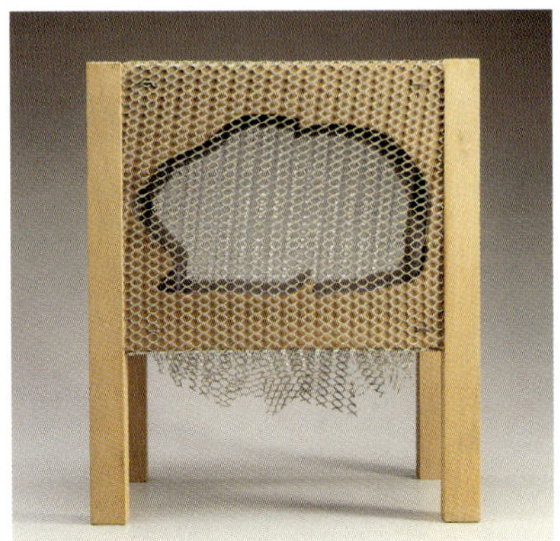

26
Gene Kangas
*Hutch*, 2000
H: 17", W: 14 1/4", D: 10 1/2"
Poplar and wire screen
lent by the artist

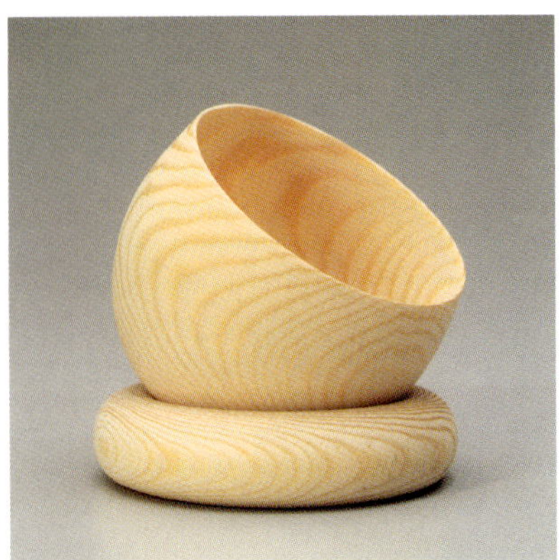

24
Peter Luisoni
*Cup*, 1999
H: 3 3/8", Diam: 3 3/8"
Pine
lent by the artist

Emptiness defines the usefulness of the vessel. Vessels are a central aspect of turning and curators Holzapfel and Tyler sought out those with something extraordinary to say. Peter Luisoni's little cup on a ring [24] initially seems understated, almost meek in attitude, but it's hard to resist the almost subliminal impulse to pick it up. This would be the model if we needed to design a pictogram meaning "turned vessel." In this object, nothing needs to be added. Nothing should be removed. Perfection.

In a completely different take on the usefulness of nothing, Gene Kangas plays with the clichéd sculptural precept that negative space is as important as solid mass and invents a world where the negative embodies positive meaning. In *Rushmore* 2000 [25], he turned the inside corners of boxes to produce a series of blocks containing negative silhouette portraits of the Mount Rushmore presidents plus Einstein and a mushroom cloud — all unique cut-outs on different surfaces of a stack of cubes. The positive segues between images have the look of chess pieces. Shifting perspectives combine the images and, by allowing the boxes to be stacked in several different configurations, Kangas leaves more possibilities open to interpretation.

In *Hutch* [26], Albrecht Dürer's painting, *A Young Hare*, is envisioned from four positions and yet, the hare has seemingly escaped through the torn wire mesh at the bottom of its "cage." This piece contains several clever references to ways of seeing. Dürer's Renaissance mastery of perspective and foreshortening is revealed as a convention, an optional method of representation, which contrasts humorously with Kangas' silhouettes which show several points of view literally, but annihilate the illusion of depth. The sculptor seems to be telling us that NO artist or method can capture the essence of experience or life through representation. The hare will always escape. Another reading suggests that just as we see through the cut-away image into another portion of our world, we project our own view of the world into our understanding of every artwork. Kangas himself describes the "ripping open of the bottom [as] an indication of potential movement outward" in the turning field. Kangas is a great example of an artist who successfully challenges himself

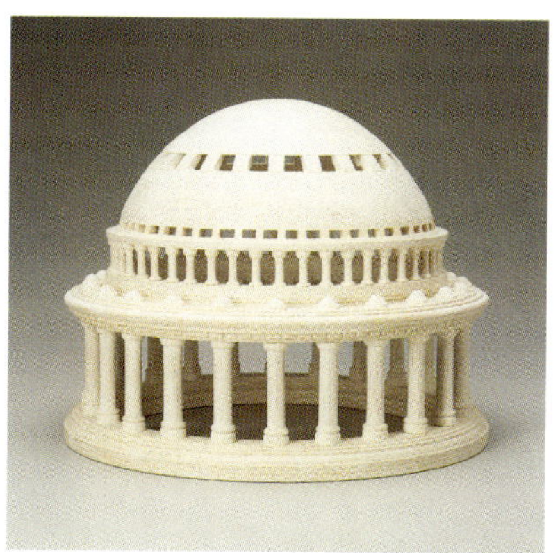

27
Dewey Garrett
*Colosseo*, 1999
H: 7 1/2", W: 13 1/2", D" 13 1/2"
Oak (bleached)
lent by the artist

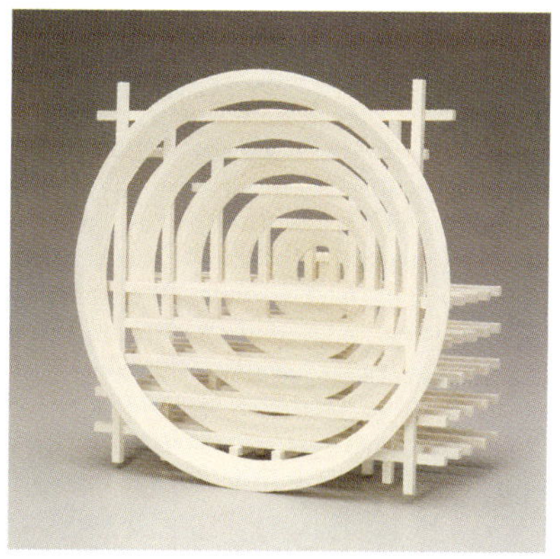

28
Dewey Garrett
*Gridded Bowl*, 2000
H: 5 1/2", W: 10 1/2", D: 10 1/2"
Oak (bleached)
lent by the artist

to transcend the expected limitations of the turning field and who is able to share his process with us.

Dewey Garrett applies his interest in light and space to vessels and architectural objects. From a classical dome [27], to lattice-based vessels [28], he explores the visual experience of moving around a complex interpenetrated space. Light and shade define the experience of shifting perspectives and even suggest the dissolution of apparent physical planes typical of Cubism. Like Cubism and Einstein's Theory of Relativity, Garrett's work challenges the validity of a single point of view. As Leonard Schlain writes in *Art & Physics*, "Explicit in Einstein's formulas and implicit in a Cubist painting is the concept that all frames of reference are relative to one another. The only unique seat from which to have a unified view of reality is the theoretical one astride a quicksilver beam of light, where front and back lose their meaning, and past and future cease to exist.... Our inability to sense these changes compels us to continue to imagine that light travels only through space in time. In fact, light just is, while space and time change in relation to it.[9] Garrett encourages us to experience this very modern truth (as a sort of illusion) while linking some of his imagery to the ancient harmonies of Roman architecture.

### Inexhaustible Sources

Though the poor workman is said to curse his tools, David Sengel gives his imaginary lathe attachment all the credit while artfully critiquing Anatole France's epigram "When a thing has been said and said well, have no scruple. Take it and copy it." In some ways, Sengel's fantasy *Dial-em-up Vessel Extruder* [29] is emblematic of the goals and challenges of *Roots: Insights & Inspirations*. Central to the work is the artist's appreciation of a particular rhododendron trunk with frothy burls, a piece of wood so beautiful that he was unable to bring himself to alter it. How ingenious to find a way to include the unscathed rhododendron in a metal and wood sculpture which simultaneously mocks those who believe Albert Einstein's sarcastic, "The secret to creativity is knowing how to hide your sources" (a "secret" which is well-nigh impossible to hide in the art world) and pays tribute to some of the "greats" of the wood turning field.

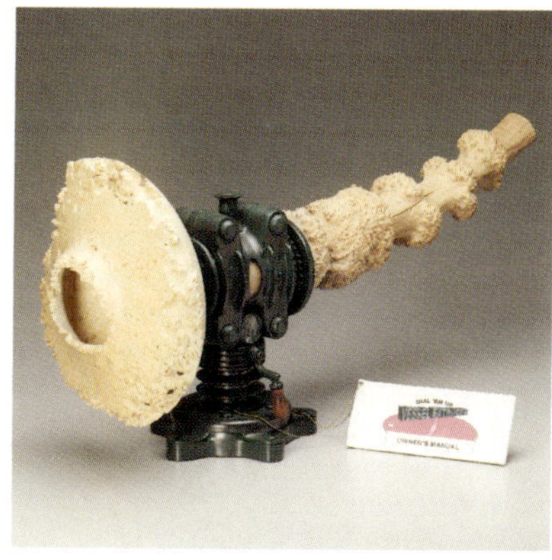

29
David Sengel
*Dial-em-up Vessel Extruder*, 2000
H: 14 1/2", W: 9 1/2", D: 7"
Rhododendron burl, maple burl, steel and paper
lent by the artist

Through their selection of *Roots: Insights & Inspirations in Contemporary Turned Objects*, Michelle Holzapfel and Chris Tyler have made a significant contribution toward the establishment of an appropriate critical practice for wood turning which, while being intellectually rigorous, is also respectful of the creative realities of the medium. This unusual and harmonious collaboration of two distinctive intellects was a pleasure to observe. Its product is *Challenge VI*, a body of work which illuminates that fruitful balance between influence and originality — between the necessary mastery of technique and the rebellion, exploration and challenge to the status quo which is intrinsic to the art-making process. Against the poet Pushkin's emphasis on freedom, one must set the limitations which inspire a creative response — even when they are galling, like the grain of sand in the oyster's shell. Creativity flowers within the restrictions and possibilities of several givens: materials, techniques, and history, both personal and cultural. Just as the martial artist exploits and transforms the power of an opponent, the craft-artist takes what is given and shapes it toward "cherished" goals.

And, just as *Challenge VI* asked each artist a question about the origins of an idea, each artist rightfully asserts the freedom to ask the questions that define the creative process. It is an open road, a process — a challenge — which is happily unending.

to sober and quiet the min**D**
so that **I**t
i**S**
in a**C**cord
w**I**th
what ha**P**pens
the wor**L**d
around **I**t
ope**N**
rath**E**r than

—John Cage[10]

1 Translation of "To the Poet," David A. Utz, with appreciation.

2 Are you satisfied by [your work], O exacting artist?
Then let the crowd curse it,
And spit on the altar where your fire burns,
And shake your tripod with childish playfulness."
The chief priestess of Apollo and mistress of its tripod seat was the powerful Delphic Oracle.

3 Marcus Aurelius, *Meditations*, trans. Maxwell Staniforth (London, New York, Toronto: Penguin Books, 1964) 170.

4 Suzannah Lessard, *The New Yorker*, 13 April, 1987: 57.

5 Dr. Jacob Goldenberg quoted in Natalie Angier, "Route to Creativity: Following Bliss or Dots?" *New York Times*, 7 September 1999: F3.

6 quoted in Schama: 9.

7 Maria van Kesteren, "Fascination for the Circle: Form, Expression, and Beauty," *Curators' Focus: Turning In Context* (Philadelphia, Wood Turning Center, Inc., 1997) 27.

8 Attributed to Lao Tzu, *Tao Te Ching*, trans. Victor Mair, *The Columbia Anthology of Traditional Chinese Literature*, Victor Mair, ed. (New York: Columbia University Press, 1994) 61.

9 Leonard Schlain, *Art & Physics: Parallel Visions in Space, Time & Light*, (New York: Quill, William Morrow, 1991)192.

10 So far, I have been unable to find a source for this little mesostic which I have had in my notes for some years.

# Index of Artists' Objects and Inspirations

Credits

**Editor**
Judson Randall

**Photography**
John Carlano
All photography except the following:

Hap Sakwa, page 164

Gene Kangas, page 118

**Design and Production**
Group M

**Printing**
Colorlith Corporation